JOURNEYS OF TRANSFORMATION

Western Buddhist travel narratives are autobiographical accounts of a journey to a Buddhist culture. Dozens of such narratives have since the 1970s described treks in Tibet, periods of residence in a Zen monastery, pilgrimages to Buddhist sites and teachers, and other Asian odysseys. The best known of these works is Peter Matthiessen's *The Snow Leopard*; further reflections emerge from thirty writers, including John Blofeld, Jan van de Wetering, Thomas Merton, Oliver Statler, Robert Thurman, Gretel Ehrlich, and Bill Porter. The Buddhist concept of "no-self" helps these authors interpret certain pivotal experiences of "unselfing" and is also a catalyst that provokes and enables such events. The writers' spiritual memoirs describe how their journeys brought about a new understanding of Buddhist enlightenment and so transformed their lives. Showing how travel can elicit self-transformation, this book is a compelling exploration of the journeys and religious changes of both individuals and Buddhism itself.

JOHN D. BARBOUR is Professor of Religion Emeritus at St. Olaf College in Northfield, Minnesota, where he taught from 1982 to 2018 and served as Martin Marty Chair of Religion and the Academy and Boldt Chair in the Humanities. He has written four scholarly books, *Tragedy as a Critique of Virtue* (1984), *The Conscience of the Autobiographer* (1992), *Versions of Deconversion* (1994), and *The Value of Solitude* (2004); he also wrote *Renunciation: A Novel* (2013).

"John Barbour's construction of the genre of the modern Western Buddhist travel narrative (that also functions as spiritual autobiography) is brilliant in drawing a circle around empirical facts and making their identity obvious in hindsight. The truth of this literary phenomenon is made unarguable, and the analytical focus on Westerners struggling between their native and Buddhist senses of personhood portrays how a foreign religion is becoming Western in the experiences and examples of actual lives. This book is a big step forward in the study of modern Western Buddhism."

— Francisca Cho, Professor of Buddhist Studies,
Georgetown University

"Focusing almost exclusively on narratives written in English since WWII, John D. Barbour does an excellent job of comparing the written record of more than thirty writers who visited Asia with the express purpose of deepening an understanding of Buddhist existential matters through hiking, pilgrimage, and other forms of travel. The writers in question are grouped according to thematic relationships, and the flow through and around different parts of Asia is entirely successful. The book will be of great interest to literary scholars interested in religion as well as to religion scholars interested in narrative and individual struggles with the central concepts of Buddhism. The research is of a very high quality and the book is also wonderfully readable. The prose style is always clear, and the flow is just right. Taken as a whole, John Barbour's book is an extraordinarily rich exploration of Buddhist-oriented travel writing. There is no other book like it."

— John Whalen-Bridge, Associate Professor of English
Language and Literature, National University
of Singapore

JOURNEYS OF TRANSFORMATION

Searching for No-Self in Western Buddhist Travel Narratives

JOHN D. BARBOUR

St. Olaf College, Minnesota

CAMBRIDGE
UNIVERSITY PRESS

University Printing House, Cambridge CB2 8BS, United Kingdom

One Liberty Plaza, 20th Floor, New York, NY 10006, USA

477 Williamstown Road, Port Melbourne, VIC 3207, Australia

314–321, 3rd Floor, Plot 3, Splendor Forum, Jasola District Centre,
New Delhi – 110025, India

103 Penang Road, #05–06/07, Visioncrest Commercial, Singapore 238467

Cambridge University Press is part of the University of Cambridge.

It furthers the University's mission by disseminating knowledge in the pursuit of
education, learning, and research at the highest international levels of excellence.

www.cambridge.org
Information on this title: www.cambridge.org/9781009098830
DOI: 10.1017/9781009106337

© John D. Barbour 2022

This publication is in copyright. Subject to statutory exception
and to the provisions of relevant collective licensing agreements,
no reproduction of any part may take place without the written
permission of Cambridge University Press.

First published 2022

Printed in the United Kingdom by TJ Books Limited, Padstow Cornwall

A catalogue record for this publication is available from the British Library.

Library of Congress Cataloging-in-Publication Data
NAMES: Barbour, John D., author.
TITLE: Journeys of transformation : searching for no-self in western
Buddhist travel narratives / John D Barbour.
DESCRIPTION: 1. | New York : Cambridge University Press, 2022. |
Includes bibliographical references and index.
IDENTIFIERS: LCCN 2021970028 | ISBN 9781009098830 (hardback) |
ISBN 9781009106337 (ebook)
SUBJECTS: LCSH: Spiritual life – Buddhism. | Buddhism – Doctrines. | Sunyata. |
BISAC: RELIGION / Buddhism / General (see also PHILOSOPHY / Buddhist)
CLASSIFICATION: LCC BQ4302 .B37 2022 | DDC 294.3/444–dc23/eng/20220129
LC record available at https://lccn.loc.gov/2021970028

ISBN 978-1-009-09883-0 Hardback

Cambridge University Press has no responsibility for the persistence or accuracy of
URLs for external or third-party internet websites referred to in this publication
and does not guarantee that any content on such websites is, or will remain,
accurate or appropriate.

For two communities that have oriented my spiritual traveling:
First United Church of Christ, Northfield, Minnesota
Northfield Buddhist Meditation Center

Contents

Acknowledgments and Author's Note		*page* viii
Introduction: A Literary Genre and Some Questions about Self-Transformation		1
1	The Origins of the Genre: John Blofeld and Lama Govinda	24
2	Peter Matthiessen's *The Snow Leopard* and *Nine-Headed Dragon River*	43
3	In a Zen Monastery: Ambiguous Failure and Enlightenment	63
4	Thomas Merton and Christian and Jewish Pilgrims in Buddhist Asia	99
5	Walking the Dharma on Shikoku and in India	123
6	Trekking and Tracking the Self in Tibet	150
7	Life-Changing Travels in the Tibetan Diaspora	179
8	Encounters with Theravada Buddhism	207
9	Searching for Chan Buddhism after Mao	243
Conclusion: Theories of No-Self, Stories of Unselfing, and Transformation		270
Bibliography		314
Index		324

vii

Acknowledgments and Author's Note

I thank Bardwell Smith for encouraging this project at a very early stage and seeing that it could be a book rather than a chapter of another book. Roger Jackson provided helpful counsel and enthusiasm and, in Northfield and Bhutan, taught me much about Buddhism. An early presentation of my ideas about Western Buddhist travel narratives took place in 2011 in a seminar led by Ronald Thiemann at the Lutheran Summer Academy at Harvard Divinity School. My focus on self-transformation began in a paper given in 2016 at the University of Navarra, and for their invitation and enthusiasm I thank a group of faculty there working on the Religious Experience Initiative, especially Rosalia Baena and Pablo Coberos. C. W. Huntington, Jr. and Ben Van Overmeier gave feedback at an early stage. I have learned much about Buddhist practice on and off the meditation cushion from Mark Nunberg, Guiding Teacher at Common Ground Meditation Center in Minneapolis. The Introduction was presented to fellow Sangha members at the Northfield Buddhist Meditation Center and to the Philosophy Discussion Group at the Kierkegaard Library at St. Olaf College. I have been supported and encouraged in countless ways by friends, family members, and colleagues at St. Olaf College.

Many Asian words are transcribed into English in varying ways, for instance, Chan/Ch'an and Daramsala/Dharamsala. Certain authors rely primarily on Pali, which uses the term *anatta* for no-self, while others use Sanskrit, which uses *anatman*. In general, I use the terms and spelling of each author in discussing that book and usually eliminate diacritical marks. I often use italics when a foreign term is introduced but not after that, especially when a term has passed into regular use by Western Buddhists. There are some inconsistencies, especially when I am discussing several authors at once or trying to balance readability with scholarly precision.

In order to reduce the number of notes, I cite page numbers in parentheses within the text when referring to the Western Buddhist travel narrative being discussed. Other references are in the traditional format.

Introduction
A Literary Genre and Some Questions about Self-Transformation

> When the moon takes over your heart,
> Where does the master of the self go?[1]

In 1973, Peter Matthiessen accompanied the biologist George Schaller to Nepal in a study of Himalayan blue sheep and to search for the rare snow leopard. Matthiessen hoped, as well, to meet a revered Tibetan lama at an ancient shrine on Crystal Mountain. Having recently lost his wife to cancer, and facing dangerous winter snowfalls and hazardous mountain terrain, he struggled with grief, regret, and fear while he attempted to better understand and practice Zen and Tibetan Buddhist teachings he had studied for several years. Matthiessen's *The Snow Leopard* (1978) describes this personal pilgrimage as a search for self-transformation and enlightenment. As he traced his journey toward these geographical and spiritual goals, he portrayed habits that made it difficult to change and intense experiences that disclosed the possibility of a radically different way of being.

The Snow Leopard is the best-known example of a literary genre that I call Western Buddhist travel narratives. These autobiographical stories describe how a journey to a Buddhist culture changed the author; they portray religious experiences and reflections in compelling and insightful ways. What can we learn from autobiographical writing about Buddhism that is obscured or neglected by the more abstract, theoretical, and systematic forms of discourse practiced by Buddhist thinkers and in academic scholarship?

Western Buddhist travel narratives often describe a transformative religious experience. A journey to the original lands of the dharma can

---

[1] Zen koan in the 2007 Korean film *Why Has Bodhidharma Left for the East?* I heard this translation at an American Academy of Religion presentation in about 2010. In the film, it is translated: "When the moon in your mind waxes beneath the water, where does the master of my being go?" The figure of the moon dancing in the water is a recurring image for the self in Buddhist texts.

change an author's understanding of Buddhism and alter his or her sense of identity in profound ways. Like Christian conversion narratives, the books examined here depict religious transformation as both a matter of new intellectual understanding and a radical reorientation of life that sometimes comes to a climax in a decisive event. In this book, I interpret diverse experiences of "unselfing," moments when a person's sense of self is radically altered. Interpreted in diverse ways, this kind of experience is a central preoccupation of many religious and ethical traditions. Such an event is believed to illuminate a fundamental human quandary: how can a person transcend the problems of narcissism, egotism, and ethical and spiritual blindness that accompany preoccupation with one's self? Western Buddhist travel narratives often address this question by focusing on the Buddhist idea of *anatman* (Sanskrit; in Pali: *anatta*), usually translated as no-self or not-self.[2] They depend on the concept of no-self to interpret certain crucial experiences, and their ideas about it are a catalyst that provokes and enables these dramatic events.

The Buddhist concept of no-self raises many questions for Westerners trying to understand it and reconcile it with their usual understanding of the self. How does an author who has come to understand the meaning of no-self in an experience of unselfing return to ordinary life, with its demands to be a family member, productive worker, and responsible agent in a society? How does an autobiographer intensely interested in depicting a personal identity portray the Buddhist insight that the self is an illusion? How does an individual's lived experience confirm, complicate, or call into doubt what they have learned about no-self?

Like William James's *The Varieties of Religious Experience*, this book examines closely how particular individuals describe religious experiences. Like James, I propose certain organizing concepts, sketch a working definition of the topic, assess the significance of specific texts, and reflect on what these books reveal about a common issue: in this case, the efforts of Western Buddhists to overcome selfishness and suffering and to find a better way to live.

This Introduction describes the subject matter and approach of this book with remarks on two issues: the characteristics of Western Buddhist travel narratives as a literary genre and source of religious insight and the relationship between Buddhist stories about self-transformation and the idea of no-self.

---

[2] When words in ancient languages are used, I have omitted diacritical marks and, depending on context, they are not always in italics.

Western Buddhist Travel Narratives as a Literary Genre

Westerners have described their perceptions of Buddhism for many centuries, and a few sympathetic travelers found personal meaning and value in Buddhist teachings. Until roughly the past half-century, almost all such accounts viewed Buddhism in a rather detached mode as an exotic worldview or a system of ideas abstracted from cultural context and unrelated to the author's own religious questions. Often, too, contemporary Asian Buddhism was viewed as a degenerate or corrupted version of an idealized version of Buddhism located in texts constructed and controlled by Western institutions such as libraries, universities, missionary societies, and government reports. The very few Westerners drawn to Buddhism before the twentieth century adopted this text-based Buddhism as a philosophy but knew little about Buddhism as a living tradition.[3] Until the last third of the twentieth century, Western appreciation of Buddhism was theoretical, advocating ideas dissociated from personal experience; or it was a matter of romantic fantasy, having little to do with the history or present condition of Buddhism in Asia. With the ambiguous exception of Alexandra David-Neel, who will be discussed in Chapter 6 on Tibetan journeys, Western authors before the 1960s rarely wrote autobiographically (except in private letters) about their engagements with Buddhism as a source of religious insight and a catalyst for transformation.[4] Moreover, even those sympathetic to Buddhism were uninterested in or puzzled by

---

[3] See Philip Almond, *The British Discovery of Buddhism* (Cambridge: Cambridge University Press, 1988). A rare exception is Henry Steel Olcott, who spent a good deal of time in Ceylon, as described in Stephen Prothero, *The White Buddhist: The Asian Odyssey of Henry Steel Olcott* (Bloomington: Indiana University Press, 1996). On other early Western responses to Buddhism, see Thomas Tweed, *The American Encounter with Buddhism, 1844–1912: Victorian Culture and the Limits of Dissent* (Bloomington: Indiana University Press, 1992).

[4] Books by Western writers sympathetic to Buddhism that hint at the author's religious leanings include Marco Pallis's *Peaks and Lamas* (1949) and Peter Goullart's *Forgotten Kingdom* (1955). In Chapter 8, I discuss three books about mindfulness written in the 1960s by the first Westerners to learn Theravada meditation methods in Burma. Farther in the past are accounts of travels such as, in the case of Tibet, by explorers (e.g. Sven Hedin), diplomats (Charles Bell, who knew the XIII Dalai Lama well), and missionaries such as Ippolito Desideri, an Italian Jesuit Father whose account of a five-year sojourn in Tibet in the early eighteenth century focuses on his desire to refute Buddhist ideas. In *Dispelling the Darkness: A Jesuit's Quest for the Soul of Tibet* (Cambridge, MA: Harvard University Press, 2017), Donald S. Lopez, Jr., and Thupten Jinpa translate and interpret the treatise (written in Tibetan!) with which Desideri attempted to debunk key Buddhist doctrines, including no-self. For a collection of Western portrayals of Buddhism to 1844, most of them quite negative, see Donald S. Lopez, Jr., ed., *Strange Tales of an Oriental Idol: An Anthology of Early European Portrayals of the Buddha* (Chicago: University of Chicago Press, 2016). These older texts are significant and fascinating, but they are not autobiographical narratives describing a personal engagement with Buddhism, that is, Western Buddhist travel narratives.

ideas about no-self, which they saw as morbidly pessimistic or nihilistic, as well as inconsistent with Buddhist claims about karma and rebirth.

In a succinct typology, Stephen Batchelor proposes that the long relationship of the West with Buddhism has been marked by five attitudes: blind indifference, self-righteous indignation, rational knowledge, romantic fantasy, and existential engagement.[5] The genre that I call Western Buddhist travel narratives tells stories of existential engagement with Buddhism. The writers of these works are not simply curious about or sympathetic to Buddhism but seriously considering or committed to it as a worldview. While there are undoubtedly elements of fantasy and projection involved in most Westerners' views of Buddhism and Asia, the writers I consider make a concerted effort to understand Buddhism on its own terms, often by textual study and especially as they encounter it during their travels. Their exploration of Buddhism often takes the form of analysis and explication, Batchelor's "rational knowledge," but their encounter is also existential in that it involves not only the intellect but the evidence of their whole being: body, mind, and spirit. These writers embed theoretical exposition and analysis within a narrative that shows what difference these ideas made in their lives.

Every theory of a literary genre is a debatable attempt to define categories of texts that could be organized differently. I will say more in the Conclusion about other texts similar to those I examine here. The point is not to classify books but to better understand them. Taken as a heuristic device, conceptions of genre can help us to discern meaning and creativity and to make illuminating comparisons and contrasts. Thinking about the genre that I call Western Buddhist travel narratives will help us do this with some interesting books that have not been understood in relation to each other or to other ways of describing Buddhism.[6]

The earliest Western Buddhist travel narratives are John Blofeld's *The Wheel of Life* (1959) and Lama Anagarika Govinda's *The Way of the White Clouds* (1966). Blofeld and Govinda were the first to write extended

---

[5] Stephen Batchelor, *The Awakening of the West: The Encounter of Buddhism and Western Culture* (Berkeley: Parallax Press, 1994), xi.

[6] For reflections on other genres, namely Buddhist fiction and poetry in the West, see Kimberly Beck, "Telling Tales Out of School," *Buddhism beyond Borders: New Perspectives on Buddhism in the United States*, ed. Scott A. Mitchell and Natalie E. F. Quli (Albany, NY: SUNY Press, 2015), 125–142; John Whalen-Bridge and Gary Storhoff, eds., *The Emergence of Buddhist American Literature* (Albany: State University of New York Press, 2009); and Lawrence Normand and Alison Winch, eds., *Encountering Buddhism in Twentieth Century British and American Literature* (London: Bloomsbury, 2013).

Western Buddhist Travel Narratives as a Literary Genre 5

autobiographical narratives about engagements with Buddhism that focus on experiences of travel. Since the 1970s, this new genre has flourished, most often structured in terms of one journey. These books explain how the author's spiritual development was influenced by encounters with Buddhism. (Such encounters also take place in the West, of course, resulting in texts that are similar to and different in various ways from those examined here.) In contrast to books that explain Buddhist philosophical ideas or the practice of meditation, travel memoirs tell a story about a pilgrimage or religious journey. These narratives do not describe Buddhism from a detached or impersonal perspective; they are introspective accounts of an author's search for religious experience, meaning, and a coherent worldview.

The authors of Western Buddhist travel narratives have diverse religious orientations. Some of them are committed Buddhists, while others are curious about Buddhism in its Asian homelands after an initial encounter with a teacher, text, or experience of meditation in Europe or America. Some writers are seekers who are sometimes called "spiritual but not religious": individuals looking for meaning and purpose in life or for contact with a holy person or place but who are unaffiliated with and often suspicious of all organized communities and institutional traditions. Since the 1970s, in dozens of book-length narratives and innumerable essays and short pieces (see the Bibliography), Western writers have described journeys to places of historic Buddhist importance, including India, Sri Lanka, Tibet, Bhutan, China, Japan, Korea, and Southeast Asia, especially Thailand. This body of literature forms a fascinating genre of religious memoir with recurring themes and preoccupations and a variety of creative literary strategies for exploring them. I focus on book-length narratives, with occasional references to essays about travel. There is considerable variety within the group of texts that I consider. Several books take the form of a diary or anecdotal travel journal rather than offering a retrospective perspective on a journey. Two works are jointly authored. A few narratives cover several journeys or an extended portion of the author's life rather than the more common focus on a single journey.

For all of these writers, a basic theme and recurring metaphor in their memoir is the analogy between an outer or geographical journey and an inner or spiritual one. Like John Bunyan's *Pilgrim's Progress*, Basho's *The Narrow Road to the Deep North*, and Muslim accounts of pilgrimage to Mecca, these texts rely on one of the most basic metaphors with which humans interpret their experience of the sacred. Getting closer to God, what is holy, or enlightenment as to the nature of ultimate reality is like moving toward – or, sometimes, arrival at – a destination in space. These

6   Introduction

stories compare religious development to travel, with a departure, various obstacles and adversities to overcome along the way, periods of feeling lost or disoriented, perhaps a pivotal decision at a fork in the road or turning point, and a final arrival at a destination, which is sometimes imagined as an open road. Using a journey as a metaphor gives a coherent shape and overarching plot to the often-confusing process of religious searching and striving. In a retrospective account of travel, a reader can compare the author at the start of and during the journey (the autobiographical writer in the role of character or protagonist) with the author who looks back on and interprets the journey (the writer as narrator) and consider how this person has changed. A somewhat different perspective is offered by a travel diary or journal, which provides a day-by-day account of the stages of a journey without a unifying retrospective view and lets us witness the incremental process of change. Like a compelling autobiography, a travel narrative shows how religious ideas and insights develop in time and make a significant difference in a person's life, portraying this in a vivid and gripping way and revealing the psychological dimensions and cultural contexts of ideas. Autobiography also discloses tensions and discrepancies between a religious tradition's normative ideals and expectations and an individual's doubts, idiosyncratic experiences, and failure to live up to the ideal.

Autobiographical accounts of Buddhist experiences are different in several ways from traditional Buddhist literature, and this is one reason why they are valuable for contemporary readers and Buddhist practitioners. In classical Buddhist texts, enlightenment is usually described as the attainment of a list of desirable attributes and the understanding of certain doctrinal truths. Such conceptual clarification is important, but it cannot do what a story does, especially an introspective first-person account. Although Buddhist tradition preserved many narratives about bodhisattvas, these figures are portrayed as beyond ordinary human limitations. Another traditional Buddhist genre is *jataka* tales, which describe how, in previous lives of the Buddha, he realized the ten perfections or demonstrated a particular virtue.[7] Some of these tales show animals or people giving up everything, including their wife and children, for the sake of enlightenment or to save others from suffering. In a past life as a rabbit, the Buddha throws himself into a fire to feed a starving wise man; as a prince, he commits suicide so that a hungry tiger can feed her cubs. In contrast with Western Buddhist travel narratives, the heroes of

---

[7] A collection of *jataka* tales is Edward B. Cowell, ed., *The Jataka or Stories of The Buddha's Former Births* (London: Pali Text Society, 1957).

these tales show little emotion, conflicted motivation, or hesitation; they practice the ideal of self-giving effortlessly. These charming didactic stories present models of virtue that demonstrate the meaning of selfless action. However, most contemporary readers will not recognize in them their own struggles along the way to enlightenment.

In Zen stories about the striking personalities of early masters, according to Dale Wright, a "focus on the distinctively human character of enlightened beings is rare ... since as Buddhism developed into the Mahayana period, characters represented in the sutras tended to take on transhuman powers."[8] When bodhisattvas resemble divine beings and don't show the characteristics of human finitude, they lose their capacity to serve as helpful models for ordinary people. It is therefore of great significance that, in the past half-century, various media, including fiction, biography, and film, have provided detailed accounts of recognizably human individuals seeking enlightenment: "Through these modern media, we now have at our disposal what traditional Buddhists could not have had—fictional and historically descriptive narratives that attempt to articulate in vivid detail what a quest for awakening would mean for actual human beings in earlier histories and in our times and places."[9] I think that for several reasons autobiographical narratives are especially valuable for exploring in depth the nature of Buddhist experience and the meaning of Buddhist ideas and insights.

Autobiography's first-person perspective offers an "inside" view of religious experience that contrasts with the descriptions of outside observers, including exalted claims about a master made by devout followers. Autobiographical writing discloses more of the full range of human emotions and struggles rather than a sanitized portrait that removes any trait deemed inconsistent with the ideal. Personal narratives reveal the larger temporal context of pivotal religious experiences: all that led up to and prepared for a moment of insight and transcendence and what followed. This contrasts markedly with the narrow focus of traditional Buddhist literature on the sudden and dramatic moment of enlightenment. Contemporary autobiographies are valuable because they give us a first-person subjective account of events, show the larger temporal context of pivotal events, and disclose not only an ideal of enlightenment but also the messy, inconclusive, and confusing aspects of transformative religious experience.

---

[8] Dale Wright, *What Is Buddhist Enlightenment?* (Oxford: Oxford University Press, 2016), 30.
[9] Ibid., 31. Wright analyses the 1981 Korean film *Mandala* as one such contemporary account of the search for awakening.

8   Introduction

Although Asian Buddhist autobiographical texts, especially in the
Tibetan and Zen traditions, are becoming better known and studied,
such works remain very challenging for most Western readers other than
advanced scholars.[10] Few of the writers studied in this book were aware
of Buddhist autobiographical writing, and they were influenced greatly
by Western examples of first-person writing. For Western readers today
who seek ways to translate Buddhism into their own cultural idiom,
the example of these contemporary travel writers has both great value
and warns of potential dangers. An analogy is when psychologists turn
to vipassana meditation as a source of strategies for improved mental
health.[11] Translation across cultures brings ambiguous transformations,
but it is inevitable and necessary when religious ideas travel. Buddhism
changed greatly when it journeyed from India and Sri Lanka throughout
Asia and to the rest of the world. It continues to be transformed, and
recognizing this cultural continuity-in-change sometimes helps a writer
understand how the self, too, can be at once the same and different as it
is transformed. This book contributes to the burgeoning scholarship on
Buddhist Modernism and Buddhism in the West.[12] I offer a fresh perspective, ask new questions, and explore a neglected source of insights:
travel narratives.

---

[10] On autobiography in traditional Buddhist cultures, see Janet Gyatso, *Apparitions of the Self: The Secret Autobiographies of a Tibetan Visionary – A Translation and Study of Jigme Lingpa's Dancing Moon in the Water and Dakki's Grand Secret-talk* (Princeton: Princeton University Press, 1998), especially chapter 1; Norman Waddell, "Translator's Introduction" to *Wild Ivy: The Spiritual Autobiography of Zen Master Hakuin* (Boston: Shambhala, 1999), vii–xlix; Miriam Levering, "Was There Religious Autobiography in China before the Thirteenth Century? – The Ch'an Master Ta-hui Tsung-kao (1089–1163) as Autobiographer," *Journal of Chinese Religions* 30 (2002), 97–122; and Sarah Jacoby, *Love and Liberation: Autobiographical Writings of the Tibetan Visionary Sera Khandro* (New York: Columbia University Press, 2014). See also the anthology compiled by Zenshin Florence Caplow and Reigetsu Susan Moon, eds., *The Hidden Lamp: Stories from Twenty-five Centuries of Awakened Women* (Boston: Wisdom Publications, 2013).

[11] For a critique of mindfulness-based psychotherapy, see C. W. Huntington, Jr., "The Triumph of Narcissism: Theravada Buddhist Meditation in the Marketplace," *Journal of the American Academy of Religion* 83 (2015), 624–648. See also Eric Braun, *The Birth of Insight: Meditation, Modern Buddhism, and the Burmese Monk Ledi Sayadaw* (Chicago: University of Chicago Press, 2013) and, for a more positive assessment, Jeff Wilson, *Mindful America: The Mutual Transformation of Buddhist Meditation and American Culture* (New York: Oxford UP, 2014).

[12] Scholarship on Buddhism in the West includes Charles Prebish and Martin Baumann, *Western Dharma: Buddhism Beyond Asia* (Berkeley: University of California Press, 2002); Jeffrey Paine, *Re-Enchantment: Tibetan Buddhism Comes to the West* (New York: Norton, 2004); Batchelor, *The Awakening of the West*; Prebish and Kenneth Tanaka, *The Faces of Buddhism in America* (Berkeley: University of California Press, 1998); Paine, *Re-enchantment*; David McMahon, *The Making of Buddhist Modernism* (Oxford: Oxford University Press, 2008); and, proposing that a postmodern Buddhism is emerging, Ann Gleig, *American Dharma: Buddhism Beyond Modernity* (New Haven: Yale University Press, 2018).

Other Western literary genres besides autobiography offer insights into Buddhist self-transformation. Gary Snyder uses Buddhist imagery and ideas in poetry such as "Smokey the Bear Sutra" and *Mountains and Rivers without End*. Allen Ginsberg's poetry and diaries reflect his deep appreciation for Buddhism and Hinduism as he encountered them in India. Fiction such as Jack Kerouac's *Dharma Bums* or Charles Johnson's *Oxherding Tale*, films such as *Mandala* and *Kundun*, and biographies of Buddhist teachers like the XIV Dalai Lama and Thich Nhat Hanh all depict how Buddhist ideas influence particular lives. Here, I consider only autobiographical narratives: books that claim to represent in prose the author's own experience. All the works discussed were published in English by persons of American or European background. I focus on a particular kind of autobiographical text, memoirs of travel to Asia, bypassing works about Buddhism by authors who describe, for instance, how in the United States or Europe they encountered a teacher or participated in a meditation retreat. The group of texts discussed here is further circumscribed in that they all explore the meaning of no-self. Not every travel writer returning from Asia is concerned with how this idea transformed their sense of identity.

Modern Buddhist journeys may seek traditional pilgrimage destinations or follow a unique personal itinerary. Traditional Buddhist pilgrimages include journeys to four sites in India and Nepal: Lumbini, where the Buddha was born; Bodh Gaya, where he attained Enlightenment; Sarnath, where he first taught; and Kushinagar, where the Buddha died.[13] Pilgrimages may be made to famous stupas (monuments honoring a relic of the Buddha), statues, monasteries, or temples. Some journeys involve arduous hiking to circle a sacred mountain, such as Kailash in Tibet, or to climb a mountain in China, where one of the two terms closest to the English word "pilgrimage" is *ch'ao-shan*, "to pay obeisances to a mountain."[14] Several writers retrace the route of Xuanzang (Hsuan Tsang), the Chinese Buddhist monk who, in the seventh century, spent seventeen years journeying overland to India, returning with hundreds of Sanskrit and Buddhist texts that he translated into Chinese.[15]

---

[13] A collection of accounts of visits to these places is Molly Emma Aitken, ed., *Meeting the Buddha: On Pilgrimage in Buddhist India* (New York: Riverhead, 1995).

[14] Pei-yi Wu, in "An Ambivalent Pilgrim to Tai Shan in the Seventeenth Century," *Pilgrims and Sacred Sites in China* edited by Susan Naquin and Chun-gang Yu (Berkeley: University of California Press, 1992), 65.

[15] For instance, see Mishi Saran, *Chasing the Monk's Shadow* (New York: Penguin, 2005) and Richard Bernstein, *Ultimate Journey: Retracing the Path of an Ancient Buddhist Monk Who Crossed Asia in Search of Enlightenment* (New York: Knopf, 2001). These books are interesting and compelling travel narratives, but their authors do not interpret their lives in light of the Buddhist idea of no-self.

Another form of traditional Buddhist pilgrimage is circumambulation of the Japanese island of Shikoku, with its eighty-eight-temple circuit and historical association with the ninth-century figure Kobo Daishi, who brought Shingon Buddhism from China to Japan. This pilgrimage, like Spain's Camino de Santiago de Compostela, attracts many walkers who are religiously unaffiliated, although unlike Santiago it has no endpoint and is conceived of as a circle that can begin and end at any point. Nontraditional pilgrimages take diverse forms and have many motivations and purposes. Like Matthiessen's *The Snow Leopard*, many accounts of journeys to Buddhist holy places merge a traditional pilgrimage with a personal quest for meaning that the author gradually discloses as he approaches a sacred mountain or temple. Like the author, the reader slowly comes to understand how traditional pilgrimage routes and rituals come to have unique personal significance for the author. Some travel memoirs describe quests for living exemplars of Buddhist wisdom. Several works depict an author's attempt to discover whether any Buddhist teachers or sages survived Communist China's relentless and brutal persecution of religion in the years since 1949, especially during the Cultural Revolution.

Certain narratives recount how the author settled into a Buddhist culture for an extended stay. Such stories explore challenges for a Westerner of putting Buddhist wisdom into practice in daily living, such as integrating ideas about no-self with ethical responsibilities and personal relationships. Works of this type include four accounts of training in a Japanese Zen monastery and Jamie Zeppa's memoir *Beyond the Sky and the Earth*, which describes two years she spent teaching in a remote village in Bhutan. Stephen Asma's *The Gods Drink Whiskey* is a collection of essays about his experiences while teaching in Cambodia and Thailand. These accounts of a lengthy residence in Asia offer a deeper understanding of a specific Buddhist culture than travel narratives that describe brief encounters during a fast-paced itinerary. Rather than extensive geographical movement, another dimension of travel is prominent in these books: a sustained encounter with a foreign culture that raises basic questions about the author's identity, values, and the self that seems at different moments so obdurate and so malleable in various environments. Still another set of books describes encounters with several religious traditions, comparing and contrasting a journey to a Buddhist destination with other "adventures from the pilgrimage trail," as Nicholas Shrady subtitles his work *Sacred Roads*. Additional examples of this kind of travel narrative include Phil Cousineau's *The Art of Pilgrimage* and Sara McDonald's *Holy*

Cow: An Indian Adventure, which describes a ten-day Vipassana retreat among other passing contacts with India's religions.[16]

Thus both the kinds of journey undertaken and the literary structures that interpret travel take many forms. Similarly, an author's religious orientation can range from a committed Buddhist such as Robert Thurman or Peter Matthiessen to a devout Christian such as Thomas Merton, and from agnostic doubt or avowed atheism to the enthusiasm of a recent convert or the bitter rejection of a disillusioned former adherent. In spite of this diversity of literary form, type of journey, and authorial background, certain issues and questions recur when Westerners encounter Buddhism. One of the most persistent, difficult, and far-reaching issues is what to make of the Buddhist idea of no-self.

No-Self, Unselfing, and Transformation

As they journey through the original homelands of the dharma, Western travelers try to correlate their experiences with Buddhist teachings about the nature of ultimate reality. All of the writers discussed here were already familiar with Buddhist ideas, some had studied and practiced meditation for many years, and several were ordained as monks. One of the primary Buddhist doctrines concerns "right understanding" of three characteristics of conditioned existence: *duhkha*, *anitya*, and *anatman*.[17] It is not difficult to see how travel often confirms the truth of *duhkha*: suffering or unsatisfactoriness. From mild discomfort or boredom to exhaustion and terror, sojourners must deal with their negative reactions to the travail that is usually part of travel. Equally important is a writer's recognition of *anitya*, the transitory and impermanent nature of things. Many aspects of travel, including its fleeting pleasures and pains and the constantly changing phases of one's thinking and moods, provoke the insight that impermanence is a fundamental characteristic of existence. A traveler may also observe how every culture, including Buddhist ones, is continually being

---

[16] Nicholas Shrady, *Sacred Roads: Adventures from the Pilgrimage Trail* (San Francisco: HarperSanFrancisco, 1999); Phil Cousineau, *The Art of Pilgrimage: The Seeker's Guide to Making Travel Sacred* (New York: MJF Books, 1998); and Sarah MacDonald, *Holy Cow: An Indian Adventure* (New York: Broadway Books, 2003). These works don't go into much depth in their presentation of Buddhism or show the author as much affected by it, so I don't discuss them.

[17] These are the Sanskrit terms for the three marks of existence; in Pali they are transliterated *dukkha*, *anicca*, and *anatta*. I will usually use the Sanskrit terms, since this is the lingua franca of Buddhism, except when I quote or refer to an author (such as Thomas Merton) who uses Pali terms. We will encounter several other closely related terms and metaphors for no-self, such as emptiness (*sunyatta* in Japanese), selflessness, and interdependent being.

Introduction

dissolved and transformed, especially under the impacts of modernity and globalization.

A Buddhist idea that is more difficult for Westerners to understand is the third characteristic of existence, *anatman*, translated variously as no-self, not-self, or selflessness. This concept holds that what we think of as the personal self is actually impersonal, without individual essence, and dependent on conditions that are always in flux. In the Mahayana concept of emptiness, this idea is extended to all things: there is no essential nature of anything, for everything that exists is conditioned and dependent on other things, as formulated in the idea of dependent arising or origination. We will see many differences of terminology, doctrine, and practice as various types of Buddhism interpret no-self.

When taken as a metaphysical doctrine, *anatman* denies a foundational assumption of Western culture: the reality of the individual personality or self. Philosophical analysis of the concept of no-self explicates its meaning and implications for understanding individual identity.[18] Several recent philosophers compare Buddhist ideas to David Hume's view of the self as a useful fiction or a convenient way of referring to a bundle of related phenomena. Yet the existential impact of recognizing that one's self is an illusion usually demands more than adopting new philosophical concepts. This is one reason why autobiographical accounts are especially valuable for understanding no-self. Roger Jackson puts it humorously: "The problem with most books about no-self … is that there aren't any people in them."[19] This book attempts to understand no-self in a new way by exploring how particular individuals have used this concept to interpret their own lives.

In Buddhist thought and practice, insight into the illusory character of selfhood is linked to awakening and brings a radical change in one's life. The emotional, intellectual, psychological, and social dimensions

---

[18] Among philosophers who see Buddhist ideas about no-self as relevant to Western questions about the self, see Derek Parfit, *Reasons and Persons* (Oxford: Clarendon Press, 1984); Mark Siderits, *Personal Identity and Buddhist Philosophy: Empty Persons* (Burlington, Vt: Ashgate, 2003); Mark Siderits and Evan Thompson, *Self, No Self?: Perspectives from Analytic, Phenomenological, and Indian Traditions* (New York: Oxford University Press, 2013); Lynn De Silva, *The Problem of the Self in Buddhism and Christianity* (New York: Barnes and Noble, 1979); Rupert Gethin, *Foundations of Buddhism* (Oxford: Oxford University Press, 1998); and Anthony Rudd, "No Self? Reflections on Buddhist Theories of Personal Identity," in *Philosophy East and West* 65 (2015), 869–891. No-self is also interpreted in relation to Western psychology, for instance in Owen Flanagan, *The Bodhisattva's Brain: Buddhism Naturalized* (Cambridge, MA: MIT Press, 2011) and Mark Epstein, *Thoughts without a Thinker: Psychotherapy from a Buddhist Perspective* (New York: Basic Books, 1995) as well as several of his later books.

[19] Roger Jackson, review of *Apparitions of the Self* by Janet Gyatso, *Journal of Asian Studies* 57 (1998), 1145.

of Buddhist transformation are in many ways comparable to Christian conversion and what in an earlier book I called "deconversion."[20] A person's former self can seem – at least for a while – to have been entirely left behind. Buddhist awakening may bring a joyful sense of new beginning and enhanced vitality, yet it frequently also involves painful feelings of loss, disorientation, and uncertainty. Although Buddhist awakening is not identical to Christian conversion, both religious traditions speak of a personal transformation that comes when a person understands the truth – even if the truth is about the nature of an illusion – and lives in accord with it. With the exception of Tibet, however, Buddhist cultures rarely produced the extended autobiographical accounts of transformation that have long been common in the West. Western Buddhist travel narratives are a rich source of insight into the process of personal transformation in its distinctively Buddhist forms. My approach to these narratives also suggests a lens that may illuminate analogous experiences described in other religious texts and traditions.

Scholarly understanding of transformative religious and spiritual experience has been dominated by the study of religious conversion. This topic, in turn, has been defined by a classical Christian paradigm established by Luke's account of Paul's conversion in the Book of Acts, the example of Augustine's *Confessions*, and the characteristics of conversion in evangelistic Protestant traditions. In the definitive study of the state of scholarship on conversion, *The Oxford Handbook of Religious Conversion*, many of the contributors reflect on problems arising from using this Christian paradigm to understand experiences of religious change in other religious traditions such as Islam, Taoism, Buddhism, and Hinduism.[21] Recognition that there are many ways Christian transformation occurs has led to new concepts such as intensification, continuous conversion, and deconversion, to theories about the stages of conversion, and to typologies and classifications of different kinds of religious change. Some of these concepts may help us understand certain Buddhist experiences, while others seem unhelpful. In the Conclusion, I reflect on how Buddhist awakening resembles and differs from Christian conversion. I hope that this book

---

[20] John D. Barbour, *Versions of Deconversion: Autobiography and the Loss of Faith* (Charlottesville, VA: University of Virginia Press, 1994).

[21] *The Oxford Handbook of Religious Conversion*, ed. Lewis R. Rambo and Charles E. Farhadian (Oxford University Press, 2014). On the problem of using traditional models of Christian conversion to study Buddhism, see Dan Smyor Yu, "Buddhist Conversion in the Contemporary World," in *The Oxford Handbook of Religious Conversion*, eds. Lewis R. Rambo and Charles E. Farhadian (Oxford University Press, 2014), 465–487.

suggests new questions and alternative perspectives with which to study religious and personal transformation in many cultures. For instance, how do various concepts of the self facilitate and shape religious experience? What ideas and experiences call a person's sense of self into question?

I will use the term "unselfing" to describe incidents that dislodge a person's ordinary and conventional sense of self and elicit some other form of consciousness. Such experiences are not unique to Buddhists and may be explained in diverse ways. The English philosopher Iris Murdoch uses this term once in passing in the context of a discussion of what helps a person become morally better: "Following a hint in Plato (*Phaedrus* 250) I shall start by speaking of what is perhaps the most obvious thing in our surroundings which is an occasion for 'unselfing,' and that is what is popularly called beauty." As an example, Murdoch describes being struck by natural beauty:

> I am looking out of my window in an anxious and resentful state of mind, oblivious of my surroundings, brooding perhaps on some damage done to my prestige. Then suddenly I observe a hovering kestrel. In a moment everything is altered. The brooding self with its hurt vanity has disappeared. There is nothing now but kestrel. And when I return to thinking of the other matter it seems less important. And of course this is something which we may also do deliberately: give attention to nature in order to clear our minds of selfish care.[22]

Murdoch asserts that, in addition to witnessing the beauty of nature, encountering art or practicing the intellectual discipline required to learn a foreign language can help a person to forget the self and perceive the world more accurately and justly. For Murdoch, there is a close connection between growth in virtue and keener vision, that is, learning to perceive accurately: "Of course virtue is good habit and dutiful action. But the background condition of such habit and such action, in human beings, is a just mode of vision and a good quality of consciousness. It is a *task* to come to see the world as it is."[23] Murdoch gives a very different interpretation of unselfing than a Buddhist would, for she connects it to Aristotelian and Platonic ideas about vision and virtue. Like Buddhists, however, she sees an experience of self-transcendence as a crucial moment in the development of right understanding and moral goodness. For this English

---

[22] Iris Murdoch, *The Sovereignty of Good* (New York: Schocken Books, 1971), 84.

[23] Ibid., 91. Interpretations of the role of unselfing in Murdoch's moral philosophy and fiction include David J. Gordon, *Iris Murdoch's Fables of Unselfing* (Columbia, Missouri: University of Missouri Press, 1995) and Maria Antonaccio, *A Philosophy to Live By: Engaging Iris Murdoch* (Oxford: Oxford University Press, 2012).

No-Self, Unselfing, and Transformation

philosopher, as for Buddhist practitioners, unselfing may happen in an unexpected moment, yet it is also a task: a matter of effort, discipline, and commitment.

The concept of unselfing seems to me a useful concept and a focus for interpreting self-transformation in Western Buddhist travel narratives. It's a participle, not a noun; it emphasizes a process, not a thing or a permanent condition. Many Buddhist experiences of unselfing are far more unsettling and disruptive of a person's sense of reality and identity than Murdoch's examples. Losing one's ordinary sense of what is real may disorient rather than clarify and be terrifying as well as liberating. Another contrast with Murdoch's concept is that, according to many Buddhist sages, the most significant change, enlightenment, is wrought by seeing into one's own nature, and it is life-transforming, not simply a moment of putting one's troubles in perspective.

Along with Murdoch's emphasis on seeing reality "as it is," which is also an important theme in Buddhism, I think self-transformation involves "seeing as," that is, learning to interpret the world in terms of a new conceptual framework, in this case Buddhist ideas about suffering, impermanence, and no-self. "Seeing as" is what religions teach their adherents to do, according to the philosopher John Hick. Relying on the works of D. T. Suzuki, Heinrich Dumoulin, and Masao Abe, Hick describes the crucial transformative insight in Mahayana Buddhism as the discovery that Samsara and Nirvana are one: "Experienced from the self-enclosed ego's point of view human existence is Samsara, an endless round of anxiety-ridden living and dying. But experienced by the ego-less consciousness of the liberated mind the same ordinary human existence is Nirvana! In enlightenment, *satori*, self and world are transformed together."[24] The Mahayana Buddhist experience and naming of reality as empty (*sunyata*) is the specific way that this tradition understands the ultimate reality that Hick calls the Real, his general term for that which in every tradition moves human beings beyond their ordinary egocentric point of view. Hick's theory of religion reminds us that unselfing is not a self-evident experience that every person would undergo and understand in the same way. Rather, experiences of unselfing are interpreted in culturally specific ways, such as, for Buddhists, in terms of the concept of no-self. A particular conceptual framework and worldview shapes the experiences of Buddhists and helps them articulate its meaning very differently than how other people

---

[24] John Hick, *An Interpretation of Religion: Human Responses to the Transcendent* (New Haven: Yale University Press, 1989), 288.

understand moments of unselfing. The Buddhist concept of no-self both precipitates certain experiences of transformation and shapes interpretation of them. After exploring Western Buddhist travel narratives, in the Conclusion I discuss relationships between experiences of unselfing and theoretical views of no-self.

The term "unselfing" helps us understand no-self not as the attainment of a quasi-divine status that extinguishes the traits of ordinary human nature but rather as a moment or process of self-transcendence, that is, an awareness that goes beyond one's former sense of self. Unselfing is a shift from a person's ordinary state of consciousness to another kind of awareness that feels extraordinary and significant and may be accompanied by a wide range of different emotions, intuitions, and sensations. What seems to be beyond all one's prior experiences of selfhood varies greatly among individuals and should not be defined at the outset of our study. Rather, how a writer understands and describes unselfing is exactly what we will explore in a number of cases. We investigate what Ann Taves calls the "deeming" of a thing – in this case an experience – as significant and the reasons for this assessment.[25] What counts as unselfing, and why?

A crucial dimension of unselfing is its ethical implications. In the West, moral philosophy, religion, and classic literary works such as George Eliot's *Middlemarch* describe the problem of human egotism and what helps a person to overcome it. Whatever the remedy is said to be – better rational thinking, God's grace, spiritual discipline, attunement to the healing powers of the natural world, or something else – hope centers on what is believed can change the self-centeredness that causes so much suffering. Shaped by their Western cultural background and by Buddhist insights, the authors of these travel narratives see selfishness as an inextricable part of the human condition, yet they also show how recognizing this reality can make a huge difference in a person's moral life. Coming to understand one's own unwarranted self-concern, egotism, or narcissism can be transformative. These Buddhist writers describe both ethical challenges rooted in human selfishness and the possibility of a transformation of moral character. They address the fundamental human problem of egotism in a distinctive way by using the Buddhist concept of no-self to interpret their lives.

For several reasons, traditional Buddhist literature was not very interested in describing in detail experiences of unselfing. Ideals of humility

---

[25] In the Conclusion, I say more about the relevance of Ann Taves's *Religious Experience Reconsidered: A Building-Block Approach to the Study of Religion and Other Special Things* (Princeton: Princeton University Press, 2009).

and modesty discouraged Buddhists from portraying their own lives or proclaiming their spiritual accomplishments. Once again, Tibetan tradition is an important exception to this generalization, for it contains autobiographical accounts that are often boastful and self-aggrandizing.[26] Usually, however, we learn about Buddhist enlightenment either in highly theoretical terms or from another person's perspective. Rather than a detailed introspective account by a person who attains enlightenment, classic texts typically describe a context, such as a monk's encounter with a Zen master, and simply declare that at this moment the monk was awakened or saw into his Buddha nature. The focus of Zen encounter narratives is not the awakened monk but rather the comportment, action, or pithy remark of a Roshi who displays the spontaneous and intuitive wisdom characteristic of Zen. A contemporary Western reader wants to know more about the person transformed by this incident: his background, suffering, questions, and hopes. What did it feel like to see into one's own nature and awaken? What happened next and in the long term? An autobiographical narrative can address such typical Western questions in ways rarely seen in classical Buddhist texts.

Stories often portray unselfing in oblique and enigmatic ways rather than with explicit analysis or conceptual precision. Western Buddhist travel narratives resemble Zen koans or encounter stories when they suggest the elusive, ineffable, and mysterious nature of unselfing. To use a common Zen analogy, they are like a finger pointing at the moon; several of our texts explain their method by using this recurring trope. Yet, at the same time that these writers stress the limitations of words and concepts, they interpret the conceptual meaning of traditional Buddhist ideas such as *anatman* and strive for as much clarity as they can render in words. I will analyze their explicit statements as well as the ways in which they point to the moon: with what gesture, in what direction, in what context, with what kind of wink or shrug? How do stories, by means of metaphors and narrative, adumbrate what cannot be stated directly? How do they suggest the contradictory truths that the self is both an illusion and a reality impossible to deny in one's ongoing life? Using various literary strategies and metaphors, Western Buddhist travel narratives dramatize truths that seem illogical or paradoxical to systematic thought.

---

[26] Gyatso, *Apparitions of the Self*, explains some of the reasons why autobiographical writing flourished in Tibet but not in other Buddhist cultures. In Tibet, there was intense competition among Buddhist teachers and an acceptance of self-promoting or boastful claims when leavened by appropriate deference to tradition and self-deprecating humor. In the Conclusion, I discuss Gyatso's study of Jigme Lingpa's texts as a parallel and precedent for Western Buddhist travel narratives.

By comparing many autobiographical narratives, we will come to understand the varieties of Buddhist unselfing. Instead of defining no-self as an ideal realized in the past by perfect beings who achieved godlike detachment from ordinary human life, and rather than looking at narratives only to confirm a particular theory of no-self, I analyze many distinct interpretations of no-self and experiences of unselfing. A moment of unselfing can arise, for instance, when a person feels merged with the natural world or absorbed into a community's performance of a ritual. It can come about through heightened awareness of one's body, through viewing the body as if from an external perspective, or by recognizing after the fact that one had in some unusual way lost ordinary consciousness of the body. Unselfing may take the form of gaining access to other minds, remembering earlier births, having a vision of a future life, or intuiting that one participates in another level of being. When a person loses the sense of agency, something other than self may seem to take over and act. A loss of ordinary selfhood may come about through scrupulous analysis of the components of consciousness or through intense emotion. The self may seem to dissolve into fragments or expand into the whole cosmos. We will explore a fascinating range of diverse experiences that authors interpret in the light of their understanding of the concept of no-self.

The authors of Western Buddhist travel narratives try to find roots in traditional Buddhism. Yet in many ways their versions of Buddhism contrast with classical texts and contemporary Asian beliefs and practices. As I will discuss in the Conclusion, traditional Asian forms of Buddhism reserved the concept of no-self for monks engaged in meditation or scholarly discourse: "Before modern times, it had never been supposed that laypersons should apply the doctrine of not-self directly to themselves."[27] In Western Buddhist travel narratives, in contrast, no-self becomes a concept used to describe desirable experiences that lay Buddhists and curious seekers hope will confirm the truths of Buddhism. Moreover, these Western writers pursue experiences of unselfing not only in the traditional practice of intensive meditation but also in a wide variety of circumstances in ordinary life. They view their travels in Asia as a quest for spiritual experience, sometimes with only a vague idea of what they are looking for, and they hope to be transformed. They seek more than a conceptual understanding of Buddhist ideas and beliefs; they want an experience that will give them

---

[27] Steven Collins, "What Are Buddhists *Doing* When They Deny the Self?" in *Religion and Practical Reason: New Essays in the Comparative Philosophy of Religion*, ed. Frank E. Reynolds and David Tracy (Albany: State University of New York Press, 1994), 68.

certainty of its truth. This orientation is characteristic of the worldview known as Buddhist Modernism, which is a hybrid synthesis of traditional Buddhist ideas with what David McMahon, following Charles Taylor, calls the discourses of modernity, such as Western theism, Romanticism, and scientific rationalism.[28] Western Buddhist travel narratives reflect many aspects of Buddhist Modernism: a shift toward interiority and self-scrutiny, distrust of institutional authority, the valorization of individual experience, and close attention to the details of ordinary life as a gateway to the re-enchantment or re-sacralization of the world. They reveal what Hans-Georg Gadamer calls a "fusion of horizons" of Western and Buddhist assumptions, values, ideas, and symbols.[29] These stories depict not only personal change but also the transformation – the identity-in-difference – of a religious tradition as it is absorbed into a new cultural setting. This book explores geographical journeys and religious changes made by individuals and by Buddhism itself.

Why should we focus on travel narratives to understand unselfing? Traveling can disrupt habits that become so engrained as to seem a permanent part of a person's identity. At its best, travel fosters alert and discriminating attention; it leads not only to seeing new sights but also to recognition of alternative ways of seeing the world and, so to speak, seeing how one sees. Travel presents opportunities to break out of unchosen fixed patterns and to experience other ways of being in the world. Of course, travelers can also form destructive habits, often without realizing it. Self-transformation of a positive kind is not automatic but only a possibility for an alert traveler. Just as often, travelers reject the alternatives offered by a foreign culture and remain stuck in their home culture's predictable ways of making sense. A journey provides an opportunity, not a guarantee, that a self-critical traveler will recognize conditioned reactions and take active responsibility for choices. Paradoxically, the Buddhist idea of no-self can influence the kind of self that is being formed by traveling and the sort of ethical character taking root. In writing about a journey, there is a second chance for a person to understand it in the light of Buddhist insights.

Travel in another culture can make one aware of how much one has been formed by one's background and that there are alternative ways of organizing gender relations, economic transactions, religious rituals, and many other things. Sometimes a traveler feels drawn to another culture's

---

[28] McMahon, *The Making of Buddhist Modernism*.
[29] Hans-Georg Gadamer, *Truth and Method*, 2nd rev. ed., trans. Joel Weinsheimer and Donald G. Marshall (New York: Seabury Press, 2004).

ways, as if a latent part of one's being has been activated or called forth. The otherness of a foreign culture can alert one to otherness within and be welcomed as not alien but potentially one's own. Encountering a foreign culture also poses the risk of projecting onto it a shadow self that one uses to shore up or define one's own identity and to justify political and economic structures from which one benefits, as postcolonial theory and studies of Orientalism have explored.[30] Some thoughtful travelers are aware of these risks; and from those who are not, there is much to learn. The ideal of transcending self leads all too often to self-deception and exploitation of other cultures in the name of one's own spiritual advancement. This is an inherent risk of pilgrimage and religious searching in another culture; it goes with the territory.

Any kind of travel can be a wake-up call. For those seeking specifically Buddhist awakening, travel to Asia involves encountering the particularity of historical Buddhism in its original setting. This can disrupt prior assumptions and understandings of Buddhism, which may be closely related to the defenses, projections, and illusions of the self one hopes to leave behind. There is something profoundly Buddhist about focusing on travel, which, especially when it involves walking, is often used as a metaphor in teaching. Walking is an established form of meditation; a guide is Thich Nhat Hanh's little book *How to Walk*.[31] Buddhist teachers frequently use journeying as an analogy in addressing philosophical or religious questions. For instance, in discussing awakening, they explore the relationship between the ultimate goal or destination and the discipline (the "way" or "path") that takes one there. One approach to this issue is to see the path as simply a technique, a means to a higher end, "a way to get there." Buddha sometimes suggested this, as when he compared his teachings to a boat that is useful for crossing a river but can be

---

[30] Postcolonial studies of travel literature explore how literary texts construct, project, and maintain white Western hegemonies and justify the subjection of the rest of the world to its interests. Among many examples of this perspective, see Mary Louise Pratt, *Imperial Eyes: Travel Writing and Transculturation* (London: Routledge, 1992); Dennis Porter, *Haunted Journeys: Desire and Transgression in European Travel Writing* (Princeton: Princeton University Press, 1991); Patrick Holland and Graham Huggan, *Tourists with Typewriters: Critical Reflections on Contemporary Travel Writing* (Ann Arbor: University of Michigan Press, 1998); Graham Huggan, *The Post-Colonial Exotic: Marketing the Margins* (London: Routledge, 2001); and James Duncan and Derek Gregory, *Writes of Passage: Travel Writing, Place and Ambiguity* (London: Routledge, 1999). Scholarship on how studies of non-Western religions reflect Orientalist assumptions includes Richard King, *Orientalism and Religion: Post-Colonial Theory, India, and the "Mystic East"* (New York: Routledge, 1999) and Donald S. Lopez, Jr., *Curators of the Buddha: The Study of Buddhism Under Colonialism* (Chicago: University of Chicago Press, 1995).
[31] Thich Nhat Hanh, *How to Walk* (Berkeley: Parallax Press, 2015).

No-Self, Unselfing, and Transformation

left behind when the river is crossed. Yet the Buddha and later sages also spoke of the path as itself the way. Path and goal cannot be separated as one makes one's way through life practicing wisdom, compassion, and mindfulness, qualities that are training for awakening and also its fruits.

In Western Buddhist travel narratives, writers apply classic Buddhist teachings to their own journeys and come to appreciate ancient wisdom in new ways. They describe an interesting geographical journey and use it as a metaphor for movements of the spirit: its progress and wrong turns, struggles with external and internal roadblocks, frustrating delays and sudden advances, and sometimes the author's transformation in the course of a journey and arrival at a longed-for destination. Then what?

A set of questions about the concept of no-self and experiences of unselfing orients my approach to Western Buddhist travel narratives. In each work, what counts as unselfing? What kind of experience allows a traveler to grasp the insight conceptualized as no-self, and how does this understanding bring change? What event brings home the truth of the doctrine of no-self? How do writers interpret its meaning and significance? How is the self that is lost or overcome described: as overly intellectual, isolated from other people, trapped in meaningless habits, either too emotional or lacking feeling, as ungenerous and without compassion, or some other miserable condition? Is the recognition or realization of no-self presented as a life-transforming event analogous to conversion? Can it fade, dissipate, or be forgotten? Is transformation all-at-once and radical or gradual, partial, temporary, or incomplete? How do authors interpret "selfing," the inevitable return to ordinary consciousness that follows incidents when self-consciousness dissolves or is radically altered? What is the role of human agency in fostering or precipitating events of unselfing? How does conceptual understanding of no-self make possible and facilitate unselfing? How do travel writers portray the long-term implications of an experience of unselfing, especially what it means to live with this insight when one returns home and resumes ordinary life as a householder, family member, and worker living in a society that expects one to be a certain sort of self and a responsible person? These questions are addressed in distinct and diverse ways by various authors, often implicitly rather than directly; they will orient my analysis of memoirs about journeys to a Buddhist culture.

Each chapter treats several narratives that explore some common issue or a particular Buddhist tradition. Chapter 1 examines the first Western Buddhist travel narratives: John Blofeld's *The Wheel of Life* and Lama Anagarika Govinda's *The Way of the White Clouds.* These were the first full-length autobiographical accounts of how Asian journeys influenced an author's understanding of and commitment to Buddhism. They change Western representations of Buddhism from the realm of pure ideas or exotic fantasy to a depiction of how Buddhist ideas shaped and are shaped by the author's experiences of travel. The first chapter explains the originality and significance of these two works.

Most later works do not survey the author's whole life, as does John Blofeld, but rather focus on a particular journey. Chapters 2–5 each begin with a groundbreaking travel narrative and then turn to later works that explore a similar journey and religious questions. We start by considering the best-known Western Buddhist travel narrative, Peter Matthiessen's *The Snow Leopard*, and his later *Nine-Headed Dragon River*, which recounts a journey to Japan after he became committed to the Soto form of Zen. In Chapter 3, I interpret Janwillem van de Wetering's *The Empty Mirror* and three other books about a lengthy sojourn in a Zen monastery by Maura O'Halloran, David Chadwick, and Gesshin Claire Greenwood. This confined setting limits geographical travel and offers fertile ground for encounters with Japanese culture that yield both frustration and ambiguous progress for authors trying to realize the meaning of selflessness.

Thomas Merton's posthumous *Asian Journal* reveals how this Trappist monk was deeply affected by his journey to India, Sri Lanka, and Thailand. In Chapter 4, I examine this influential text and those by two other writers – William Johnston and Bardwell Smith – who try to integrate Christian commitments with the wisdom they find in Buddhism. I also consider a comparable Jewish encounter with Buddhism, Rodger Kamenetz's *The Jew in the Lotus*. Chapter 5 considers Oliver Statler's account of his circuit of Shikoku's eighty-eight temples, turning then to two other narratives in which the meaning of Buddhism, especially with regard to no-self, is realized during a long and arduous walking tour. Robert Sibley retraces the classic Shikoku route, offering a contrasting perspective on how this traditional pilgrimage became meaningful to him. In *Rude Awakenings: Two Englishmen on Foot in Buddhism's Holy Land*, Ajahn Sucitto and Nick Scott alternate as narrators in recording their difficult journey through sites associated with the Buddha in India and Nepal. The first five chapters, then, discuss how an influential early work defined an issue or topic that later writers also explored, sometimes in a different location and Buddhist tradition.

Chapters 6–9 are organized in terms of the main traditions of Buddhism and the lands in which they predominate. More travel narratives have been set in Tibet and the Tibetan diaspora than anywhere else, and two chapters analyze encounters with Tibetan traditions, which are

No-Self, Unselfing, and Transformation   23

usually referred to as Vajrayana Buddhism. I first examine narratives by Jim Reynolds (now Ajahn Chandako), Robert Thurman and Tad Wise, Ian Baker, and Matteo Pistono that describe challenging treks in Tibet. Chapter 7 interprets how encounters with the Tibetan Buddhist diaspora in India, Bhutan, Nepal, and Europe led to life-changing transformations for Andrew Harvey, Jamie Zeppa, Jan Willis, and Stephen Schettini.

In Chapter 8, I explore two contrasting kinds of engagement with Theravada Buddhism. Tim Ward and Phra Peter Pannapadipo describe their lives in a Thai monastery, while Rudolph Wurlitzer and Stephen Asma reflect on a brief journey and an extended teaching stint in urban centers of Burma, Thailand, and Cambodia, where Theravada Buddhism is pervasive, deeply rooted, and interacting in striking ways with the forces of modernity. Chapter 9 follows several authors who journey through the People's Republic of China in search of what remains of Buddhism, especially Chan (Chinese Zen), after the traumatic destruction inflicted under Mao's rule. Gretel Ehrlich's *Questions of Heaven*, George Crane's *Bones of the Master*, and Bill Porter's *Road to Heaven* and *Zen Baggage* reveal how these authors' journeys through China engendered responses to Chan that, like all the narratives considered here, center on the meaning of no-self.

In the Conclusion, I reflect on theories of no-self, stories about unselfing, and the distinctive value of autobiography, especially travel narratives, for understanding religious transformation. I draw conclusions about how these topics are related and develop the theory that orients my approach to Western Buddhist travel narratives, which I hope might be useful in other fields of study. An important part of this theory is my understanding of autobiographical writing as a religious activity or practice and a search for further transformation.

CHAPTER I

The Origins of the Genre
John Blofeld and Lama Govinda

The prototypical works of Western Buddhist travel narrative are John Blofeld's *The Wheel of Life* (1959) and Lama Anagarika Govinda's *The Way of the White Clouds* (1966). These books are the first to exhibit the essential features of the genre, although they differ in one important way from most later works. Blofeld and Govinda integrated the genre of travel narrative – which, especially in the case of Tibet, had until then been for Western writers a tale of adventure and fantastic otherness – with the genre of spiritual autobiography, the introspective exploration of the authors' search for ultimate meaning. Spiritual autobiography has deep roots in Christian confessions and conversion narratives but also encompasses later developments, when the search for self replaces the desire to know God and when the goal of defining a unique personal identity becomes more important than salvation or fidelity to a religious community.[1]

Blofeld and Govinda depicted compelling experiences of transformation and interpreted them in Buddhist terms. For both of them, travel was a crucial catalyst for transformation. Blofeld and Govinda put new wine in the old wineskins of spiritual autobiography to create something new: Western Buddhist travel narratives. They made their case for Buddhism not by moral exhortation or explication of doctrines, but, rather, by dramatizing how it transformed their identity. Their works are spiritual autobiographies that survey much of their lives, but they each begin and end their book with a scene from a pilgrimage that symbolically expresses their understanding of Buddhism. Blofeld and Govinda condense into a climactic moment the outcome of a long process of learning and practice, much as Augustine constructed a conversion scene set in a garden in Book 8 of the *Confessions*. Their narratives begin and end with a crucial scene that recounts an experience of unselfing.

---

[1] See John D. Barbour, "Spiritual Autobiography," in *Encyclopedia of Life Writing: Autobiographical and Biographical Forms*, ed. Margaretta Jolly (London: Fitzroy Dearborn, 2001).

The Origins of the Genre

Most later Western Buddhist travel narratives are not complete autobiographies, but rather accounts of a particular journey, several expeditions to the same place, or a series of related pilgrimages, with scattered references to the rest of the author's life. They are memoirs, not autobiography: travel narratives that depict just enough of the writer's past so that the reader understands how a journey changed him or her, and perhaps, too, how life was different after the journey. Blofeld and Govinda, in contrast, each wrote an autobiography about a life full of travel and focused on Asian journeys that illuminated their understanding of Buddhism.

*

John Blofeld's *The Wheel of Life*, first published in 1959, is the spiritual autobiography of a life (1913–1987) packed with travels throughout Asia on a prolonged search for Buddhist enlightenment. His autobiography could also be discussed in the context of several later chapters of this book, for Blofeld encountered Buddhist, Taoist, and Confucian sages in China and Hong Kong, studied Theravada traditions during many years of residence in Bangkok, stayed for nine months in a Chan monastery in Yunnan, and made a pilgrimage to the classic sites associated with the Buddha's life in India. He witnessed the transition to Communism in China, the traumatic event that shapes the works discussed in Chapter 9. Blofeld had a comprehensive knowledge of the many forms of the Dharma and translated or wrote twenty books about Buddhism and other Asian religious traditions. He is a fascinating and neglected figure worthy of a full biography assessing his significance.[2] Here I consider him, far too briefly, primarily in the context of Western encounters with Tibetan Buddhism. Even while Blofeld was deeply involved with other forms of Buddhism, he believed that his ultimate spiritual destination was Vajrayana Buddhism. When he finished a somewhat disappointing "Great Pilgrimage" to India, "the certainty dawned in my mind, not for the first time, that the turning point of my life would be reached somewhere in the Himalayan borderlands of Tibet" (233).[3] Thus, he

---

[2] The only biographical accounts of John Blofeld I know of are a brief entry in Wikipedia and Reid's "Translator's Introduction" of *My Journey in China: Old Pu's Travel Diary*, translated from the Chinese by Daniel Reid (Rochester, VT: Inner Traditions, 2008), xv–xxvi. This work, originally published in Mandarin in 1990, is more clearly structured as a chronological series of travel narratives than *The Wheel of Life* and provides additional information on many aspects of his journeys, although it is not as revealing about his religious experiences. Written for a Chinese audience, it is nostalgic, appreciative, and enthusiastic about all things Chinese, but it does not describe unselfing or what Buddhism meant to him personally.

[3] John Blofeld, *The Wheel of Life: The Autobiography of a Western Buddhist*, third edition (Boston: Shambhala, 1988). The original publication was in 1959, and the second edition in 1972. Numbers in parentheses refer to this text. Throughout this book, I will follow the practice of citing page numbers in parentheses when referring to the Western Buddhist travel narrative being discussed.

was also the predecessor of the writers I discuss in Chapter 7, who encounter Tibetan traditions in diaspora after the Communist takeover in 1951.

The Wheel of Life begins and ends with a scene at Tashiding monastery in Sikkim, probably in 1957, with Blofeld watching a sunrise and expecting to receive that day an initiation from the Tangku Lama. He depicts a moment of unselfing when, "if I had retained my powers of reflection, I might have been conscious of an almost egoless state" (17). This was not the only time that Blofeld knew a state of deep contemplation when "there remained no individual entity to be conscious of its own absence." The timeless moment is recognized only when it is over and self-consciousness returns: "My 'I' tried in vain to capture the nearly reached state of 'no-I.' Little remained but a swiftly fading memory of infinite stillness and blissful tranquility, a feeling of having touched the rim of a great and inexpressible mystery" (17). Feelings of regret, nostalgia, and sadness recur in Blofeld's narrative as he recounts his "many backslidings" (18) after peak moments. Compared with other accounts of unselfing, including Lama Govinda's, Blofeld's emphasizes the difficulty of going back to ordinary life and his painfully frustrated longing to return to an egoless state.

The unlikelihood of Blofeld's long journey to Vajrayana Buddhism, given his childhood upbringing in an English middle-class family, is evidence for him of the truth of the Buddhist idea of reincarnation: "How could my chosen mode of life or even my presence there in Sikkim, under such circumstances, be explained in the light of my upbringing and family background, except as the logical result of trends stretching back past my birth?" (18). As a child, he had several experiences of altered perception that he later interpreted with the help of Buddhist ideas such as "the Mahayana doctrine concerning the subjectivity of phenomena" (20). At the age of ten, he was unaccountably moved to purchase a small statue of the Buddha, to revere it, and to invoke its aid against bullies. Sitting on the sacred mountain in the Himalayas, Blofeld realizes that this and other childhood incidents, such as the strong impression made by an Indian film, mean that he must have been a Buddhist in a previous life:

> It was as if "something in the air" at Tashiding had sharpened my perceptions, enabling me to see that Buddhism had played so great a part in my immediately previous incarnation that the "memory" of a well-loved symbol had lain near enough to the surface of my child's consciousness for me to be able to "recognize" it at first sight. (24–25)

Although he had believed in reincarnation before, at this moment what had been purely intellectual adherence became a matter of faith based on a personal experience that stretched his sense of self.

The Origins of the Genre 27

The opening chapter of *The Wheel of Life* explains the major transformation in the author's life, his commitment to Buddhism, as closely linked to these experiences of connectedness to lives distant in time and space: "My conversion to Buddhism was in fact a RECONVERSION, which took place after the veil separating me from a conscious recollection of my previous life had now and then been momentarily blown aside. This explains why I became a Buddhist in a manner that was neither clearly reasoned nor the result of logical argument" (30). Blofeld had long sensed that his being was larger than the individual self, and at Tashiding, he interprets these experiences in terms of his belief in reincarnation. He is one of the few Western writers for whom the meaning of no-self is linked to experiences presented as evidence for the truth of reincarnation – or, put more modestly, as Blofeld's reasons for "reconversion." Certain other authors we will consider discuss karma and argue for the continuing influence of past lives, but Blofeld, like Govinda, is unusual in his explicit affirmation of reincarnation.

At the end of the first chapter, Blofeld leaves the reader with a spiritual cliffhanger, as "the hour of my (perhaps final) initiation was at hand" (30). He prepares to meet the Tibetan Buddhist lama whom he hopes will help him gain the "insight into Reality which would make me the equal of a Buddha!" (15). But before he returns, at the end of the book, to this initiation in Sikkim, Blofeld tells the story of his religious searching and travels up to this climactic moment.

He had attended Cambridge University for two years, leaving in 1932 for Hong Kong and China, where he lived until he moved to Bangkok in 1951. During his initial stay in Hong Kong, he encountered monks from the Gelugpa sect and was initiated into this form of Buddhism.[4] In spite of his reservations about the rituals and complex symbolism of Vajrayana, he had an intense experience when the presiding Rinpoche (an honorific term for a prominent Tibetan Buddhist teacher) rested his hands on Blofeld's head:

> At the touch of those hands, a shock of frightening strength shot through my body, racing down from head to throat and onwards through heart and solar plexus to the base of my spine, and simultaneously shooting out along my arms and legs, penetrating as far as my fingers and toes. My body must have shaken visibly with its violence. The room swam before me and a darkness, shot with fire, rushed upon me. (55)

This version of unselfing takes the form of a sudden access of power. When he returned to ordinary consciousness, he was at once exhausted

---

[4] He spells the sect "Gelugspa."

and aware of "a hidden but enormous reserve of strength," mixed pleasure and pain, and mingled joy and disquiet. In spite of this mysterious yet compelling event, the fading away of the sense of empowerment and the fact that he understood little of what the lama told him led Blofeld to reject Tibetan Buddhism "in favor of what *seemed* to me the nobler simplicity of Zen Buddhism" (55; all italicized words within quotations are italicized in the original). Yet the memory of that event in Hong Kong stayed with him, reminding him of another reality that he had briefly known.

Blofeld uses the titular image of the wheel of life to characterize his failure to understand that an extraordinary state of mind cannot be sustained:

> I had half expected to be permanently uplifted and set free once and for all from desire for purely worldly pursuits. As nothing of the kind had happened to me, I began to tell myself that perhaps I was still too young to see life as a wheel revolving amid an ocean of sorrows; but, at the same time, I realized that until I did see life that way I had no hope of reaching a state of mind capable of yielding the fruits of Nirvana. I was like a schoolboy who well knows that, if he does not soon begin to work for his examination, he will risk failure and perhaps dismissal from the school, but who goes on postponing the task until tomorrow and tomorrow. (56)

This passage reveals a continuing conflict in Blofeld's understanding of Buddhism. He knows that attaining and maintaining the condition where self-consciousness dissolves is not something he can do simply as an act of will. On the other hand, he cannot deny that he is disappointed about this, and he blames himself for procrastination and laziness when faced with the need for demanding and disciplined effort. He remembered his experience of unselfing with gratitude and also felt frustrated and guilty that he could not find a way to return to this state.

As Blofeld traveled throughout Asia during the next several decades, he sought out Confucian, Taoist, and Buddhist hermits and teachers. He asked them how he should understand ultimate reality and practice a spiritual life. He tried many practices and reproached himself for not sticking to one, exerting himself with greater effort, and making clear progress toward enlightenment. The ideal of renouncing the world appealed strongly to him, and he sometimes describes as impediments his family life and work for the United Nations in Bangkok. Yet he was equally attracted to the Tibetan Buddhist ideal, which, in contrast to what Blofeld says is the Chinese Buddhist emphasis on renunciation of the world, "teaches the realization of *Nirvana* through *Samsara* or 'seeking truth *through* life'" (139). He studied and practiced many traditions but

The Origins of the Genre 29

did not commit himself to any one, perhaps because nothing else quite measured up to the overwhelming experience of unselfing that he had with the Tibetan monks.

At the end of *The Wheel of Life*, Blofeld returns to the scene described in the first chapter, the initiation ceremony at Tashiding. He had finally come to the firm conclusion that Vajrayana was "best suited to my attainments and spiritual capacities" (238). Because he could not go to Tibet after the Chinese takeover, his choices were limited to the Tibetan borderlands. He secured an audience with the Rinpoche living at the monastery of Tashiding and convinced him of his sincerity and commitment. Blofeld is reticent about the details of his initiation and says that it would not be proper to share them with the reader, for without a teacher's instruction the outer form of the ritual would mean little. After the ceremony he muses: "This *could* be the turning point of my life.... Henceforth, my fate rested, not in other hands, but in my own" (252). But as he concludes the original edition of *The Wheel of Life*, published two years after the initiation, Blofeld laments squandering a precious opportunity:

> Back in Bangkok amid the clamorous surroundings of a worldly city, with few friends to share my enthusiasm or to drive me forward with stern words of encouragement and by high example, the great urge which lay upon me daily in the mountains has sadly declined. No longer am I blessedly tormented by the Great Thirst; no longer do I maintain iron control over the sinews of body and spirit.... Whether I shall gather strength to press the great assault, steeling the will to gain it all or perish—time alone will show. (258)

The transformation he hoped for had not taken place; his glimpse of his own Buddha nature as "One with Ultimate Reality" was obscured by his feeling that he was separated from other beings. Although Blofeld knew that, for a Buddhist, "Ultimate Unity" is to be recognized rather than attained or possessed, he views his failure to live according to this truth as a moral and spiritual fault that betrays the potential for a radical transformation that he sensed in moments of unselfing, such as his initiation into Vajrayana.

A second edition of Blofeld's autobiography in 1972 includes two new chapters that continue his rueful, wistful tone. "The Ox-drawn Spacecraft," the title of one chapter, is a metaphor for himself that captures both the dynamic power of Vajrayana to take him to a new place and "the fetters forged by my own karma—outstanding among them the fetter of sloth" (259). He has greater understanding of enlightenment but fails to live in accord with this knowledge. Enlightenment depends not only on intellectual comprehension, but also, he suggests, on further experiences of unselfing:

> Every step forward in the understanding of such matters as non-duality, the egolessness of all compounded entities, the fundamental identity of Nirvana and Sangsara [*sic*], the folly of longing for extinction on the one hand or eternal life on the other—every such step, *provided the understanding is at least partly experiential and not merely intellectual*, brings one nearer to liberation. Above all, the egolessness or *voidness* of all compounded entities must be directly experienced. (263)

By this time, Blofeld had enough direct experiences to be committed to Buddhism, and he found Tibetan practices and rituals to be the best way of living the Dharma. But without further experiences of unselfing, he feels stuck at the level of intellectual understanding. Meeting "Three Grand Lamas" (the second added chapter), including the XIV Dalai Lama, provides welcome assurance that what he hopes for is possible: human beings can realize and embody the unity of wisdom and compassion that is the central meaning of the Dharma.

In "A Farewell Letter," written shortly before his death in 1987 and appended to the third edition of *The Wheel of Life*, Blofeld remarks on his astonishment that Buddhism is now flourishing in the West just as it is rapidly eroding in Asia, especially in urban areas and among younger people. He encourages Westerners who practice Buddhism but warns against attempts to create a ritual-free meditation practice. Blofeld affirms that humility and reverence are at work in the Tibetan love of rituals and supernatural beings, which have parallels in all dharma traditions: "Asian Buddhists bow to the ground, burn incense before the Three Jewels, the departed Patriarchs, teachers and so on, believing that success in meditation without the practice of reverence tends to inflate the sense of egohood and thus eliminates whatever good effects may accrue from meditation" (291). Ritual helps guard against ego inflation and nourishes "a wholesome spirit of reverence, awe, humility or whatever, for someone or something greater than little me" (291). Participating in ceremonies was the occasion of several experiences of unselfing for Blofeld, and he hopes that Western adepts, impatient with Buddhism's ritual expressions, will not forgo similar possibilities. Ideas about self and no-self shape his perspective on this and many other questions about Buddhist thought and practice.

Blofeld is a groundbreaking figure for several reasons. His autobiography is the first Western autobiography to explain in detail how the author's experiences led him to become a Buddhist. He followed Buddha's advice to study and revere the words of sacred texts and contemporary teachers, "but only to accept such teachings if we have put them thoroughly to the test and thus gained evidence of their merit in the light of direct experience" (290).

The Origins of the Genre

Many Westerners are attracted to this "try it and see for yourself" approach to Buddhism, which they see as a stark contrast with monotheistic admonitions to submit in faith to what cannot be understood. This way of thinking provides a distinctly Buddhist rationale for writing autobiographical narratives that interpret Buddhist concepts in light of the author's experience.

Blofeld's pioneering way of combining vivid details of far-flung travels with introspective reflection on Buddhism's personal meaning was a model for later travel narratives, even if few people could match his lifetime of geographical wandering and deep exploration of diverse Buddhist traditions. His focus on unselfing and his search for experience as well as theoretical understanding exemplifies the orientation of all of the writers I examine here. *The Wheel of Life* set a precedent for other writers who discover Tibetan Buddhism in its diaspora after the Chinese takeover of Tibet, and also for the authors discussed in the final chapter, which deals with the search for what survived Mao. Like Blofeld when he wrote *The Wheel of Life* and *My Journey in Mystic China*, their narratives explore not only a place but also the lost time when Chinese Buddhism flourished before the onslaught of Communist orthodoxy. When Blofeld wrote about Chinese religions as he had known them in the 1930s and 1940s, he questioned whether they would survive. For a younger generation writing several decades after the Cultural Revolution, the impetus for a journey to China was certain knowledge that traditional Buddhism had been devastated by the Red Guard, yet they hoped to salvage fragments for a future recovery. For them as much as for Blofeld, a Chinese journey would lead to experiences of unselfing and unfinished transformation.

*

Lama Govinda's *The Way of the White Clouds* focuses on a spectacular and hazardous journey to western Tibet in 1948.[5] Compared with Blofeld's autobiography, Govinda says relatively little about the rest of his life, and almost nothing about the eighteen years before the book's publication. His more focused depiction of two journeys to Tibet prefigures and shapes the explosion of travel memoirs by Westerners beginning in the 1970s. He took the traditional tale of a trek in a new direction, going deeper into the personal and Buddhist meanings of what had been for earlier Western writers a story of adventure and exploration and an outsider's report on an exotic religion.

[5] Lama Anagarika Govinda, *The Way of the White Clouds: A Buddhist Pilgrim in Tibet* (London: Rider and Company, 1966).

32 The Origins of the Genre

Lama Anagarika Govinda (1898–1985) was born in Germany as Ernst Hoffmann. In 1928, after serving in World War I and several years of painting and studying, he went to Ceylon.[6] A convinced Buddhist since he was eighteen, he had intended to become a Theravada monk, but instead decided to become an *anagarika*, a homeless layman, and took the name Govinda. Convinced that Theravada was the original and purest form of Buddhism, he went in 1931 to a Buddhist conference in Darjeeling, planning to convert the adherents of other traditions. Unexpectedly, he found that Tibetan Buddhism was not, as he supposed, simply a degenerated mixture of fantastic beliefs and magic rituals to propitiate demonic beings. At a Tibetan monastery at Ghoom, he encountered a Gelugpa teacher with the name Lama Ngawang Kalzang and the title Tomo Géshé Rinpoche, who inspired him and became his primary spiritual mentor for the rest of his life. Tomo Géshé had meditated alone for twelve years in remote mountains. At the heart of his vision of life was the inseparability of self and world: "What actually he had forgotten was not the world but his own self, because the 'world' is something that exists only in contrast to one's own ego" (7). The pivotal moment in Govinda's spiritual trajectory was this encounter with a guru who showed him the possibility of enlightenment not only in the distant past or after many future lives, but also here and now. He subsequently became a Tibetan Buddhist, although he remained appreciative of other forms of the Dharma and saw their common core as direct insight into the emptiness and relatedness of all things.

Lama Govinda was hugely influential in the early transmission of Buddhism to the West, inspiring John Blofeld, Baba Ram Dass (Richard Alpert), Timothy Leary, Daniel Goleman, Joseph Goldstein, Sharon Salzburg, Gary Snyder, Allen Ginsberg, Huston Smith, and others. Many of these individuals visited Govinda at a Bohemian colony in northern India known as Crank's Ridge. Several American professors of Religious Studies told me that reading books by John Blofeld and Lama Govinda was their first exposure to Tibetan Buddhism, motivating them to study it and travel to Asia in search of teachers and opportunities to practice. Govinda was the first Western lama, and, although he did not speak Tibetan and interpreted Buddhism in debatable ways,

---

[6] For biographical details of Govinda's life, see Richard Power, "Within the White Cloud: Life and Work of Lama Govinda," in *The Lost Teachings of Lama Govinda*, ed. Richard Power (Wheaton, IL: Quest Books, 2007), xvii–lviii.

he was accepted and respected by Tibetan teachers.[7] From 1931 to 1962, Govinda made his home in northern India, including a period of internment by the British during World War II. From India, Govinda traveled with his wife, a painter from Bombay named Li Gotami, to Tibet on several journeys. *The Way of the White Clouds* describes these travels, climaxing with an extraordinary journey in 1948 to Tsaparang, a remote abandoned city and monastery in western Tibet.

In the Foreword, Lama Govinda says that his book is not a travelogue, but the description of "a *pilgrimage* in the truest sense of the word, because a pilgrimage distinguishes itself from an ordinary journey by the fact that it does not follow a laid-out plan or itinerary, that it does not pursue a fixed aim or a limited purpose, but that it carries its meaning in itself, by relying on an inner urge which operates on two planes: on the physical as well as on the spiritual plane. It is a movement not only in the outer, but equally in the inner space" (xiii). In terms remarkably similar to Thomas Merton's view of pilgrimage, Govinda sketches the kind of travel at the heart of the genre of the spiritual travel narrative: a journey that is related to a historical religious tradition and also involves an idiosyncratic itinerary and an inner voyage of self-discovery.

Tsaparang was an abandoned fortress, city, and monastery in desiccated western Tibet that had been the capital and religious center of the ancient kingdom of Guge. *The Way of the White Clouds* begins with a section recounting three visions that inspire Govinda to form a plan to save the beautiful artworks of this place from oblivion. In "The Poet's Vision," he describes an experience in the ruins of Tsaparang when he receives the protection and help of Tara, a female Buddha and deity. In "The Guru's Vision," Govinda recounts how Tomo Géshé witnessed a pantheon of Buddhas. Govinda then goes back in time to explain how he reached Tsaparang, reporting how he became a Buddhist and encountered Tome Géshé. Partly because of his guru, he learned to appreciate artistic representations of the Dharma in dance, music, theater, and visual arts, in contrast to the stark and ascetic Theravada tradition:

---

[7] Donald Lopez, Jr. *Prisoners of Shangri-La: Tibetan Buddhism and the West* (Chicago: University of Chicago Press, 1998), 60, challenges Govinda's claims to have been initiated into several Tibetan Buddhist orders: "It is difficult to imagine what transpired between the Tibetan monk and the German traveler (dressed in the robes of a Theravada monk, although he seems not to have been ordained), who spoke no Tibetan, or what this 'initiation' may have been (it was perhaps the most preliminary of Buddhist rituals, the refuge ceremony). Govinda's description of any instruction he may have received is vague."

The Origins of the Genre

> The images and frescoes around me were not merely beautiful decorations of aesthetic value but representations of a higher reality, born from visions and inner experience. They were put into as precise a language of forms as is contained in a geographical map or a scientific formula, while being as natural in expression and as direct in appeal as a flower or a sunset. (54)

Tibetan Buddhism's prolific expressions of artistic creativity deeply appealed to Govinda, tapping into youthful aesthetic experiences that he had not been able to integrate with his life as a Buddhist. Now he could affirm that art is not a dangerous sensual pleasure but has potential to awaken a person to other realities and to precipitate transformative experiences. Art is a catalyst for unselfing.

The first section of *The Way of White Clouds* closes with "The Chela's Vision." As a *chela* (disciple or devotee), Govinda decides to do in his own way what his guru did for him: communicate the Dharma to others by strengthening their visionary powers and their capacity to discern the truth revealed in artistic forms:

> I now saw clearly the message which he had communicated to me through this vision; and out of the wish to convey to others what I had seen and experienced the idea was born in me to follow the way of the Lama-artists of yore and faithfully to reproduce in line and colour the traditions of a great past, which had been treasured in the temples and mountain fastnesses of Tibet. (55)

The rest of *The Way of the White Clouds* recounts Govinda's efforts to accomplish this mission by journeying into Tibet in search of Buddhist art. Along the way, he encounters remarkable hermits and teachers, esoteric rituals and teachings, and sweeping mountain vistas. The form of a travel narrative allows Govinda to describe his interpretations of encounters and spectacles that are opportunities for unselfing. Diverse Tibetan Buddhist practices can transform ordinary perception and engender unusual states of consciousness. Unselfing is not a rare or unusual experience for Govinda but a regularly recurring event in the rhythm of Tibetan Buddhist life and in his own itinerary.

Without using the term no-self, Govinda interprets how ritual practices, art, and personal encounters can transform a person by altering their sense of their relation to the world. These experiences challenge conventional Western ideas about the self's identity, boundaries, and capacities. For example, consider how Govinda describes his reaction when a hermit takes over his consciousness:

> I had the sensation that somebody took possession of my consciousness, my will-power and my body—that I had no more control over my thoughts,

The Origins of the Genre 35

> but that somebody else was thinking them—and that, slowly but surely, I was losing my own identity. And then I realised that it could be none other than the hermit, who, by directing his attention upon me, had entered my body and taken possession of it, probably quite unintentionally, due to the power of his concentration and my own lack of resistance in the moment while I was hovering between the waking and the sleeping state. (101)

Frightened by his sense of lost identity, Govinda frantically draws a self-portrait "to assure myself of my own reality" (102). The next day, the hermit suggests that Govinda meditate on the subject of "The Eighteen Kinds of Voidness" (103). Govinda feels both an intense desire to keep a firm grip on his sense of personal identity and a yearning for the hermit's apprehension of a far greater reality. As in this situation, Govinda usually begins with terror and then emphasizes that loss of self brings liberation and fulfillment. The hermit taught him that "we cannot face the Great Void before we have the strength and the greatness to fill it with our entire being. Then the Void is not the negation merely of our limited personality, but the Plenum-Void which includes, embraces, and nourishes it, like the womb of space in which the light moves eternally without ever being lost" (103). Many other experiences, such as several times when he witnesses telepathy, involve similar feelings of fright and then exhilaration at what violates his usual sense of his capacities and boundaries.

Govinda's version of unselfing resembles and was surely influenced by the Romantic experience of the Sublime, in that what at first overwhelms or terrifies the self leads to exaltation and a sense of increased power. In this spiritual death and rebirth, what must be left behind is the self as ego: "The root of suffering is man's egohood, which separates him from his fellow-beings and from the sources of reality" (113). The ego, the deepest source of suffering, can only be overcome by regression to a preconscious, subhuman state of awareness or by being "fully born" so that one transcends the egocentric relation to the world. The purpose of Buddhist meditation is "a process of *transformation*, of *transcendence*, in which we become fully conscious of the present, of the infinite powers and possibilities of the mind, in order to become masters of our own destiny, by cultivating those qualities which lead to the realization of our timeless nature: to enlightenment" (114). Govinda speaks of self-transformation with the rhetoric of fulfillment, liberation, and empowerment, as when he says that meditation builds "already *now* the bodies of future perfection in the image of our highest ideals" (114). He never speaks, as John Blofeld does, of disappointment or frustration that he must return to ordinary life or cannot return to the moment of unselfing.

The Way of the White Clouds explores why long-distance walking in Tibet nurtures a state of mind conducive to unselfing. It is partly the mountain setting, where the grandeur of the landscape suggests human limitations; here, ordinary human preoccupations seem petty and one feels called to greater things and a higher purpose. The uncertainties of a trek, if faced with resilience and courage, strengthen one's independence and freedom:

> When every detail of our life is planned and regulated, and every fraction of time determined beforehand, then the last trace of our boundless and timeless being, in which the freedom of our soul exists, will be suffocated. This freedom does not consist in being able 'to do what we want,' it is neither arbitrariness nor waywardness, nor the thirst for adventures, but the capacity to accept the unexpected, the unthought-of situations of life, good as well as bad, with an open mind; it is the capacity to adapt oneself to the infinite variety of conditions without losing confidence in the deeper connections between the inner and the outer world. (60)

These passages echo evocations of the Romantic Sublime by Alpine climbers and wandering poets since the nineteenth century, which were part of Govinda's education in Germany. At many points, he uses the customary rhetoric of earlier adventurers in Tibet without adding specifically Buddhist meanings.

Govinda also attributes the trek's potential for unselfing to the quality of the atmosphere, the luminosity of colors ("the living language of light"), and the thin air and low humidity of high altitudes, which he speculates may facilitate telepathy. A trekker's long stretches of solitude and silence induce concentration, introspection, and sensitivity to impressions that would be dissipated by interactions with other people. The combined influence of all these factors on a mountain walker stimulates a form of consciousness that he compares to the ideal state of mind realized in meditation:

> Thus a strange transformation takes place under the influence of this country, in which the valleys are as high as the highest peaks of Europe and where mountains soar into space beyond the reach of humans. It is as if a weight were lifted from one's mind, or as if certain hindrances were removed. Thoughts flow easily and spontaneously without losing their direction and coherence, a high degree of concentration and clarity is attained almost without effort and a feeling of elevated joy keeps one's mind in a creative mood. Consciousness seems to be raised to a higher level, where the obstacles and disturbances of our ordinary life do not exist, except as a faint memory of things which have lost all their importance and attraction. At the same time one becomes more sensate and open to new forms of reality;

The Origins of the Genre 37

the intuitive qualities of our mind are awakened and stimulated—in short, there are all the conditions for attaining the higher stages of meditation or *dhyana*. (62)

Here, Govinda describes the preconditions for a form of unselfing unknown to traditional Buddhist monks or Romantic poets, but drawing from both East and West to create a distinctive new version of spiritual transformation.

Govinda's account of mountain trekking will be echoed by many later writers who compare it to meditation. Tibet's geographical features foster an altered state of consciousness because of the way they condition walking. At high altitude, one must regulate one's breathing and movements carefully. Govinda learns to walk with a slow and steady pace and to breathe in harmony with his steps. "Walking, therefore, becomes almost a kind of conscious *hatha-yoga* or breathing exercise, especially when accompanied by rhythmic recitations of sacred formulas (*mantras*), as is the habit with many Tibetans. This has a very tranquillizing and energizing effect, as I found from my own experience" (63). Walkers in other settings, such as India's baking plains or Japan's Shikoku pilgrimage circuit, will explore other ways in which peregrination can induce unselfing.

Govinda inadvertently performs *lung-gom*, the Tibetan practice of trance walking. This spiritual exercise, vividly described by Alexandra David-Neel, involves traveling for many hours at great speed over rough territory in a manner that seems superhuman. In a trance, the walker moves across a field of stones as if bouncing or dancing, finding sure footing and miraculously avoiding injury. One day while Govinda was exploring a remote mountain alone, he was overtaken by darkness. Without food, water, or shelter, he was in deadly peril. Somehow he found the strength to keep going, no longer picking his way but jumping from boulder to boulder in a pair of flimsy sandals:

> And then I realized that a strange force had taken over, a consciousness that was no more guided by my eyes or my brain. My limbs moved as in a trance, with an uncanny knowledge of their own, though their movement seemed almost mechanical. I noticed things only like in a dream, somewhat detached. Even my own body had become distant, quasi-detached from my will-power. I was like an arrow that unfailingly pursued its course by the force of its initial impetus, and the only thing I knew was that on no condition must I break the spell that had seized me. (78)

In this situation of imminent death, Govinda duplicated the feats of those who do trance walking as a yogic practice:

> Unwittingly and under the stress of circumstance and acute danger I had become a *lung-gom-pa*, a trance walker, who, oblivious of all obstacles and fatigue, moves on towards his contemplated aim, hardly touching the ground, which might give a distant observer the impression that the *lung-gom-pa* was borne by the air (*lung*), merely skimming the surface of the earth. (78)

After many miles of sure-footed leaping in the darkness, when a misstep would have meant dying from exposure, Govinda found his companions' camp.

He disagrees with David-Neel's explanation of trance walking as involving anesthesia that deadens pain. Not less than ordinary consciousness, but much more, is required for such feats. At yogic training centers, he witnessed adepts learning trance walking with spiritual practices that overcome the separation of mind and matter: "The deeper meaning of *lung-gom* is that matter can be mastered by the mind.... *Gom* (*sgom*) means meditation, contemplation, concentration of mind and soul upon a certain subject, as well as the gradual emptying of the mind of all subject-object relationship, until a complete identification of subject and object has taken place" (81).

A similar form of spiritual practice is *tum-mo*, the generation of inner heat that allows Tibetan yogis to expose themselves to extreme cold and even to produce steam from wet shirts donned in freezing temperatures. David-Neel had reported on this striking phenomenon, too, looking for a rational explanation of what seemed to be magic; for instance, *tum-mo* may be motivated by the need to survive Tibet's harsh conditions. Govinda goes deeper into the spiritual meaning of practices such as *lung-gom* and *tum-mo*; their purpose is "the attainment of inner unification or integration, which brings about the state of enlightenment and the wholeness of being" (82). These practices are not feats of bravado or reasons for pride because a person's training for them "is based on the giving up and not on the strengthening of his ego, in which pride and ambition have their origin" (82). Demanding training is required for these exercises, yet Govinda was somehow able to perform them inadvertently. In the instance of unselfing when he trance-walked, his body seemed to take over as his mind watched, yet the accomplishment of an apparently impossible task suggests an intuitive wisdom based on a hidden unity of matter and mind. Unlike earlier Western travelers, Govinda does not just describe what Tibetans believe or do; he presents his own experience of performing an action that depends on "wholeness of being."

Like John Blofeld, he affirms that "for myself rebirth is neither a theory, nor a belief, but an experience" (147). When he was twenty-one and living

The Origins of the Genre

on Capri, Govinda read to a friend a story he had written. The friend already knew the story, which had been written a century earlier by a German mystic and poet. Govinda does not say who this writer was, but one scholar identifies the earlier writer as Novalis.[8] The Tibetan belief in reincarnation helps Govinda understand this puzzling experience: "This is what Tibet has taught me, where the saints and Siddhas of old kept on returning through ever new incarnations, in ever new forms until the present day" (149). If anything directly challenges Western concepts of individual selfhood, it is reincarnation. Unlike Blofeld and Govinda, later travel writers drawn to Buddhism have rarely described experiences that they believe validate belief in reincarnation, although many think they discern the effects of karma in their own lives. This characteristic of Western Buddhist travel narratives contrasts with the many claims about reincarnation in New Age spiritual writings.

Govinda was one of the first Westerners to present from the inside what it is like to be devoted to a guru. He asserts that in meditation the guru, the Buddha, and one's own individual identity become merged:

> One should imagine the Buddha in the form of one's Guru, and having done so to a degree that one feels his very presence, one should visualize him seated in the posture of meditation above one's head and finally merging into one's own person, to take his seat on the lotus-throne of our heart. For, as long as the Buddha is still imagined outside ourselves, we cannot realize him in our own life. (35)

In the book's final chapter, when Govinda says farewell to his guru, "lo!— without knowing how it happened—the deep voice of the Guru sounded from my own chest!" (281). Others hear the voice, too, and "since then the voice has come back whenever I remembered the Guru" (281). It's not clear how literally Govinda means this claim; in any case, he tries to show that love and devotion to a guru overcome the ordinary sense of discrete and separate identities. No Western writer before Govinda shows so well the deep bond between guru and *chela*; this merging of identities is one of the main ways that the sense of ordinary selfhood is transcended in later narratives about Buddhism.

The Way of the White Clouds combines descriptions of Govinda's extensive travels in Tibet with interpretations of architecture, artwork, dances, rituals, and performances of "mystery plays." Using the structure

---

[8] Wikipedia article on Lama Govinda, note 20, referring to Hellmuth Hecker's *Lebensbilder Deutscher Buddhisten Band* (1990).

of a travel narrative, Govinda strings together his reflections on these arts like beads or jewels on a necklace. He believes that such arts stimulate enlarged consciousness and engaged imagination. Encounters with artistic beauty are openings to spiritual truth. His accounts of witnessing these events merge into a theory of how the ideal watcher, hearer, or believer should be affected by the symbolism of art or ritual. Always it is the overcoming of ego and the intuition that a person is ultimately at one with the world that is offered to those willing to give themselves to the experience. For instance, an oracle who undergoes a violent possession by an unknown power is not simply a spectacle, but a role model for the surrender called for in those who witness the ordeal: "We ourselves could feel how we were lifted out of our own consciousness and seized by an upsurge of uncontrollable emotion, so that we threw ourselves like the others at the feet of the Oracle, oblivious of anything else around us, except the reality of a power beyond our understanding" (186). The oracle-priest who falls into an unconscious state after being violently possessed is not a case of primitive demon worship, as earlier Western observers had held. Govinda compares the ordeal to Christ's sacrifice: "the crucifixion of a human being, sacrificed on the altar of primeval powers in the service of a higher ideal to which even those powers had to submit for the welfare and guidance of men, who still were struggling in the meshes of samsaric life" (187). Tibetan rituals and art provide regular occasions for believers to recognize the limits of selfhood by enabling them to undergo an experience that is at once aesthetic and religious as it brings about transformed consciousness.

Pilgrimage effects a similar unselfing that leads to bliss. When pilgrims circumambulate Mount Kailash, they give up comfort and safety for danger and hardship. Govinda explicitly links this form of travel with transformation:

> Their mental faculties seem to be heightened, their awareness and spiritual sensitivity infinitely increased, their consciousness reaching out into a new dimension, so that many of them see wonderful visions and hear strange voices and fall into trance-like states, in which all their former obstructions and difficulties disappear like in a flash of light that suddenly lights up what was hidden hitherto. It is as if their individual consciousness, which obscured or distorted their views or their conception of the world were receding and giving place to an all-embracing cosmic consciousness. (204)

Govinda merges his own autobiography with quasi-ethnographic interpretation in this account of "the pilgrim" who must leave behind his ego to endure suffering.

The final section of *The Way of the White Clouds* describes the stunning art and architecture of Tsaparang and the efforts of Govinda and Li Gotang to document it. They photographed, sketched, traced the frescoes, and described ancient works of art that were soon to be destroyed during China's Cultural Revolution. Li's spectacular photographs enrich *The Way of the White Clouds* and she also published *Tibet in Pictures: A Journey into the Past.*[9] The couple worked frantically from September to December 1948, trying to finish their work before winter set in or they were expelled. Sheltering in a crude stone hut, eating only chapattis and porridge, drinking tea before it froze in their cups, suspended from improvised scaffolding, and struggling to find enough light to sketch and photograph frescoes, they painstakingly documented the precious images surviving in the ruins of Tsaparang. The narrative closes with Govinda asserting that he discovered a vocation for the rest of his life and the motivation to write the book:

> We knew that the Gurus and the treasures of memory that this unforgettable country had bestowed on us would remain with us till the end of our days and that, if we succeeded in passing on to others even a part of those treasures and of our Gurus' teachings, we would feel that we had repaid a little of the debt of gratitude that we owe to Tibet and to our Teachers. (282)

He and Li Gotang dedicate the rest of their lives to conveying to the world the heritage of Tibet in "word, line, and colour."

In an epilogue, he expresses gratitude to Tomo Géshé Rimpoche and connects his guru's example and teaching to his own deep appreciation for art. The Vajrayana path leads right through the world of color and appearance, passing forms of beauty both natural and humanly created. One can meditate upon "the Buddha of Infinite Light" while facing the setting sun, a mandala, a mighty peak, or a statue. For Lama Govinda, unselfing is a frequent experience prompted by encounters with a guru, natural beauty, and many artistic forms. All of these occasions beckon one to forget the self and recognize one's participation in a greater life and a process of constant change. His many accounts of unselfing always culminate in statements about its uplifting, lofty, or ennobling effect. His version of unselfing echoes the rhetoric of the Romantic Sublime expressed by earlier Western explorers, but Govinda knew far more about Buddhism than they did. In this spiritual autobiography, which takes the form of a travel

---

[9] Li Gotami, *Tibet in Pictures: A Journey into the Past*, 2 volumes (Cazadero, CA: Dharma Publishing, 1979).

narrative, it was how Buddhism shaped and made sense of his experiences of unselfing that Govinda most wanted to convey. Like John Blofeld, Lama Govinda gave a distinctively Buddhist interpretation to experiences of unselfing that were the high points of a much-traveled life.

Their common emphasis on religious experience as contrasted with theory and theology is a common trait of spiritual autobiographers. It is also one of the primary traits of Buddhist Modernism, as argued by scholars such as David McMahon.[10] The most significant form of experience for these writers is pivotal moments of unselfing, which play a crucial role in personal transformation. Here is Govinda reflecting on his encounter with his Tibetan guru:

> I realized that religious truths and spiritual life are more a matter of transcending our habitual consciousness than of changing our opinions or building our convictions on the strength of intellectual arguments and syllogisms, of the laws of reasons, which will never lead us beyond the circle of what is already known in the form of ready-made concepts: the cut-and-dried bricks with which we have constructed the present world of "material reality" and "common sense." (16)

Whatever else modern Westerners believe in – God, science, Buddhism, or the primacy of the human heart – they believe in transformation, by which they mean a reorientation of their whole being. The autobiographical writing that describes transformation explores not only its intellectual components and what an author believes, but also other existential dimensions, such as emotions, psychology, intuitions, and relationships with other people. The cult of experience, the sense that much more is involved in religion than ideas and belief, can lead to an anti-intellectual stance. Or it can indicate appreciation of the need to integrate the intellectual aspects of a religious tradition with its wisdom about other dimensions of human existence. Blofeld and Govinda, who each gave his whole life to the study and practice of Buddhism, showed how an autobiographical writer can provide a rich and compelling account of experiences – above all, transformation – with many dimensions and inexhaustible meaning and mystery. In addition, they reveal how much Buddhism is transformed as it is interpreted by Western adherents.

[10] David McMahon, *The Making of Buddhist Modernism* (Oxford: Oxford University Press, 2008).

CHAPTER 2

Peter Matthiessen's The Snow Leopard *and* Nine-Headed Dragon River

Peter Matthiessen's *The Snow Leopard* (1978) is a masterpiece that won the National Book Award in the United States. It defined Western Buddhist travel narratives as a recognizable genre and remains the most admired and influential example of this kind of literature. The quest for self-transformation is central to its plot and theme. Matthiessen's more diffuse and uneven *Nine-Headed Dragon River* (1985) covers a thirteen-year period and includes portions of *The Snow Leopard*; it has not received much notice or acclaim. This work culminates in a journey to Japan that reveals changes in Matthiessen's understanding and practice of Buddhism and his search for experiences of unselfing and transformation. I devote an entire chapter to Matthiessen's works because *The Snow Leopard* remains the best known and arguably the most compelling Western Buddhist travel narrative and the classic that for most readers defines the genre, and because his two narratives explore both Tibetan and Zen Buddhist traditions.

In the autumn of 1973, Peter Matthiessen accompanied biologist George Schaller on a field trip to Nepal to study the Himalayan blue sheep. The two men hoped, as well, to spot the rare snow leopard. Matthiessen was also pursuing two spiritual goals on this journey: to further his knowledge and experience of Buddhism, which he had been practicing since December 1970, and to come to terms with the recent death of his wife, Deborah Love. These several purposes are related in many ways. The search for the snow leopard becomes a symbol of the quest for enlightenment and prompts reflections on the conditions that make possible a vision of ultimate truth. The physical challenges of the two-month trek are a testing ground for the practice of Buddhist mindfulness, patience, compassion, and other virtues. The process of working through his grief for his wife's death demands emotional vulnerability and acceptance, which were unfamiliar to him. To meet these challenges, he had to grow and adapt in ways that stretched him to become a different sort of person.

44   *The Snow Leopard* and *Nine-Headed Dragon River*

In charting his journeys toward these geographical and spiritual goals, Matthiessen portrays both the habits that make it so difficult to change and experiences of unselfing that disclose the possibility of a radically different way of being.

Although *The Snow Leopard* takes the form of a travel journal, with daily entries from September 28 to December 1, 1973, the book was heavily edited before publication in 1978. Matthiessen wrote elsewhere that for two years (1974–1976), "polishing my Himalayan journals had become my practice, taking the place of the intense sesshin attendance of the past four years."[1] *The Snow Leopard* has the fragmentary, detailed, day-to-day quality of a diary written in the midst of unfolding events in the author's life. It also has characteristics of an autobiography or memoir, offering a retrospective perspective and assessment of the long-term significance of events. *The Snow Leopard*'s hybrid literary form – a heavily revised journal – is common in travel narratives, including many of the works to be examined in later chapters. Matthiessen showed what could be accomplished in a Western Buddhist travel narrative, most notably a compelling depiction of significant changes in an author's sense of self, moments of unselfing, and the continuing preoccupations and habits of mind that define individual character.

In the first day's entry in *The Snow Leopard*, Matthiessen describes his understanding of the Buddha's "creed" as an attempt to apply the serenity of yogic states attained in meditation to all of life, "until the transparent radiance of stilled mind opens out in *prajna*, or transcendent *knowing*, that higher consciousness of 'Mind' which is inherent in all sentient beings, and which depends on the unsentimental embrace of all existence" (18).[2] The experience of enlightenment or liberation brings transformation: "a profound vision of his identity with universal life, past, present, and future, that keeps man from doing harm to others and sets him free from fear of birth-and-death" (18). Ten days earlier, at Bodh Gaya, where the Buddha had attained enlightenment, Matthiessen sat at dawn with three Tibetan monks under the bodhi tree, but "came away no wiser than before" (19). These reflections on the journey's first day show a pattern that runs through the book: passages suggesting genuine and increasing understanding of the dharma are juxtaposed with remarks denying that the author has made any progress in comprehending or practicing Buddhist wisdom. *The Snow Leopard*'s narrative arc follows and links the

---

[1] Peter Matthiessen, *Nine-Headed Dragon River* (Boston: Shambhala, 1985), 67.
[2] Peter Matthiessen, *The Snow Leopard* (New York: Penguin, 1978).

author's outer journey and the shifts in his character and consciousness, interpreting these events in terms of Buddhist ideas.

The expedition that Matthiessen and Schaller undertake to Inner Dolpo in northwestern Nepal involves many hazards and logistical difficulties. Porters threaten to quit, food is so scarce that by the end of the trek they must subsist on rice and lentils, and winter's cold and snow threaten to trap the party in an inaccessible remote area. Matthiessen worries about his children, especially the youngest, eight-year-old Alex. He cannot keep his promise to his son to return by Thanksgiving. He worries about the weather, being stranded, and the constant danger of injury or death. All these concerns challenge his capacity to be fully present as a witness to the extraordinary beauty of the Himalayan Mountains. Moreover, grief for his wife's recent death often pulls him into melancholy or consoling memories of the past. Vivid descriptions of high passes, local people, and birds and animals alternate with portrayals of incidents in his past life, expositions of Buddhist ideas, and comparisons between Zen and Tibetan Buddhist traditions. Matthiessen feels too scattered to be fully present: "One 'I' feels like an observer of this man who lies here in this sleeping bag in Asian mountains; another 'I' is thinking about Alex; a third is the tired man who tries to sleep" (41).

In contrast to this distracted state of mind, Matthiessen describes several incidents when an experience of unselfing has occurred. While very different from each other, these events all contrast with the fragmented consciousness that Matthiessen wants to escape. The first account of unselfing is Matthiessen's interpretation of what his son experienced when playing in a sandbox before a sense of self emerged:

> In his first summers, forsaking all his toys, my son would stand rapt for near an hour in his sandbox in the orchard, as doves and redwings came and went on the warm wind, the leaves dancing, the clouds flying, birdsong and sweet smell of privet and rose. The child was not observing; he was at rest in the very center of the universe, a part of things, unaware of endings and beginnings, still in unison with the primordial nature of creation, letting all light and phenomena pour through. Ecstasy is identity with all existence, and ecstasy showed in his bright paintings; like the Aurignacian hunter, who became the deer he drew on the cave wall, there was no "self" to separate him from the bird or flower. (41–42)

A child's unselfconscious wonder, joy, and immersion in the world dissipate as he learns to protect himself: "The armor of the 'I' begins to form, the construction and desperate assertion of separate identity, the loneliness" (42).

Yet if backing away from identification with the world is a necessary part of human development, in scattered moments a person can recapture the sense of oneness that becomes lost. A second portrayal of unselfing is Matthiessen's recollection of a night in a storm on the high seas when he was battered into another state of consciousness:

> One night in 1945, on a Navy vessel in Pacific storm, my relief on bow watch, seasick, failed to appear, and I was alone for eight hours in a maelstrom of wind and water, noise and iron; again and again, waves crashed across the deck, until water, air, and iron became one. Overwhelmed, exhausted, all thought and emotion beaten out of me, I lost my sense of self, the heartbeat I heard was the heart of the world, I breathed with the mighty risings and declines of earth, and this evanescence seemed less frightening than exalting. Afterward, there was pain of loss—loss of *what*, I wondered, understanding nothing. (42–43)

Much of the literature to which Matthiessen was drawn, including works by Hesse, Kierkegaard, and Gurdjieff, described a search for mystical experience resembling this exaltation, as well as unbearable pangs of loss when the yearning is not satisfied.

For ten years Matthiessen had experimented with hallucinatory drugs, confusing beautiful and grotesque visions with religious experience. He fell in love with his future wife, Deborah Love, who was engaged in a similar search for "the path home" to one's true nature. On one drug trip he and Love seemed to have had one mind and to have become trees growing into each other. But the self always returned: "at no time did the 'I' dissolve into the miracle" (47). The insights and delusions of drug experience could not be carried into daily life, and "the alien chemical agent forms another mist, maintaining the separation of the 'I' from the experience of the One" (47). Matthiessen's use of drugs and turbulent relationship with Love expressed his yearning to transcend ordinary selfhood. But the self always returned.

Matthiessen and Love turned to Zen Buddhism with the hope that its disciplined practice might provide a way to find unity with all Being. In December 1970, he went to his first weekend retreat at the New York Zendo. *The Snow Leopard* reveals glimpses of Matthiessen's Buddhist practice during the three years preceding the Himalayan trek and articulates his early understanding of Zen. A central theme is his view that Zen provides a way to transcend the selfhood that obscures ultimate truth. What the Buddha perceived was "his identity with the universe ... that Mind which is shared with all of existence, that stillness, that incipience which never ceases because it never becomes but simply IS" (66). The ultimate

The Snow Leopard *and* Nine-Headed Dragon River   47

reality is different from "the illusion of the ego, the stuff of individual existence, the dream that separates us from a true perception of the whole" (66). Meditation, in Matthiessen's view, attempts to intuit the true nature of things and our unity with all being.

He sees the search for self-transcendence arising in every culture and forming the core of religious experience. The goal of every religious practice is obliteration of the ego, the falling away of the self, and dynamic resting in lucid consciousness of the present moment. Religious traditions, including different versions of Buddhism, have sought to induce this state using various means:

> Among Hindus and Buddhists, realization is attained through inner stillness, usually achieved through the *samadhi* state of sitting yoga. In Tantric practice, the student may displace the ego by filling his whole being with the real or imagined object of his concentration; in Zen, one seeks to empty out the mind, to return it to the clear, pure stillness of a seashell or a flower petal. (91)

Central to Matthiessen's understanding of Buddhism is his claim that ultimate reality is screened by ordinary self-consciousness and his belief that Buddhism offers several disciplined methods of overcoming the limitations of this perspective. His view that Zen provides the clearest understanding of the essential and universal substrate of all religious traditions remains widespread among Westerners attracted to Zen Buddhism, reflecting the enormous influence of D. T. Suzuki.[3]

A final incident of unselfing took place at a weekend retreat in November 1971, when the shock of confronting Love's imminent death struck Matthiessen forcefully. During a period of furious chanting, "I 'lost' myself, forgot the self—a purpose of the sutra" (106). At the same time, he felt "a Presence of vast benevolence of which *I was a part*" and a sense of belonging that brought tears of relief. "For the first time since unremembered childhood, I was not alone; there was no separate 'I'" (107). Here is one of many paradoxical aspects of no-self that recur in Western Buddhist travel narratives: Matthiessen asserts that he had no consciousness of self, yet he was aware of being not alone but in the company of something that seemed to embrace, reassure, and bless him. Consciousness of unity or "being with" a Presence seems to require the self-awareness that he claims was overcome or dissolved.

---

[3] An influential criticism of Suzuki's reliance on Western terms to interpret Zen, such as a transcendental notion of experience beyond culture, is Robert H. Sharf, "Buddhist Modernism and the Rhetoric of Meditative Experience," *Numen* 42 (1995), 228–283.

48   *The Snow Leopard* and *Nine-Headed Dragon River*

This powerful experience, which Matthiessen calls a state of grace, continued throughout the winter when Love was dying. He felt an inner calm and "perhaps because no ego was involved, the one who acted in this manner was not 'I'" (107). When his Roshi tells him "You have transcended," Matthiessen takes this to mean "transcended your ego." He felt forgiven, by Love and by himself, for all the difficulties and pain of their contentious relationship: "This forgiveness strikes me still as the greatest blessing of my life" (107). Yet the state of grace faded; the experience of unselfing did not become a permanent condition. Matthiessen makes a crucial point about the limitations of *kensho*, that is, seeing into one's original and true nature:

> A *kensho*, or *satori*, is no measure of enlightenment, since an insight into "one's True Nature" may vary widely in its depth and permanence: some may overturn existence, while others are mere tantalizing glimpses that "like a mist will surely disappear." To poke a finger through the wall is not enough—the whole wall must be brought down with a crash! My own experience had been premature, and a power seeped away, month after month. This saddened me, although I understood that I had scarcely started on the path; that but for D's crisis which had cut through forty years of encrustations, I might never have had such an experience at all; that great enlightenment was only born out of deep *Samadhi*. (108–109)

It was at this point that Matthiessen was invited to accompany Schaller on the Nepal trek. His motivation was in large part to discover whether a selfless condition could be recovered, deepened, and extended to fill all his life.

Interspersed with flashbacks showing earlier moments of unselfing and expositions of Buddhist ideas, *The Snow Leopard* depicts a number of occasions when Matthiessen's Himalayan trek presents opportunities for unselfing, only some of which he can embrace. The vast emptiness and silence of the mountain setting induces states of consciousness similar to meditation. A hiker must tread carefully on steep or slippery slopes and be attuned to the present moment and his or her exact place. The mind may wander or float free but returns to the path as does a meditator to breathing or a mantra. The challenge is to extend this acute awareness to every moment of ordinary life. Even the danger and extraordinary setting of a Himalayan journey cannot hold the mind's attention. Matthiessen tries to stay focused on the present by not opening a packet of letters received from family and friends. Either good or bad news would intrude, "spoiling this chance to live moment by moment in the present by stirring up the past, the future, and encouraging delusions of continuity and

The Snow Leopard *and* Nine-Headed Dragon River

permanence just when I am trying to let go, to blow away, like the white down feather on the mountain" (234).

Matthiessen's journey releases waves of emotion that he had not felt for many years. Sometimes for no apparent reason, tears come to his eyes. Some of this outpouring of feelings is undoubtedly related to the work of mourning. His deep emotional responses are also facilitated by freedom from ordinary social roles and interactions: "mail, telephones, people and their needs" (115). While the social self develops defensive postures, screens, and "encrustations," a trekker in remote Nepal can respond to events or people in an unguarded way. Matthiessen admires the Sherpas who serve as guides and porters because of their emotional spontaneity and resilience: "so open, so without defense, therefore so free, true Bodhisattvas, accepting like the variable airs the large and small events of every day" (168). To become like a Sherpa would be to become another person and at the same time to realize his deepest self, able to recognize and express feelings as they arise and pass.

Although Matthiessen often describes his journey as a form of pilgrimage, he is uneasy about using this term because a pilgrimage may or may not bring the self-transcendence that is his greatest hope. A pilgrimage should be undertaken with a purpose but not reflect spiritual pride, ambition, or even a fixed idea of what one is looking for. As when searching for the yeti or the snow leopard, so on a spiritual journey: one should not be certain about just what one will find, or when or where. Asked by Schaller why he is walking hundreds of miles on the Tibetan Plateau, Matthiessen is reluctant to speak of a pilgrimage: "And so I admitted that I did not know. How could I say that I wished to penetrate the secrets of the mountains in search of something still unknown that, like the yeti, might well be missed for the very fact of searching?" (125–126).

The danger that his preconceptions will blind him is illustrated in Matthiessen's search for a Lama. He arrives on November 2 at Crystal Mountain, the site of Shey Gompa, a monastery of the Kagyu sect of Tibetan Buddhism. He is disappointed that the Lama of Shey, whom he had hoped would be his teacher, was absent. "That the gompa is locked and the Lama gone away might be read as a karmic reprimand to spiritual ambition, a silent teaching to this ego that still insists upon itself, like the poor bleat of a goat on the north wind" (191–192). At a nearby hermitage, Matthiessen encounters two monks sitting quietly, mending boots and curing a goat hide. A few days later he learns that one of the silent monks was the Lama of Shey. He had not perceived what was right in front of him. A true pilgrim must undertake the journey with right intention and clear purpose, and at the same time cultivate receptivity and discern what does not fit prior expectations. Like the gaze that scans a distant slope for a flicker of motion revealing the presence of a blue sheep or snow leopard, a spiritual seeker must practice alert watchfulness rather than attempting to confirm what he already thinks or knows. Yet watchfulness must be guided, oriented, and directed by training and aspiration.

Just before he departs from Crystal Mountain, Matthiessen encounters the Lama of Shey. Because he is crippled, the Lama has not left this place for eight years and will probably never leave again. Yet he joyfully points to his twisted legs, the snowy peaks, and brilliant sunlight and cries: "Of course I am happy here! It's wonderful! *Especially* when I have no choice!" (246). This effusive affirmation of existence in all circumstances, a "wholehearted acceptance of *what is*," is exactly what Matthiessen strives for. For a moment he adopts this perspective on his own journey, even anticipating one way he might respond to the question of whether he found the snow leopard: "No! Isn't that wonderful?" (246). With this portrayal of the ambiguous failure and success of the author's journey, *The Snow Leopard* elucidates one of the great challenges of pilgrimage: combining deliberate pursuit of specific goals with the capacity to let them go when the journey offers something even more significant than that one had imagined at its outset.

As he was about to depart for the Himalayan journey, Matthiessen was given a koan by Eido-roshi, his primary Zen instructor: "All the peaks are covered with snow—why is this one bare?" (130). The Roshi advised him to expect nothing. Matthiessen reminds himself of this admonition as he meditates on and chants his koan daily. He never "solves" the meaning of the koan or even speculates explicitly about its meaning, yet several incidents in the book suggest its relevance. The bare peak refers not only to Crystal Mountain, but to his own "bareness," his lack of spiritual attainment. Can he be content, even joyful, about this failure, too? He links not solving the koan to not seeing the snow leopard, which indicates that he is not yet ready:

> All the peaks are covered with snow—why is this one bare? To resolve that illogical question would mean to burst apart, let fall all preconceptions and supports. But I am not ready to let go, and so I shall not resolve my *koan*, or see the snow leopard, that is to say, *perceive* it. I shall not see it because I am not yet ready. (256)

That the snow leopard exists, probably watching him, and that he lives with the enigma of the unsolved koan – "that is enough" (242), enough for him to rest content with not-seeing and not-knowing. At other moments, the drive to solve the koan, like the hope of seeing the snow leopard, seems necessary to fuel his quests. Here is another paradox of the Buddhist path (and

The Snow Leopard *and* Nine-Headed Dragon River   51

any spiritual journey) that perhaps only a narrative can adequately portray: One must somehow – at different moments, or with different parts of one's being – restlessly desire and seek something beyond what one has, and also be able to appreciate whatever the journey brings or withholds. The barren peak in Matthiessen's koan signifies the kind of open receptivity that is not a lack of attainment but the very nature of the enlightened state.

The quest for unselfing in *The Snow Leopard* is related to another important theme: wildness. Links between natural wilderness and human wildness run through all Matthiessen's writing, for instance, his *Shadow Country* trilogy, which revolves around the murder of the violent protagonist, Edgar Watson, and the furious destruction of the creatures and natural environment in southwestern Florida.[4] In *The Snow Leopard*, the transformative potential of the Himalayan region is rooted in its stark and soaring natural beauty and its remoteness from civilized life. Yet the condition of this wild region is fragile and temporary. Although the mountain setting seems eternal, "the wilderness will certainly be gone by the century's end" (49), given the relentless pressure of people seeking agricultural land, game, wood, and other natural resources. Humans fear and destroy wilderness, and they also desire and seek it, partly to find contact with repressed wild parts of themselves. In the Himalayan mountains, Matthiessen experiences moments of danger that terrify him and intensify his desire for self-preservation. Yet danger, like violence or lust, can precipitate a moment of unselfing that reveals the limitations of one's ordinary sense of identity. The desperate will to survive in what he calls "extreme moments" seems to come from a different part of one's being that is more real and alive:

> Perhaps this dread of transience explains our greed for the few gobbets of raw experience in modern life, why violence is libidinous, why lust devours us, why soldiers choose not to forget their days of horror: we cling to such extreme moments, in which we seem to die, yet are reborn. In sexual abandon as in danger we are impelled, however briefly, into that vital present in which we do not stand apart from life, we *are* life, our being fills us; in ecstasy with another being, loneliness falls away into eternity. But in other days, such union was attainable through simple awe. (248–249)

---

[4] William Dowrie (1991), argues that the central theme of Matthiessen's work to that point in his career is the attainment of unity with nature, and his fiction's central characters must experience themselves as part of nature and recognize the wildness of their own nature. See also Ihab Hassan, "The Writer as Seeker: The Example of Peter Matthiessen," in *Morphologies of Faith: Essays in Religion and Culture in Honor of Nathan A. Scott, Jr.*, ed. Mary Gerhart and Anthony C. Yu (Atlanta: Scholars Press, 1990), 245–265. Like most studies of Matthiessen, these studies do not fully reckon with the role of Buddhism in shaping his work.

Matthiessen wants to extend to every moment this vivid awareness of mortality linked to a wild desire to live. This is the true purpose of meditation, he asserts: not enlightenment, but to pay attention at every moment, to be mindful of the present. Because we fail to do this, ordinary life becomes habitual and boring; the spirit sleeps. Then an encounter with wildness, that of the natural world and that in our own nature, may elicit the unselfing that wakes us up.

In the final part of *The Snow Leopard*, "The Way Home," Matthiessen hikes out of Inner Dolpo. He returns many times to the questions of what he has learned and whether he has been changed by the journey. In response to this question, like so many others, the book gives contradictory answers. For instance, Matthiessen ponders changes in his relationship to his companion, George Schaller. Although the two men were often withdrawn or irritated with each other, they developed a strong unspoken bond. Bidding farewell to Schaller, Matthiessen says: "I am moved from where I used to be, and can never go back" (265). Yet it seems to him inevitable that when they return from their journey, the two will return to old patterns of interaction: "For want of words, we shake hands once more, knowing that when we meet next, in the twentieth century, the screens of modern life will have formed again, and we may be as well defended as before" (265). Whether his relationships with people will have changed remains an open question.

As Matthiessen crosses the last high passes and anticipates reunion with friends and family, he feels a surge of love and joy and affirms everything that has happened to him. He remembers one of Deborah's favorite Zen sayings: "No snowflake ever falls in the wrong place" (285). Yet later the same day, he feels angry that there is so little sunlight in the mountains in November. Annoyed at his own moodiness, he reinterprets his giddy exhilaration, suggesting that perhaps it was only relief at crossing the pass:

> If so, how sad it seems to celebrate the end of precious days at Crystal Mountain. Perhaps I left too soon; perhaps a great chance has been wasted; had I stayed at Shey until December, the snow leopard might have shown itself at last. These doubts fill me with despair. In worrying about the future, I despoil the present; in my escape, I leave a true freedom behind. (289)

His fickle moods of elation and despondency belie any claim of long-term gains in equanimity, patience, or serenity. He doubts that he has learned anything at all.

Returning from a pilgrimage is like coming out of a meditation retreat, with the shock of re-entry threatening to undo whatever spiritual gains have been realized. Descending from the mountain plateau brings a crash

The Snow Leopard *and* Nine-Headed Dragon River 53

of Matthiessen's spirits. His harshest judgment on himself comes after an outburst of fury at a porter who intrudes into his tent. Matthiessen condemns the aspiration for spiritual attainment that motivates his quest but betrays his Roshi's warning to expect nothing:

> The path I followed breathlessly has faded among stones; in spiritual ambition, I have neglected my children and done myself harm, and there is no way back. Nor has anything changed; I am still beset by the same old lusts and ego and emotions, the endless nagging details and irritations—that aching gap between what I know and what I am. (298)

At this, the low point of his journey, he feels utterly defeated and depressed at his failure to fulfill his hopes and his squandering of a great opportunity.

The next day, November 25, he begins to relax into and find solace in hopelessness, and this returns him to the present moment: "Already the not-looking-forward, the without-hope-ness takes on a subtle attraction, as if I had glimpsed the secret of these mountains, still half-understood. With the past evaporated, the future pointless, and all expectation worn away, I begin to experience that *now* that is spoken of by the great teachers" (300). Walking onward, he accepts the failures of the journey along with its wonder, knowing that his feeling of serenity will pass but enjoying it while it lasts. To affirm and bless the present moment is the highest wisdom of all spiritual teachers, he asserts, including Jesus, the Lama of Shey, and the figure who unexpectedly emerges at the end of the book as Matthiessen's true spiritual mentor: the enigmatic and charismatic porter Tukten.

The characterization of Tukten, who dominates the last pages of *The Snow Leopard*, links many of the motifs and themes that have emerged on the journey. Tukten acted as a Bodhisattva, courageous, uncomplaining, and gentle to all. He embodies selflessness: "There are no boundaries to this man, he loves us all" (270). Back at the trekking company, Matthiessen tries to get Tukten promoted to head porter. But "our evil monk" (242) with the Bodhisattva smile has a bad reputation, swears and drinks alcohol, and is a loner among the clannish Sherpas. He has the provocative antinomian "crazy wisdom" of Tibetan outsiders. When Matthiessen's proposal comes to naught, Tukten's gracious manner epitomizes the ease and resilience with which he meets all obstacles. Their journey completed, Matthiessen finally recognizes that Tukten is the spiritual guide and exemplar he had sought, but not seen: "Without ever attempting to speak about it, we perceive life in the same way, or rather, I perceive it in the way that Tukten lives it. In his life in the moment, in his freedom from attachments, in the simplicity of his everyday example, Tukten has taught me over and over,

54   *The Snow Leopard* and *Nine-Headed Dragon River*

he is the teacher that I hoped to find" (316). The "leopard-eyed" porter is linked to the snow leopard that Matthiessen sought but never saw.

In his last journal entry on December 1, Matthiessen goes to meet Tukten at a Buddhist shrine. His guide is not there, and in the nearby village "no one knows of Tukten Sherpa" (321). This ending epitomizes the paradoxes of self-transformation involved in his journey through Nepal. Matthiessen failed to recognize his true teacher, and it is too late now to learn from being in his presence. Yet this recognition scene shows that Matthiessen has come a long way, so to speak. According to a Buddhist saying, when one is ready, the teacher will appear. That Matthiessen now beholds his teacher in memory shows that he is ready – if not for enlightenment, then for the next step on the path that will go on for the rest of his life. He will be guided by all he takes away from his teacher and his journey, especially the memory of moments of unselfing that opened glimpses of what is possible for him.

*

Like *The Snow Leopard*, Peter Matthiessen's *Nine-Headed Dragon River* takes the form of an edited journal. It covers a much longer period of thirteen years (1969–1982) and focuses not on the challenges of a geographical journey but rather on Matthiessen's deepening understanding of Zen Buddhism. The first of the book's three sections is set in America between 1969 and 1976, when Matthiessen practiced in the Rinzai tradition. The second part, "Nepal: Himalayan Journals 1973," consists of extracts from *The Snow Leopard*. The final section, "Japan: Soto Journals, 1977–1982," recounts a trip to Zen monasteries in Japan and explores Matthiessen's relationship to several contemporary teachers and his interpretation of classic Zen patriarchs, especially Dogen Zenji, a thirteenth-century master considered the founder of the Soto school of Zen Buddhism. Journeys are important in two ways. The Himalayan trek now helps explain Matthiessen's transition from Rinzai to Soto Zen, which involves a shift in his understanding of the path to awakening. And the book culminates in a journey to Japan that is much less dramatic than the search for the snow leopard, but just as significant. *Nine-Headed Dragon River* questions the pursuit of intense experiences of unselfing that dominate *The Snow Leopard*. At the same time, it explores the meaning of unselfing in two new ways: as an aspect of student–teacher relationships and as a metaphor for transformations of Zen within Chinese and Japanese history and as Zen moves to America.

The book opens in August 1968 with a scene of Matthiessen unexpectedly encountering in his driveway three Zen masters who were guests of his wife, Deborah Love. In greater detail than in *The Snow Leopard*, he describes how his initial experiences of Buddhism were connected to his stormy relationship with Love and helped him cope with her dying. He repeats the earlier work's account of accepting her death as an opening or *kensho*, although he adds that "that small opening was very far from great enlightenment, *dai kensho*, in which the self dissolves without a trace into the One" (27). The index lists twenty-five references to *kensho*, which he defines in the glossary as "literally, *ken* (seeing into) *sho* (the original nature, one's true nature). Enlightenment-experience, the opening of the Buddha-eye; not yet true enlightenment, which requires the maturing of this opening and the shedding of all traces of it" (277–278). In this book, the Japanese concept of kensho is crucial for understanding experiences of unselfing and their limitations. Seeing into one's own nature involves letting go of false understandings and is a genuine experience of unselfing. Yet because this moment of insight may not last or be integrated into one's ongoing life, it must be distinguished from satori, full enlightenment. A teacher distinguishes between one of Matthiessen's partial and uncertain realizations and the great or true kensho that "wipes away the last traces of doubt" (131). The difference between them is like that between glimpsing an ox and seeing "what color it was, whether male or female, fat or thin, poor or healthy" (132).

Can one be enlightened without kensho, a moment of opening or unselfing? Eido-roshi, one of Matthiessen's teachers, tells a story about a monk who said he had never had a kensho, yet showed "moment-by-moment enlightenment in everyday life" (41). Eido-roshi clearly admires this monk's dedication more than "a superficial kensho after a few months of sitting." Yet he urges his disciples to strive for the crucial moment of seeing into one's own nature, saying "Zen cannot be truly apprehended without kensho" (41). As these remarks indicate, the meaning and value of kensho is contested in Zen tradition, so it is difficult to measure one's own condition against various characterizations of it. Doubt is inevitable until the final breakthrough.

Experiences of unselfing are desirable, perhaps necessary, but not sufficient for full enlightenment. Hence, Matthiessen is sometimes encouraged to seek them, while in other interviews teachers discourage him from pursuing them. He is told both to strive persistently for kensho and to stop trying so hard for a particular result. This makes for a confusing orientation to meditation and many moments of exhilaration and disappointment. Eido-roshi's pep talk inspires Matthiessen to try once again to "burst through the iron wall of 'self,' through moment-by-moment emptying of mind" (41–42). Yet his teacher soon warns him that he is too anxious about making progress, too greedy for spiritual attainment. He advises Matthiessen to "expect nothing." It was at this point in 1973 that he made the Himalayan journey with Schaller. As we saw in *The Snow Leopard*, he struggled throughout that journey with the paradoxes of spiritual ambition to overcome the limitations of selfhood. After returning from Nepal, he was "cast down" for a year by the lack of a profound experience of enlightenment in the high mountains. Given the many moments of insight and clarity recorded in *The Snow Leopard*, this comes as a surprise.

The first part of *Nine-Headed Dragon River* concludes with a ceremony marking the opening in New York's Catskill Mountains of Dai Bosatsu, the first traditional Rinzai Zen monastery in the United States. Matthiessen hints at tensions with Eido-roshi, who demanded submission from American students who questioned his authoritarian demands. (Much later, in 2011, Eido Shimano stopped teaching Zen at this organization because of a controversy about his sexual relationships with several students.)[5] Without explaining this situation or his own views, Matthiessen says that he withdrew as a student from Eido-roshi and did not return to Dai Bosatsu for more than two years. Instead of *sesshin* (meditation retreats), his primary spiritual practice shifted to working on his Himalayan journals.

In introducing the extracts from *The Snow Leopard* that form the second section of *Nine-Headed Dragon River*, Matthiessen describes himself in 1973 as "still stuck in that wide-eyed early stage of practice in which one yearns for 'miraculous' experience of the universal self, for so-called 'enlightenment.' And the journals reflect the inevitable struggle to apply such insights as have been attained on the black cushion to the more rigorous Zen of everyday life" (72). This rather detached perspective on his earlier drive for experiences of unselfing, combined with a new focus on everyday life, reflects his shift from Rinzai Zen to Soto Zen, a transition that began with a retreat at the Los Angeles Zen Center in 1977. An important theme in Matthiessen's account of this change is the contrasting ways that Rinzai and Soto view attempts to bring about unselfing.

Matthiessen contrasts "the intensity of relentless zazen" (119) in Rinzai practice, with its koan study, shouting, and use of a stick to arouse sleepy meditators, and Soto Zen, which emphasizes "just sitting" and

---

[5] See Mark Oppenheimer, *The Zen Predator of the Upper East Side* (Washington, DC: Atlantic Books, 2013).

The Snow Leopard *and* Nine-Headed Dragon River 57

seems gentle, undramatic, and content with silent contemplation. The two schools tend to stress, respectively, sudden and gradual enlightenment, although in practice they have both found ways to reconcile these emphases.[6] Most of the third part of *Nine-Headed Dragon River* describes the differing perspectives of various historical figures, monasteries, and schools of Zen Buddhism. This chronicle of Zen history largely displaces the introspective spiritual questioning of *The Snow Leopard*, as well as any sustained narrative drive, and may not hold the attention of readers who do not have a keen interest in the varieties of Buddhism. Beneath the descriptions of different genealogies of Zen, however, one senses Matthiessen's attempt to understand his movement from a spiritual practice focused on attaining intense experiences of unselfing toward the view that enlightenment cannot be found apart from everyday life and ordinary consciousness. His search for unselfing is not abandoned, but it becomes more subtle and diffused throughout daily life, and it is not primarily a matter of will power, technique, or achievement.

Matthiessen's shift from Rinzai to Soto Zen is not directly described and does not resemble a sudden conversion. Instead, as he describes the history of Zen Buddhism, he obliquely suggests changes in his own spiritual practice. He patterns his narrative as a series of fleeting insights or openings, what one Zen patriarch called "the moment-by-moment freshening of the mind" (156). Matthiessen's repeated use of the phrase "moment-by-moment" in this work emphasizes the ongoing and constant opportunity for overcoming fixed routines and perceptions, rather than an intense, once-and-forever breakthrough. This perspective resembles the idea of "continuous conversion" that some Christians have proposed as an alternative to the traditional concept of conversion as a single event. The form of *Nine-Headed Dragon River*, which turns away from the author's spiritual high points to the steady development of Zen Buddhism in history, thus exemplifies the proper focus of Zen: not the individual's introspective examination of particular experiences, but rather deepening understanding of how one participates in a community of practice guided by historical exemplars and contemporary teachers. What displaces the self is not consciousness of an altered state of body or mind but one's teacher and religious tradition. Instead of sudden, all-or-nothing enlightenment, Matthiessen depicts a gradual process that admits of degrees of awakening. In this work he shows little anguish that moments of unselfing

---

[6] Peter Gregory, ed., *Sudden and Gradual: Approaches to Enlightenment in Chinese Thought* (Honolulu: University of Hawaii Press, 1987).

cannot be maintained in "the more difficult zazen of daily life," where (repeating a phrase from *The Snow Leopard*) he continues to encounter "a dismaying separation between what I know and what I am" (148).

The shift in Matthiessen's understanding of Buddhism is accompanied by his reorientation toward two revered teachers, Eihei Dogen (1200–1253) and Tetsugen, a contemporary American Soto Zen master. He describes Dogen Zenji as the most significant Zen thinker and "one of the most exciting minds in the history of thought" (137). Matthiessen's 1982 journey to Japan visits places associated with Dogen, climaxing at Eihi-ji, a temple located in the valley of Nine-Headed Dragon River. Every chapter of the book he named after this place begins with an epigraph by Dogen. These teachings, discussed by several of Matthiessen's instructors, often concern the self's relationship to the world. For instance:

> To study the Buddha Dharma is to study the self
> To study the self is to forget the self
> To forget the self is to be enlightened by all things.   (59)

Dogen advises both relentless self-examination and forgetting the self as equally necessary for enlightenment. For Matthiessen, Dogen's crucial significance is his emphasis on the immanence of enlightenment in life's ordinary activities: the perception of Buddha-nature in "the wonderful precision of this present moment, moment after moment—*now!*" (167). Instead of striving for intense moments of oneness with the world, what Dogen calls for is a receptive opening to the reality that is already present apart from one's efforts and one's ideas about what enlightenment should look like:

> In effect, Dogen had freed himself of all ideas and preconceptions about Buddhism, about enlightenment, about the true nature of all reality, all of which had "dropped away with body and mind." There was simply the fact of his vertical nose and horizontal eyes, of the sun and moon rising and falling, moment by moment, day by day. With the opening of his true Dharma eye, he perceived the extraordinary within the ordinary, and realized with all buddhas and patriarchs that everything, everywhere, in every moment, is "nothing special," as is said in Zen, being complete and perfect just-as-it-is. (169)

This orientation made Dogen less judgmental and demanding than some other masters; the Soto teacher's "tender spirit" contrasts with the Rinzai school's sometimes harsh methods.

Matthiessen's contemporary teacher, a Zen master in the Soto lineage, was Bernard Glassman (1939–2018), known by his Dharma name, Tetsugen. This American Roshi feels great affinity for Dogen's emphasis on "the everything-as-it-is" (189) and asserts that Dogen's greatest

The Snow Leopard *and* Nine-Headed Dragon River 59

contribution, expressed in his own life, is "the perception that daily practice and enlightenment are one" (190). Matthiessen became the head monk in the Soto Zen community in New York founded by Tetsugen in 1979, and he was ordained as a Zen priest in 1981. In describing the journey to Japan that he undertook as Tetsugen's assistant, Matthiessen devotes more attention to his relationship to his teacher than he does to the details of travel. The dynamics of the Zen student–teacher relationship offer the possibility of unselfing, given the ideal of becoming one with the teacher and his spiritual lineage. To transmit the dharma, a master must recognize and approve of the disciple's understanding and practice of the teachings and assess his experiences of kensho and satori. In the ideal master–student relationship, two individual personalities dissolve in a common understanding and experience of the Buddhist dharma. In actuality, however, prickly defensiveness, pride, and other human foibles continue to remind teacher and student of their individual differences and character. When Matthiessen is moved by a wild duck descending to a river, Tetsugen is amused, lacking his student's interest in the natural world. Matthiessen acknowledges that being more than a decade older than his mentor and certain personality differences make it difficult to realize the ideal of oneness that Tetsugen had found in relation to his teacher, Maezumi:

> I knew that he had 'become one' with Maezumi-roshi in a way and to a degree that was probably not possible in our case, given not only my life apart from his Zen community (which meant that except in intense bursts, such as this journey, we spent too little time together), but also discrepancies in age, outlook, and temperament, including my stubborn resistance to authority and a notable lack of the proper devotional attitude. (180)

Although the ideal of becoming one with one's teacher is the form that unselfing now takes for Matthiessen, he accepts with equanimity his failures to realize this aspiration.

In addition to exploring the student–teacher relationship in Zen, *Nine-Headed Dragon River* uses the ideal of no-self to interpret another issue: the question of whether Zen tradition has a character or identity (a metaphorical "self") that pervades its many forms in Chinese and Japanese history and its new expressions in America. This issue is explored in several other Western Buddhist travel narratives when writers discern analogies between the emptiness of the self and that of Buddhism itself. They use the idea of no-self to interpret the transformation of Buddhism as it travels and adapts to Western culture.

60 *The Snow Leopard* and *Nine-Headed Dragon River*

As Matthiessen and his teacher discuss periods of stagnation and renewal in Zen Buddhism, Tetsugen affirms the need for both structure and creativity. Rinzai, Soto, and other Zen sects and schools arose as protests against routinized and lifeless practice, whether based on koan study, particular techniques of meditation, doctrines, ceremonies, or hierarchies of authority. Tetsugen describes "an endless, intertwining dualism, in which one element seeks to maintain its structure and the other tries to keep it from petrifying; if either fails, the whole will die" (200). He does not use the terminology of self in tension with no-self, but that is what he describes: the ceaseless interaction between form and emptiness, or between identity and transformation, which shapes the evolution of a religious tradition as it does the spiritual growth of an individual.

If Zen must transform itself as it comes to America, certain questions arise: What is Zen? Does it have an essential nature? Or can it mean anything at all? Is everything that claims to be Zen in America really Zen? These issues underlie many of Matthiessen's reflections on Zen history. He does not say explicitly what the essence or identity of Zen is through its manifestations, just as a person's selfhood cannot be identified with any specific condition of body, mind, memory, or aspect of human nature. Both individual selfhood and Zen religious tradition are empty of permanent substance, yet narratives about them show forms of continuity and persistence along with change.

Matthiessen describes his uncertainties about how to integrate Zen practices with his American life. He has a public identity and interacts with American Indians, commercial fishermen, and others who do not understand Buddhist practices. Visiting a Japanese monastery, he is reluctant to shave his head, for this would "draw unwelcome attention, making people uneasy and flaunting my 'Zen' in a way that I very much dislike" (187) – although he had shaved his head earlier, when becoming a monk. His involvement in various political movements – especially groups devoted to environmental preservation, peace, and the rights of Native Americans – contrasts with the apolitical orientation of Tetsugen and other teachers. His vocation as a writer seems to him to violate the silence and anonymity required of a Zen monk. He reports several disdainful comments by Zen masters about the folly of devoting one's life to writing, at least until one can do so in the spirit of Zen. He takes exception to one such remark: "Presumably Master Muso railed at dilettantes, not true poets – though the work of both is an expression of their Buddha nature. Since the ground of Zen is life itself, neither murderers nor poets are excluded" (188). Here is another irony: Matthiessen surely hoped that *Nine-Headed Dragon River* would express Buddha nature rather than simply displaying a flailing ego. Yet nothing is excluded from revealing the ground of Zen in life itself, including the writing of an unenlightened person.

The form and focus of *Nine-Headed Dragon River* reflect a change in Matthiessen's ideal of no-self, as well as a different strategy for expressing it in autobiographical narrative. In 1978, he abandoned keeping a journal about his meditation sessions: "I resolved, once and for all, to drop the practice of these sesshin notes, with their hoarding of miraculous states and 'spiritual attainments,' with their contaminating clinging, their insidious fortification of the ego. I never kept a journal of sesshin again" (130). The third part of *Nine-Headed Dragon River* reflects a turn away from introspective examination of states of his own mind and a redirection of attention to the history of Zen. This shift in focus disappointed readers hoping for a more personally revealing story. Many readers and reviewers criticized the book's overwhelming detail about the history of Japanese Buddhism. I think the book reflects Matthiessen's attempt to express the meaning of no-self in a new way – even though he knows that a writer's distinctive selfhood constantly shapes his writing, whatever form it takes.

Nine-Headed Dragon River ends in 1982 with Tetsugen and Matthiessen visiting their old teacher Soen-roshi, a lively, eccentric, and playful master who had withdrawn into seclusion. The Roshi's exuberant appreciation of all of life seems to epitomize Matthiessen's view of the Dharma's essential meaning: "The sun, the moon are buddhas, all the human beings of this earth are buddhas, *all* is Buddha! Everything and everybody is a teacher. Sometimes you are my teachers, *you* are so-called roshi! Everybody is so-called roshi, okay? *All* is enlightened, as-it-is-now!" (258). Every person is one's roshi, demonstrating clear teaching by example, and everyone is also a koan: enigmatic, obdurate, and elusive. As they depart from Soen-roshi, Tetsugen feels sad that Soen-roshi does not have long to live, and in his weakening condition seems like a ghost. Yet the dharma will be taught by another teacher in another place. The book's final paragraph gratefully affirms Tetsugen as Matthiessen's teacher:

> In the sadness attending our visit there was also freedom. The wonderful teachers who had brought the Dharma from Asia to the West would appear no more, but in another sense, they would be with us forever. In Western as in Eastern lands, the Buddha Way might need centuries to become established, so the sooner we got on about it, the better. It was time to step forward from the hundred-foot pole as the fortunate student of this American-born Buddha who sits here beside me in this present, first, last, past, and future moment of my life. (259)

Like the ending of *The Snow Leopard*, with its turn to the elusive figure of Tukten, this final scene dramatizes the Zen saying: "Only be ready, and the teacher will appear" (157). Both works shift focus from the author to his spiritual guide, from self to what is not the self, yet will henceforth shape it. Both works also suggest that Matthiessen has undergone a significant change to be able at last to recognize the teacher he has sought for so long.

In this travel narrative that traces Zen Buddhism's journey from China to Japan to America, the ending depicts a new home as the setting for an authentic transformation of Buddhism and a vital expression of the freedom of the dharma. Matthiessen suggests the importance of appreciating ancient Chinese and Japanese masters while affirming new ones such as Tetsugen, whose presence now pervades all the moments of his life and with whom his identity is merged. Thus Matthiessen shows that "the Buddha way," like an individual traveler, changes in the course of journeying to another place yet maintains continuity with a past identity. The paradox that self and no-self are both valid insights into a complex reality is also expressed in the student–teacher relationship that honors the idiosyncrasies of each person and unites them in something larger than themselves: common dedication to the Buddhist Dharma. The dialectic between self and no-self also shapes Matthiessen's representation of American Zen as preserving Buddhism's essential character even as it becomes fresh and vital in a new context. *Nine-Headed Dragon River* continues the quest for experiences of no-self that animates *The Snow Leopard*, yet it turns away from analyzing intense moments of self-transcendence and from disappointment when they fade. Instead, Matthiessen emphasizes the challenge of being present in every moment. The idea of no-self is still crucial in the later work, not as a state to be achieved, but rather as a lens through which Matthiessen views his relationship to past and present Zen masters and the journey of Zen to America.

CHAPTER 3

In a Zen Monastery
Ambiguous Failure and Enlightenment

One of the earliest Western Buddhist travel narratives, Janwillem van de Wetering's *The Empty Mirror* (1973), describes eighteen months he spent in a Zen monastery in Kyoto. Before van de Wetering's book, there had been brief autobiographical accounts of transformative Buddhist experiences, such as "Eight Contemporary Enlightenment Experiences of Japanese and Westerners" in Philip Kapleau's *The Three Pillars of Zen*.[1] Van de Wetering wrote a much longer narrative about his experiences on and off the meditation cushion, and he emphasized failure, not the attainment of enlightenment. In contrast to external perspectives of enlightened masters, short accounts culminating in enlightenment, and the expectations created by D. T. Suzuki's theoretical works about Zen, van de Wetering depicted a long and frustrating period of monastic training that did not end in awakening yet revealed insights into no-self and a questionable, ambiguous transformation.

The Empty Mirror and three later works by Maura O'Halloran, David Chadwick, and Gesshin Claire Greenwood show how living in a Japanese monastery influenced their understanding of Zen and changed them. These and other works form a genre that Ben Van Overmeier calls "Zen monastic memoirs."[2] In autobiographical accounts of residence in a Japanese monastery, there is usually little physical movement; the author

---

[1] Philip Kapleau, ed. "Eight Contemporary Enlightenment Experiences of Japanese and Westerners." In *The Three Pillars of Zen: Teaching, Practice, Enlightenment* (New York: Harper & Row, 1965). Kapleau's own narrative, "Mr. P. K.," is on pp. 208–229.

[2] Ben Van Overmeier, "Modern Zen Buddhist Autobiography As Utopian Narrative," (unpublished book proposal, 2017) also discusses the short excerpts in Kapleau's *Three Pillars of Zen*; Robert Aitken's *Taking the Path of Zen* (San Francisco: North Point Press, 1982); Natalie Goldberg's *The Great Failure: A Bartender, a Monk, and My Unlikely Path to Truth* (New York: Harper, 2004); Shozen Jack Haubner's *Single White Monk: Tales of Death, Failure, and Bad Sex* (Boulder, CO: Shambala, 2017); and an anthology, Zenshin Florence Caplow and Reigetsu Susan Moon (eds.), *The Hidden Lamp: Stories from Twenty-Five Centuries of Awakened Women* (Boston: Wisdom Publications, 2013).

64 In a Zen Monastery

may make a brief excursion or explore the neighborhood, but he or she is basically stationary. The urge to go elsewhere is significant because of what it reveals about the mind. It is not geographical journeying but another dimension of travel narratives, immersion in an unfamiliar culture, that precipitates self-discovery. Experiencing Zen Buddhism in its Japanese setting may bring surprise, confusion, loneliness, boredom, or frustration; it can also engender moments of delight, amusement, or joy. An author may puzzle over how much of Zen is Japanese cultural baggage that is not a necessary part of her future Buddhist path. She may reconsider her prior understanding of and practice of the Dharma and adopt new ways. In various ways, transformations grow out of the determined attempt to achieve satori (enlightenment), understood as selflessness, emptiness, or another version of no-self. A central theme in many Zen memoirs is the deeper meaning of the author's professed failure to achieve satori.

In *The Empty Mirror*, Janwillem van de Wetering begins with his arrival in Kyoto in 1958, when the Dutchman was twenty-six years old, and ends nearly two years later with his departure on a ship bound for Marseilles. His spiritual reckoning with Zen Buddhism focuses on the meaning of this worldview and the question of whether and how he was changed by monastic training. Van de Wetering's practice of Rinzai Zen involved intensive meditation on a *koan*, sometimes for up to eighteen hours a day. A koan is a mental puzzle that defies logic and is supposed to help the adept break through dualistic thinking. It is a gift from a master that a disciple may struggle with in meditation for many years and perhaps never "solve." Van de Wetering links intense engagement with a koan to the shattering of ordinary self-consciousness:

> One tries to become one with the koan, to close the distance between oneself and the koan, to lose oneself in the koan, till everything drops or breaks away and nothing is left but the koan which fills the universe. And if that point is reached enlightenment, the revelation, follows… In every training the ego is broken, the "I" is crushed. (17)[3]

His goal is to experience this distinctive form of unselfing. In the discipline of koan meditation, what displaces ordinary consciousness is an enigma that cannot be comprehended and fills the adept's awareness. Van de Wetering does not reveal what his koan was, but he describes many famous ones such as: What is the sound of one clapping hand? Another one: Show me the face you had before your parents were born.

---

[3] Numbers in parentheses refer to Janwillem van de Wetering, *The Empty Mirror: Experiences in a Japanese Zen Monastery* (New York: St Martin's Press, 1973).

The Empty Mirror includes many koan-like anecdotes told by the Zen master, other monks, or Western friends. The meaning of these stories and their connection with the author's situation is often enigmatic. Although van de Wetering does not claim to be a Zen master or to have achieved enlightenment, his regular use of these unofficial koans suggests one significant way in which his worldview was influenced by Buddhist practice: he learned to interpret the world by framing puzzling events and encounters as if they are koans. He starts to see his life as a series of situations calling for an immediate, intuitive response rather than a controlled, rational one. Zen training gives him a way to comprehend strange incidents and cryptic conversations and to live with unresolved questions. The koan is his model for describing and interpreting the enigmas of living in a foreign culture. Moreover, *The Empty Mirror* itself seems to be a koan that poses the question of what it means that the self is empty. Van de Wetering's central metaphor for no-self is an empty mirror.

Although the young Dutchman frequently asks himself whether he is making progress in his practice, the master warns him that attempting to measure it is foolish. The idea of progress in Zen training seems to depend on the concept of a self that claims ownership of certain properties such as the correct understanding of a koan. This idea of an enduring self with a fixed character assumes a worldview that Zen practice should dissolve.

Van de Wetering shows two ways in which Zen teaching challenges or undermines the usual Western idea of the self. He hears about "a Zen master who said that his first *satori* experience consisted of recognizing all people as himself. Everybody had his own face" (96). As in this case, enlightenment is sometimes described as a person's identification with what is usually thought to be outside of or beyond the self, in this case other people. The sense of self is expanded or stretched beyond its normal boundaries.

A second way of dissolving the self is to deny its reality not by expanding it but by a direct negative challenge. The title of *The Empty Mirror* refers to a koan about a woman who sees herself reflected in fifty mirrors. Another Zen student discerns in this story "that everything which happens is reflected in everything else" (124). The master approves of this interpretation but says that the student still has much to learn. Discussing this koan with his friend Peter, van de Wetering asserts: "These mirrors are empty ... Nothing reflects, nothing can be reflected." Peter affirms this view and suggests that, if van de Wetering could understand the empty mirror, "there would be nothing left here for you to look for" (125). The central meaning of satori is identified with understanding the self's

66   In a Zen Monastery

nonreality or illusoriness. There are different strategies for eliciting the moment of insight when an adept grasps the truth of no-self. We can call these contrasting forms of unselfing the way of expansion and the way of dissolution of ordinary self-consciousness.

Of course, the very notion of "grasping" this insight into no-self and holding on to it suggests clinging and attachment, which will bring suffering and prevent the release from it that is the goal of the Buddhist path. Self and no-self are human concepts, not the final or ultimate truth, not dogmas that must be believed. They are "skillful means," insights that may help a person along the path toward self-transformation. Contrasting strategies for unselfing and various metaphors for no-self will be expedient for different individuals, or for the same person at different times.

A paradox of Zen practice is the combination of long and intensive practice and the high value placed on satori, a sudden moment of enlightenment. Like the Christian concept of conversion, satori is a turning point of spiritual transformation, the climax of a longer story. *The Empty Mirror* includes many accounts of such moments, usually linked to a monk solving his koan. One such story concerns a Zen master who after many years in a monastery has satori when having sex with a prostitute. Van de Wetering, who at this point is weary of his demanding training, asks a monk whether this story shows that "Zen training can be really free." The monk responds: "Water suddenly boils, but the kettle must have been on the fire for some time" (102). Long preparation and arduous training facilitate the flash of insight. Like Christian conversion narratives, Western Buddhist travel narratives describe, often in the same text, both moments of sudden transformation and a person's arduous struggles over a long period of time. This tension between contrasting views of transformation – as gradual or sudden – is necessary to do justice to a recurring paradox: A person who has struggled long and hard to change feels as if an entirely new orientation abruptly comes into being.

In the last pages of *The Empty Mirror*, van de Wetering reflects on what he learned from a year and a half of Zen training. On one level, he seems not to have progressed or changed much. He hasn't solved his koan. He is still intermittently depressed and, on a last motorcycle ride into the mountains, he contemplates suicide. The reasons he leaves the monastery are as vague as was his motivation for entering it. He says he never became a Buddhist, although by this he means he did not participate in a formal ceremony. After several inconclusive conversations with the master about his desire to perform this ritual, he asks the head monk whether he is a Buddhist. The monk, Han-san, responds: "'I' don't exist.

In a Zen Monastery

I change all the time. Every moment I am different. I exist in the way a cloud exists. A cloud is a Buddhist, too" (139–140). Van de Wetering drops the subject and never again mentions the ceremony. This enigmatic exchange suggests that becoming an official member of "the brotherhood of Buddhists" in a formal ritual is less important than practicing meditation, sharing a worldview, or partaking in the Buddha-nature of all things. The passage suggests that the cloud-like impermanence of the self makes the question of community membership, even when undertaken with vows of commitment, a matter with little long-term significance. This downplaying of the institutional forms of Buddhism looks like typically Western individualism, yet van de Wetering continues to subordinate his own needs and desires to strenuous discipline and hierarchical authority.

The ideal of equanimity is a recurrent theme throughout van de Wetering's narrative, for instance in his admiration of the head monk: "His equanimity impressed me most. He, rather than the master, was the example which I used in my routine... He slipped through life easily; he was free, kind, quiet, perhaps even careless or indifferent. Nothing touched him" (48). A Zen master never rushes or worries about accomplishment: "Masters are never in a hurry, and a disciple, provided he is in the later stages of his training, isn't in a hurry either. Everything comes, if you do your best. And if it doesn't come, that's all right too" (106). The book's final chapter, entitled "Whatever Ends Begins," summarizes what van de Wetering learned in the monastery in terms of the ideal of equanimity: "Not only has one to do one's best, one must, while doing one's best, remain detached from whatever one is trying to achieve" (142). He tries to apply this lesson to the questionable results of his efforts to attain enlightenment:

> So that's what matters. To do your best and be detached. To come to the point where everything you have been trying to do comes to nothing, and be unmoved. Equanimity. That's all I have been able to learn. A little theory. It has taken me a year and a half. I doubt whether I can practice the theory. (143–144)

The conclusion of *The Empty Mirror* poses the question of whether or not van de Wetering learned not only to understand but also to practice equanimity. After he resolves to meditate for seventy-two hours but gives up after half a day, he feels depressed and concludes "the whole Buddhist adventure now seemed one huge failure" (144).

In contrast to his own negative view is his Zen master's affirmation that van de Wetering has been changed by monastic training. When saying farewell, the master gives him the stick with which monks hit each other to encourage alertness, writing on it a proverb: "A sword which is well

68   In a Zen Monastery

forged never loses its golden color." In this way, the master affirms that
van de Wetering's character has been forged in the monastery. He gives a
final blessing: "By leaving here nothing is broken. Your training continues. The world is a school where the sleeping are woken up. You are now
a little awake, so awake that you can never fall asleep again" (146). The
master suggests that his student's Zen training is a step in a long-term
process whose outcome will be realized elsewhere and later. Hearing this,
van de Wetering's gloomy feelings fall away. The book's final paragraph
depicts the Dutchman on a departing ship, ordering a cold beer. He seems
remarkably detached from his disappointment at not accomplishing much
after prolonged effort, his failure to solve his koan or even concentrate on
it in meditation, and his recent suicidal thoughts. It may be that the master's affirmation simply reassures van de Wetering that he has indeed made
progress, so he is back in the cycle of hope and disappointment. Yet I think
that van de Wetering's depiction of his final state is supposed to represent
equanimity, and perhaps even satori. What looks like indifference may be
equanimity, in contrast to a person who is elated at his or her Buddhist
accomplishments or broods over and laments failures. Van de Wetering's
stance resembles that of many other writers who apparently dismiss the
question of whether or not they have been transformed by Buddhism and
by their Asian journey, while raising questions about what this really means.

In *A Glimpse of Nothingness*, van de Wetering's later memoir about living in an American Zen community, he more explicitly links satori to
detachment from achievement. Although he learned that "solving a koan
is accompanied by satori, enlightenment," van de Wetering solves his koan
but finds that his life changes only slightly, if at all:

> I had to admit that nothing had changed very much. Perhaps I might
> now have a more intense realization of relativity, a better idea of the non-
> importance of what concerned me. But that was nothing new. Detachment
> is caused by a slow process, and the results of this process, if any, are gradual.
> It was quite possible that I was merely imagining my improved sense of
> detachment.[4]

This memoir, too, emphasizes the importance of detachment from clinging to the results of practice and his uncertainty about whether he made
progress.

The Empty Mirror suggests that equanimity is not a permanent achievement or condition but a moment of relative tranquility that passes. With
practice, it can come again more easily. Van de Wetering's training will

---

[4] Janwillem van de Wetering, *A Glimpse of Nothingness: Experiences in an American Zen Community*
(New York: Pocket Books, 1975), 73.

continue outside the monastery, and now he knows what to watch and hope for. At the end of his narrative, he is still the same person that he was at the beginning of the book, with characteristic moods, thoughts, and anxieties. Yet in certain ways he has changed. In particular, he has learned to frame and interpret incidents in his life using Zen koans and concepts, including the idea of the empty mirror, a direct experience of the world unobstructed by the ordinary self. Although van de Wetering does not point to any single moment of satori when a permanent shift of orientation took place, a gradual change has come about. The way he turns away from the monastery, almost with a shrug, might be interpreted as cynicism or despair. I see it as his interpretation of the meaning of equanimity, which came when he stopped asking whether or not he was transformed into a better Buddhist or human being. To claim a better character or an altered sense of self as an achievement or permanent possession would surely demonstrate that he does not understand the meaning of the empty mirror. For van de Wetering to have gotten to the point where he can drop the question of progress toward enlightenment shows a significant change of orientation and, ambiguously, a transformation of self. It is ambiguous because at the end of the book he still shows many of the same characteristics as he did at the outset, including a flip, devil-may-care, and irreverent manner.

Theravada tradition formulates four "divine abidings" or virtues and what are called their "near enemies": qualities that resemble the virtues but actually undermine them. The near enemy of equanimity is indifference, the absence of caring. It's hard to tell whether van de Wetering's attitude at the end of *The Empty Mirror* is equanimity or an unwholesome state of indifference that resembles it.

The Empty Mirror does not show the long-term consequences of his sojourn in Japan. We can make inferences about this based on his much later book *Afterzen: Experiences of a Zen Student Out on His Ear* (1999). This work is structured as a series of autobiographical stories, each of which is paired with a koan that both influences his understanding of his life and is partially illuminated by it. "Some koans will, at least in my experience, come up again in unexpected circumstances, and may finally clear up just a tad of ignorance or stubborn denial" (60).[5] Again, he links the method of koan study to overcoming the self:

> As soon as the monks say yes to anything, the teacher denies its existence; when the monk says no, the teacher affirms existence. The monk can't win and he isn't supposed to win. A good monk is a complete loser. The entire

---

[5] Janwillem van de Wetering, *Afterzen: Experiences of a Zen Student Out on His Ear* (New York: St. Martin's Press, 1999).

> Buddhist discipline is aimed at having the inquirer truly realize that as long as he holds on to anything, whether a positive or a negative, he will suffer. Only extinction of the self culminates in a state of illumination. (110–111)

Here enlightenment is linked to a total destruction of the self.

In the final chapter, "Emptiness Is Form," van de Wetering qualifies this view. He acknowledges that he succumbed to a nihilistic danger in Zen: "the possibility of being absorbed by the shadow side of negation, a weakness I saw in several teachers and also in my own approach, preferring self-centered lazy indifference to a state of mental freedom" (183–184). Analyzing his attraction to Zen, he suggests that the idea that "nothing matters" because all things are ultimately empty allowed him to avoid pain and suffering. The book ends with a description of a moment of callous indifference in Central Park, followed by a joyful affirmation of children playing jazz. "Emptiness took form" in this moment when he passed from self-protective disengagement to genuine equanimity (which he calls detachment and some other Buddhists would call nonattachment). A moment of unselfing led to engaged participation in life rather than cold withdrawal. Describing this experience and perhaps offering advice to the reader, van de Wetering concludes: "Fall into the big hole of not caring, fly out on the cloud of detachment" (187). Forty years after his experiences in Japan, van de Wetering was still thinking about the meaning of detachment and its close resemblance to cynicism, indifference, sloth, and other defensive strategies that try to protect the self from the world. If he has not attained a selfless condition, the question of what that would mean, not simply as an abstract ideal but as a way of living, continues to preoccupy him long after he left the Zen monastery. In his depiction of the ambiguous failure of a person whose life is nonetheless transformed by Buddhism, van de Wetering's example prefigures and contrasts with later narratives about Zen monastic life.

*

In November 1979, Maura O'Halloran arrived at Toshoji Temple in Tokyo. The twenty-four-year-old Irish-American woman was accepted as a student by the Roshi, Tetsugyu Ban, and spent three years training there and at Kannonji Temple in Iwate Prefecture. In contrast to Janwillem van de Wetering's ambivalence and inconclusive training, O'Halloran committed herself wholeheartedly and was quickly declared to be enlightened by her Zen master, who authorized her to teach as his heir. She was traveling to Ireland to start a Zen center when, on October 22, 1982, she died in a traffic accident in Chiang Mai, Thailand. Since her death, O'Halloran has been recognized in Japan as a bodhisattva. Her example has inspired

Western spiritual seekers from many backgrounds since the publication in 1995 of *Pure Heart, Enlightened Mind: The Life and Letters of an Irish Zen Saint*, edited by O'Halloran's mother, Ruth. The 2007 expanded edition of this book includes O'Halloran's diary, letters to family and friends, a chapter from an unfinished novel, and other documents by and about her, including a letter from Roshi Tetsugyu Ban. This material provides a fascinating account of an extraordinary woman's Buddhist experiences. The contrasts between her self-assessments and other people's views of her raise profound questions about enlightenment. O'Halloran's reflections on her Zen practice, both in meditation and in daily life, reveal wisdom, compassion, and a joyful, energetic, life-affirming spirit. Her journal shows a woman with a strong and confident sense of self trying to realize the ideal of no-self.

O'Halloran's motivation for committing herself to intensive Zen training is obscure. A recent honors graduate of Trinity College, Dublin, she was not unhappy with her life or wanting to renounce the world. In a letter to her family, she describes how on her way to Japan she stopped at a Hare Krishna temple in Hawaii. She criticizes this movement's view of the world as an illusion and place of misery: "They were in a mini-paradise, Hawaii, and couldn't even enjoy it ... They'll never convince me that I'm in misery" (16).[6] She rejected the Hare Krishna "line that women were of a lower order than men," a view that she would again confront in the Zen temple. "But I got away" (17). The documents at the end of *Pure Heart, Enlightened Mind*, including her mother's recollections of O'Halloran's youth and O'Halloran's journals from travel in Canada and Latin America and a sojourn in Boston and Maine, show her enjoying parties, food and drink, the natural world, adventurous travel, and music. She has warm relationships with her family and male and female friends. She is not particularly religious, and her attraction to Zen does not grow out of disillusionment or deconversion from her Catholic upbringing, a sense of guilt or shame, or fear of death. She is what William James calls a "once-born" convert rather than a "twice-born" conflicted soul whose transformation involves rejecting an earlier life. A few months after arriving in Japan, O'Halloran reflects on her lack of suffering in relation to her aspirations:

> Spiritual liberation, but from what? ... Those who suffer want liberation from suffering, but I seldom suffer. My life has been wonderful, blessed. Who could enslave me? I did as I wished when I wished. Now I feel gratitude

---

[6] Maura O'Halloran, *Pure Heart, Enlightened Mind: The Life and Letters of an Irish Zen Saint* (Boston: Wisdom Publications, 2007).

that this Zen way took me, because I consciously, fervently, could not be
said to have taken it. Now I feel there is no turning back. (75)

This way of describing her commitment to Buddhism is strikingly passive, as if something beyond her own agency, the spirit of Zen itself, was
at work in her life. Rather than fleeing from suffering, she is drawn to a
spiritual freedom that she cannot define.

With no hint of unhappiness or desire to renounce the world or her
past, and no account of how she picked a particular temple, the journal
begins with her arrival at Toshoji Temple in Tokyo. O'Halloran trained
in the Soto school of Zen with a master, Tetsugyu Ban, whom she usually refers to as Go Roshi. In her first *dokusan* (interview) with him, a
week after she entered the monastery, Go Roshi gave her the customary first koan, which concerns "mu." This word, which means "not" or
"nothing," is a famous Zen master's response to the question of whether a
dog has Buddha nature. O'Halloran concentrates on mu until it fills her
consciousness: "All the time my pulse beats 'nothingness, nothingness.'
Poems have come to me between the beats of mu … It's like a jungle
drum beating through my veins, but I must fight for it. I sleep in a frenzy.
I keep awakening hearing 'Nothingness, nothingness'" (23). Seeing and
feeling mu everywhere, she describes this experience, relying especially on
water imagery: "My body. Inside and all around is nothing. No thing. No
separation. A geyser in a lake appears to be a separate thing but is the lake"
(23). She describes self-consciousness as like an ice cube, an apparently
separate but temporary form. When the sun shines, the state of this water
is transformed, as well as the person who beholds it: "Our consciousness
changes with the form. Thus there is nothing left of the ice cube. We are
all nothingness" (23). Waves on the ocean seem distinct, but only for a
moment. Metaphors of dissolving and liquefaction express O'Halloran's
experience of unselfing: becoming other than she was.

When she tells another monk her understanding of the mu koan, he
declares that she is enlightened. O'Halloran is elated, but Go Roshi rejects
her answer because it has been reached through logic. A few days later,
after she learns to breathe in a new way, she suddenly understands mu in
a way that is embodied, emotional, and overwhelming:

> Takeo suggested how I should breathe. I tried and gradually got more and
> more excited. Mu rose vibrating up my spine, exploded in my head. Every-
> thing was simple. I was laughing. Mu was only mu. I felt ecstatic, couldn't
> contain my joy. I ran out of the hall, kissed the trees, stood in the garden and
> was the garden, really was it. All though dinner I beamed. Jiko kept staring.
> The others had described enlightenment. This was so much stronger. (24)

This incident, which takes her beyond what she had been told about enlightenment, happened after only two weeks in the monastery. Her conception of enlightenment deepened and developed as her practice matured and prompted introspective reflections. Dale S. Wright describes how every ultimate ideal, including enlightenment, is a moving target that is altered by achievement: "Whenever it occurs that through practice, energetic effort, or some other mechanism of change we alter ourselves by moving toward such an actual and plausible ideal, something extraordinary occurs. In acts of practice, the foundations are established for the projection of a new and somewhat transformed version of that ideal."[7] O'Halloran's several experiences of unselfing and their influence on her evolving understanding of Buddhism are evidence that, for her, enlightenment was not the achievement of a permanent condition but rather a process of continuing transformation.

One of the most intriguing aspects of O'Halloran's story is her struggle to reconcile self-knowledge with various outside perspectives. She is confused and upset by books about "all the conflicting theories of Zen and schools" (24) that she found at an English bookstore. She decides not to read a book because she wants not "words" but "to know from inside." O'Halloran is uneasy that other monks see her as nearing enlightenment when she harbors many uncertainties and doubts. When others praise her, she is not sure whether they accurately discern real progress or are simply fascinated by a woman and a foreigner. She realizes that several television interviews of her are primarily interested in her gender and Western background. After recording monks' admiration and praise, she notes "how easily people are fooled in spiritual affairs. They want to believe people have attained depths and to feel associated with the extraordinary... It made me wonder if there are hundreds of unscrupulous people with as little insight and understanding as me, masquerading as being in some way developed and capable of teaching" (117). When psychologists conduct scientific tests on meditating monks, they found that after only three months O'Halloran was having "deep meditations that are normally reached after years of practice" (51). This surprises her, but she is skeptical that physiological measurements mean much; these data are by-products that have no correlation with insight and understanding.

Especially important to her is Go Roshi's assessment of her practice. She is alternately elated, disappointed, and skeptical about his comments on her progress. When he does not accept "my experience of 'enlightenment'"

---

[7] Dale Wright, *What Is Buddhist Enlightenment?* (Oxford: Oxford University Press, 2016), 131–132.

74 In a Zen Monastery

and doubts that she apprehended mu, O'Halloran wonders how he could know this. Discouraged, she decides "to hell with koans" (27) and concentrates for a while on breathing and being in the present moment. When her sense of self keeps returning, she notes this sometimes with sadness or frustration, at other moments with calm acceptance. She understands that "form is emptiness" and all things are constantly changing, including the self; "but bang into the wall, of course form is form" (39). Daily interactions continually challenge her ability to put in practice the ideal of no-self: "The thing to which I am most attached, can least give up, least admit its transience, is myself" (39). In spite of what others say about her, she believes that she is a long way from enlightenment.

Three months into her training, O'Halloran performs a thought experiment to "redefine" herself. She imagines stretching the boundary of her body until it encompasses all that surrounds her:

> Each noise, sight, movement was me. I was tremendously excited, quivering, smiling. As if there was a statue, my physical body, with a cloth draped over it, hanging close around my body; it was what I defined as self. Now a tack through the head and cloth, someone is raising it and stretching it; it's still attached to my body but covers more and more, and that is me. How can I die or cease to be? I am eternal; I am process and thing. I am my mother. I am Roshi. I left the hondo, a new I; every noise and sight caught my notice, being incorporated into myself. (41)

After this unselfing through identification with the world, she goes shopping, cooks dinner, and "soon my self-conception was back to its usual stifling structure" (41). O'Halloran's doubts about her training focus on the discrepancy between her continuing sense of selfhood and her aspiration to realize the ideal of no-self, which she feels she attained momentarily. She tracks the ups and downs of her moods, one day knowing "calm, big mind" and the next day feeling "trivial and frazzled" (58). Through it all, she persists: "Keep at it, m'dear."

Many, although not all, of O'Halloran's doubts and questions are resolved in an experience of kensho in May 1980, about six months after she began Zen training. This initial flash of enlightenment, a moment of seeing into Buddha nature, comes when she has been feeling dejected and hopeless about her practice and progress. In an interview with Go Roshi, she responds to his command to shout "mu" several times with all her strength. Suddenly he grabs her and says, "This body is muji, this head, eyes, ears" (78). O'Halloran responds: "Suddenly I'm laughing and crying muji. I don't even realize 'Now I am muji,' but I simply was muji and everything around me" (78). When Go Roshi tells her that she has realized her Buddha nature, she is at first "too self-conscious even to know that it was kensho." She quickly accepts his judgment that this was a genuine kensho, and when she leaves the interview, she perceives mu in everything. She links this apprehension to compassion and care: "Suddenly I understood why we must take care of things just because they exist; we are of no greater and of no lesser value" (79). Feeling keenly the desperation of other monks striving for kensho, she cries and shouts with them, urging them on.

Two weeks later, O'Halloran questions her breakthrough experience and rapid progress through koans:

> At first I was so exhausted I felt neither joy nor sorrow, just relief. The next day I was ecstatic, couldn't stop smiling. Then all was as before—or at least, so it seems. Everyone tells me I look different. It's hard to be sure. I can't be bothered looking for big changes. I began the koans and flew through about twelve. Maybe they came easily because of my reading. I don't know. (79)

There is a striking contrast between her own tentativeness and the certainty of Go Roshi and the monks that she was transformed. O'Halloran resolves to stop trying to discern change but soon resumes doing so, although with less emotion and more detachment. In spite of her doubts, she accepts Go Roshi's judgment that her kensho was authentic, as well as her new role and status in the temple. The verdict of an authority figure and spiritual guide has a clarity and decisiveness that are not duplicated by her vacillating moods and thoughts.

O'Halloran suggests that her extensive reading about Zen (she mentions D. T. Suzuki) may have influenced her sudden and rapid progress through a dozen koans. It would be revealing to know exactly which intellectual resources shaped her understanding of mu, koans, and enlightenment. O'Halloran understood the difference between a merely rational understanding of Buddhist ideas and the deep existential knowledge that makes possible a spontaneous and often nonverbal response to a Zen master's questioning. Yet her remarks suggest that there are standard "answers" to koans that must be grasped and articulated in order to make progress.[8] She worries that by giving these stock responses she is not going deep enough: "I hope I'm not cheating myself by knowing some of the answers, but am afraid that I am" (79).

---

[8] See Yoel Hoffmann, (ed. and trans.) *The Sound of the One Hand: 281 Zen Koans with Answers*, (New York: New York Review of Books, 2016). When this book was originally published in 1916, it caused a scandal in Japan because it implied that rote learning, not an experience of enlightenment, was the basis for advancement in Zen institutions.

76   In a Zen Monastery

Go Roshi was seriously ill with cancer during O'Halloran's sojourn, although he lived until 1996. His sense of mortality, as well as his enormous confidence in O'Halloran's spiritual capacity and potential for leadership, motivated him to move her rapidly through training that took most monks much longer. Six months after her initial kensho, O'Halloran remarks that her teacher explained things to her in an unusual way:

> Maybe because my teacher's due to die soon and figures I'd better push on with my training—I don't know—but stuff that normally he wouldn't explain, but says himself that he usually gives a student months to work on, he was just shooting out like ping-pong balls—ping-pong balls with the force of bowling balls. I could hardly digest it all. (120)

A few days after her kensho, O'Halloran remarks that the only change she notices is that, when reading the sutras, she now loves "to shout in a booming voice. Previously I simply could not" (81). She finds relief in this shouting, compares it to "screamers" in Ireland, and "can see shades of many therapies in Zen" (81). The lack of self-consciousness that enables full participation in shouting "mu" or the sutras seems to be a condition of progress in this kind of training. A Zen master performs ritualized actions with ease and confidence. His words and gestures are not impulsive or wild spontaneity, as Westerners often think, but a kind of improvisation that builds on disciplined training and mastery of ritual acts. It is the result of persistent self-conscious effort, like the intuitive performance of a skilled athlete or musician. In the unselfing that can take place in a ritual, a person participates in a performance without feeling that she is acting, as if ritual has a momentum and purpose that replace individual agency.

O'Halloran tried with mixed results to live out the implications of her powerful kensho experience of unselfing. She participates in *takuhatsu*, ritual begging rounds, in frigid conditions, sometimes in sandals and without gloves. She learns to feel the cold without adding a layer of judgment: "These days I feel cold, but that's all. There's no comment; my self isn't resisting it nor having to persuade it" (109). When she feels irritation or resentment at monks who don't do their share of work, she does their chores for them with forbearance or resentment. When she gives way to what she considers selfish reactions, she is dismayed and depressed: "Every time I think I've progressed, I seem to mess it up again" (107). Infuriated that she feels a victim of her moods, she judges her Zen training as a failure. At other moments, she accepts that vacillating states of mind, including cheerful and optimistic ones, reveal the self's impermanence:

In a Zen Monastery 77

> I, me, my ego-self, was the mood; now it's over and that self is over. The "I" constantly mutates. It has no "essence." Yesterday, alone, I felt very happy, very at peace. "What is it that I lack?" Nothing, absolutely nothing. But that is equally a mood. Because it is more pleasant, I would like to see it as somehow more real, truer, always there behind, but in the same way it will come and go. (108)

Like a hawk hovering above its prey, she scans her mind's wayward movements between a sense of accomplishment and feelings of futility, serenity and disillusionment, discriminating judgment and acceptance of whatever is. The concept of no-self helps her to understand these inner conflicts and turbulence as ephemeral and to persist steadily on her chosen path.

A great challenge for O'Halloran in living out her Zen insights is deciding how to respond to Japanese expectations about gender roles. In two contexts, she feels strong pressure to conform to norms about women's proper role that conflict with her own values. First, the male monks often treat her as if she were a maid who should wait upon them. Sometimes O'Halloran does not challenge these expectations and even sees cheerful submission as part of Zen training: "I reckon in the long run it's I who gains and he who loses, I who'll get my ego battered and he whose will grow more entrenched" (141). Giving up her own wishes will bring long-term gain, she hopes, while the bossy monk forgoes this possibility. In other situations, she resists or disobeys male commands or requests. Once when she does this, she admits: "Hee, hee, hee, I'm a bitch, I'm terrible, but chuckle, chuckle, I enjoyed that" (142). Then, noticing an old woman earnestly scrubbing the floor, she feels ashamed. Gazing at bent bodies working in rice fields, she wonders if these humble people were "Zen monks, living their koans—digging and digging and only digging" (142). Throughout her residence in the temple, O'Halloran tries to reconcile her goal of transcending self with her strong reactions when men make demands that seem to her not simply forgivable expressions of a different culture's norms but unjust and harmful.

The second gender-related challenge that O'Halloran confronts is relentless pressure to marry. She is not attracted to several monks who pursue her and disdains what she calls the unromantic, businesslike Japanese idea of marriage. Her dilemma becomes acute when Go Roshi urges her to marry a particular monk. He tells her that he wants to make her the head priest of the temple at Kannonji and that only her children would be worthy successors. O'Halloran realizes that Go Roshi's primary intention is to establish a spiritual dynasty: "I finally clicked on the reason for all the marriage bit: My purpose is to make kids" (140). She nods her assent, trying to conform to the ideal that "everything, anything was okay." Then she rebels: "I caught myself. Wait, hold it, no, that's not what I want. Stop. I thought of my ego, of discriminating consciousness, etc., but still, it's not the life for me" (140). O'Halloran informs Go Roshi that instead of his plan she wants to go back to Ireland to start a Zen practice center. She continues to observe her "almost allergic reaction to the mention of marriage" (139), trying to determine whether it reflects the discriminating judgments of an ego that should be overcome or a deep intuitive knowledge of the way she must follow.

Go Roshi's insistence that O'Halloran marry Tetsugen-san, a man she did not love, precipitates a crucial breakthrough in July 1981. "He was pushing me, pushing hard. It was killing me to refuse him … I begged him not to ask, no, not that" (161). After leaving this interview with her teacher, she becomes hysterical, while at the same time she thinks she is overreacting and "being ridiculous." Then, as several monks attend to her, she has an experience of unselfing:

> Something left me, some huge oppressive weight that I'd never even known was there and only recognized in its lifting. I felt so light. I was laughing and crying. Euphoria. They were alarmed. I assured them I'd never felt so wonderful in all my life. (Tetsugen-san had nothing to do with it any more; he was merely the trigger.) My breathing was a kind of panting as if mounting to some emotional climax. Galli told me to breathe deeply, to do zazen. I tried. My breathing stopped. My mind never felt so clear or lucid. The voices were very far away. I was in a crystal paradise. Galli was screaming at me to breathe. From somewhere I heard my voice softly answering, "hai." In the distance Tetsugen was calling the hospital. What an effort. But I'd have to show them I was okay. I snapped out of it, sat up, normal as hell. (162)

The monks' reactions and her claim that she stopped breathing suggest that O'Halloran appeared to be near death. Yet her mind remained lucid and she felt as if she was hearing others from a great distance. To reassure the monks, she forced herself to break out of the blissful crystal paradise and act "normal as hell." This incident is described as a symbolic death and return to life. In the context of intense pressure to marry coming from the teacher she loved and respected, she lost the ability to function normally, as if her ordinary self had vanished. When she returns to normal consciousness, she resumes her identity and holds firm to her refusal to marry. O'Halloran comes back to her ordinary sense of herself with new resolution and the self-knowledge that she is a modern Western woman who, for all her acculturation to Japanese ways and commitment to Zen ideals, cannot fit into an alien system of marriage without violating her sense of integrity and well-being.

In a letter to a friend about six months later, O'Halloran reflected on this pivotal experience of unselfing:

> They put on a lot of pressure for me to marry this kidney-machine monk and live here and start a dynasty. Was I not into that! In fact I fainted, blanked out three times at the very prospect. All of this triggered some psychological mechanisms of which I have neither understanding nor control, but there seemed to be an actually physical weight lifted off me, followed by an ecstatic euphoria that I wouldn't mind repeating—but without the threat of marrying Tetsugen-san. Anyway, that resolved itself. (173)

Although she remained puzzled by this incident, her dilemma about whether to submit to Go Roshi's pressure to marry was "resolved." It is as if the life-determining decision was made for her and she passively yielded to what was too difficult for her to affirm. After this crisis, O'Halloran committed herself to Zen on her own terms, without having to obey her mentor's oppressive directive. The incident of unselfing allowed her to stay on the path she had chosen without having to disobey or disappoint Go Roshi.

This incident marks a turning point in O'Halloran's story. The next day after her euphoric trance, her mentor says to her: "Until last night you were human trying to become God; now you're God. I'm Buddha" (162). Go Roshi says that they must "help the others" and consents to her proposal to go back to Ireland to start a Zen center after three years of training. She is "the only one who is his equal" (164). From this point on, Go Roshi assumes that she is his spiritual heir. Although he sometimes tries to influence her, he accepts her choices.

O'Halloran demonstrates renewed commitment to her practice and to helping others. She begins to sleep sitting up for only a few hours each night. She frequently says that she is exhausted, and this condition surely affected her altered states of consciousness and sudden shifts of mood. She observes that her mind can focus only on peeling potatoes and wonders if she is close to awakening or to "sleepening." For no apparent reason, she is frequently bursting with joy. In the same entry that reports her trance and euphoria, she says she feels close to death, as if she had fulfilled all her hopes and ambitions and has nothing to strive for. Yet she is completely content: "At 26, a living corpse and such a life!" (165). Desiring nothing more for herself, O'Halloran vows to help others save themselves from suffering:

> I have maybe 50 or 60 years (who knows?) of time, of a life, open, blank, ready to offer. I want to live it for other people. What else is there to do with it? Not that I expect to change the world or even a blade of grass, but it's as if to give myself is all I can do, as the flowers have no choice but to blossom. At the moment the best I can see to do is to give to people this freedom, this

bliss, and how better than through zazen? So I must go deeper and deeper and work hard, no longer for me but for everyone I can help. And still I can't save anyone. They must work themselves, and not every one will. (165)

In a way at once forceful and humble, not formally but writing in her journal, O'Halloran makes the vow of a bodhisattva. She expresses a striking combination of decisive agency and a sense of not being able to help herself, as if her choices are an unwilled expression of her nature like the blossoming of a plant.

Although the final chapter of the book is entitled "Completion," O'Halloran's future was wide open as she wrestled with several issues during her last months in the temple. In particular, she tried to reconcile the ideal of no-self with her affirmation of her worth as a woman. In a letter to her friend Sean, O'Halloran condemned the system that made her "a man's servant" even as she viewed her judgmental attitude as "a middle-class Western luxury" compared to "how the majority of women in the world really live" (177). She both criticizes and acquiesces in the patriarchal system:

> I'd never choose to bind myself into such a relationship, but I feel free in that I can actually do it … It's crap; it's unjust, but I'm living it and totally happy. Don't get me wrong—it's no perverse, masochistic, always-secretly-desired-the-whip joy—but in spite of that I'm quite aware that the universal implications of such a view would be reactionary and I would hesitate to recommend it, but it sure makes life easier. (178)

I don't know if this kind of double consciousness – obligingly fitting into a system she condemns as wrong – is evidence of moral hypocrisy, a form of self-deception, cultural relativism, or the detachment of an enlightened person. O'Halloran says that she is happy to conform to a pattern of gender relationships that is not simply conservative but unjust. She knew that she could neither single-handedly reform a complex social system nor give up her feminist ethical perspective. She found a way to participate in the institutions of Zen Buddhism without compromising her integrity. As we will see for Gesshin Claire Greenwood, other women authors of Western Buddhist travel narratives have wrestled with similar challenges as they tried to live according to the ideal of no-self while resisting patriarchal attempts to deny their choices or worth.[9]

---

[9] The scholarly literature on the role of women in Buddhism is immense; a good starting place is Rita Gross, *Buddhism after Patriarchy: A Feminist History, Analysis, and Reconstruction of Buddhism* (Albany: SUNY Press, 1993). Another Western travel narrative set in Japan is Tracy Franz, *My Year of Dirt and Water: Journal of a Zen Monk's Wife in Japan* (Berkeley: Stone Bridge Press, 2018). In this work, a central metaphor for the author's changing sense of self is the practice

In a Zen Monastery

Although Go Roshi said he accepted her desire to return to Ireland, he later resumed his pressure on O'Halloran to marry a Japanese man and become his successor. After an interview with him, she felt disoriented and wondered what she should do: "In the real world, Roshi's and my ideas are so different. But it seems I have no criteria left by which to make a decision. Anything is okay. It's a strange feeling, not a problem, but definitely disorienting" (196). O'Halloran wants to embrace whatever life brings as "okay." Yet to submit to Go Roshi's wishes would require her to violate crucial values and goals and undermine her capacity to make meaningful decisions. As she tries to function within the monastery's hierarchical system and stand her ground as an independent woman, O'Halloran must make intentional choices and also have equanimity and adaptability, come what may. Her journal does not explain how she resolved this issue in theoretical terms, for instance by establishing clear principles or criteria. Instead, she shows how different values that were important to her conflicted and how she resolved her dilemmas with decisions. O'Halloran's story makes vivid the challenges involved in living out the implications of insights gained in moments of unselfing. She gives us not an ethical theory but a striking example of practical wisdom: a Zen master's union of intuitive knowledge with decisive action.

The last few months of O'Halloran's journal are sketchy, and the final section was stolen after the bus crash that killed her. In April 1982, she went through a ceremony marking her graduation from koan study, and in June, she participated in a ritual affirming the transmission of the Dharma to her. With no mention of further conflicts with Go Roshi, she persisted in her plan to return to Ireland to start a Zen center and translate Japanese texts into English. O'Halloran made decisions that reflected her core values and aspirations even as she recognized the limited perspective and transitory nature of these expressions of her selfhood.

The contrast between outer views of O'Halloran as an enlightened person and her self-description is especially intriguing because of Go Roshi's claims about her after she died. The epilogue of *Pure Heart, Enlightened Mind* includes his inscription on a statue dedicated to her at Kannonji Temple. This memorial states that O'Halloran completed 1,000 days of continuous Zen practice involving "three hours of sleeping in the zazen position and twenty hours of devotion to her studies in order to attain

---

of making pottery from "dirt and water." Franz struggles to make identical pots and then breaks them down into formless clay. Although she does not discuss no-self explicitly, many of her experiences suggest insights about this, such as when her teacher says of a teacup: "It is the nothingness in the middle that determines the true size of the vessel" (75).

salvation not only for herself but also for all people" (294). An authorized certificate of "Enlightenment Achieved" was conferred on her before she died, and she was posthumously given the name "Great Enlightened Lady, of the same heart and mind as the Great Teacher Buddha." Go Roshi affirms that O'Halloran was an "incarnation of Kannon Bosatsu to be loved and respected forever." (This is the Japanese name for the female Bodhisattva of Compassion, known in China as Guanyin.)

Go Roshi's letter of condolence to the O'Halloran family, also included in the epilogue, declares that O'Halloran's training for 1,000 days followed the example of Dogen, the founder of the Soto school of Zen: "She was the modern Dogen" (293). Go Roshi pinpoints O'Halloran's enlightenment as a decisive event on May 2, 1980: "There was a spring training at Kannonji from May 2nd for five days. O'Halloran reached her enlightenment on the first day. She went in for meditations twice, three times a day, and solved all three thousand koans" (293). There is no ambiguity, uncertainty, or suggestion of future development in this portrayal of O'Halloran; she was well on her way toward becoming a divine figure in the eyes of many devout Buddhists.

Go Roshi's view contrasts markedly with O'Halloran's description of later insights that deepened and developed the earlier kensho. For instance, in May 1982, she describes "two minor awakenings" at a meditation retreat in Kyushu, "the best sesshin I'd ever experienced" (199). About the second of these experiences, O'Halloran wrote: "On the fourth day, my awakening began in the corridor and became intense while I was eating. Everything is perfect. Everything is enlightening, just as it is by virtue of being" (200). Here, she refers to "my awakening" as occurring at that time, two years later than the first day of the 1980 training exercise that Go Roshi described as the moment of "her enlightenment."

Two weeks later, O'Halloran looked back on her recent insights as at once "tenuous" and abiding: "Old habits die hard but the experiences are there, I now really know what I had theretofore assented to as being true" (202). This remark suggests that she understood enlightenment as a gradual process of deepening, like what Christians call continuous conversion, rather than the sudden decisive turning point implicit in Go Roshi's statement or the certificate of "Enlightenment Achieved." Her reflections on the meaning of her experiences would continue to develop, rather than being completed and permanent. O'Halloran's remarks are in this way more faithful to the deepest insights of Zen than are those of her teacher, who wished to place his stamp of approval on her as the recipient of the mind-to-mind transmission of the Dharma handed down by the Buddha.

O'Halloran is uneasy when Go Roshi praises her to other monks at the temple. She feels ashamed when he says that, like Dogen, she "hadn't slept lying down for a thousand days," which was not the case. When one monk makes a speech saying that he is "justifiably put out by Roshi's exaggeration of my worth and his condemnation of the Japanese" (200), she wishes that her mentor would not do this. These remarks suggest that Go Roshi's elevation of O'Halloran may have been motivated not only by his recognition of her unusual spiritual gifts and his desire for a successor but also as a strategy to inspire flagging Japanese monks to work harder. The Roshi's emphatic declaration contrasts strikingly with O'Halloran's confession of doubts, uncertainties, and occasional feelings of inadequacy.

The status of "Enlightenment Achieved" is an honor bestowed by an authority figure and a role within an organized community. It is doubtful that an individual's self-examination can ever attain such a clear and certain judgment about one's own spiritual condition. If it did, we would wonder whether a person who believed this about herself lacked self-critical awareness and scruples about self-deception. A Western individual with the status of a Zen master is in an awkward position where reputation and self-knowledge are sometimes at odds. Enlightenment can be understood in many ways, including the perspectives of various Buddhist traditions, intellectual disciplines, and stories about individuals by their associates or, rarely, by themselves. What does O'Halloran's personal diary reveal about this acclaimed bodhisattva? Her journal shows her unusual openness to experiences of unselfing and her keen insight into their significance and limitations. It depicts enlightenment as not a reified state, divine status, or unsurpassable knowledge but rather, like everything else from a Buddhist perspective, a process of continuing transformation shaped by underlying conditions. It involves, among many changes in the consciousness of an awakened person, a dialectic or rhythm between times when social identity predominates and times of unselfing when conscious selfhood is abandoned, effaced, or given up. Unselfing is not completely subject to a person's choices or controls, yet a person can influence the conditions that make it possible. For instance, there are subtle shifts of awareness and patterned ways to train attention that help a person become more conscious of dependence on the world, more perceptive of the fleeting nature of identity, and more compassionate. Maura O'Halloran had unusual gifts for feisty assertion, yielding dispossession of her sense of selfhood, and rapid assimilation of the Zen worldview. Her journal reveals an openness and alert receptivity that facilitate the breakthrough events that sometimes seem to befall and overpower a Zen practitioner. She depicts a constant interplay between selfing and unselfing in her practice: a rhythm that alternates between periods of self-reflection and events she understands as loss of self. O'Halloran deeply understands the human condition's full range of emotions and challenges and embraces her own particular form of it, sometimes with ecstatic abandon and exuberant gestures, at other times in quiet and subtle ways such as a feeling that her heart opened or melted.

O'Halloran understood the value of narrative in presenting Zen insights. The expanded edition of *Pure Heart, Enlightened Mind* includes thirty pages of an unfinished novel that O'Halloran was working on in 1982. It portrays a Western woman, Annie Shaw, who enters a Zen monastery and asks many of the questions that O'Halloran lived with, for instance whether one should participate in a ceremony without fully understanding its meaning. One voice inside Annie tells her that she will get nowhere "by endless questioning and rejecting" and that "the only way to understand this thing is not by analysis but by immersion" (272). Rather than simply portray Zen wisdom as abandoning the intellect's questions, however, O'Halloran also depicts a skeptical side of Annie that reminds the first voice that "immersions have resulted in drownings" (272). This vignette suggests not only Zen wisdom but also wisdom about the need to integrate Zen with other perspectives: a multifaceted awareness of complexity that is best rendered in narrative. In a letter to her mother that describes her novel, O'Halloran explains how reading fiction requires an imaginative movement that is more Zen-like than analytical discourse:

> I always thought that writing analytical books about Zen seemed so un-Zen. It set up structures, distinctions, and invited argument and speculation. The novel, on the other hand, requires the sympathetic understanding of the reader. If it's successful, he'll leave his own ego and "become" the character suggested, at least for the length of reading. This is much closer to a Zen understanding (intuition, even?). (174)

Like fiction, compelling works of autobiography and memoir stretch a reader to understand another person's way of being, such as the embodied wisdom of a Zen master. Such reading calls for forms of intuition that are intellectual, emotional, and spiritual, and perhaps for something like unselfing. O'Halloran's moving narrative of her Buddhist training portrays moments of unselfing within the larger context of her life as a very distinct individual, the Irish-American woman who became a Zen master and saint: "Sure and begorra, let me tell you the tricks" (16). *Pure Heart, Enlightened Mind* invites the reader to "leave his own ego" and learn from O'Halloran's unique way of living Zen, as rendered so memorably by this wise, compassionate, and joyful bodhisattva.

*

David Chadwick's *Thank You and OK!: An American Zen Failure in Japan* (1994) also explores the ambiguity of success and failure in Zen monastic training, as this is revealed by changes and continuities in the author's sense of selfhood. This memoir's narrative structure alternates between chapters that describe two different periods of residence in Japan. One set of chapters recounts seven weeks in 1988 when Chadwick lived in a small mountain temple on Kyushu that he calls Hogoji. Forty-three years old and originally from Texas, Chadwick had studied Zen for twenty-two years at the San Francisco Zen Center, including five years with Shunryu Suzuki Roshi, who ordained him as a Soto Zen priest.[10] He also practiced for five years with Richard Baker Roshi, Suzuki's successor there, and intermittently for many years with Dainin Katagiri Roshi, the founder of the Minnesota Zen Center, who often visited the San Francisco Center. While Katagiri was in residence at Hogoji, he encouraged Chadwick to join him there to experience Soto Zen monastic life.

Another series of chapters, organized chronologically but interspersed with sections about the 1988 monastic residence, tells the story of three years (May 1989 to April 1992) that Chadwick lived with his wife Elin in the suburbs of a city in western Honshu that he calls Maruyama. They lived next door to a large Rinzai temple that he calls Daianji, where he meditated and chanted, had dokusan (private interviews) with teachers, and learned about the Rinzai approach to Zen practice. A keen observer of Japanese ways, Chadwick describes shopping habits, bureaucracy, etiquette, marriage customs, dress, food, and daily interactions with neighbors, portraying "a place full of wonders, delusion, tradition, pretense and the dance of life— just like the States, only completely different" (x).[11] *Thank You and OK!* is likely the funniest Western Buddhist travel narrative, with Chadwick portraying himself as a bumbling *gaizin* (foreigner) who is confused but good humored as he struggles to get a visa, puzzles over indirect communications, or makes embarrassing mistakes using the Japanese language. He explores similarities between monastic and lay life and reflects on which aspects of its Japanese cultural heritage can or should be adopted by Western adepts of Zen. In spite of two decades of prior Buddhist study and practice, Chadwick

---

[10] Chadwick edited two books about Suzuki, *Crooked Cucumber: The Life and Zen Teaching of Shunryu Suzuki* (New York: Broadway Books, 1999) and *Zen Is Right Here: Teaching Stories and Anecdotes of Shunryu Suzuki, Author of "Zen Mind, Beginner's Mind,"* (Boulder, Colorado: Shambala, 2007).

[11] David Chadwick, *Thank You and OK!: An American Zen Failure in Japan* (New York: Penguin, 1994).

86 In a Zen Monastery

demonstrates a refreshing "beginner's mind" (one of Suzuki's key concepts) as he depicts Zen monastic life and his sincere efforts to be a good Buddhist. Like van de Wetering, he has a Zennish appreciation for quirky irony and absurdity and is not pedantic or pretentious. He quotes Roshi Baker's comment – serious or joking? – about the results of Chadwick's practice: "Years of expensive Zen training gone to waste."[12]

The concept of no-self underlies and shapes Chadwick's story in several ways. In order to understand Japanese culture and to practice Zen in the prescribed way, he must become aware of and overcome ingrained habits of mind and cultural assumptions. To fit in, he has to become, or at least act like, a different person. For instance, he must learn the elaborate ritual choreography of meals and ceremonies, which is the last thing his "friends back in Texas would have imagined me doing with large chunks of my life" (117). This is not simply a matter of absorbing new information but requires patience, deference to others, obedience to authority, conformity to incomprehensible rules, and other attributes of character that feel foreign to his nature. As he learns to function in the monastery and as a householder in an ordinary Japanese neighborhood, Chadwick demonstrates remarkable perceptiveness and adaptability. He practices new ways of living in Japan as if he were donning a change of clothes or taking a role in a performance. Is this adaptability a new expression of a persisting character, a sign of a new self coming into being, or evidence that there is no stable self? His story suggests all of these interpretations.

A recurring challenge is dealing with bureaucracy, which takes "time, experience, and patience—maybe some courage too" (154). Chadwick visits the Immigration Office several times as he tries to get the right kind of visa. He puzzles over regulations for marriage ceremonies, housing, and banking. In a hilarious episode at the Driver's License Office, he cheerfully answers interview questions such as whether the test he took in California was conducted in Japanese and the number of ccs in the test vehicle's engine. His friend and fellow American monk Norman counsels him that inside and outside the monastery an essential feature of Japanese culture is to "torque-the-individual" to induce conformity: "The group is all that matters. 'Enlightenment' is just the substitution of the group ego for the individual one ... The purpose of the training in Japanese Zen temples isn't to help you along the path to enlightenment—it is to cultivate you into a refined and obedient Japanese priest for Japanese temples" (164–165). Yet if one goal of Zen training is to produce docile

---

[12] Cited online at Chadwick's website, www.cuke.com, and several other websites.

Japanese temple priests, the monastery nonetheless offers an opportunity to follow the way of the Buddha. Monastic discipline teaches Chadwick how much he prefers his own way, yet he usually submits and tries to follow the rules and live in harmony with others. His individual desires, not just for comfort or pleasure but simply to do what he wants, do not vanish, but he watches them arise and pass while he follows the myriad rules and regulations governing how to arrange utensils at a ritual, care for his robes, or respond to a monk's petty bossiness. Occasionally he just does as he pleases, enjoying alcohol or goofing off with no residue of guilt.

The tension between demands of the ego and of the group that is an inherent part of monastic life is also a dominant theme in Chadwick's engagements with secular Japanese culture. He goes beyond the predictable contrast between Western individualism and Japanese group consciousness, for example, when he shows how he and his friend, the Japanese monk Koji, realize that they are both searching for a balance between We and Me. The presence of foreigners and Japanese in Hogoji brings many conflicts but also the possibility of new understanding for each of them:

> "Balance," said Koji.
> I took a deep breath and droned, "WE, WE, WE, WE, WE, WE, WE, WE."
> "ME, ME, ME, ME, ME, ME, ME, ME," he responded with perfect timing.
> "WE, WE, WE, WE, WE, WE, WE, WE," we sang together followed by "ME, ME, ME, ME, ME, ME, ME, ME." And so down to Ryumon we marched chanting the Japanese-American cultural balance sutra. (324)

Monastic life brings moments when Chadwick's sense of selfhood is not destroyed but transfigured by participation in community. Although he sometimes feels confined and claustrophobic when living communally, he also finds that "when we function smoothly as a group, our differences and gripes become irrelevant, but we do not lose our distinctness. It's transformational. The very substance that was an irritant becomes a note in a harmonious chord" (348). In the end, he concludes that the Japanese and their Western guests need each other to spark a transformation that can come out of the tension between me and we, individual self-assertion and communal belonging:

> They need us as much as we need them. I mean, they don't need us if they just want to be good Japanese monks and irrelevant to the present tense and the rest of the world. And we don't need them if we just want to be cowboy iconoclasts without regard for tradition and harmony—but we need each other to get out of our ruts and get on with it, get on with creating this diverse unity. Maybe we are each other's secret ingredient—to metamorphose. It's butterfly time. (437)

When the friction between individual and group brings about a shift in how one understands one's relationship to others, then a transformation may take place.

Like other Western authors of monastic memoirs, Chadwick views the contrasts between Rinzai and Soto Zen in terms of their differing understandings of which practices best elicit unselfing. In the United States, he had followed Soto practices. In Maruyama, he learns firsthand about Rinzai and, like Maura O'Halloran, meditates on the mu koan: the famous response (nothingness) to the question, "Does a dog have Buddha nature?" Compared to Soto Zen's emphasis on "just sitting," the more vigorous and energetic pursuit of enlightenment taught in Rinzai temples is "gangbuster Zen." In Rinzai, you "try to do it as hard as you can every instant" (29). From the Soto perspective, this active seeking can express and nurture the egotistic self: "We regarded Zen-that-ran-after-enlightenment as goal seeking, or 'having some idea,' as Suzuki said" (250). An old saying has it that "Rinzai picks the fruit off the tree and that Soto lets it fall" (300). In Japan, however, Chadwick learns to appreciate Rinzai methods: "it was good to have something definite to chew on for a change" (250). He realizes that there are dangers in being either an eager beaver or – his own proclivity – the type of person who likes to let his/her mind wander freely, sometimes in order to avoid the task at hand in the present moment. Hard-core Rinzai practitioners and the more relaxed and receptive Soto forms of Zen may alike express the ego's attempt to control experience rather than being open to what the present moment offers: "It could be said that the avoiders are seeking and that the seekers are avoiding. They're merely different expressions of the age-old near-impossibility of just being" (299). The monastery's rituals and routines offer each of these human types an opportunity to be absorbed in something beyond personal ideas and assertions: "Due to the softening effect of zazen, sweeping, and the peaceful environs, both types of people may enter into less cerebral states and just be sitting or sweeping, aware of the motions of the body, the contours of the ground being appreciated and the borders of consciousness slipping away" (299). This description of sweeping suggests an imminent moment of unselfing. Chadwick depicts many similar brief moments as part of the rhythm of Zen life, rather than focusing on one of them at length or presenting a single incident as a turning point or awakening. Compared to van de Wetering and O'Halloran, he is much more relaxed about attaining a breakthrough experience. He is older and wiser, or older and less energetic.

Dogen, the founder of Soto Zen, described the "dropping away of body and mind." Chadwick recounts similar moments when he becomes

In a Zen Monastery 89

completely absorbed in a task, meditation, or perception. Following Dogen, Suzuki, and Katagiri, he says that attaining such moments of unselfing is not the point or purpose of Zen training. Just sitting is enough, without trying to realize a particular subjective state of being: "My teachers imparted the empowering teaching that we are fine as is. No need for something extra: just us as we are is all we need to stand in the footsteps of the saints and to sit on the zafu of the masters" (300). For Dogen, taking the posture and proper mindset of meditation is itself enlightenment, not a means to it. When Chadwick stops trying to produce a particular experience such as some version of unselfing, then willing and desiring cease and he relishes "the joy of continuing this bumbling unseen path of me as I am and us as we are" (364).

During Chadwick's sojourn in Japan, Roshi Katagiri was slowly weakening from cancer, and he died in 1990. Writing a few years later, Chadwick reflects at length on this beloved teacher and his legacy. A Zen master's followers often perceive him as the perfect exemplification of the ideal of noself. In certain ways, Katagiri represents that ideal for Chadwick because of his humility and generous way of relating to others; he said little and inspired by example. Yet even as he depicts the Roshi as a selfless and compassionate teacher, Chadwick compensates for the tendency to idealize a spiritual leader, especially when grieving his death. Don't confuse the teacher with the absolute truth, he warns himself; don't take the finger pointing to the moon to be the moon. Whether or not his teacher was or was not a bodhisattva and an actualization of no-self, he was a vivid, unique individual with a distinctive character: a certain kind of self.

Chadwick emphasizes Katagiri's sense of failure, and this helps him to see his own lapses in a larger context. The Roshi sometimes felt he had not done a good job of translating Zen Buddhism into terms Americans could understand and had not created a cohesive sangha that would survive his death. Katagiri suffered when Shunryu Suzuki died; he was deeply attached to his friend and mentor. He was hurt that Suzuki never thanked him for years of dedicated service, an assertion that Chadwick disputes. Trying to reassure Katagiri, Chadwick claims that Suzuki, too, could be said to have failed: "What of Suzuki's so-called success? Look what's happened. We've got fine buildings and many students, but we're all a bunch of idiots. Nothing to brag about here. Just a lot of depressed dopes and infighting. Who of us understands anything? So didn't Suzuki fail?" (399). At the end of the book, Chadwick reflects on what it means that he and his American Zen companions failed to realize "our early pure and simple expectations and the clear-cut enlightenment of the story books" (434). This kind of failure is actually a form of success: "It seems to me that all our endless failures are adding up to a magnificent success. It's just not what we had in mind. It's real" (434).

This avowal makes explicit what was only implied in van de Wetering's portrayal of his failure to achieve enlightenment. To have attained "what we had in mind" would not be an expression of selflessness but rather the fulfillment of expectations and grasping desires. Chadwick and van de Wetering each find a contemporary Western idiom for the traditional Soto critique of Rinzai practice. Each author's professed failure to achieve his original idea of enlightenment is an ambiguous sign that he may have moved beyond concern with his own spiritual condition. Or not. Who can know about other people's or one's own deepest motivation and achievement? Like many other Western Buddhist travel narratives, these memoirs of Zen monastic life turn away from offering a firm conclusion about whether the author attained the goal that was a chief motivation for pursuing Zen. This reorientation signals an important transformation: a diminished concern with one's spiritual progress or condition. The authors do not explicitly claim as much; their stories suggest what they do not say.

The way in which Chadwick concludes his narrative depicts another way that his years in Japan changed him. He learns that the house in Maruyama where he and his wife had been living and raising a child would soon be sold. He had come to love the home on which he was laboring, so the eviction comes as a blow. Although sad, he quickly realizes how much he had been burdened by this project:

> Why do I let such trivia get to me? I wondered. After all these years of Zen. What good is it? What have I learned. I shook my head. Looking into the evening sky, I felt light and imagined my family and me going way, way up there in a balloon, empty and free.
>
> Then I glanced down at the wood before me and smiled. It looked so good I wanted to eat it. And so, returning to the full life I am enslaved by, I picked up a board and went back to work. (446)

He is remarkably resilient, able to acknowledge and let go of attachments and then participate in daily life in a lighter, freer way. This is not the same as not caring and very different from van de Wetering's callous indifference. A capacity for resilience is a significant marker of selflessness, showing that a person has not invested all of his/her identity and sense of value in a project or pursuit that comes to naught.

In their final interview, his Rinzai instructor tells Chadwick that he does not need to work any longer on the mu koan. Because he never experienced

In a Zen Monastery

a breakthrough, Chadwick asks his teacher for clarification. The Roshi responds that Chadwick's future way will be followed not in a temple but in everyday life. His zendo (meditation hall) is wherever he is. Instead of concentrating on mu, Chadwick should do something else: "Open your ears!" (447). This final vignette suggests the unfinished nature of Chadwick's spiritual quest as well as a genuine change in him that his teacher discerns. Although he did not have a dramatic moment of satori, he came a long way on a wandering path and, more important, he knows how to go on.

The title of this travel narrative takes on new meaning at the end of the book. "Thank you and OK!" refers to a Japanese matchbox depicted on the book's cover. This unusual object is an A-frame structure six inches high with a picture on the box that shows a smiling Japanese man giving a thumbs-up sign: "He's winking, sticking his chin out and tightening his lips in a beaming smile—all in a way that immediately conveys a gung ho, agreeable attitude" (70). This incongruous item sat on the altar in Hogoji Temple next to 500-year-old scrolls and ancient utensils arranged according to Dogen's instructions. The matchbox and the phrase "Thank you and OK!" recur several times in the book and suggest a whimsical but positive attitude that acknowledges and then passes over ironies, contradictions, and conflicts. It is a helpful attitude for both Westerners and Japanese to adopt in the monastery as they butt heads about how to pursue their practice, each insisting that their own culturally distinctive way of doing things is superior. In a funny but telling incident, Norman, who is more adamant and exasperated than Chadwick about the need to leave behind Japanese cultural baggage attached to Zen, nearly comes to blows with a fellow monk, Shuko, as the two of them squabble about whether rice can be served mixed with pine nuts. Norman climbs a tree and refuses to come down unless he gets his way. As he ends his residence in the monastery, Norman says it will take him a long time to heal. He and his nemesis Shuko both need to learn to say, "Thank you and OK!"

Chadwick proposes a distinctly Buddhist meaning of this phrase. He tells Norman that the matchbox symbolizes the core of their practice: "'Thank you' is gratitude, the gateway to religious joy, and 'OK,' which comes from 'all correct,' represents the perfection of wisdom. This is our mantra" (311). "Thank you and OK!" expresses Chadwick's final blessing on Japan for all the ways in which, while driving him crazy (or by driving him crazy), it deepened his understanding of Buddhism and enriched his life. Chadwick does not claim to have achieved selflessness, or even to have made progress toward it, but the way he understands and practices Zen was transformed by his sojourn in Japan. He seems to have transcended two basic dualisms that had fragmented his life. First, he found a way to reconcile the dueling approaches of Soto and Rinzai, which respectively emphasize either just sitting without expectation or active and energetic pursuit of enlightenment. He now appreciates both approaches and sees how each of them can be subverted by the self's desire to control experience. Second, his future path and practice will combine all that he learned in the monastery with a life outside it, which his teacher calls "the One Drop Zendo—and that of course is you. It will be wherever you are" (447). The split between monastic and lay life is overcome in this call to overcome isolated selfhood by participating in a big zendo, an extended community larger than the one he came to appreciate at the Zen temple.

*

Like Maura O'Halloran's journal, Gesshin Claire Greenwood's *Bow First, Ask Questions Later* (2018) depicts a woman's distinctive experience of Zen monastic life. Greenwood, too, is a young, feisty, candid, and often irreverent writer who received traditional Zen training for years in Japan and puts her understanding of it into the sometimes startling idiom of a Western feminist in her twenties. Born in 1986, Greenwood grew up in San Francisco, where her parents were part of the Spirit Rock community practicing the Vipassana tradition. After graduating from college, she went to India and in Bodhgaya was temporarily ordained as a Theravada nun. She moved to Japan and was ordained in 2010 by the Soto Zen priest Seido Suzuki Roshi, the abbot at Toshoji, one of the temples where O'Halloran practiced. Greenwood received dharma transmission in 2015, completed her training at several monasteries, and became an *osho*, a fully authorized Soto Zen priest. For three years she lived in Nisodo, a women's convent led by Shundo Aoyama Roshi. She left the convent to study in a Japanese university and started a blog. As the memoir ends, Greenwood has returned to the United States, married, enrolled in graduate school to study Japanese Buddhism, and is deliberating about her future as a twenty-nine-year-old married Zen priest with literary ambitions.

Bow First, Ask Questions Later is structured as a series of short (6–8 pages) thematic essays that usually explore a puzzle in understanding Zen or a practical difficulty in implementing a Buddhist rule or idea. The book's title suggests one of the many ways that questions about no-self arise in these situations. When Greenwood asks questions about the meaning of various monastic practices, she is usually told to go ahead without full understanding of what she is doing or saying. This pattern recurs in many contexts as she learns to make tea, take care of her robes, perform complex rituals, meditate, and so forth. In the chapter that provides the book's title, Greenwood is about to "receive the precepts" as a layperson at Toshoji. She is not taught the meaning of the sixteen bodhisattva precepts; when she asks, she is told that they are difficult to translate. Basic ambiguities and uncertainties nag her. For instance, the Roshi interprets the vow not to use alcohol as "don't drink too much." She thinks about various meanings of "Do not misuse sexuality." Greenwood realizes that her American orientation, including her need to understand what she is saying when making a vow, differs from the Japanese focus on observing the correct form of behavior:

> In the Japanese context there is an understanding that participating in the ceremony—such as a precept ceremony or ordaining—itself has meaning, that the ceremony engenders the vow and practice through embodying form, not the other way around. In the West, we usually approach the precepts as promises we make first, bolstered and strengthened by the precept ceremony; in the West, receiving the precepts is descriptive, rather than prescriptive. (38)[13]

In Japan, in contrast, a person grows into a role by performing it. When Greenwood asks what it means to be a nun, Seido Roshi tells her: "you'll know after you become one" (39). This Soto Zen perspective reflects Dogen's assertion that practice and realization are one. Moreover, a monk should not expect special experiences to result from practice; "just sitting" is itself the embodiment of enlightenment. We saw how Peter Matthiessen's understanding of Zen practice changed as he turned to Soto and away from his earlier Rinzai quest for intense experiences of unselfing. For Greenwood, too, proper Zen practice involves suspending her own agenda and submitting to the forms and rules established by a tradition: "Japanese monastic practice purposefully collapses the distinction between ceremony and meaning, between bodily form and understanding, in order to arrive at something close to the unity of practice and realization. This is why receiving the precepts in a ceremony, no matter what your mind is doing, is seen as more important than believing or thinking about the precepts" (38–39). Striving to have a particular kind of experience and needing to have one's questions answered are demands of the self that Soto Zen tries to deflect or diminish.

A similar issue arises when Greenwood participates in a ceremonial "Dharma combat," a ritual when monks respond to challenging questions, supposedly in a spontaneous way. In contemporary Japan, these events

---

[13] Gesshin Claire Greenwood, *Bow First, Ask Questions Later* (Somerville, MA: Wisdom Publications, 2018).

94   In a Zen Monastery

are scripted: a monk learns the questions beforehand and memorizes the correct responses. This does not mean that a Dharma combat is not "authentic" or "real" (terms that Greenwood uses with reservations). The meaning of her own participation in this ceremony is different than what she initially expected:

> The meaning for me was not about me showing how mature and advanced I am as a practitioner. It was actually the opposite. For me, the meaning was about realizing that I am a very, very small part in a much larger tradition, and that at all times I depend on dozens of other people to help, teach, support, and encourage me. (30)

A conception of no-self explains Greenwood's emphasis on the discipline and denial – not only of bodily desires but also of intellectual understanding – that were crucial in her Zen monastic training.

Yet although she learns to postpone getting an answer, her questions do not go away. Her memoir presses for clear understanding, expresses her doubts, and interrogates the meaning of moral integrity. Like O'Halloran, she subjects Buddhist ideas, including no-self, to critical examination and explores tensions between no-self and other ideas and ideals. For instance, she argues that the Japanese emphasis on observing the correct form of behavior entails several dangers, such as producing "mean and ill-spirited practitioners. There is little space for confusion or doubt. Form is privileged over emotional or psychological processing" (39).

Western Buddhist travel narratives by women tend to be more aware of the dangers of no-self than are those by male writers. Perhaps having struggled in a patriarchal society to find and express an identity, women authors are more skeptical about the ideal of giving up self. Gender differences play a significant role in their narratives about the Zen monastic system. Greenwood realizes that dharma transmission in Japan is usually "patrilineal, from father to son, in order to secure temple inheritance" (26). This political and bureaucratic aspect of lineage is forceful, whether or not a dharma heir has had spiritual experiences or is fully enlightened. Just as O'Halloran's breakthrough came about when she resisted a Roshi's pressure to marry and inherit his temple, Greenwood, too, must establish boundaries with a teacher rather than submit to his wishes. Compared to most male authors, these women carefully distinguish selflessness from self-effacement or betrayal of their core values. Without going into detail about a painful incident, Greenwood says that she fell in love with Seido Roshi and that he "loved me back … He was incapable of escaping from his conditioning, the way he could hurt me without realizing. He stopped being able to view me objectively—that is the saddest part" (41–42). The

In a Zen Monastery 95

ideal of selflessness makes it difficult to negotiate proper boundaries in relationship to her teacher and mentor:

> The relief that Buddhist practice brings, after all, is loosening our grasp on the small self; we find that we can separate from our personal views, and this brings tremendous peace of mind. So in the beginning of practice, thrilled by the potential of separating from our ego, many of us are willing to give up large chunks of our personality or identity. And yet, the more we progress down this path, the better we get at understanding when the sacrifices being asked of us are too much, when endurance is hurting rather than helping. We become more skilled at understanding what our best self needs. (42–43)

Greenwood sets the ideal of loosening the hold of "small self" alongside the goal of strengthening her "best self."

This incident is recounted in a chapter entitled "Buddha Never Told Me to Be Stupid," which articulates a nuanced response to the Zen emphasis on "not thinking." There can be great value in practicing without full comprehension of what one is doing, so that growing understanding arises from engagement. Yet doing one's best to learn through practice is not the same as being stupid. Questions and doubts need to be addressed sooner or later; scruples of conscience and one's need for understanding can be postponed but not denied. In various contexts, Greenwood affirms both the value of Buddhist traditions and practices that "show me that I am not the Center of the Universe" (46) and the necessity of a strong sense of self based on knowledge of personal boundaries and values. Certain interpretations of no-self, including the attempt to make the experience of unselfing a permanent condition, are not conducive to a right understanding of self: "It's important to establish these boundaries, and I think I caused myself a lot of pain and suffering because I used to think that the solution to my problems was to get out of my intellect and to be in some nondualistic state of being all the time" (46). Greenwood balances appreciation of Buddhism's challenge to the self with what she has learned about healthy selfhood from feminism, psychology, and relationships with family and friends. Her commitment to Buddhism does not mean renunciation of everything about the self but self-transformation through insight and right understanding.

One of Greenwood's central concerns is understanding the rightful place of rules and precepts in Zen practice. She engages in blatant violations of some of her vows, especially by having a sexual affair. She sometimes describes breaking a precept as an opportunity to define for herself the standards of ethical behavior. American readers applaud this freedom: "When I write about how traditional Buddhism is crap and we can make everything up as we go along, people love it. Because ... it's *America!* And we had the *fucking tea party!* We dumped that tea in the fucking *BAY!* So take THAT Buddhism and your *RULES! I DUMP YOU IN THE BAY!*" (118–119). Americans don't want to read about celibacy and renunciation, much less practice monastic life. Greenwood criticizes this antinomian celebration of personal liberty. So, her attitude to rules is complex and conflicted. She is an American individualist who wants everything on her own terms, right away. Yet Buddhism helps her see the limitations of this perspective: "I am skeptical of a view of Buddhism that places the individual self at the center and allows the individual self to act as the ruler by which everything else is measured" (119). Buddhism provides a form, a container, and a structure that help her to see things from a perspective older, wider, and wiser than her current opinions.

As the book concludes, Greenwood has returned to the United States after six years in Japan. Like several other authors who write about the impact of travels when they were relatively young (such as Maura O'Halloran, Jim Reynolds, and Jamie Zeppa), and because of the long period she spent in Japan and the demanding Zen training, Greenwood's life was significantly transformed by her encounters with Buddhism in Asia. More changes seem imminent as she experiments with new forms of North American Buddhism. Her need to ask questions is juxtaposed with learning to live with unanswered questions. When the abbess at Green Gulch Farm suggests that she start her own temple, Greenwood responds that she thinks she is too young. The abbess tells her that she must do things in her own way. To Greenwood's response that she has always been told to follow tradition, the abbess says: "To be a true bodhisattva in the world, we have to do things in our own way" (213). She will follow a venerable tradition of breaking with tradition as she models her life on the bodhisattva who breaks the mold.

In the book's final scene, Greenwood goes out to dinner with her future husband, her head shaved and wearing a green satin dress and high heels; she feels "very much in love and how a normal twenty-nine-year-old woman is supposed to feel, sitting across from a man who loves her, looking forward to a blossoming professional career—confident and happy" (213). The next morning, during zazen, she is struck by the question that drove Dogen: "What about the great matter of life and death?" (214). Then she realizes that another question (or two) lies beneath all her other ones: "How can I be happy? What does it mean to live a good life?" (214). Although she does not know the answer to these questions, she feels gratitude for them, for they motivated her travels in India and Japan and her commitment to Zen training. The same questions will determine her own future and the new forms of American Zen that she will help create. "We can make our questions into strength," she concludes: "I've kept my question close to me, letting it drive me forward" (214).

This ending conveys a delicate balancing of self and no-self in Greenwood's version of American Zen. Monastic training taught her to discipline the imperious demands of "small self," as expressed among other ways in the demand to have her questions answered immediately. She learned to bow first. Yet "bow first, ask questions later" does not mean "don't ask questions." Rather, ask them when the time is right. In her reflective memoir about her spiritual journey, the intellect's doubts, distinctions, and demands for clarity take a prominent role, as does her need to address questions of conscience related to personal integrity and proper Buddhist moral conduct. Greenwood found a creative way to reconcile the seemingly incompatible needs to renounce the self and to discover and affirm a transformed self, one that knows its own nature. The title's central metaphors of bowing and questioning placed in tandem convey the need to renounce self and to assert oneself, and the narrative as a whole depicts how tensions and interactions between these impulses shaped Greenwood's experience.

*

These four narratives set in a Japanese monastery, like Peter Matthiessen's two travelogues, juxtapose the authors' professed failure to achieve enlightenment with hints of a significant transformation. Although we see the motif of failure in other Western Buddhist travel narratives, it is especially prominent in memoirs about Zen, probably because of the Soto Zen emphasis on the dangers of active seeking for enlightenment or even having a fixed idea of what it is. They all depict a Western person with a strong commitment to individuality struggling in a social system that is set up to dissolve egoism or, as Chadwick's fellow monk puts it, to "torque-the-individual."

Unselfing takes various forms in these books. The authors depict moments when they are not aware of body or mind. They describe times when consciousness expands and seems to encompass dimensions of reality beyond the ordinary self's usual awareness so that one feels part of a greater whole, either a human community or the natural world. The authors may become fully absorbed in rituals, chores, or meditation. O'Halloran depicts a climactic moment when another part of her being empowered her to say "no" to her mentor's pressure to marry at a time when her ordinary self could not do this. These books also portray selfing, the inevitable return to a personal identity with its conditioned limitations. Extended autobiographical accounts are thus very different as forms of literature and sources of religious insight in comparison to traditional Buddhist writings such as koans, brief reports of enlightenment, legends about great masters, and short accounts focused on meditation such as those Philip Kapleau compiled in *The Three Pillars of Zen*. They contrast, as well, with modern theories and interpretations of enlightenment, especially the influential works of D. T. Suzuki, which were many Westerners' first encounter with Zen.[14]

The autobiographical portraits in these Western Buddhist travel narratives question or criticize the ideal of no-self that many practitioners strive for. They are often skeptical about whether no-self can be realized or even understood. The narrators of these monastic memoirs describe how they failed to become enlightened; they also raise doubts that this ideal can ever be fully realized. Nonetheless, incidents of unselfing experienced in a Zen monastery were crucial catalysts for personal transformation, providing a glimpse of what is possible and motivating continued practice. Each author's confession of failure to attain no-self reflects an abandonment of self-centered striving, or at least a significant change in their Buddhist orientation and practice. If the hints of transformation suggested are signs of what was to come, each writer's Zen practice would henceforth not focus on attaining a goal defined as a matter of personal achievement. Although van de Wetering, O'Halloran, Chadwick, and Greenwood assert that they failed to achieve enlightenment, they were each significantly transformed by their experiences in a Japanese monastery. For each of them, departure from the monastery means that selfless practice may take place anywhere and everywhere, expressed both in Japanese cultural forms and in other ways yet to be discovered.

---

[14] See Ben Van Overmeier, "Portraying Zen Buddhism in the Twentieth Century: Encounter Dialogues as Frame-Stories in Daisetz Suzuki's *Introduction to Zen Buddhism* and Janwillem Van de Wetering's *The Empty Mirror*," *Japan Studies Review* (2017) 21: 3–24. There are six essays by Suzuki in another early and influential work on Zen: Nancy Wilson Ross (ed.), *The World of Zen: An East-West Anthology* (New York: Vintage Books, 1960).

CHAPTER 4

Thomas Merton and Christian and Jewish Pilgrims in Buddhist Asia

During the last two months of his life, in the autumn of 1968, Thomas Merton undertook a journey to India, Nepal, Sri Lanka, and Thailand. *The Asian Journal of Thomas Merton*, a posthumously edited version of his travel journal, contains descriptions of daily sightseeing and meetings, reflections on religious matters, and quotes from readings, dreams, and poems. With its hurried jottings, sometimes cryptic allusions, and occasional tedious sections, it is unlikely that Merton would have published this writing. Yet the journal offers a fascinating if fragmentary account of an experience of pilgrimage to Buddhist cultures by one of the most profound and influential religious thinkers of the twentieth century. It shows the transformative effect of his encounters with Buddhism as Merton sought to integrate the insights he garnered in Asia with his Christian faith. Many of the crucial events and unresolved questions presented in the *Asian Journal* concern Merton's depiction of experiences that I will interpret as versions of unselfing.

In an address he delivered in Calcutta in October 1968, Merton called his journey a pilgrimage: "I come as a pilgrim who is anxious to obtain not just information, not just 'facts' about other monastic traditions, but to drink from ancient sources of monastic vision and experience. I seek not only to learn more (quantitatively) about religion and about monastic life, but to become a better and more enlightened monk (qualitatively) myself" (313).[1] His pilgrimage was not to the geographical source of his own religious tradition; rather, it meant learning from another tradition in order to become more committed to his own. He wanted to drink deeply from another spiritual well, to assimilate its insights into his worldview and faith. The transformation Merton imagined for himself was not

---

[1] Numbers in parentheses refer to Thomas Merton, *The Asian Journal of Thomas Merton* (New York: New Directions, 1973).

99

conversion to another tradition but more meaningful commitment to his own:

> I think we have reached a stage of (long-overdue) religious maturity at which it may be possible for someone to remain perfectly faithful to a Christian and Western monastic commitment, and yet to learn in depth from, say, a Buddhist or Hindu discipline and experience. I believe that some of us need to do this in order to improve the quality of our own monastic life and even to help in the task of monastic renewal which has been undertaken within the Western Church. (313)

Merton's understanding of pilgrimage is unusual and creative in three ways. The destination is not a place but other people; pilgrimage can deepen one's faith through encounter with another tradition rather than the historical roots of one's own tradition; and the journey is not institutionalized but a matter of individual choice and creativity. Merton's desire to learn all he could about the religions of Asia expressed his hopes to broaden his capacity for religious experience and approach God in new ways.

Interest in Asia was not a passing fancy for Merton; he had long been a student of Asian religions. He was especially drawn to Chinese religious traditions and Zen Buddhism. He edited a collection of Chinese stories and teachings, *The Way of Chuang Tzu*, and gathered many essays on Zen in *Zen and the Birds of Appetite* and *Mystics and Zen Masters*. In one essay, Merton describes the purpose of pilgrimage as a physical movement to a place that expresses an "inner journey" of self-discovery and religious intensification: "The geographical pilgrimage is the symbolic acting out of an inner journey. The inner journey is the interpolation of the meaning and signs of the outer pilgrimage. One can have one without the other. It is best to have both."[2] He used the same terms to describe his Asian travels.

Merton's understanding of Buddhism was decisively shaped by D. T. Suzuki, whom he had met and frequently refers to in several of his books. He published a lengthy dialogue with Suzuki on "Wisdom in Emptiness," which compares the insights of the Desert Fathers and Zen masters.[3] Merton saw commonality between the Zen experience of awakening and the purity of heart sought by early Christian hermits and monks.

---

[2] Thomas Merton (ed.), "From Pilgrimage to Crusade," in *Mystics and Zen Masters* (New York: Farrar, Straus, and Giroux, 1967), 92. Compare this to Merton's letter to friends just before he departed for Asia in *Asian Journal*, 296: "Our real journey is life is interior: it is a matter of growth, deepening, and of an ever greater surrender to the creative action of love and grace in our hearts."

[3] Thomas Merton, *Zen and the Birds of Appetite* (New York: New Directions, 1968), 99–138.

He understood the similar dimension of contemplative experience in each religious tradition as a wordless loss of subject-object consciousness. In his essay "Transcendent Experience," he refers to "an experience of metaphysical or mystical self-transcending and also at the same time an experience of the 'Transcendent' or the 'Absolute' or 'God' not so much as object but Subject."[4] Merton's understanding of Buddhism, heavily influenced by Suzuki, strips away all doctrinal, historical, and institutional context, leaving only a momentary experience of detachment from ordinary self-consciousness.[5]

There are contrasts and contradictions in the diverse ways in which Merton characterizes self-transcendence. For instance, he sometimes emphasizes negation of the self and sometimes stresses its fulfillment in something like a true self. At certain points, he stresses similarities between Christian and Buddhist experiences of self-transcendence; in other passages, he contrasts them.[6] What is significant for this study is Merton's intense focus on the experience of overcoming the ordinary self, his version of unselfing, which he describes in various ways in his essays and the *Asian Journal* and is always the *sine qua non* of authentic religious experience.

One way in which Merton's prior thinking and writing about Buddhism framed his travel experience is his critique of the way a person may try to turn the self-emptying dimension of "transcendent experience" into "the crowning glory of egohood and self-fulfillment" and to "chalk up another experience on the scorecard."[7] This perspective is expressed in the title of *Zen and the Birds of Appetite* in the metaphor of a "buzzard hovering around a corpse" that characterizes those who approach Zen

---

[4] Ibid., 71.

[5] For an analysis of how Suzuki's version of Zen relies on terms alien to that tradition, especially a transcendental ideal of experience, see Robert H. Sharf, "Buddhist Modernism and the Rhetoric of Meditative Experience," *Numen* 42 (1995), 228–283 and John P. Keenan, "Thomas Merton's Unfinished Journey in Dialogue with Buddhism," *Buddhist-Christian Studies* 37 (2017), 103–128.

[6] This passage in Merton, *Zen and the Birds of Appetite*, pp. 71–72, stresses the commonality between Christian and Buddhist "transcendent experience": "These metaphorical expressions all point to the problem we have in mind: the problem of a self that is 'no-self,' that is by no means an 'alienated self' but on the contrary a transcendent Self which, to clarify it in Christian terms, is metaphysically distinct from the Self of God and yet perfectly identified with that Self by love and freedom, so that there appears to be but one Self. Experience of this is what we here call 'transcendent experience.'" A second passage, pp. 117–118, contrasts the distinctive forms of transcendent experience in the two religions: "The great difference between Christianity and Buddhism arises at this juncture. From the metaphysical point of view, Buddhism seems to take 'emptiness' as a complete negation of all personality, whereas Christianity finds in purity of heart and 'unity of spirit,' a supreme and transcendent fulfillment of personality."

[7] Merton, *Zen and the Birds of Appetite*, 73.

hoping to gain something from it. Zen does not enrich the voracious self. Only when the ravenous birds go elsewhere does the "'nothing,' the 'no-body' that was there, suddenly appear. That is Zen. It was there all the time but the scavengers missed it, because it was not their kind of prey."[8] Well before his journey to Asia, Merton was thinking about how to displace his desire to profit from his encounters with Buddhism. To Suzuki's emphasis on the emptiness of the Zen experience, Merton adds a scrupulous examination of motivation and an ascetic renunciation of any benefit, concerns that he sometimes expresses with a harshly judgmental rigor that recalls the tone of his rejection of the world in *The Seven Storey Mountain*.

Merton's *Asian Journal* records day-to-day experiences while traveling, in contrast to the unified retrospective perspective of an autobiography or memoir. A travel journal captures a journey's uncertainties, searching, and contrasting impressions, and it is written before the author knows how the journey ended or what turned out to be most significant in the long run. Unlike other journals discussed here, such as Matthiessen's *The Snow Leopard*, Merton did not edit and revise his work, and the several editors of the journal affirm that, with minor exceptions, "no substantive changes were made in the text" (xiv). Merton's contrasting opinions and shifting perspectives, his unanswered questions and unresolved dialogues with himself, and his vital and complex personality make it impossible to draw firm conclusions about how he would have been changed in the long run by his Asian pilgrimage. Nonetheless, we can discern in the *Asian Journal* how encountering Buddhism "on the ground" affected him and precipitated transformation.

Merton sought to understand both commonalities and differences between Christianity and Buddhism. For instance, he likened the Zen experience of emptiness to the Christian apophatic tradition of negative theology. In three interviews with the Dalai Lama, he compared the vows and practices of Tibetan and Benedictine monasticism. Merton thought that the Tibetan ideal of the "child mind" to be recovered after experience was analogous to an insight of early Christian monks: "So too, a Desert Father came to freedom by weaving baskets and then, at the end of each year, burning all the baskets he had woven" (84). He quotes a book discussing whether there is "grace in Buddhism" (114) and searches for other analogies with Christianity. At the same time, Merton was keenly aware of the dangers of facile comparison or reducing all religious traditions to

---

[8] Ibid., ix.

some simplified common denominator. He agreed with his translator in Nepal, a lay Tibetan monk who was "against the mixing of traditions" and argued that "we should not try to set up a pseudocommunity of people from different traditions" (85). Without claiming that all religions are basically the same, Merton searched for fundamental human experiences underlying diverse cultures: "Even where there are irreconcilable differences in doctrine and in formulated belief, there may still be great similarities and analogies in the realm of religious experience ... Cultural and doctrinal differences must remain, but they do not invalidate a very real quality of existential likeness" (312). The overcoming of self was, for him, the crucial common experience that Christianity and Buddhism understood in contrasting ways.

An intriguing theme in Merton's journal is his view of his Asian pilgrimage as both a homecoming and a practice of homelessness. As he flew eastward on the first stage of his journey, Merton wrote, "I am going home, to the home where I have never been in this body" (5). As he traveled through Asia, he was actively considering whether to leave the Trappist monastery of Gethsemane after twenty-seven years and searching for a new place to live. He yearned for a new spiritual home, an actual or symbolic place to which he would feel deeply connected. At the same time, being a pilgrim meant not having a settled home as he wandered through unfamiliar places. A month before he left on his Asian journey, Merton wrote a journal entry that expresses the idea that travel is an exercise in homelessness and a form of symbolic dying:

> A journey is a bad death if you ingeniously grasp or remove all that you were before you started, so that in the end you do not change in the least. The stimulation enables you to grasp more raffishly at the same, familiar, distorted illusions. You come home only confirmed in greater greed—with new skills (real or imaginary) for satisfying it.
> I am not "going home." The purpose of this death is to become truly homeless.[9]

Homelessness means dispossession, letting go of one's notion of stable identity, and loss of self, all of which Merton contrasts to the illusory permanence of home. This understanding of the goal of pilgrimage as homelessness implies the need for a form of unselfing. A pilgrim's temporary homelessness can teach important lessons about finitude, impermanence, mutual human dependence, gracious acceptance of hospitality, and

---

[9] Merton, journal entry dated September 13, 1968, in Patrick Hart and Jonathan Montaldo (eds.), *The Intimate Merton: His Life from His Journals* (San Francisco: Harper, 1999), 337.

nonpossessiveness. Yet Merton's ideal pilgrim is also impelled by longing for a perfect place where he will finally rest in peace. He shares Augustine's understanding of pilgrimage as a metaphor for the restless heart, wandering unhappily until it finally rests in God.

As Merton traveled through Asia, Buddhist ideas became more and more important in his reflections; he started to write not only about them but as if viewing the world from their perspective. For instance, he describes his "mandala awareness of space," which enabled him to discern the geographical organization of a Tibetan community as a sacred space with the Dalai Lama at the center. He becomes extremely self-critical about how preconceptions shape experience of a foreign culture. At a tea estate in Nepal, he considered his travels up to that point:

> Reassessment of this whole experience in more critical terms. Too much movement. Too much "looking for" something: an answer, a vision, "something other." And this breeds illusion. Illusion that there *is* something else. Differentiation—the old splitting-up process that leads to mindlessness, instead of the mindfulness of seeing all-in-emptiness and not having to break it up against itself. (148)

Merton internalized Buddhist ideas so that he saw his own searching as a form of desire leading to illusion and suffering.

To search assumes that one knows what one is looking for, which may prevent direct perception of what one actually encounters. On several occasions, Merton criticizes his typically Western search for "the real Asia." He is dubious about attempts to distinguish a pure essence of Asia uncontaminated by Western influences and reminds himself to be open to all that he sees:

> I am at a loss to know what one means by "the real Asia." It is *all* real as far as I can see. Though certainly a lot of it has been corrupted by the West. Neither Victorian Darjeeling nor the Kennedy-era Oberoi [hotel] can be called *ideal* Asia. I remember Deki Lhalungpa laughing at the phony American minarets in the Taj dining room at the Oberoi. Still, that is Asia too. (150)

He wonders whether he has experienced Asia or only recognized his erroneous preconceptions about Asia. "Did I find an illusion of Asia, that needed to be dissolved by experience? *Here?*" (150). Merton realized that a Western person's reactions to and judgments about Asia reflect prejudices and political interests. He was struck by a question asked of him by a Tibetan rinpoche: "Have you come to write a strange book about us? What are your motives?" (89). Merton's attempt to criticize how Western preconceptions are connected with power relationships anticipates later critiques of Orientalism.[10]

Merton made an intriguing series of journal entries about the peak called Kanchenjunga in Nepal. He wondered how accurately he perceived this mountain and saw his reactions to it as a struggle with *anicca*, impermanence. He noticed his dismay at landslides, reforestation projects, and other evidence that Kanchenjunga is not as permanent as it appears:

> The place is a frightening example of anicca—impermanence. A good place, therefore, to adjust one's perspectives. I find my mind rebelling against the landslides. I am distracted by reforestation projects and other devices to *deny* them, *forbid* them. I want this all to be *permanent*. A permanent post card for meditation, daydreams. The landslides are ironic and silent comments on the apparent permanence, the "eternal snows" of solid Kanchenjunga. (150)

He praised the mountain's unsurpassable beauty, and then called his focus on Kanchenjunga a delusion: "When you begin each day by describing the look of the same mountain, you are living in the grip of delusion" (161). He took dozens of pictures of the mountain. In a dream he heard a voice tell him: "There is another side to the mountain" (152). He mused about the limits of photography and suggested that it can never capture what is most important: "There is another side of Kanchenjunga and of every mountain—the side that has never been photographed and turned into post cards. That is the only side worth seeing" (153). As he reflected on Kanchenjunga, vision, perception, and photography, Merton pondered the relationship between the mind and "the real Asia" – and, I think, ultimate reality. We never fully grasp the nature of reality because we see it from just one perspective and because of our illusions, those mental "postcards" that tell us how a view ought to look. Yet discipline and self-awareness can help us recognize at least some of our illusions. "The best photography is aware, mindful, of illusion and uses illusion, permitting and encouraging it—especially unconscious and powerful illusions that are not normally admitted on the scene" (153). There is a profoundly Buddhist character to these reflections on the possibility of becoming mindful of illusions through discipline and insight.

---

[10] See John D. Barbour, "Thomas Merton's Pilgrimage and Orientalism," in *Literature, Religion, and East/West Comparison: Essays in Honor of Anthony C. Yu*, ed. Eric Ziolkowski (Newark: University of Delaware Press, 2005), 243–59. See also Judith Simmer-Brown, "Ambivalence in Shangri-La: Merton's Orientalism and Dialogue," *Buddhist-Christian Studies* 37 (2017), 93–101.

Christian and Jewish Pilgrims in Buddhist Asia

In a direct and fervent address to the mountain, which he calls the "Testament of Kanchenjunga," Merton rhapsodically praised it as a revelation of the paradoxical nature of ultimate reality, a vision that unites apparent opposites:

> O Tantric Mother Mountain! Yin-yang palace of opposites in unity! Palace of anicca, impermanence and patience, solidity and nonbeing, existence and wisdom. A great *consent* to be and not-be, a compact to delude no one who does not first want to be deluded. The full beauty of the mountain is not seen until you too consent to the impossible paradox: it is and is not. When nothing more needs to be said, the smoke of ideas clears, the mountain is SEEN. (156–157)

Aware that his perceptions of Asia and Buddhism were influenced by prior knowledge and expectations, Merton tried to be open to people and events that would challenge his preconceptions and blow away "the smoke of ideas." For a week, he interspersed ecstatic praise of majestic Kanchenjunga with internal debates about whether he was finding "the real Asia" or "an illusion of Asia, that needed to be dissolved by experience" (150).

Merton thought he found an answer to that question in a powerful experience of Buddhist art. The climax of his Asian journey was a visit to the huge Buddhist figures at Polonnaruwa in Sri Lanka. The profundity of this experience for him was such that he did not write about the event for several days and commented that he may have spoiled it by trying to explain it at a dinner party. He had approached the statues alone, while the vicar general of the local Catholic diocese remained behind, averse to "paganism." Merton describes an overwhelming moment of insight and illumination:

> Looking at these figures I was suddenly, almost forcibly, jerked clean out of the habitual, half-tied vision of things, and an inner clearness, clarity, as if exploding from the rocks themselves, became evident and obvious. The queer *evidence* of the reclining figure, the smile, the sad face of Ananda standing with arms folded (much more "imperative" than Da Vinci's Mona Lisa because completely simple and straightforward). The thing about all this is that there is no puzzle, no problem, and really no "mystery." All problems are resolved and everything is clear. The rock, all matter, all life, is charged with dharmakaya … Everything is emptiness and everything is compassion. I don't know when in my life I have ever had such a sense of beauty and spiritual validity running together in one aesthetic illumination. Surely, with Mahabalipuram and Polonnaruwa my Asian pilgrimage has come clear and purified itself. I mean, I know and have seen what I was obscurely looking for. I don't know what else remains but I have now seen and have pierced through the surface and have got beyond the shadow and

the disguise. This is Asia in its purity, not covered over with garbage, Asian or European or American, and it is clear, pure, complete. It says everything; it needs nothing. And because it needs nothing it can afford to be silent, unnoticed, undiscovered. It does not need to be discovered. It is we, Asians included, who need to discover it. (233–236)

This passage describes a moment of intense aesthetic experience closely related to religious insight. The sculptural qualities of the figures, with their massive size and delicate lines, give Merton a sense of beauty and spiritual truth conjoined in an aesthetic epiphany. The statue's enigmatic smile does not hide a mystery but clearly reveals "what matters." Merton compares his experience of the statues to "a Zen garden, a span of bareness and openness and evidence, and the great figures, motionless, yet with the lines in full movement, waves of vesture and bodily form, a beautiful and holy vision" (236). The statues combine massive solidity with a sense of flowing motion, suggesting the paradox of form and emptiness in endless succession. His encounter with these Buddhist statues shows Merton's responsiveness to art and his appreciation of the ways in which another culture communicated its apprehension of ultimate reality in a nonverbal medium.

Merton appreciated and internalized Buddhist ideas as he described the way the statues incarnate the view that "everything is emptiness and everything is compassion" (235). When Merton says that "all matter, all life, is charged with *dharmakaya*," he refers to the Sanskrit term for "the cosmical body of the Buddha, the essence of all beings."[11] The faces of the statues are "filled with every possibility, questioning nothing, knowing everything, rejecting nothing, the peace not of emotional resignation but of Madhyamika [the 'middle path' school of Buddhism, founded by Nagarjuna], of sunyata [emptiness], that has seen through every question without trying to discredit anyone or anything—*without refutation*—without establishing some other argument" (233). Merton does not simply describe how this art embodies a religious vision; he views the world in these terms. He not only appreciates a Buddhist perspective on the world but shares that perspective. He has made it his own, and by so doing fulfilled his hopes for his journey; he has drunk deeply from a different spiritual well, seen life from the perspective of another culture, and not simply learned interesting facts but been transformed in the way he sees. This came about in a moment of unselfing when, forgetting himself, he was totally absorbed in aesthetic contemplation.

---

[11] See the glossary in Merton, *Asian Journal*, 372, quoting Tirupattur Ramaseshayyer Venkatachala Murti, *The Central Philosophy of Buddhism*, second edition (London: Allen and Unwin, 1960).

108   Christian and Jewish Pilgrims in Buddhist Asia

Exactly what Merton thought he saw at Polonnaruwa remains enigmatic and somewhat confusing for several reasons. The climactic passage about viewing the statues says that he was only "obscurely looking for" what he found, implying that he could not have formulated his discovery before he found it. He realized that he needed to learn more about Buddhism before he would have the conceptual framework to understand his encounter with the statues. The experience confirmed many of his earlier reflections about the limitations of language to render the most important truths and the need to go beyond words: "the deepest level of communication is not communication, but communion" (308). The passage is puzzling in that its assertion that he found "Asia in its purity" contradicts his recognition two weeks earlier that "it is all real," not just the parts uncontaminated by Western influences, modernization, or "garbage." Equally surprising, given his view that pilgrimage is primarily not to a place but to dialogue with people, is that this moment of epiphany involves solitary communion with statues. Finally, Merton's statement that the meaning of his Asian pilgrimage was now clear to him stands in tension with a journal entry made two days later (December 6) that indicates his willingness to let the meaning of the journey continue to unfold. He looked forward to going to Indonesia, where "a whole new journey" would begin. "And I am still not sure where it will take me or what I can or should plan on. Certainly I am sick of hotels and planes. But the journey is only begun" (238). Merton held in creative tension two equally important aspects of pilgrimage: journeying in pursuit of a definite goal and openness to discoveries that lead to reorientation and redefinition of what goals, values, or visions should henceforth be sought. As he pondered his Asian travels, he knew that he was changing, but he didn't know how. He was reluctant to articulate the meaning of his travels, even in a private journal, as if conceptualization might preclude further discoveries.

Merton's Polonnaruwa experience involved an understanding of *sunyata*, the Mahayana concept of emptiness. This concept, which developed out of the idea of *anatman*, extends beyond persons to all phenomena the idea that every entity is relative and conditioned rather than having an abiding essence. The *Asian Journal* contains fifteen references to this concept (see the book's index). Merton holds that emptiness is not "another truth," or a dogma to be believed, and quotes an ancient Buddhist source: "Sunyata is the antidote for all dogmatic views, but him I call the incurable who takes sunyata itself as a theory" (118). Merton reports the Dalai Lama's assertion that "the greatest error is to become attached to sunyata as if it were an object, an 'absolute truth'" (125). Although the concept of sunyata is often treated as a doctrine, underlying this move to philosophical discourse is an insight into the nature of reality as a continual emptying out and transformation of all things into something new. In his epiphany at Polonnaruwa, the experience of the statues was the gateway for Merton's conceptual understanding that "everything is emptiness and everything is compassion" (235).

This understanding of emptiness influenced Merton's striking openness to Buddhism at the end of his journey and his new perspective on his commitment to the Christian faith. Appreciation of the Buddhist view of emptiness opened Merton to the possibility of transformation on the institutional as well as the personal level. He asserted the need to transcend one's religious tradition by enriching it with new insights. A monk "must be wide open to life and to new experience because he has fully utilized his own tradition and gone beyond it. This will permit him to meet a discipline [*sic*] of another, apparently remote and alien tradition, and find a common ground of verbal understanding with him" (315).[12]

In "Marxism and Monastic Perspectives," a talk delivered to a group of Buddhist and Christian monks in Bangkok on the day he died, Merton said that the purpose of monastic life in both Asia and Western Christianity is "commitment to total inner transformation" (337) and that monks must henceforth "travel light," not relying on institutional structures. Merton quoted with approval Chogyam Trungpa Rinpoche, a Tibetan lama whom he met by chance early in his journey and with whom he formed a strong bond. Merton described how, when Trungpa was deciding whether to leave his homeland, he was told by an abbot: "From now on, Brother, everybody stands on his own feet" (338). According to Merton, this statement captures "what Buddhism is about, what Christianity is about, what monasticism is about—if you understand it in terms of grace ... we can no longer rely on being supported by structures that may be destroyed at any moment by a political power or a political force. You cannot rely on structures" (338). Merton describes how Trungpa Rinpoche fled Tibet with a train of twenty-five yaks. In order to escape the Chinese Communists, he had to leave the yaks behind and travel light. Merton comments: "I think there is a lesson in there somewhere, too. We can ask ourselves if we are planning for the next twenty years to be traveling with a train of yaks. It probably is not going to work" (339). Trungpa Rinpoche learned

---

[12] On Merton's enrichment of Christian contemplation through learning from Asian sources, see Francis X. Clooney, S. J., "Thomas Merton's Deep Christian Learning across Religious Borders," *Buddhist-Christian Studies* 37 (2017), 49–64 and Thomas Forsthoefel, "Merton and the Axes of Dialogue," *Buddhist-Christian Studies* 37 (2017), 65–72.

English, got a degree from Oxford, and established a Tibetan monastery in Scotland that Merton intended to visit.[13] Merton takes Trungpa's history of geographical mobility and intercultural fluency as evidence that what is most essential in monastic life is "this business of total inner transformation" (340). He sees a commitment to freedom and self-transcendence as shared by Buddhism and "the Christian monastic view of reality."

Merton's assertion of the need to "travel light" with regard to institutional forms reflects his understanding of emptiness as a characteristic not only of selves but also of all reality. Just as a person must not cling tightly to any particular conception of self, so a religious tradition must be willing to find new forms of expression and be open to transformation. Like Trungpa, Merton was suspicious of institutional forms of religion and made iconoclastic remarks intended to provoke fellow believers who clung to particular ways of expressing spiritual truth. To be sure, Merton was also appreciative of traditional forms. At the end of his Asian journey, his emphasis was clearly on being willing to change, on both personal and institutional levels.

The two men were alike in their constant awareness of what Trungpa would later term "spiritual materialism," that is, the ways that ego manifests itself in religious forms, ambitions, and achievements.[14] This critique of self-seeking is similar to Merton's warning about the "birds of appetite" looking for carrion in Zen. Religious aspiration is, in part, longing to be a different self, with qualities such as wisdom, compassion, ecstasy, certainty, peace, and release from fear and anxiety. This striving sometimes becomes completely focused on the self, hence the need for an alert conscience and a sense of humor about the ways in which religious practice may express in disguised ways a person's needs to build up, protect, and flatter the ego. Trungpa's typical response to this danger was deliberate transgression of his followers' expectations of an enlightened master. For Merton, the best antidote was an introspective conscience that punctured inflated views of one's spiritual condition. His scrupulous conscience is

---

[13] Chogyam Trungpa went on to become an influential and controversial Buddhist teacher in the United States, introducing Vajrayana practices to the West, writing many books, and founding Shambhala Buddhism and the Naropa Institute. On Merton's relationship to Trungpa, see Jack Downey, "'We Drank Many Gin and Tonics': Desire and Enchantment in Merton's Buddhist Pilgrimage," *Buddhist-Christian Studies* 37 (2017), 73–92; and Simmer-Brown, "Ambivalence in Shangri-La."

[14] Chogyam Trungpa, *Cutting through Spiritual Materialism* (Boston: Shambhala Publications, 1973), 17: "It is important to see that the main point of any spiritual practice is to step out of the bureaucracy of ego. This means stepping out of ego's constant desire for a higher, more spiritual, more transcendental version of knowledge, religion, virtue, judgment, comfort or whatever it is that the particular ego is seeking."

a different kind of "bird of prey," hovering like a hawk, ready to swoop down on the slightest movement of ego.

While devoted to Christian faith and monastic life, Merton stressed the need for individual freedom and transcendence of the institutions and structures of organized religion. He spoke of a spiritual liberty valued by both Asian and Christian traditions that lies deeper than or beyond cultural differences: "The combination of the natural techniques and the graces and the other things that have been manifested in Asia and the Christian liberty of the gospel should bring us all at last to that full and transcendent liberty which is beyond mere cultural differences and mere externals—and mere this or that" (343). The *Asian Journal* shows Merton trying to reconcile the deep human needs for cultural identity and communal commitment with the equally significant human capacities for growth, freedom, and self-transcendence. His encounter with Buddhism helped him to appreciate the value of its distinctive forms of religious thought and practice as well as the importance of transformation, which depends on not clinging to any particular form as if it were the only way that human beings can encounter the holy. Merton's final address presents Trungpa as a good example of the freedom to "travel light" in relation to the baggage of one's religious tradition, linking travel and transformation.

Because of Merton's untimely death (by electrocution from the faulty wiring of a fan, in Bangkok, on December 10, 1968), we do not know how he would have understood his homecoming or integrated his pilgrimage with the rest of his life, including his Christian and monastic commitments. In the terms of the theory of pilgrimage proposed by Victor and Edith Turner, he remained in the liminal stage of freedom from established social structures and never went through homecoming and rejoining his original community.[15] His *Asian Journal* reveals that Merton believed that he was undergoing a profound experience of transformation that was not yet complete. This conviction was based on his encounters with several Buddhist teachers, the holy mountain Kanchenjunga, and the statues at Polonnaruwa, all experiences that helped Merton grasp the understandings of reality conceptualized as *anicca* and *anatman*, impermanence and no-self. The *Asian Journal* records several moments of unselfing when Merton recognized his desire to enrich himself or profit from his journey and tried to disable that self-interested motivation. He learned to respect and appreciate Buddhists and their culture, listening to and communing with them

---

[15] Victor Turner and Edith Turner, *Image and Pilgrimage in Christian Culture: Anthropological Perspectives* (New York: Columbia University Press, 1978).

and finding that he had begun to see the world, himself, and God in a different way.

*

Like Merton, other Christians have discussed whether and how the concept of no-self is compatible with Christian faith and values. Usually, such reflections are made at a theoretical level without describing the author's life. William Johnston's *Mystical Journey: An Autobiography* is a rare example of Christian writing about personal experiences that the author sees as resembling or the same as what Buddhists mean by no-self.[16] Not a traditional travel narrative but an autobiography, this book is germane to our study because Johnston uses the journey metaphor to describe his lifelong religious development and because he was decisively influenced by extended study of and encounter with Zen Buddhism during many years of living in Japan. *Mystical Journey* presents the emptying out of selfhood as a common emphasis of Buddhist enlightenment and Pauline Christology and interprets several events in Johnston's life in these terms.

Born in Belfast in 1925, Johnston became a Jesuit priest and in 1951 volunteered to go to Japan, where he spent most of his career as a professor at Sophia University in Tokyo. He had a strong interest in Christian mysticism, especially St. John of the Cross and *The Cloud of Unknowing*, and eventually wrote several books about Western and Eastern mysticism. When he arrived in Japan, Johnston discovered forms of contemplation very different from the highly intellectual practices of the Ignatian Spiritual Exercises. Asian religious traditions, especially Zen Buddhism, offered practical knowledge and wisdom about deeper levels of consciousness that can arise in meditation. Johnston began to meditate in the traditional Zen posture, combining concentration on his breath with "prayer before the Blessed Sacrament" (127) and reciting distinctively Christian mantras such as the repetition of "Jesus" or "Come, Holy Spirit" (126). He developed a form of Christian contemplative practice focused on the love of God, drawing on writings by St. Francis of Assisi, St. John of the Cross, Meister Eckhart, and the Canadian theologian Bernard Lonergan, who described the effect of conversion as "my being becoming being-in-love." While Johnston did not become a Buddhist or practice "double belonging" (118), he asserts "there is much to learn from Buddhism, particularly in the area of purification" (136). For many decades, he led contemplative retreats in which people from various traditions, using

---

[16] William Johnston, *Mystical Journey: An Autobiography* (Maryknoll, NY: Orbis Books, 2006).

the mantra of their choice, enter into silent meditation: "I could not teach my students Zen but I could teach a Zen-influenced meditation that they could practice as Christians, Buddhists, or agnostics" (151). Like Thomas Merton, he sought to enrich his own tradition by learning from Asian religions, practicing and teaching "Christian contemplation in dialogue with Zen and other Asian forms of prayer" (189).

Johnston describes several experiences when he felt he could let go of attachments to a person, long-standing ideas, concern about how other people saw him, and the passport and visa that were stolen with his briefcase in India: "I had to lose everything; I had to be attached to nothing" (175). These incidents involving moments of dispossession, uncertainty, and loss of identity resemble what he sees as the heart of mystical experience. He describes the theft as "a real experience of emptiness and nothingness—*mu* and *ku*" (174–175), using the Japanese terms. Like Merton, he sees Christian theology's apophatic traditions, which insist on God's unknowability, as akin to the Zen rhetoric of enlightenment. The Pauline idea of *kenosis*, God's self-emptying by taking human form in Christ, resembles the emptiness discerned in an experience of awakening. Johnston follows Masao Abe's interpretation of the crucial passage in Philippians in which Paul tells Christians to model their lives on Christ's self-emptying:

> Masao Abe says that this text is a beautiful expression of the Zen experience wherein one recites "*mu*" ("nothing") again and again and again, leaving everything and coming to utter emptiness (*ku* in Japanese or *sunyata* in Sanskrit) and to the immense joy of *satori*. In this way, Abe points to a remarkable similarity between Buddhist and Christian mysticism. (153)

According to Johnston, the common core of mystical experience in every religion is self-emptying, which he links to nonattachment and compassion for all beings.

This emphasis on transcending selfhood by negation, leaving it behind as one becomes aware of a greater truth, stands in tension with other passages in which Johnston describes the emergence of a deeper or true self. Using Carl Jung's psychological theories, Johnston adopts the distinction between the ego shaped by personal experience and an underlying self rooted in deeper levels of consciousness that may emerge in dreams and intuitions and calls into question one's sense of identity. Mystical traditions try to nurture this true self through meditation practices. In Zen, the awakening of the true self in enlightenment is sometimes spoken of as knowing one's "original face" or the face one had before one's parents were born.

Christian and Jewish Pilgrims in Buddhist Asia

Johnston holds together beliefs that most Christians would consider antithetical, contradictory, or at least paradoxical, including the need to transcend self and the ideal of finding a true or deeper self. Another example is his juxtaposition of traditional theological affirmations about God and his view of meditation experience as culminating in awareness of nothingness rather than divine presence. For Johnston, the paradoxes of theory and theology are attempts to express insights arising when meditation leads to a state of consciousness that discerns the coincidence of opposites, or nondualism. Because the human psyche is multilayered, statements that seem illogical to rational consciousness are necessary to make sense of deeper levels of awareness. Zen tradition embraces seemingly contradictory truths:

> It is at the deeper layers that one realizes the saying of the *Heart Sutra* that "form is emptiness and emptiness is form." Or one realizes that every day is a good day and yet every day is not a good day. Or one realizes that yin and yang are one and not one. Nishitani quotes a Zen master who said, "Separated from one another by a hundred million *kalpas* [eons], yet not apart for a single moment; sitting face-to-face all day long, yet not opposed for an instant." I began to see that the aim of koan practice is to bring one to the deep level of awareness where we will see that things are one and not one. (154)

Although Johnston does not explicitly connect the concept of the coincidence of opposites to the question of the self's reality, I think he would agree with Buddhist philosophers who argue that at different levels self is both real and unreal, a truth and an illusion. The essence of his own development, the mystical journey of his whole life was – at different levels – both an emptying of selfhood (his version of unselfing) and a slow realization of a deeper self that is interconnected with all of reality.

Johnston describes several occasions when he felt he could move "From Ego to Self," as he titles the final chapter of his memoir, adopting Jung's language for the individuation process. Throughout his life, he struggles with his vow of celibacy as he enjoys a close friendship with a Japanese woman. He learns to accept sexual energy, purified of selfish desire, as energizing spiritual life: "The challenge is to love without clinging, to let go of the other, to let her have other friends while I have other friends. For me this has been a lifelong struggle" (172). Jealousy and sexual desire continue to challenge his ideal of self-emptying, and the times when he can overcome them are one form that unselfing takes in his life.

His mystical path took William Johnston far from the pre–Vatican II Irish Catholicism of his early life. It brought about transformation in several ways, above all in his appreciation of Zen wisdom as a matter of practice

Christian and Jewish Pilgrims in Buddhist Asia

and experience rather than doctrine. The effects of unselfing include greater compassion for all, which he affirms as mysticism's crucial gift to the world. In the book's final chapter, Johnston dramatizes the change in himself when, at the age of eighty, he walks the streets of his childhood's Catholic neighborhood in Belfast. Signs saying "BRITS OUT" rekindle his anger and sympathy for those who resort to violence. Yet he realizes how much he has changed, in that he now affirms that the only way to a united Ireland, or to reconciliation anywhere in the world, is through peaceful dialogue: "For the big thing in my life of meditation has been the death of the ego and the birth of the true self. In childhood my ego cried for a united Ireland and I admired the gunmen who sacrificed their lives for this noble cause. Now my ego was dying—or was it being transformed?" (216). In closing, Johnston expresses his hope that the world's conflicts might be healed by shared experiences of the deeper levels of consciousness (the true self) realized by meditation and mystical traditions.

Unselfing, the movement from ego to true self, is the essence of mystical experience in every religion. Johnston learned to appreciate experiences of unselfing through decades of Zen practice that transformed how he understood his own Christian faith. In many ways, his story can be summed up with the title of a book by another Catholic theologian: *Without Buddha I Could Not Be a Christian*.[17] Yet Johnston's use of the journey metaphor emphasizes that the self continues to change and does not arrive at a final, fixed identity or destination, and he expresses his ideas in the form of an autobiography that centers on his life and learning in Japan.

Comparisons between Buddhism and Christianity focus on many topics, including meditation and prayer, ethics and social engagement, monasticism, and philosophical and theological analysis of whether ultimate reality is personal, impersonal, or empty. While these reflections often discuss no-self, extended autobiographical accounts are rare.[18] A personal account of a Buddhist pilgrimage by a Christian is Bardwell Smith's essay entitled "In Contrast to Sentimentality: Buddhist and Christian Sobriety."[19] Smith was Professor of Religion at Carleton College

---

[17] Paul Knitter, *Without Buddha I Could Not Be a Christian* (London: One World, 2009).

[18] An outstanding forum for comparative studies of Buddhism and Christianity is the journal *Buddhist-Christian Studies*. This journal is also receptive to autobiographical reflections, unlike many scholarly journals.

[19] Bardwell Smith, "In Contrast to Sentimentality: Buddhist and Christian Sobriety," in *Christians Talk about Buddhist Meditation; Buddhists Talk about Christian Prayer*, eds. Rita M. Gross and Terry C. Muck (New York: Continuum, 2003), 45–52. This book includes several autobiographical accounts comparing prayer and meditation, although Smith's is the only one that explores pilgrimage.

Christian and Jewish Pilgrims in Buddhist Asia

and a scholar of Buddhism in Sri Lanka and Japan. He participated in the Shikoku pilgrimage seven times and walked part of the Camino de Santiago de Compostela in northern Spain. In the worldviews underlying these two pilgrimages, as well as in the practice of meditation, Smith discerns a sober view of the human condition that is shared by Buddhism and Christianity and contrasts with "sentimental" perspectives. In Buddhism's healthy respect for the "three poisons of anger, greed, and ignorance" (45), Smith sees an analogy to "Augustinian, Kierkegaardian, and Niebuhrian reflections on man's capacity for evil and self-deception" (46). In their acute awareness of "the roots of suffering within each person and as magnified in social institutions and values" (46), both religious traditions discern how illusions about the self fuel misery and brutality. There can be no spiritual growth without sober realism about the sources of these evils in conceptions of the self.

Buddhism and Christianity also hold that there is a doorway out of suffering, and they affirm "the human capacity for transformation" (46). While they express this insight in different ways, both traditions speak of another kind of selfhood that is found in community with other beings:

> Realizing that there is no selfhood except through our relationships constitutes the path to genuine freedom. Having had H. Richard Niebuhr as a teacher over many years, when I first encountered Buddhist visions of the interdependence of all reality, it was not difficult to see them as correlative with biblical metaphors about the kingdom of God. (46–47)

Buddhism and Christianity are at once realistic and hopeful about the human condition. Illusions and desires based on individual selfhood inevitably persist, yet there is always the possibility of another way of being based on "an awakening of the spirit to its inseparability from all other beings" (47).

This way of understanding the human condition becomes transformative when it is expressed in the practices of pilgrimage and meditation, which attempt to realize and sustain awareness of the wholeness and interconnectedness of life. When Smith discusses his participation in the Shikoku pilgrimage, he focuses on the fleeting but significant experience of camaraderie and openness that Victor Turner termed *communitas*:

> Even though the sensation is transitory, it is genuine. In fact, its ephemerality is a powerful commentary about the difficulty of sustaining community in complex, conflicted, and ever-changing circumstances. The pilgrim's experience provides a modest vision, a taste of alternatives to mistrust and bias. Its very uncommonness is the other side of the dual vision mentioned above. Rather than ruing its passing as one returns to one's daily routine,

one is led to wonder more about what constitutes authentic community. However briefly savored, one's hunger for extended forms of justice, peace, and kindness in our communal life and body politic is increased. (48)

Although a pilgrim's sense of connectedness with others fades and the boundaries of individual selfhood are restored, moments of *communitas* leave their mark in further thinking about the nature of community and in searching for renewed occasions of it. This alteration of a person's relationship to other people, which stretches one's sense of kinship, is the form that unselfing takes in Smith's account of pilgrimage.

Finding community with others does not mean loss of individuality or blurring of what is distinctive about specific selves and cultures. When Smith discusses walking on the Shikoku pilgrimage circuit with people who were variously Buddhist, Christian, or with no religious commitment, he found that their unique characteristics were enhanced as the pilgrims found common ground: "The metaphor that came to mind was the familiar one of apprentice monks (*unsui*) in a Zen monastery who serve as diamonds polishing each other's experience in ways that make uniqueness shine more brightly in a communal setting than when alone" (49). In a similar manner, when walking as a Protestant with a pilgrim group on the Santiago path, Smith felt he was an outsider to Roman Catholic tradition and also a participant in a common quest. He compares this aspect of the Camino pilgrimage to Thomas Merton's encounter with Buddhist monks:

> As one participates in the specific forms of another's tradition, it does not take long to become part of some larger human pilgrimage. In this experience there is a process of instantaneous translation from one symbol system to another, which is in no sense a scrambling of metaphors or ritual expressions. It is, instead, similar to what Buddhist monks in Sri Lanka and Thailand felt instinctively when they met Thomas Merton, as he did with them. It was a resonance in the reciprocity of being. It was the quality of respecting each other and being transformed by the meeting. The openness that exists in such meetings is as unforced as the opening of a flower to the warmth of sunlight. (49)

The transformative effect of pilgrimage for Smith was a stretching of the spirit as he engaged in a traditional practice that, while not his own, summoned a "capacity for faith and for seeing the oneness behind the many" (50). Thus Smith finds in the communal dimension of pilgrimage both an overcoming of isolated selfhood and the discovery of another kind of self formed in relationships to others, and that he compares to a unique gem resting with others in a bowl.

118   Christian and Jewish Pilgrims in Buddhist Asia

When Smith describes meditation practice, he similarly stresses the way it changed him by creating a yearning for more, even when the gap between his aspiration to mindfulness and his actual achievement remained substantial:

> Paradoxically, with cumulative practice I felt a deepening of spiritual hunger and that this hunger was healthy and appropriate. It was not a hunger for what I did not have, but a hunger for what I truly am yet have not nearly become ... With a taste for the real, one is no longer willing to settle for what is illusion. (51)

For Smith, the transformative effects of the unselfing experienced in pilgrimage and meditation include a strengthened commitment to seek commonality and community in encounter with others, at the same time that he gained greater appreciation of the distinctive qualities of individual persons and particular cultures.

As the examples of William Johnston and Bardwell Smith show, Thomas Merton continues to inspire many Christians encountering Buddhism because of his emphasis on experience, openness to dialogue, and ability to learn from non-Christian traditions. His *Asian Journal* provides a striking depiction of a transformation in process, an awakening precipitated by a journey with outer and inner dimensions. These three Christian travelers explain how they were profoundly influenced by journeys to Buddhist lands by using metaphors and stories that reckon with problems of selfhood even as they point beyond the self.

*

Rodger Kamenetz's *The Jew in the Lotus: A Poet's Rediscovery of Jewish Identity in Buddhist India* (1994) resembles these three works by Christians in that it tells the story of how the author's understanding of his own religious tradition was transformed by an encounter with Buddhism in Asia. In October 1990, Kamenetz, a professor of English at Louisiana State University, traveled to India to participate in a religious dialogue between a diverse group of Jewish thinkers and rabbis and the XIV Dalai Lama. The Dalai Lama had seen parallels between Tibet's contemporary suffering under Chinese occupation and the long history of Jewish persecution. He asked the Jewish thinkers for help: "Tell me your secret ... the secret of Jewish spiritual survival in exile" (2).[20] For several days in Dharamsala, Kamenetz and his colleagues did their

---

[20] Rodger Kamenetz, *The Jew in the Lotus: A Poet's Rediscovery of Jewish Identity in Buddhist India* (New York: HarperCollins, 1994).

Christian and Jewish Pilgrims in Buddhist Asia

best to respond to this request. The conversation explored many other topics as Tibetan Buddhists and Jews discussed commonalities, differences, and the challenges posed by modernity. Kamenetz was deeply moved by what he learned about Tibetan traditions and began to search for analogies in Judaism. What is there in Jewish history, and what possibilities for Jewish renewal might be imagined, with equivalent power to transform individuals and the religious community? The interreligious dialogue in India precipitates a change in Kamenetz from an essentially secular and ethnic Jewish identity to one committed to creatively renewing Judaism.

Kamenetz unexpectedly discovers suppressed spiritual longings in himself and other contemporary Jews. "So many Jews had been turned off, not only to Judaism, but to any sort of spiritual experience. I was such a Jew" (144). He valued the Jewish commitments to social justice and intellectual and educational achievement, and he identified with Jewish culture and history. Kamenetz, though, was not interested in Judaism or any other religion. It was the Dalai Lama's spiritual wisdom and charismatic presence, as well as what he learned about Tibetan Buddhist practices, that prompted him to recognize his own unfulfilled longings for religious meaning and commitment.

One of the organizers of the dialogue was Dr. Marc Lieberman, a San Francisco ophthalmologist who described himself as a JUBU: a Jewish Buddhist. JUBUs have played a huge role in the development of Western Buddhism as founders of meditation centers, teachers, translators, and publishers. Among the early leaders of American Buddhism with Jewish backgrounds are Joseph Goldstein, Jack Kornfield, Sharon Salzberg, Sylvia Boorstein, and Peter Matthiessen's Roshi, Bernard Glassman (Tetsugen). The poetry and popular writings of Allen Ginsberg and Richard Alpert (Ram Dass) made Hindu and Buddhist ideas accessible to the American counterculture. Jewish participation in American Buddhist groups has been measured variously at 6–30 percent, in significant contrast to their proportion of the American population (about 2 percent). In American universities, "perhaps up to 30 percent of the total faculty in Buddhist Studies" (9) have a Jewish background. Among the delegates to the Dharamsala dialogue, several in addition to Lieberman had studied Buddhism and practiced forms of meditation, and several other JUBUs living in India also participated. What explains this pattern of Jewish attraction to Buddhism?

Exploring this question, Kamenetz confronts the grief, sense of loss, and estrangement between Jews and JUBUs. At the conference and in interviews he conducts after his return, he asks JUBUs why they felt disillusioned by what they knew of Judaism and why they found in Buddhism a vital and joyful spiritual life. Many of them wanted direct contact with a spiritual teacher and personal experience, in contrast to obeying ancient rules and having to believe what was prescribed. As Joseph Goldstein put it: "Insofar as I understood it, the path of Judaism involved following the vision, the law, of someone else's experience. I used the Old Testament prophets as an example. I was interested in having that experience. I wasn't interested in taking it on faith and trying to live up to it" (149). To those who became Buddhists, Orthodox Judaism seemed trapped in an irrelevant and oppressive past, symbolized by an old man saying "no." Reform Judaism, like the worldview of secular Jews who dropped their religious identity altogether, seemed overly rationalistic, this worldly, and preoccupied with fitting in with American culture. Many Jews abandoned distinctive aspects of Judaism, including its emotional, experiential, and mystical dimensions. What was left of the religion lacked the sense of play and wonder, the spiritual discipline, the mystery, and the emphasis on personal development that JUBUs longed for. Searching for transformative experiences of unselfing, they turned to Buddhism. According to Kamenetz, Tibetan Buddhists have preserved these crucial elements of religion, even in exile. The vitality of this religious community provides clues to what a renewed Judaism must offer contemporary people.

As Kamenetz and the other Jewish representatives grasp this insight, their purpose in India changes: they are no longer simply giving helpful advice but learning and deliberating about their own future. Having come as "missionaries of the secret of survival, … bringing their Torah to Dharamsala" (116), they discovered that "true dialogue goes both ways." All of them were profoundly affected by the encounter: "Every participant from the Jewish side felt transformed by the dialogue experience" (279). Kamenetz doubts that this could have happened by means of dialogue with Christians; there is just too much baggage, bitterness, and anger at the long history of anti-Semitism. It seems unlikely that the compelling power of this encounter could have been equaled in the United States. Being on unfamiliar ground and away from the constraints of their usual Jewish community, as well as the total impact of India's religious pluralism (for instance, visits to a Sikh temple and other sites of worship), played an important role in opening up Kamenetz and his companions to new experiences and possibilities. Travel was a crucial factor in their transformation.

Kamenetz does not discuss the Buddhist concept of no-self. Yet one point of contact that he finds in the two religions is their common interest in a closely related idea: emptiness. In the Jewish esoteric tradition of kabbalah, God is sometimes referred to as *ain sof* ("without bounds") to

Christian and Jewish Pilgrims in Buddhist Asia

acknowledge that, about God, nothing can be said or thought. Following suggestions of the Dalai Lama, Kamenetz sees analogies between this idea and the Tibetan Buddhist doctrine of *shunyata* that derives from Nagarjuna's teachings: "Maybe where *shunyata* meets *ain sof*, I would find the high place where Jews and JUBUs and Buddhists could dance together again" (157). Because Buddhists do not believe in a Creator, one cannot dismiss crucial differences between their worldview and Judaism. Nonetheless, as the Dalai Lama held, "if God means truth or ultimate reality, then there is a point of similarity to *shunyata*, or emptiness" (85). The Dalai Lama and the Jewish participants were fascinated to discover analogies between certain Buddhist perspectives and Judaism's mystical traditions. In response to the Dalai Lama's question about the "inner life" of Jews and their methods of spiritual transformation, one rabbi describes the mystical writings of kabbalah and another explains little-known Jewish meditation practices. This theme in *The Jew in the Lotus* resembles William Johnston's efforts to reconcile Buddhism with Christianity by exploring the latter's apophatic and mystical ideas and practices. Kamenetz asserts that the kabbalah can correct and enrich simplistic notions of God and that a renewed Judaism must make esoteric traditions more accessible. Learning about emptiness in Tibetan Buddhism reorients Kamenetz's understanding of what Judaism has meant and might become in a vital renewal movement.

Although he hopes that the concept of emptiness will redirect thinking about God, Kamenetz does not connect it with ideas about human selfhood or his own sense of identity. He does not reflect on the emptiness of self or experience a dramatic moment of unselfing when ordinary awareness is transfigured. Nonetheless, Kamenetz shows how the Dharamsala conference engendered significant changes in his sense of identity. Before the trip, "I was basically an unthinking agnostic—I neither believed nor disbelieved in God" (251). Contact with Buddhism "opened me up," he says, freeing him to be interested in and committed to Judaism. By the end of the narrative, Kamenetz has become a questioning, doubting, sincere, and passionate seeker of God and a way of life infused with a sense of the holiness of ordinary existence. "Seeing Judaism in the light of Tibetan Buddhism, I realized that the religion of my birth is not just an ethnicity or an identity, but a way of life, and a spiritual path, as profound as any other" (280). After the journey to India, Kamenetz is no longer a materialist and skeptic who thinks that only science can explain reality. "The transformation in my own life tells me that the subtlety of consciousness—the quiet mind—that a Dalai Lama develops cannot be denied. It is as real as anything—it is as real as any *thing*. And far more precious" (288).

I take Kamenetz's discovery and affirmation of unfamiliar spiritual dimensions of his own being as a form of unselfing, a process that leads to a new sense of who he is as a Jew. *The Jew in the Lotus* focuses less on the unraveling of an older sense of the self than on the emergence of a new identity, elements of which were latent but repressed all along – just as the mystical side of Judaism has been hidden in modern America. His narrative focuses on the discovery of true identity, not on an ordeal that shatters a false identity. Kamenetz's identity is still taking shape at the end of the narrative, just like the new forms of Judaism that he hopes will flourish in the United States. As was the case for Thomas Merton, William Johnston, and Bardwell Smith, Kamenetz was personally transformed by experiencing Buddhism in Asia, and his depiction of this encounter is inextricably connected with reflections about the past and future of his own religious tradition, which he came to view as analogous in crucial ways to Buddhism.

CHAPTER 5

Walking the Dharma on Shikoku and in India

Of the many ways to travel on a Buddhist pilgrimage, walking is usually considered to be the most challenging, rewarding, and meritorious. It has the greatest potential to transform the pilgrim. In this chapter, I consider three accounts of long walking pilgrimages: two following Japan's eighty-eight-temple Shikoku circuit and a foot journey to sites in Nepal and India associated with the Buddha's life. In contrasting ways, the authors of these Western Buddhist travel narratives affirm the reality of personal transformation in the course of a demanding long-distance walk. At the same time, each author shows that striving for enlightenment continues and bad habits are still deeply entrenched. A common concern in these narratives is how walking leads to both unselfing and self-understanding, experiences that seem contradictory or incompatible yet are linked.

The most famous Buddhist pilgrimage is the 1,000-mile circular route around the Japanese island of Shikoku, which visits eighty-eight temples associated with Kobo Daishi (774–835), also known as Kukai. He traveled to China to study Tantric (sometimes called Esoteric) Buddhism and when he returned to Japan organized the Shingon school. One of its main centers is Koya-san (Mount Koya), not far from Osaka and Nara, which is considered the start of the Shikoku pilgrimage route. Kobo Daishi is often called the greatest figure in the history of Japanese religion. He was a priest, wandering holy man, poet, scholar, calligrapher, artist, and a civil engineer and social worker who benefited many people's lives. Shikoku pilgrims have faith that this "great master" (Daishi) accompanies or may encounter them along their route.

In 1985, Oliver Statler published *Japanese Pilgrimage*, a book that combines his own experiences walking the Shikoku circuit with historical reconstruction of what is known about Kobo Daishi, interpretation of how the pilgrimage evolved over centuries, and impressions of contemporary Japanese religious life. Born in 1915, Statler began working in Japan in a civil service position with the US Army in 1947. He lived in Japan

124   Walking the Dharma on Shikoku and in India

for most of the next three decades, eventually settling in Hawaii until his death in 2002. *Japanese Pilgrimage* grew out of Statler's research for an earlier book, *Japanese Inn*, because the ways that travelers are housed and cared for originated in lodging for pilgrims. As explained in the postscript, Statler visited Shikoku many times beginning in 1961 and completed the entire pilgrimage in 1968. A second full circuit in 1971, accompanied by Nobuo Morikawa, was the source of most of the autobiographical incidents he recounts. *Japanese Pilgrimage* describes Statler's encounters and acute observations along the route, but it is reticent about his own religious orientation. While it is evident that he understands and appreciates many aspects of Japanese religious life, it is not clear whether or to what extent he considers himself a Buddhist. Statler does not discuss the idea of no-self or portray dramatic moments when ordinary consciousness was altered. Nonetheless, in several ways his descriptions of the Shikoku pilgrimage in the past and the present revolve around the topic of personal transformation as a result of walking the path. As his personal engagement in the pilgrimage increases, Oliver Statler seems to be considering whether he, too, could be transformed.

Another kind of transformation that Statler traces involves the figure of Kobo Daishi. The first of the three sections of *Japanese Pilgrimage*, "Master," distills what can be discerned about the historical Kobo Daishi in the many legends and stories about him: "Though such tales interest me I keep searching for the flesh-and-blood Daishi, the man who lived from 774 to 835" (35).[1] Like the search for the historical Jesus, certainty about most of Kobo Daishi's life is impossible. Ancient legends were grafted on to the figure of the Daishi, and stories were invented later to promote certain temples or political or religious interests. Tales about the Daishi and Shikoku locations reflect the heritage of Shinto, with its shamans and reverence for mountains and other sacred places. Legends about the Daishi's services to the common people are influenced by his precursors and later holy men who organized villagers to build roads, bridges, dams, and dikes. Although Statler shares most Western readers' interest in distinguishing the historical Kobo Daishi (his "true self"?) from myths about him, he makes it clear that this quest is probably futile and misses what is most important about the Master's presence on the Shikoku pilgrimage trail.

The book's second section, "Savior," describes how Kobo Daishi took on a salvific role in Japanese popular religion. Stories about the holy man reflect the influence of other figures associated with Mount Koya who

---

[1] Oliver Statler, *Japanese Pilgrimage* (New York: William Morrow and Company, 1983).

Walking the Dharma on Shikoku and in India 125

wandered freely through the countryside, independent of the court and priestly hierarchy. "The Daishi's life was one of the greatest that any Japanese has ever lived but as it receded into the mists of time the great master that he had been was forgotten. In his place the holy men evoked a miracle worker, a deity, a savior" (159). The figure of Kobo Daishi fuses several different paths to salvation: austerity and asceticism, meditation, reliance on supernatural power, and service to the common people. Many stories about miraculous events attributed to the Daishi began as legends about other heroes, saints, and local deities such as Kokuzo. Like selves, stories mutate. Guidebook accounts, temple priests' anecdotes, and local legends diverge, and multiple versions of key events arise, fade, or merge with other stories. The many tales about the holy man reflect the diverse ways in which the Japanese people have sought and found salvation from various forms of suffering. Like selves, stories mutate, and Kobo Daishi continues to be transformed.

Stories about various *henro* (pilgrims) also dramatize transformation. Emon Saburo, the archetypal first pilgrim, models the connection between walking and personal change. He was a rich and greedy man who refused to give alms to the Daishi. When his children died, he was stricken with remorse. Emon Saburo set out to find Kobo Daishi and beg for forgiveness. He circled Shikoku many times until, near death, he finally met the Daishi and was granted absolution. The most significant change in Saburo did not come when he was forgiven or faced death but when he set forth on his journey, humbled and repentant. His legend inspires a central theme in the Shikoku pilgrimage: seen or unseen, Kobo Daishi always accompanies the henro. He can encounter a pilgrim at any moment, in any guise. The Emon Saburo story stresses the importance of generosity for pilgrims and for residents of Shikoku, who often bless passing henro, ask for a blessing, and assist in material ways. At the heart of the Shikoku pilgrimage is the transformation of the human heart that accompanies a compassionate response to need or suffering.

In the final section of the book, "Pilgrims," Statler recounts stories of henro who experienced transformation, most often in the form of healing. Local legends and temple attendants describe miraculous cures of disease. Passing henro explain their motivation in terms of a search for improved health, pregnancy, or better employment. Others walk to express gratitude for success or recovery, or they are escaping a meaningless job or empty relationship and trying to discern their future direction. An extract from a young woman's diary describes a 1918 pilgrimage when she was suffering from depression. At the outset, she forms several resolves, including

126 Walking the Dharma on Shikoku and in India

"to accept whatever happened, however unexpected, without anxiety" and "not to cling to life tenaciously" (273–274). She describes agonizing loneliness and concerted efforts to change herself into a stronger person. We do not learn whether this woman believed that she had been transformed, but her resolution and courage as she walks are a striking contrast with her past self. Her persistence in spite of suffering marks a turning point in her life; she later became a prominent writer. In various ways, then, henro seek and often experience a fundamental change in their lives.

All this detailed information about Kobo Daishi, Japanese religion, and the stories of individual henro is interwoven with Statler's account of his own circuit of the eighty-eight temples, which synthesizes incidents from several walking tours and two years of residence on Shikoku. The personal religious dimensions of this travel narrative are a significant if understated dimension of *Japanese Pilgrimage*. There are several ways in which Statler explores the possibility of transformation in his own life, even though he tells us very little about himself before or after the pilgrimage. The most dramatic incident in his journey comes when he fails to heed a request to act as a healer. Having accepted an invitation to have tea in a woman's home, he is asked to examine his host's daughter, who suffers from a chest condition. When he thinks he is about to be asked to perform a prayer ritual, Statler becomes intensely uncomfortable with the role of faith healer or shaman:

> As a man with hair gray enough to imply some wisdom; as a stranger—there is mystery in that word, the mystery of a person unknown unexpectedly appearing from a world unknown—and doubly a stranger, a foreigner; and above all as a henro, I am being asked to minister to a sick girl.
> I panic, utterly at a loss. Nothing I have studied has prepared me for this. Suddenly I am not a henro, I am a misplaced doctor's son from Illinois (one who instinctively shied away from his father's profession). I have no religious power, I tell this woman. I am wearing a henro robe but I have no religious power. I have no ability to diagnose an illness or to cure it. (191)

Statler apologizes, tells the family to call a doctor, and flees. The doctor's son who avoided his father's profession refuses to act like his father, as if he were stuck in a conception of himself as "not like Dad."

He soon regrets his hasty escape and learns what he should have done: pass over the girl's body his copy of the album that pilgrims carry. When he did not perform this shamanic ritual, which might have helped the sick girl, he avoided the transformation that can come with becoming a henro. A change in one's identity is symbolized outwardly when one dons a pilgrim's white robe and carries a staff; a pilgrim's inner change should include accepting that others may respond to one as Kobo Daishi and acting appropriately.

Walking the Dharma on Shikoku and in India 127

When Statler refused to act as a healer who performs a ritualized role, he failed to act as Kobo Daishi to a faithful believer. He turned away from an opportunity for unselfing. Taking part in a ritual can alter one's sense of self and lead to transformation. Statler had realized this earlier when he described how, when Kobo Daishi imitated the deity Kokuzo, he took on his virtues and powers: "Imitation, emulation, identification—these are steps we all take in one way or another as we are molded or mold ourselves" (64). That he fails to put in practice this understanding of performative action teaches as much about transformation as would a more willing and graceful adaptability to the role that he was asked to play.

In the same chapter as his encounter with the sick girl, Statler witnesses a fire ritual (*goma*) performed by the priest of a *bangai*, an unofficial temple off the main pilgrimage route. The goma ritual, practiced in various ways by different priests, involves mysterious rites of exorcism, healing, purification, and "making our wishes come true" (202). The priest prays that Statler and Morikawa will complete their pilgrimage safely and then, to Statler's amazement, lifts and holds him outstretched over the fire. The priest answers questions from local people about their health, troubles, and future fortunes. Statler is disturbed by this ritual and wonders if the priest abuses people's faith in him: "Is this priest exploiting superstition or do people need what he offers? I truly believe that faith can work miracles. I know that all religion has an element of magic. But how slippery is the line between seeking enlightenment in this world and seeking favors—the priest said 'happiness'" (204). He asks several other priests about the place of faith and esoteric rituals in Shingon Buddhism and continues to be troubled. Near the end of the pilgrimage, he decides to return to the priest who did the goma ritual, to do so crossing the island on a train. Statler asks the priest a question that has haunted him: "If someone comes to you with a disease that a doctor could help, do you recommend that he or she see a doctor—as well as offering your help through prayer?" (206). The priest replies that he always asks first if they have been to a doctor, and if not he urges them to do so. This answer satisfies Statler. The priest values scientific medicine and also believes that there are things that cannot be explained by science. In this conversation and other ruminations, Statler emphasizes the important role of faith in personal transformations, including healing. He also points out the limits of faith and the necessity of human efforts in healing and in any serious quest for transformation.

Statler's interest in faith is unusual among Western travel writers drawn to Buddhism, many of whom see that tradition as utterly different from monotheism's demand for belief in God. Westerners tend to stress motifs such as the Buddha's advice to verify his teachings in one's own experience and his dismissals of otherworldly speculation. The appeal of meditation for many Western adherents is that one relies not on supernatural power to find peace of mind but rather on one's own persistent practice. Statler, however, sees in the Shikoku pilgrimage and in the figure of Kobo Daishi a blending and synthesis of religious impulses that are often set against each other: faith in a power beyond the self and the importance of willed effort. Throughout *Japanese Pilgrimage*, he documents both the indispensable role of faith in Kobo Daishi and the need for a pilgrim's deliberate striving.

Statler explores conflicting Japanese views of whether personal transformation comes about through human initiative or faith in divine action. Many pilgrims avow faith in the power of Amida Buddha, in keeping with a primary emphasis in Pure Land Buddhism but in contrast with certain of Kobo Daishi's teachings. The hymns sung at many Shikoku temples express faith in Amida: "The words of almost all of them are deeply dyed not with Kobo Daishi's assurance that man can attain Buddhahood in this existence, but with the holy men's faith in Amida's paradise of the next world" (156). Priests and holy men created myths about Kobo Daishi that portray his supernatural powers or represent him as a deity, such as Miroku, the future Buddha. Statler expresses reservations about the way these priests stress the importance of faith, and he even asserts that this is inconsistent with Kobo Daishi's approach: "Their message was incompatible with the Daishi's teaching. Dainichi, not Amida, was central in the Daishi's thought; to the Daishi, Mount Koya was a place for intense meditation, not a gateway to paradise; the Daishi had not spoken of a paradise after death. These distinctions were beyond the holy men" (99). Even with these reservations, Statler's appreciation of the central place of faith in Japanese pilgrimage is unusual among Western travelers, most of whom, in keeping with their own religious orientation, dismiss theology, the supernatural, and future worlds and instead describe Buddhism as a way of life that depends on one's own efforts and perhaps a supportive community.

One can hardly ignore the necessity of human effort in the 1,000-mile Shikoku pilgrimage or the Shingon Buddhism established by Kobo Daishi. The essence of Shingon Buddhism is "the conviction that man can attain Buddhahood 'in this very existence'—not after traditional Buddhism's countless cycles of birth, rebirth, and misery, but, with faith and practice, in the here and now" (77). Although Statler points out the contrast between the Daishi's example of struggle to attain enlightenment in this world and faith in a future rebirth in a Pure Land, he tries to reconcile these differing understandings of how transformation comes about. One temple priest emphasizes a "both/and" approach: "To intellectuals, religion seems strange. But the point of the religious life is mental and spiritual training, and that cannot be achieved by oneself. We need help from some source like Buddha or Kobo Daishi .... The point of the pilgrimage is to improve oneself by enduring and overcoming difficulties" (260). Statler eventually comes to a similar view. Having set forth a stark choice between reliance on faith or on human effort, Statler reconciles these two dimensions of religion not in thought or doctrine but in the act of pilgrimage. The lesson of Emon Saburo, the paradigm for later henro, is to put one's faith in Kobo Daishi and keep walking:

> Salvation came to Emon Saburo not through study of doctrine but through hard practice. Morikawa and I have learned that the essence of the pilgrimage lies in treading a route that tradition says the Daishi trod, and in the conviction that, spiritually at least, one walks in the Daishi's company. The henro puts his faith in the Daishi. Beyond that, doctrine is for priests. (292)

Strenuous effort and reliance on powers beyond the self are for most people both necessary aspects of a quest for transformation.

Walking the Shikoku pilgrimage expresses this ideal unity of faith and human effort in search of transformation. Statler criticizes those who make the circuit by motorized vehicle. Riding is a travesty of the true meaning of pilgrimage, which is linked to asceticism: "The pilgrimage is ascetic exercise for the layman. Its essence lies in the physical, mental, and spiritual demands made on the henro, and the physical, mental, and spiritual rewards that accrue" (298). Although Statler respects the earnest devotion of henro on a bus pilgrimage he once took, he could not believe that Kobo Daishi was with them "on that sense-numbing, sleep-inducing, dyspepsia-causing bus" (298). He mentions several reasons why walking is helpful in the process of healing: "I know that there are diseases it can cure. Polio or a stroke, for example, if the victim can walk at all, then the hard physical exercise (some would call it therapy) and the getting out into nature (for nature has therapeutic powers), if accompanied by faith, can work miracles—but not without faith" (195).

We can speculate further as to why prolonged walking may bring transformation. An extended walk may be beneficial because fresh air, natural beauty, exercise, and simple food on the pilgrimage route remedy the effects of urban life. A simple change of scene and clear focus on getting to the next temple may alleviate mental strains, distraction, and anxiety. For some people, the sense of accomplishment involved in completing an arduous journey provides a boost of self-confidence. Encounters on the pilgrimage route with other people, both local residents and other henro, may bring a renewed sense of connection with strangers and the special bond among travelers that Victor Turner calls *communitas*. The relaxed sense of time on a walking pilgrimage is different from the tight schedule of an organized motor tour of temples. A meditative, contemplative mood needs time and space to develop. The mind works differently at three and at sixty miles per hour.[2]

Toward the end of his journey, Statler meditates on the pilgrimage of a prominent Kabuki actor, Ichikawa Danzo, which culminated in his suicide. In 1966, at the age of eighty-four, Danzo retired from the stage and undertook the Shikoku pilgrimage. When he was finished, he spent a few days on Shodo Island, where there is a several-days-long condensed replica of the Shikoku pilgrimage. Then he boarded a midnight ferry and in the darkness entered the water. His body was never recovered. This enigmatic suicide fascinates Statler. He collects stories about Danzo on Shikoku, visits Shodo Island, and goes to Tokyo to conduct interviews about the Danzo, looking for clues as to why he committed suicide. He learns that the great actor dreaded "becoming unpresentable" like his father, also a Kabuki legend, who when he was elderly once dozed off during a performance. Danzo explained his retirement by saying that he wanted never to exhibit any sign of senility. Statler thinks that Danzo "must have thought about death often on his pilgrimage" (313). By all accounts, he was "convincing in the role of henro" (313), and when he died in his chosen way he fulfilled his desire never to have given a poor performance. "In that respect he was spared: he was never seen unpresentable. His was an act not of desperation but of resolution. He walked out of life as he had walked off the stage, with composure. He never became a burden" (318).

Statler does not explain why he devotes so much attention to Ichikawa Danzo. In the context of this study of unselfing, the Danzo's enigmatic suicide raises the question of whether or not he went through a transformation on his pilgrimage. In order to make his decision about how to die, perhaps he had to go through a process of unselfing, letting go of his identity, success, and fame as a renowned Kabuki actor. Statler admires the resolution with which the Danzo foresaw his inevitable decline and chose to end life on his own terms. Yet that the Danzo was terrified of giving a bad performance and could not imagine a new identity after retirement suggests desperate clinging to his conception of himself as a superlative actor. He could not learn a new role, improvise another self,

---

[2] On the psychology of walking, see Rebecca Solnit, *Wanderlust: A History of Walking* (New York: Penguin, 2001), especially her chapter "The Mind at Three Miles an Hour."

or allow himself to be transformed. Danzo's performances as actor, henro, and suicide raise questions about how much he linked his conception of his identity to these roles. At the end of his life, did he experience a radical unselfing that was necessary to choose suicide, or did he cling desperately to the identity threatened by aging? This enigmatic story is a fitting conclusion to Statler's study of pilgrimage, in that the question of whether or not a person has been transformed is finally unknown to an outside observer, however much we may want to know this. Did Danzo successfully perform the new role of henro and become other than his former self, or does his suicide show that he was unable to realize the pilgrim's essential goal, self-transformation in a new life? Statler's narrative suggests this question but does not answer it.

In the final chapter of *Japanese Pilgrimage*, as he approaches Temple Eighty-Eight, endings of several kind loom. Statler notices many henro graves and learns that at this point many pilgrims feel unable to complete the pilgrimage. He thinks about the conclusion of his pilgrimage and how the journey has affected him. He mentions the deep connection he feels with his companion, Morikawa: "a bond forged of shared delights and discomforts, of mutual dependency, of search and discovery, each into himself and together into a new landscape" (327). Statler refers vaguely to a process of reevaluating one's life during a pilgrimage: "They say a henro carries the baggage of his life: true, and the pilgrimage gives him time to sort out some of it" (327). He does not reveal the nature of his own "baggage," how he sorted it, or what he dropped or carried with him into the next phase of his life.

Shikoku's circular route symbolizes the nature of spiritual life: "This Shikoku pilgrimage is the only pilgrimage I know of that is essentially a circle. It has no beginning and no end. Like the quest for enlightenment, it is unending" (320). Statler quotes Joseph Kitagawa on the importance of the Path in Buddhism: "The important thing in Buddhism is not dogma but practice, not the goal—the mysterious and unascertainable Nirvana—but the Path … The Path is not the means to an end: the Path is the goal itself."[3] Given the nature of the Shikoku circuit, the transformation wrought by walking it cannot be a completed and final condition, for it is an initiation into an ongoing practice. In the book's final paragraphs, Statler heads back to Temple Number One as if he is about to begin again.

---

[3] Statler, *Japanese Pilgrimage*, 337, indicates that this quote is from Joseph M. Kitagawa's *Religions of the East* (Philadelphia: Westminster Press, 1960). *Japanese Pilgrimage* is dedicated to Kitagawa, who gave Statler "counsel and enthusiasm" and "invaluable advice" (335).

He remembers a priest's final blessing: If he is earnest, he will "to some degree be transformed." Using this partial and enigmatic phrase, Statler assesses his own pilgrimage:

> This I know to be true. Anyone who performs the pilgrimage seriously must be to some degree transformed. But in my own case, to what degree? Of one thing I am certain: the transformation I yearn for is incomplete. I do not know whether I am any closer to enlightenment—I do not really expect to achieve it—but I know that the attempt is worth the effort.
> The pilgrimage is addictive, as a henro we met some time back remarked. This circuit around Shikoku will pull me back to try again. And again. It is a striving, and that goes on. What is important is not the destination but the act of getting there, not the goal but the going. (327)

Thus does he reconcile his sense of the genuine benefits of his walking pilgrimage and the unfinished character of his lifelong spiritual journey. He is "to some degree" transformed, most evidently in his commitment to further walking on Shikoku and continued striving on a nameless spiritual path.

*

Three decades after Oliver Statler, Robert Sibley walked the entire Shikoku pilgrimage circuit continuously in fifty-four days and published *The Way of the 88 Temples: Journeys on the Shikoku Pilgrimage* (2013).[4] The Ottawa newspaper journalist had previously written about walking the Camino de Santiago de Compostela.[5] Although Sibley refers to himself as a skeptic with a secular orientation, he found a sense of peace and detachment on the Camino: "My mind emptied of the clatter and crush of everyday life, and I felt that some epiphany, some brief transcendence, was at hand" (25). He "awakened to the spiritual life" (31) and wanted more of it. He was haunted by memories of the Santiago walk, fleeting moments when a passing sight or incident suddenly seemed tremendously significant. In contrast to these events, the things that he had been pursuing – money, a career as a journalist, and reputation – seemed of little value. He sets out on Shikoku in search of more moments of illumination and greater understanding of their pattern and meaning. Sibley is not a Buddhist and initially thinks of his walk as "a secular journey to sacred places" (4). His journey changes, however, as he learns more about the pilgrimage route and its inspiration, Kobo Daishi: "I set out on one kind of journey but ended up on a very

---

[4] Robert C. Sibley, *The Way of the 88 Temples: Journeys on the Shikoku Pilgrimage* (Charlottesville, VA: University of Virginia Press, 2013).
[5] Robert C. Sibley, *The Way of the Stars: Journeys on the Camino de Santiago* (Charlottesville, VA: University of Virginia Press, 2012).

Walking the Dharma on Shikoku and in India 133

different one" (5). Along with the meaning of his walking, his sense of himself was transformed. When Sibley describes how he changed, he does not employ the concept of no-self or use the Japanese terms *mu* (nothing) or *ku* (emptiness). He remains firmly committed to the Western idea of a coherent self. Yet he portrays several experiences when his sense of selfhood was radically altered, and he interprets these moments of unselfing using both Western concepts and certain key Japanese ideas that reflect Buddhist influence and are closely related to no-self.

After several weeks of arduous walking, Sibley begins to develop a "pilgrim mind." This orientation is partly a matter of learning that the physical challenges and psychological difficulties of walking will pass. He must accept what can't be changed: "My ego, that fantasy of myself as the center of the universe, had to humble itself before a reality it couldn't control ... In short, I had to get over myself" (41). An inevitable part of a long trek is pain: blisters, aching joints and muscles, periods of boredom or discouragement. Yet one need not turn pain into suffering. In non-Buddhist language, this is basic Buddhist wisdom about the ways aversion and desire can change hardship into anguish and misery.

Pilgrim mind involves resilience, equanimity, and attentiveness to hidden meanings, coincidences, and beneficial occurrences. Sibley encounters many fortuitous events. A taxi driver gives him a ride when he is exhausted, a Buddhist nun provides timely religious instruction, a fellow pilgrim helps him find new shoes to replace his too-tight boots, and local residents of Shikoku give him offerings (*settai*) of food, salve for his feet, or other comforts. In like manner, Sibley provides crucial assistance and encouragement to fellow pilgrims. These encounters suggest that Kobo Daishi does indeed walk the trails of Shikoku in disguise, helping pilgrims to continue their outer and inner journeys.

Pilgrim mind means openness to seeing the ordinary as extraordinary. Although Sibley worries that he is "drifting close to the shoals of mysticism" (70), he notices how small events, passing encounters, and commonplace situations inspire him to continue. At certain moments he is completely immersed in seeing his surroundings:

> The event I most remember from that day, however, was a ten minute rest I enjoyed while squatting on a street-side curb outside a Tosa City postal station while Shūji used a cash machine inside and Jun phoned his mother. It was a narrow street of houses set behind whitewashed walls and largely empty of traffic. The only passersby were two middle-aged women who nodded and said "konnichi wa," "good afternoon," as they passed. Nothing happened, and yet there was poetry in the images before me: the green

> No. 32 bus rumbling past, with children in their dark blue school uniforms leaning out the windows; the rain-wet yellow curb lines running down the length of the road, bright under the sun; a spider's web of electrical wiring, silhouetted against the pale sky; tiled roofs and tidy shrub gardens, shining after the rain; a woman's lilting voice from the dark interior of a nearby house—everything seemed to hum and glow with intense significance, the ordinary transformed into the extraordinary. (77)

Sibley is reading Basho's *Narrow Road to the Interior* along the way. The great Japanese poet models keen perception of the everyday world and concise, startling writing: "From this attention to the everyday world, he turned ordinary experience into poetry. Bashō attempted to capture the effervescent quality of that everydayness. And that, I thought, is what made his poems a kind of pilgrimage" (80–81). When Sibley pushes beyond tiredness, he sometimes finds moments of clear vision when he glimpses the radiance of everyday life overlooked because of habits, busyness, and distraction; or pain breaks through his dim awareness of bodily sensation. Basho teaches him how to travel with a pilgrim mind that appreciates the details of everyday life and their resonances in one's inner being. This state of mind, so poignant, uncontrollable, and fleeting, seems to heighten or extend ordinary self-consciousness so that it becomes something else.

In epiphanic moments of vision, Sibley's ordinary sense of the division between self and world is overcome. Alone in the rain on a hill overlooking the ocean, he has an overwhelming feeling of being fully present in that obscure spot: "I exulted in the sheer awareness of myself being in the place. It was as if I were merging osmosis-like with what I saw, heard, and smelled, as if there were no veil of self-consciousness to separate me from the experience, no gap between self and world" (86). Seeing the beauty of gnarled branches in ancient forests, Sibley thinks that he understands the Japanese belief in *kami*, spirits that take palpable form in the natural world. While his modern, scientific, and secular outlook disdains belief in *kami*, another part of his being moves through the forest watching for these spirits and those of Basho and Kobo Daishi.

In the middle of the two-month walk, absorbed in the landscape and his basic needs for food and rest, Sibley feels that his former life in Canada is unreal and he has become a different person. Referring to Victor Turner's theory of the liminal condition of the pilgrim, Sibley describes his altered sense of selfhood:

> Now, halfway along the Henro Michi, I was increasingly conscious of myself disappearing into the peripatetic existence of a pilgrim. I was entering what anthropologists have described as a "liminal state" in which I moved beyond

Walking the Dharma on Shikoku and in India

> the normal strictures of my everyday life and into a psychological condition in which I no longer felt bound by the constructions of my normal social order or by the sense of identity and belonging that I derived from that order. In this state of displacement I had acquired a new, if temporary, sense of identity and belonging. (99)

Pilgrim mind involves a different sense of temporality: the henro learns to slow down, observe the natural world more closely, and be grateful for small comforts and gestures. As the journey approaches its finish, this present-moment awareness becomes harder to attain as Sibley begins to think about what he will do after the walk and as the clustering of temples at the end makes him inattentive to their subtle differences. The experience of walking changes as the goal of completing the pilgrimage displaces receptivity to whatever comes his way.

Sibley uses both Western and Asian frameworks to explore the meaning of his brief epiphanies. For instance, he has a momentary vision of his bento box lunch as a tiny landscape:

> For a few seconds I was looking down on a Japanese landscape from a great height: the white rice from the valley fields, the raw fish from the sea, the slices of bamboo from the mountain slopes. But then the vision blinked out like a lighted room suddenly darkened by the flick of a switch. Still, I continued to eat slowly, savoring the flavors—the melt-in-your-mouth *maguro*, the crunch of the bamboo shoots, the sweet sashimi that complemented the sour vinegar taste of the rice—hoping the light might go back on again. (125)

Sibley calls his bento box vision a moment of *yoin*, using a Japanese term for moments of intense awareness. This word can refer to the resonance or reverberation of a bell, to moments of deep feeling between loved ones, or to "situations where the ordinary turns extraordinary—where, as it seems, you are on the threshold of some degree of transcendence, modest or otherwise" (126). This kind of experience is rendered in Basho's haiku when a grazing horse is surprised to pull up a mouthful of roses, and when Basho perceives the laces of his sandals as iris flowers. Basho's poems record and transmit a moment of vivid apprehension when ordinary self-consciousness drops away: "a second or two when the gap between the perception of the object and the awareness of the experience disappeared, and we knew the essence of that thing" (126). When a bell sounds, a coincidence resonates, or omens and portents hum with significance, then attention is so focused on that event or image that the observer feels merged with the world.

Another way in which Sibley interprets his experiences of "the mysticism of the ordinary" (using a phrased coined by James Carse) is to see them in terms of Carl Jung's concept of synchronicity. Sometimes a person feels that outer and inner events have a meaningful relationship even though there is no causal connection between them. Jung was keenly interested in these intuitions of an uncanny equivalence or relationship between physical and psychic events. For Sibley, beneficial coincidences and his sense of inner resonance with certain sights and images elicit a feeling that he is part of a hidden wholeness. During one such moment of intuited connectedness, he views himself walking as if from another place: "I seemed to float above myself, watching as my body did the hard work of climbing up a slope or scrambling over rocks while my mind wandered on its own" (135). Like the concept of *yoin*, Jung's ideas about synchronicity are a possible lens for making sense of experiences of unselfing when a person senses the interdependence of all being and the resonance of an outer event and an intuition.

Another example of how Sibley interprets an experience of unselfing with contrasting intellectual frameworks concerns what happens in a *bangai*, an unnumbered temple off the official pilgrimage circuit, when Sibley tries an ascetic meditative technique. For Zen monks, standing under an ice-cold waterfall is supposed to shock one into greater awareness. Referring to Ian Reader's study of Japanese religions, Sibley describes the goal of pushing the body to its limits as the "dropping off of body and mind" (137).[6] Three times he steps into the icy water. Stunned and woozy, he slowly recovers his wits; then, sitting alone in the twilight, he has a flashback memory of losing consciousness as a child: "slowly, through some alchemy of solitude, silence, and the day's exertions, stillness settled on me. The world fell away, and the memory of an all-but-forgotten incident from my childhood took over my mind: the day I fell off a playground swing and knocked myself out" (140). Viewing himself as a boy and as a tired but exhilarated pilgrim, Sibley feels dislocated, at once a child, a man, and a distant observer of both. This perspective seems placed outside his usual self and is both intimately engaged in the world and curiously detached from it.

Interpreting this out-of-body, atemporal awareness, Sibley compares it to *makyo*, a Zen term for the point in meditation when hallucinations, buried memories, and strange mental phenomena arise. This is not enlightenment, but it is sometimes a stage on the way, for it suggests that

---

[6] Sibley quotes Ian Reader, *Religion in Contemporary Japan* (Honolulu: University of Hawaii Press, 1991), 121. Sibley acknowledges his dependence on several of Reader's studies and other scholarship. He also refers many times to Oliver Statler's experiences in the same places he walks on Shikoku.

Walking the Dharma on Shikoku and in India

the mind's insistence on logic and rational consistency is breaking down. Sibley takes this unusual event as a sign that his pilgrimage, and perhaps he himself, is changing. When he began the Shikoku circuit, he saw his walk as "an adventure in cultural exoticism" (142). At this point, he realizes that the real purpose of his journey is self-transformation: "It seemed to me at that moment that if the real purpose of my pilgrimage, however inchoately acknowledged, had been to cross some liminal threshold within myself, then this *okunoin* [the waterfall as an inner sanctuary] had fulfilled it" (142). His new sense of self recovers boyhood's wide-eyed curiosity and returns to the world with a deeper sense of connection and being at home: "as I gazed around the temple, I felt as though I'd returned to the world after a long absence. I didn't hear ash falling, but there was the rustle of leaves on an overhanging branch, the grate of gravel beneath my shoes, and the slow thudding metronome of my heart. The boy was home" (142). Sibley uses both a Japanese term deriving from Zen practice (*makyo*) and a Western anthropologist's theory (Turner's concept of the "liminal" identity of a pilgrim) to interpret this experience of an uncanny alteration of consciousness.

As Sibley's pilgrimage draws to a close, his appreciation of community and relationships with other people becomes emphatic. He connects this to Turner's ideal of *communitas* and to a distinctive aspect of Buddhist thought: karma. When he began the Shikoku circuit, Sibley intended to enjoy the company of others but to remain independent and usually solitary. However, he grows intimate with fellow pilgrims Shuji and Jun, a father and son. Jun is an impulsive and often irresponsible young man who cannot find his place in the adult world. Shuji takes him on the Shikoku pilgrimage in the hope that it will give him confidence and nurture their fragile relationship. Sibley speculates that Shuji was making the pilgrimage "to exorcise whatever bad karma he and his family had inherited in the hope of changing his fate and Jun's" (145). The notion of karma holds that the consequences of action reverberate in the world, including effects on a person's later reincarnations. The idea that a person inherits and influences the karma of other people contrasts starkly with the modern Western belief in a discrete, independent self. Although Sibley wants to dismiss the idea of karma, he finds himself acting as if it were true as he tries to help Shuji and Jun, encouraging them to continue and reciting chants and prayers with them. He participates in ritual actions that nurture the bond among companions and shows increasing awareness of how much fellow henro care about and need each other. When Jun strikes his father and runs away, it is Sibley who insists that the son apologize to his father and to Sibley and another fellow traveler. Jun had disturbed *wa*, group harmony: "*Wa* privileges good relations with others over notions of individual self-assertion. It's not that the Japanese deny individuality; rather, they recognize that individuality depends on relationships. Without others, there is no self. *Wa* is the glue that gives Japanese society its sense of cohesion" (149). Sibley challenges Jun to consider the consequences of his impulsive acts and make amends for selfish behavior. In this and other incidents, Sibley demonstrates that he has learned to care as much about the well-being of other people as about fulfilling his original intention to simply enjoy the scenery, learn about Japanese culture, and have a few pleasant encounters. These shifts in his orientation take place partly because of the conceptual framework he learns in Japan, which holds that there is no self apart from relationships. Sibley comes to understand interdependence and to practice compassion, both crucial Buddhist ideas connected with overcoming the illusory limits of the egoistic self. When his pilgrimage ends, Sibley affirms that one of its chief blessings was having as companions Shunji, Jun, and another pilgrim, a retired engineer named Tanaka-san. Deep friendships established on the road show the reality of *communitas* in pilgrimage. When vulnerable travelers depend on kindness and compassion, they make vivid the insights latent in the idea of karma. Actions have far-reaching consequences beyond what we understand, and our choices have long-term effects on our own well-being and that of others.

Sibley's feeling of connectedness to fellow henro endures after their Shikoku circuit. He visits them in Tokyo and, when he is back in Canada, receives their letters, including thirty-three haiku that Shuji wrote during the pilgrimage that resonate with his own responses to the same places. The poems show that Shuji had been present and attentive as he walked, having his own epiphanies and finding words that take Sibley back in memory to Shikoku. This happy ending of Sibley's travel narrative is shattered when, a few months after his return home, Sibley receives a letter from Shuji's niece, informing him that Shuji had killed Jun and committed suicide. Like the eminent Kabuki actor Danzo, with whose story Oliver Statler ended *Japanese Pilgrimage*, Shuji had made the Shikoku pilgrimage as an act of expiation before he took his life. He hoped to purify himself before his horrific act of violence. So Sibley surmises, and he finds confirming details in the niece's further account of Jun's destructive acts after the pilgrimage.

Deeply saddened by this tragedy, Sibley wants to do something for Shuji and Jun. Working within their cultural worldview, which has come to be part of his own, he wants to "ease their karmic burden" (167), assisting

Walking the Dharma on Shikoku and in India

in Shuji's purpose on Shikoku. Sibley bears witness to his friendship with fellow pilgrims by participating in a ritual that would be meaningful to them. In the epilogue, he describes how, a few months after his return from Shikoku, he went to Point-No-Point, on the western coast of Vancouver Island, and gazed outward toward Japan. This journey took place within the period of seven weeks during which, many Japanese believe, a soul is judged to determine how it will be reborn. Family and friends of the deceased hold memorial services and beseech the deities to intervene in this rebirth. *Way of the 88 Temples* ends with Sibley on the Canadian beach by a pounding sea, reciting the Heart Sutra and reading Shuji's haiku: "Then I bowed my head and prayed that the gods, if any existed, would give my friends a better fate in the next life" (171). Although he is not a Buddhist, Sibley's sincere and heartfelt participation in this ritual shows how he has been changed by his pilgrimage. He is tied to his fellow pilgrims by their common endeavor, by compassion for their suffering, and by the knowledge that his being is connected to others in ways more mysterious than his secular worldview can explain. Without giving up the Western concepts and frameworks that make sense and are useful to him, he has learned to understand his experience from the perspective of Japanese cultural beliefs that bear the imprint of Buddhism. He uses a Buddhist lens to interpret many of his experiences: his increased sense of interdependence with others, moments of discerning the ordinary as extraordinary, his awareness that any particular sense of the self is variable and fleeting, and the striking incidents when awareness of mind and body simply drops away. Robert Sibley shows the validity and value of Buddhist ideas related to no-self as one way of making sense of the occasions of unselfing he experienced on his Shikoku pilgrimage.

*

A very different walking pilgrimage is depicted in *Where are You Going: A Pilgrimage on Foot to the Buddhist Holy Places*, which comprises two separate volumes. *Rude Awakenings: Two Englishmen on Foot in Buddhism's Holy Land* (2006) recounts the first half of a six-month, 700-mile slog through Nepal and India that visits sites important in the Buddha's life. In November and December of 1990, Ajahn Sucitto and Nick Scott flew to New Delhi and traveled by train to India's border with Nepal. From there they walked to Lumbini, where Siddhattha Gotama was born, across the Ganges plain and through Kushinagar, where he died, to Vaishali, where he first set forth his teachings, and ended at Bodh Gaya, the setting of the Buddha's awakening. Although the narrative concludes in the middle of their journey, *Rude Awakening* is presented as a self-contained travel narrative, with "all the difficulties and comedy of the pilgrimage plus a climax and resolution" (xv).[7]

The alternating voices of the two authors express "the Buddhist understanding that realities depend on perspective" (xv). Ajahn ("revered teacher") Sucitto is an English Theravada monk born in 1949 who later served for a decade as the abbot of Chithurst Buddhist Monastery and wrote and edited many publications on Buddhist teachings. Nick Scott, a plant ecologist and nature reserve warden of about the same age, had previously studied and practiced Buddhism as a layman. The two men had known each other for about ten years before their pilgrimage, and after it they worked together at Chithurst Monastery, running that institution and writing their travel narratives. Ajahn Sucitto characterizes their different temperaments: "I was more reticent, plodding, and tenacious by nature as befitted my birth sign of the Ox. Nick was definitely a Dragon—spontaneous, ebullient but erratic, but then, as he put it later, we made a 'dangerous combination'—he would come up with crazy ideas, and I would resolve to stick to them, come what may" (9). Sucitto's strong ascetic drive and strict regimen made their journey painful and difficult. He focuses relentlessly on spiritual goals and takes precautions "against being hypnotized by the spells of India" (9). He is not adept in practical situations and needs a lot of looking after. Scott, in contrast, is fascinated by sights, smells, and sensations along their route and keen to observe birds and wildlife. He handles the food and logistics, navigation, and financial transactions. While sometimes exasperated, he admires and is fond of Sucitto. The relationship between the two men demonstrates the respect and mutual dependence of monks and laity that is central in Theravada Buddhism, as well as Scott's ideas about spiritual friendship.

A particular conception of their journey shapes the two men's walk. "We were going on a pilgrimage, not a sightseeing tour; so the logic was to walk and be absorbed into India as much as absorbing it. A pilgrimage has to be about surrendering oneself, to allow a new centre of being to develop. To realize, rather than to travel, is a pilgrim's aim and momentum" (5). Because they do not want to be separate from or protected from India, they make themselves vulnerable. Walking in intense heat through the rural poverty and destitution of Bihar, India's most crowded and backward state, they endure many forms of suffering. They must deal with aversion, distress,

---

[7] Ajahn Sucitto and Nick Scott, *Rude Awakenings: Two Englishmen on Foot in Buddhism's Holy Land* (Boston: Wisdom Publications, 2006).

Walking the Dharma on Shikoku and in India 141

and fear many times every day. Surrounded by curious Indians who try to engage them as they pass by, stop to eat, or camp, the two Englishmen long for privacy. Trying to protect a tiny personal space, even in the mind, creates tension and pain, and the only antidote is to let go of this craving.

As Sucitto and Scott walk across the endless fields and flat plains along the Ganges River, everywhere they go appears much the same and unremarkable. They try to focus on inner movements of heart and mind: "Progress was a matter of being undone and swallowed by the forces around me: the bantering inner and outer voices, the sweat and grime, the grit in the throat. The balance came through simply focusing on these things" (131). They are repeatedly asked: "Where are you going?" This question, which furnishes the title of the two volumes, cannot be answered in terms of spatial movement or a final spiritual goal. They try to focus on the going, not the goal, like Statler and Sibley on Shikoku. Yet much more than the pilgrims in Japan, they confront impediments, distractions, and hindrances to following their planned itinerary. They try not to resist what thwarts them but keep on keeping on. Unlike Shikoku's well-established circuit, their route through India involves periods of wandering, getting lost, arriving at a dead end, backtracking, and reorienting their course to the next holy site.

One of the most difficult aspects of the journey is finding and consuming food according to monastic regulations. As a monk, Ajahn Sucitto does not handle money and made a vow not to request anything. He must wait for Scott or other people to offer him food, tea, or water. Scott, too, adopts the practice of not eating after midday. Sucitto wants to get all of his food in the traditional way, by receiving it on alms rounds. The strict rules for alms gathering and uncertainty about whether they will get enough to eat by noon make for many anxious and several hungry days. Unsanitary conditions mean that the two men are often weak or sick with intestinal illnesses. Tensions arise between them, for instance when Scott tries to get villagers to offer Sucitto milk mixed into their afternoon tea. Sucitto had wanted to eliminate milk as a food, but a monk may not refuse what he is offered. Suffering from dysentery and protein deficiency, the companions eventually give up their attempt to survive on alms food alone, and Scott purchases a few additional items.

Walking in India would be challenging in any case, given the searing heat, limited opportunities for washing, hazardous traffic, no reliable maps, and the threat of thieves and robbers. Making a pilgrimage while obeying monastic rules is an exhausting and debilitating ordeal. Incredibly, Sucitto vows not to lie down to sleep and spends much of every night trying to sit upright. He tries to follow all the Vinaya's requirements, including meditating all night at the time of a full moon and half-night vigils every new moon. He plans to sleep under trees rather than under a roof and to perform lengthy chants three times a day. Seeing other monks playing volleyball and enjoying themselves, Scott comments wryly that "they seemed to be having a much easier time of being a monk than my companion ... Why did it have to be so hard? Ajahn Sucitto seemed even to *want* it to be difficult" (216). Sucitto did become less demanding in the course of the journey, to Scott's relief. He hints tactfully that "kindness to ourselves" is appropriate for Westerners driven by the need to accomplish something, including spiritual goals. Although neither author reflects much on this issue, their journey shows that the will asserts itself forcefully, if in disguise, in efforts at self-denial.

The pilgrimage depicted in *Rude Awakenings* reveals several connections to no-self and, at the end, a dramatic incident of unselfing. The contrasting temperaments of the two men sometimes grate on and irritate each other; each must overcome aversion – or better, notice and let it pass. After one grumpy moment, Sucitto consoles himself: "We were probably helping each other through all kinds of attachments if we could only realize it!" (111). The motif of developing patience recurs in the narrative, and the ideal of the Buddha as "Great Patient One" furnishes the title of the subsequent volume. In the context of this grueling ordeal, patience is a hard-won personal virtue that slowly becomes part of character. It requires overcoming one part of the self and strengthening another part; hence, it is related to both no-self and self-formation. Patience requires deliberate self-transformation as the travelers must let go of their resistance or aversion to many things encountered on the path.

Sucitto and Scott discern analogies between how Buddhism and other religions understand selflessness. For instance, Sucitto describes the origins of the Sikh religion as an attempt "to purify and point to the truths—and the false grasping—in current practices and ideas" (183). Like Buddhism, the vital spiritual impulse of the Sikh Gurus burst the bounds of Vedic Brahmanism, which had become static and inert. After an excursus on Sikh history and the hardening of identity linked to conflict with the Mughals, Sucitto laments continuing violence by and against Sikhs in India. He sees the source of violence as "the hypnosis of history fixing the future into the pattern of the past," in contrast to the only sane alternative to fixation on brutal memories: "opening into the present" (191). A religious practice that invites such an opening is the *langar*, the communal Sikh meal that the travelers gratefully receive in "a Sangha of sorts" (191). Sucitto sees the heart of all religion as a yielding of the self to others, and he evaluates traditions by how well they foster this orientation and disposition.

In the chapter "Dark Angel," Sucitto points out parallels to no-self in the history of religions, especially in relation to the Hindu goddess Kali. This fearsome figure, with her hideous fangs, garland of skulls, and bloody rituals, embodies Shiva's relentless energy, which eventually destroys every form, including those taken by Shiva himself. "Call her Fate, Kamma, or all-devouring Time, she is the power that shapes and undoes lives that we long to call our own" (196). According to Sucitto, the "angels of transcendence" in every religious tradition have a terrifying dimension:

> Jehovah had no more scruples about ripping people apart than Kali. Come to think of it, following the Dhamma was no pushover either. The angels of transcendence have their dark side. If you could take it, all this getting beaten up was about giving up ownership of the birth-death thread. The impeccable few who let go come to a life beyond the web; flawed aspirants grasp wildly and go under in the darkness. In the eyes of the Transcendent, that's fair—compassionate even. (198)

Buddhism's formalized teachings about no-self are its distinctive way of conceptualizing the awareness of finitude that Sucitto discerns in other religious traditions. He asserts that a vision of the self's annihilation can be liberating if it helps one to stop grasping at life. Let go, let go, he repeats like a mantra throughout his journey. "How you come out of the unknown, transfigured or destroyed, must depend on how you go into it. After all, dark angels always play fair. You can trust them to shatter your world" (218).

This understanding of the self's dissolution and Sucitto's resolution to be prepared to let it go are put to a dramatic test in the climax of the narrative, when the lives of the two travelers are threatened. They had left the Gangetic plain for forested uplands and were just three days from Bodh Gaya when they were attacked by dacoit (robbers). When bandits armed with axes and machetes try to steal their bags, Sucitto immediately offers his life:

> The only freedom was to go without fear. I bowed my head and pointed the top of my skull toward him, drew the blade of my hand along it from the crown of my head to the brow. "Hit it right there." Something shifted; he backed off, waving his axe and muttering angrily. I stepped forward and repeated the action. Give it away; let it all go. (238)

Luckily, the assailants grab his bag and go into the forest. Meanwhile, Scott resists them and runs away, pursued by the bandits. After a struggle, he loses the bag containing their passports, money, relics given to them as offerings, and the diary and rolls of film documenting their journey that

144   Walking the Dharma on Shikoku and in India

they intended as an offering to their English sangha. Scott is seriously injured when he falls down a ravine. Surviving this nearly fatal incident makes the travelers laugh with relief. Sucitto affirms that it is good to be alive and yet "when it comes down to it, nothing really matters—all you can do is die, which you're going to do anyway" (242). Offering his head to a man with an axe, a startling example of letting go of self, brings an exhilarating feeling of lightness and appreciation of life.

This confrontation with imminent death may be the most dramatic instance of unselfing in Western Buddhist travel narratives. Sucitto's instinctive reaction to the threat reveals how deeply he has internalized the meaning of taking refuge and is prepared to accept whatever comes:

> And as for myself, refuge had become very clear. Something in me on that dusty track handed over my life rather than go into fear. When I looked back on my mindstate at the time, the dominant mood had been to maintain calm and introspection ... I had not done anything against Dhamma, so my mind had remained clear ... The past—gone; the future—gone; and the present wonderfully free and unformed, unformable. We are going nowhere. I felt no need for direction. Just to rest in the Way It Is. To know that as my heart's intention was worth travelling for a lifetime to discover. I felt dangerously pleased with myself. (245)

Sucitto displays a remarkably undefended response to the possibility of being murdered and, so quickly, the inevitable arising of delicious self-approval. The incident depicts both the possibility of letting go by an act of unselfing and the inevitable "black hole" one falls into when, by determining to learn from a mistake and take control of future experience, one thereby sets up again the cycle of expectation and disappointment: "'I'll remember and do better next time,' chirps the mind, assuming ownership and authority, and thereby paves the way for the next black hole when it can't bring about the same process. The whole trap was set around 'I am': the need to get life under control by figuring it out or attaining something" (230).

Nick Scott asserts that Sucitto did the right thing in the forest when he stayed calm and gave the robbers what they wanted. In contrast, his resistance created a frenzy that could have gotten them both killed. When they survived the attack, he, too, felt jubilant. Having lost all their possessions, he felt released from care, floating free of this bond to ordinary selfhood. However, the travelers soon return from this moment of unselfing to the world of decisions, assertion, and ownership. When they report the crime to the police, a comedy of bureaucratic evasion and inefficiency turns tragic: the police jeep in which they are speeding strikes and kills a pedestrian. Sucitto and Scott believe that their own impatience and agitation

Walking the Dharma on Shikoku and in India 145

goaded an unskilled police officer to drive the jeep. By their fierce desire to recover their stolen things, they created as much frenzied energy as the robbers. After the interlude of detached floating, says Sucitto, "I had landed in India" (250). He feels responsible for a brutal death.

Giving up on dealing with the police, the two men decide to resume their pilgrimage for at least a few more days to Bodh Gaya. They are given a few clothes by other Buddhists and walk to the place where the Buddha was enlightened. They try to take with them their new perspective, "to go back with kindness to the human realm: whatever happened, to connect to it; not to fight, not to complain, not to push" (254). Instead, they fall back into old patterns of aversion and attachment: "How quickly, how effortlessly, the world arises!" (256). The mind, ever moving like a stream, can no more rest in a moment of unselfing than in any other condition.

The final chapter of the book, "The Time of Gifts," describes the arrival of the two Englishmen in Bodh Gaya at Christmas. The motif of gifts refers both to generous donations the two men receive and to the Buddha's Awakening. Sucitto's characterization of the enlightenment of Siddhattha Gotama stresses a dialectic of self and unselfing. At the root of the problem of life is "the creation of a self that is both alienated from life and besieged by it" (264). At Bodh Gaya, Siddhattha had "seen through the picture show of identity" and "the self-perpetuating road of damma" (269). The alternative is not to try to get off this road but to understand what is happening: "To reject the process, to think of getting off the road, is just another road, another becoming, another birth. Knowing there's no person on the road, that is Awakening" (269–270). This knowledge makes a difference in life, interrupting one's fixation on satisfying desires. Awakening came to Siddhattha unexpectedly, like a gift or grace, and his teaching passes the gift on to his followers. A second "time of gifts" is a Christmas gathering when a group of Westerners in Bodh Gaya exchange presents that replace all the things lost in the robbery. Sucitto and Scott are deeply moved by this kindness and generosity, which enables them to pursue their original plan for the pilgrimage.

Did their travels transform these two individuals? Sucitto thinks that "the robbery had made us more fragile and open, and hence more capable of living as a samana should" (272). As they resume their foot journey, he hopes he will be more open to the unexpected and less resistant to whatever confronts and challenges them. He realizes that, with all its maddening chaos, he loves India. "All that was certain was that it would now be a 'who knows' pilgrimage" (280). Yet he knows that his ability to live according to the Way of the Buddha is limited. The fallibility and fragmentation of his life seems mirrored in the many other Buddhists gathered at Bodh Gaya. *Rude Awakenings* ends with a glimpse of differing Buddhist groups who comment, argue, speculate, prove, and rebuff interpretations of the Dharma, all the while continuing to suffer: "Thousands of years later, after the suttas and the sutras and the Abhidhamma and the Great Vehicle and the Thunderbolt Vehicle and Zen and Salvation Buddhism and Western Buddhism and Buddhaless Buddhism, it is still raining. In all that splash and fragmentation we forget where Awakening comes into the world" (284–285). Sucitto seems resigned to an endless cycle of remembering and forgetting the Dharma, both on his own part and in the Buddhist sangha as a whole. This recognition qualifies any claim to have been permanently transformed by a moment of unselfing or the entire journey.

The epilogue indicates that the pilgrimage continued but shifts its focus to the authors' later activities. Ajahn Sucitto became the abbot of Chithurst Monastery, in West Sussex, England. Nick Scott joined him there, managing building projects and the woodland. They worked on the manuscript of *Rude Awakenings*, which was published just as both men departed from Chithurst after ten years: "Perhaps all this book and the pilgrimage ever were, were the means by which we ended up working together to complete the establishment of this monastery so it can benefit others" (288). The authors turn away from the question of whether and how travel changed each of them, instead conveying their hope that their pilgrimage, the book about it, and Chithurst Monastery will spread the Dharma to others. Rather than focusing on changes in individual character, they emphasize the hope that their common work will have beneficial effects for others. This exemplifies a different meaning of selflessness: not a personal virtue but an orientation to how one's life affects others. In common with several other Western Buddhist travel narratives, Sucitto and Scott suggest that the most important transformation and the deepest meaning of selflessness is turning away from pondering one's own spiritual progress.

In a second volume, *Great Patient One* (2010), Sucitto and Scott trace the rest of their journey: to Calcutta to replace passports and travelers' checks, back to Bodh Gaya, and on to Varanasi, Lumbini, Katmandu, and Nepal's border with Tibet.[8] As they set forth, they raise the question of whether the rest of the journey will be any different: "Perhaps the next

---

[8] Ajahn Sucitto and Nick Scott, *Where Are You Going: A Pilgrimage on Foot to the Buddhist Holy Places. Part II: Great Patient One* (West Sussex: Cittaviveka Monastery, 2010). This is a self-published book available for download at www.forestsangha.org.

Walking the Dharma on Shikoku and in India   147

part of the pilgrimage, if we were allowed to do it, would be different—wiser, more compassionate—even the way a pilgrimage should be" (xiii). They may be a little more flexible and patient and a bit better at observing their environment, but the changes are not striking. At the end of the book, Scott reflects on the meaning of the whole journey. As he enjoys the natural beauty and solitude of a remote valley in the Himalayas, he realizes that he had spent most of the pilgrimage looking for experiences of the sublime. This orientation resembles the way he had participated in meditation retreats by seeking a particular state of mind and suffering if it did not come. Scott recognizes this conditioned pattern without remorse or fruitless second-guessing the past:

> That realization was very powerful, but it came, was acknowledged, and passed just as the other perceptions of the afternoon did: the beauty of a waterfall we crossed beneath or the deep blue of the sky between the high wooded valley sides. From the perspective of centred-ness there was no regret, and no need to dwell on it. That was just the way it was. (342)

The hope that life will be different in the future depends partly on being able to see habits of past conditioning with this kind of equanimity.

The self is expressed even in unselfing. The differences between Scott and his companion are epitomized by the ways in which they each spend a free morning in the mountains. Sucitto sits meditating in a cave while Scott climbs a boulder and gazes in wonder at the valley below them:

> Everywhere were trees, most of them conifers, and the recent rain had left them all glistening in the morning sun. Tiny droplets of water hung from the pine needles beside me, and I sat in silence, delighting in it all. My mind had emptied, leaving a sense of vastness and awe and no feeling of a boundary between me and the world about me. It felt very profound, and I sat like that for two hours or more drinking from that spiritual well that I had been a long time in re-finding, until Ajahn Sucitto called, and I had to go down to pack up our things and set off down the valley. (340–341)

Bounding down the trail to lower elevations, he has "no perception of anyone at all doing it" (341). Scott experiences unselfing as a joyful feeling of merging with the natural world. The contrasting ways in which each man finds release from self are as distinctive as their conscious identities. Unselfing comes in different ways to an ascetic and a sensualist. Sucitto tends toward absorption or abstraction, while Scott is drawn by sensual delights.

Although the monk and the naturalist often grated on each other, Scott affirms that his friend's differences furthered his own spiritual development: "Had I done the pilgrimage with someone like me, I would have learnt little and let nothing go" (345). Their journey and joint writing project "turned out to be about two people struggling to do something together rather than about what we actually achieved" (346). The often-conflicted relationship between these spiritual friends generated a subtle transformation, as if friction slowly wore away or refined their rough edges and prickly irritability.

Like Christian conversion narratives, Western Buddhist travel narratives usually portray both transformation and continuity with the author's previous character. At the end of the book, the writer resumes ordinary life, but a Christian conversion experience or a Buddhist moment of unselfing suggests a possibly different future without claiming it. The last incident in *Great Patient One* shows Scott's middle way between asserting too little or too much personal change. He has just affirmed the Buddha's conclusion that neither sensuality nor asceticism is the right way to live. Neither self-indulgence nor rejecting the world brings serenity but rather learning to enjoy pleasures and accept difficulties without desire or aversion. He seems to have thoroughly internalized this central component of the Buddhist dharma. On the airplane back to England, however, the entire twelve-hour flight occurs between dawn and noon, the period when the Buddhist monk and his precept-observing lay companion are permitted to eat. Famished from the long ordeal in India, Scott devours his own food, requests seconds, and repeatedly raids the passing food trolley, stuffing himself until he is nauseous. Thinking he never wants to eat again, he is greeted in the airport by a group of monks bearing gifts of food. Scott is not only physically ill but feels "that sensation so familiar from the pilgrimage, that sinking feeling of having blown it again" (350). He doubts that anything has changed as he returns to the cycle of birth and death created by greed, aversion, and delusion.

Yet the final paragraph of the book affirms otherwise:

> But something, somewhere, had changed. Maybe it wasn't at the front of my mind then, but somewhere there was now the knowing that it is here that I have to work it all out. For it is here that *nirvana* is, not some other place that I had striven for. I just had to work at the illusion. (350)

Like Statler's assertion that he was "to some degree transformed" by his long pilgrimage, Scott affirms limited but significant personal change. The crucial knowledge that he must return again and again to the present moment is with him, even if not always "at the front of my mind." Even as he foresees that illusion will be part of his future life, he redirects his attention to the present moment and the knowledge that *nirvana* is here and now. Thus does Scott suggest both that travel transformed him and that the basic contours and habits of his character remain much the same, for instance a sensualist's overindulgence in the pleasure of eating.

For Scott and Sucitto, as for Oliver Statler and Robert Sibley, a long walking pilgrimage provides a crucial opportunity to realize again and again the paradoxes involved in the self's ceaseless arising and dissipation. The act of walking, with its rhythm of unselfing and return to self, becomes a metaphor and a vehicle for the continual practice of returning to the present moment. There one begins again, patiently persisting in the attempt to leave behind all that one has strived to attain.

CHAPTER 6

Trekking and Tracking the Self in Tibet

Tibet has long posed an irresistible challenge to Western travelers as an alluring destination, a blank slate on which to project Orientalist fantasies, and a catalyst for many kinds of personal transformation. For both geographical and political reasons, it was far less accessible than other Buddhist regions. No British delegations, for example, entered Tibet between 1784 and 1904. Because of its remoteness and mystery, Westerners could imagine Tibet as the mythical world of their fantasies. In the popular mind, it was viewed as the land of the highest spiritual attainments and a place populated by superstitious primitives practicing black magic and sexual depravity. Since James Hilton's 1933 novel *Lost Horizon*, Tibet's mystique has been linked to apocalyptic and utopian ideas about what might survive the self-destruction of the modern world. In *Prisoners of Shangri-La*, Donald Lopez, Jr., examines several emblems of the Western romance with Tibet, including the term "Lamaism," the uses of *The Tibetan Book of the Dead*, the history of the famous mantra *om mani padme hum*, and the academic discipline of Tibetan Buddhist Studies.[1] Becoming captivated by myths about Shangri-La seems inevitable as Westerners encounter Tibet.

When Westerners write about the religions of Tibet, it is usually as a foil for their own spiritual transformation. Tibetan Buddhism, often called "Lamaism," is the backdrop for the author's personal epiphany, which until the last few decades was usually the recognition of a secular humanist faith in the spiritual capacity of all human beings, coupled with skepticism about organized religion. The author seeks not Buddhist

---

[1] Donald S. Lopez, Jr., *Prisoners of Shangri-La: Tibetan Buddhism and the West* (Chicago: University of Chicago Press, 1998). In a note (213n23), Lopez lists many Western travel narratives and fiction about Tibet and writing by Protestant missionaries. Scholarly work on travel literature includes Peter Bishop, *The Myth of Shangri-La: Tibet, Travel Writing, and the Creation of Sacred Landscape* (Berkeley: University of California Press, 1989), Peter Hopkirk, *Trespassers on the Roof of the World* (Los Angeles: Tarcher, 1982), and Thierry Dodin and Heinz Räther (eds.), *Imagining Tibet: Perceptions, Projections, and Fantasies* (Boston: Wisdom Publications, 2001).

enlightenment but rather the ideals of the European Enlightenment. He contrasts his independent thinking and individual searching with the rituals and clerical domination of Lamaism, which usually looks suspiciously like the Catholic Church. Francis Younghusband's *India and Tibet* (1910) reveals links to colonialism, in that the author's epiphany affirms the value of secular relationships and the duty of useful work, implicitly justifying the purpose of the 1903–1904 Younghusband Expedition from India to Tibet, which was to open this area to British influence and control.[2] In these early works of Tibetan adventure, travel is linked to transformation and the author's realization of his true self, but these matters are not linked to understanding Tibetan Buddhism.

Even Alexandra David-Neel's extraordinary *My Journey to Lhasa* (1927) presents Tibetan Buddhism as a collection of exotic rites to be explained, not the spiritual tradition to which she was herself committed. David-Neel (1868–1969) converted to Buddhism in 1889. She made her first journey to Buddhist Asia in 1891 and returned to Europe to become an opera singer and journalist. Leaving her husband behind, she returned to India in 1912 to collect and study Buddhist texts. She made several brief forays into Tibet through Sikkim, defying British prohibitions of travel there. In 1914, David-Neel was made a female lama by Sikkimese monks, and in 1916 she visited the Panchen Lama and the monastic university of Tashilhunpo, near Shigatse in southeastern Tibet. David-Neel was a committed Buddhist (she called herself a "rational" one) who was accepted by Tibetan Buddhists as a spiritual teacher; the XIII Dalai Lama, whom she met in Sikkim in 1912, decided that she was an emanation of Dorje Phagmo, a popular female Tantric deity in Tibetan Buddhism.

The colonial British authorities had prohibited all Westerners from entering Tibet. When they learned of David-Neel's travel there, they banned her from Sikkim. This incident and another foiled attempt to enter Tibet from the Chinese side are the starting point of *My Journey to Lhasa* and her explanation of her motivation for a long trek. What prompted David-Neel's harrowing journey was "above all, the absurd prohibition which closes Tibet" (xxxiv).[3] Turned away at the border, "I took an oath that in spite of all obstacles I would reach Lhasa and show what the will of a woman could achieve!" (xxxix). She portrays her journey not

---

[2] Laurie Hovell McMillin, "Enlightenment Travels: The Making of Epiphany in Tibet," in *Writes of Passage: Reading Travel Writing*, eds. James Duncan and Derek Gregory (London: Routledge, 1999), 49–69.

[3] Alexandra David-Neel, *My Journey to Lhasa* (New York: Harper and Brothers, 1927). My quotations are taken from the 2005 Harper Perennial Edition.

152 Trekking and Tracking the Self in Tibet

as a search for religious meaning but as vindicating the principle that "any honest traveler has the right to walk as he chooses, all over the globe which is his" (xxxix).

My Journey to Lhasa is an amazing adventure story, packed with mysterious encounters, grueling ordeals, and close escapes from death. It records only the final part of a circuitous journey of many years that began when David-Neel could not return to Europe during World War I. She traveled from India through Burma, Japan, and Korea to China, where she spent three years at Kum Bum Monastery, on Tibet's eastern frontier. She then made her way by mule and yak to the Mekong River in the mountains of Yunan province. Her travel narrative begins at this point. Disguised as a beggar and accompanied only by Yongden, a Sikkimese monk whom she later adopted, she endured an astounding series of challenges over the course of four months, dodging authorities who would expel any foreigner and surviving bandits, many illnesses, frozen mountain passes, leech-infested jungles, scorching desert heat, protracted hunger, and utter exhaustion. David-Neel takes well-earned pride in what she went through to become the first Western woman to enter Lhasa.

David-Neel does not explain what Buddhism meant to her and hides her adherence to this worldview. A biography says she aimed her book at "an audience interested in the East but by no means specialists or necessarily inclined to Buddhism."[4] She knew that her potential audience was not ready for the story of a Western convert to Buddhism but would devour a tale of dangerous adventures and heroic triumph, spiced with glimpses of exotic religious practices. David-Neel describes many incidents when she witnessed or engaged in Tantric rituals that were part of the "short path" to awakening in one lifetime. She saw *lung-gom-pas*, men who could leap across the ground rapidly for days on end without a break for water or food. She encountered lamas and hermits who apparently knew things by telepathy. She kept herself alive more than once by *tum-mo* breathing, the generation of inner heat in frigid conditions that would ordinarily kill a person. She also recounts serene moments when, even at a time of life-threatening peril, she enjoyed "the delights of my solitude in the absolute silence, the perfect stillness of that strange white land, sunk in rest, in utter peace" (164). These various experiences may be taken as events

---

[4] Barbara Foster and Michael Foster, *Forbidden Journey: The Life of Alexandra David-Neel* (San Francisco: Harper and Row, 1987), 252. The Forsters' extensive research in David-Neel's private letters to her husband reveals sides of her character very different than the heroic image presented in *My Journey to Lhasa*.

of unselfing when the ordinary limits of human capacity and perception are transcended. Yet her vivid account of these events provides only hints about how her journey affected her understanding of Buddhism, and the concept of no-self is not important to her. *My Journey to Lhasa* proclaims the triumphant entrance of a woman into the all-male club of world-conquering adventurers. The Fosters' biography notes an irony about this Buddhist heroine: "Above everything, this willful woman who could beat a recalcitrant servant, this beneficiary of turn-of-the-century imperialism who defied an empire, stands for individual liberty, for the full expression of 'I' that her Buddhist philosophy denied."[5] Many Western Buddhist travel writers reveal their sense of conflict between attraction to the idea of no-self and their intense autobiographical focus. Some of them explore this paradox, but for David-Neel this is not an issue.

Just as David-Neel veils her participation in Tantric sexual practices and other episodes that would have shocked her audience, she may have been influenced by ideas about no-self to a greater degree than is apparent in what she published. For instance, a Buddhist recognition of the arbitrary nature of constructions of identity may have been a factor in David-Neel's remarkable capacity to step outside approved gender roles and go where no Western woman had set foot. *My Journey to Lhasa* is a fascinating adventure tale packed with information about Tibet in the 1920s, but it does not depict the author's religious experience, which I take to be constitutive of the genre of Western Buddhist travel narratives.[6]

Another travel narrative that contrasts with later works is Heinrich Harrer's *Seven Years in Tibet* (1953). This book recounts a two-year trek to Tibet and the five years Harrer spent there from 1946 to 1950, immersing himself in the culture and becoming a teacher of the XIV Dalai Lama. The story of his harrowing journey from a British internment camp in India through the Himalayas is an exciting story of survival and perseverance in brutal conditions. His glimpses of Tibetan religion along the way are evidence for him of the Tibetan people's "childlike mentality" (89).[7] Although Harrer says that "all my life I have been a seeker" (67) and he learned to meditate, he does not consider Tibetan Buddhism to be a spiritual path for himself. He criticizes Tibetans' superstition, fatalism, and

---

[5] Foster and Foster, *Forbidden Journey*, 315.
[6] David-Neel's later work *Magic and Mystery in Tibet* (New York: Dover, 1932; first published in French in 1929) conveys much information about "the doctrines and practices of the mystics and magicians of Tibet," including a discussion of how in meditation practice one realizes that the self does not exist (277–279). Is she speaking of her own experience? She doesn't say.
[7] Heinrich Harrer, *Seven Years in Tibet* (New York: Penguin, 1953).

resistance to progress, even though, like so many Occidental visitors, he also envies their deep faith and freedom from the vices and materialism of Western societies. Although fascinated by this unique culture, Harrer and his companion view it with detachment: "We contented ourselves with studying their customs, visiting their temples as spectators, and making presents of white silk scarves as etiquette prescribed" (202).

The aspect of Buddhism that most intrigues him is the people's faith in the divinity of their religious leader. Harrer develops a deep bond with the fourteen-year-old Dalai Lama, who he knows is lonely. For Harrer, adherence to Buddhism would require him to view his friend as a god. At one point he says, presumably in jest, that the young man's intelligence and wisdom "almost persuaded me to believe in reincarnation" (254). The Dalai Lama hopes to convert Harrer to Buddhism by sending him to distant places and directing him from Lhasa. This would demonstrate the truth of ancient Tibetan stories about saints who perform actions far from their physical bodies. Harrer responds with a laugh: "All right, Kundün, when you can do that, I will become a Buddhist, too" (287). In spite of Harrer's great affection for the Dalai Lama and the Tibetan people and his lifelong work to create understanding and sympathy for their situation since the Chinese invasion, he does not consider their religion as a live option for himself. His understanding of Buddhism focuses on faith in the divinity of the Dalai Lama, and he never mentions the concepts of suffering, impermanence, and no-self or selflessness. Harrer does not use Buddhist ideas to interpret his own experience but rather presents his story in the form of heroic adventure and immersion in an exotic culture. His story, too, is very different from travel narratives beginning with Lama Govinda's *The Way of the White Clouds* and Peter Matthiessen's *The Snow Leopard*, which both explain Tibetan Buddhism to outsiders and interpret the author's life using Buddhist ideas.

Many travel narratives set in Tibet, like those mentioned so far, involve a "trek." This was originally an Afrikaner term for their organized migration to settle (and conquer) a new area. This word became used for other long journeys that involve arduous walking, complex logistical arrangements, and interaction with local guides and inhabitants. A Tibetan trek provides the setting and plot for many Western interpretations of Tibetan Buddhism and is often the catalyst for the author's transformation. In this chapter, I examine four travel narratives by writers who understand their experiences in Tibet in terms of ideas about no-self or selflessness. For Jim Reynolds (Ajahn Chandako), Robert Thurman and Tad Wise, Ian Baker, and Matteo Pistono, the tale of a trek provides an opportunity to track the self. Excellent narratives about trekking in Tibet have also been written by those committed to other religious traditions or by agnostics such as Colin Thubron, who, in *To a Mountain in Tibet* (2011), considers Buddhist ideas about impermanence as he mourns a sister who died many years earlier on a Swiss mountain.[8]

*

Jim Reynolds's *The Outer Path: Finding My Way in Tibet* (1992) shows a clear and decisive change in the author's life as a consequence of travel in Buddhist lands. From July to November 1987, Reynolds traveled from Hong Kong across China and entered eastern Tibet through Yunan province. Walking, bicycling, and hitchhiking on trucks, he traversed Tibet, visited Lhasa and the traditional pilgrimage site Mount Kailash, and left the country via Nepal. During this brief period, Tibet was relatively accessible to Westerners. While Reynolds was there, Chinese suppression of Tibetan culture took a violent turn in response to protests in Lhasa, and China expelled all foreign tourists from Tibet. The "outer path" in Tibet was a crucial stage in the transition from twenty-four-year-old Jim Reynolds to Ajahn Chandako, as the Theravada monk is now known.

At the time of his Tibetan journey, Reynolds had recently practiced Vipassana meditation for several months at Wat Pah Nanachat in Thailand, the forest monastery founded by Ajahn Chah to instruct Westerners. He wanted to commit his life to Buddhism but hesitated, still uncertain. The Tibetan journey was partly a test to see whether the mental awareness he had cultivated at the monastery would continue: "I was still filled with a restless energy, so I decided to reenter the world of distractions to see whether my mind was any more calm, any less troubled by the defilements of anger, greed, and delusion, than it was before I had gone to Thailand" (3).[9] Reynolds could have traveled anywhere or simply tried to live a secular life, but he was drawn to Tibet for two reasons. He shared the usual Western fascination with its remote mountains and rugged people: "I wanted to explore Himalayan reaches long forbidden to Western eyes and to see areas nearly untouched by Western influence"; and he deliberately chose a place where travel was difficult and suffering would test what he had learned in the monastery: "I was ready for *dukkha* travel" (4).

---

[8] Colin Thubron, *To a Mountain in Tibet* (New York: Harper Collins, 2011).
[9] Jim Reynolds, *The Outer Path: Finding My Way in Tibet* (Sunnyvale, California: Fair Oaks Publishing, 1992).

156   Trekking and Tracking the Self in Tibet

Suffering and dissatisfaction were not hard to find. Lacking official permission to travel in Tibet, Reynolds was always anxious about being arrested. He forges a phony document saying he is authorized to study plants and animals in Yunan, and on the first part of the journey disguises himself as a peasant riding a bicycle. At many junctures, he is told to return the way he had come, held captive for several days, or forced to hole up and hide. He encounters incessant rain for days on end, altitude sickness, scanty or inedible food, numerous physical ailments, and winter conditions that bring frostbite, snow blindness, and several times nearly fatal exposure. Vicious dogs attack. He encounters a wide range of responses from local people and Chinese officials. Through all these ordeals he plods on, and at the end of his journey, crossing the Himalayan mountains alone at night in brutal winter conditions, he realizes: "I am learning nothing if not patient endurance on this trip, and for that alone my time has not been wasted" (164–165). These many forms of *dukkha* disclose his attachments, including to self: "I'm trying to use this experience as an opportunity to contemplate Dhamma, the teachings of the Buddha. I know that it is my attachment to things, people, even my 'self,' that is the cause of my discontent" (28). In spite of frequent lapses when he is disappointed or despairs, Reynolds affirms, in Lhasa at about the midpoint of his journey, that he is making progress in being able to observe suffering and let it go: "What I've discovered is that when I don't fight the discomfort, when I let it go, my suffering is less. When I accept the problems that arise, they lose their power over me" (79).

The climax of the journey takes place at Lake Manasarovar, near Mount Kailash, when Reynolds takes shelter for a few days in a cave and reflects on his journey. Settling down helps him realize that he had lost the "meditative stillness" he knew in Thailand and that as he traveled he was "sucked back into old habits, caught up in goals, worries, excitement, and disappointment" (128). He questions his life on the outer path as "half monk and half adventurer." The appeal of a whole-hearted dedication to an inner path becomes stronger, and he realizes that it requires stability and tranquility. With this new readiness for Buddhist monastic life comes an appreciation for the ethical vows and behavior that are prerequisites for inner peace. When he was first drawn to Buddhism, Reynolds admired Jack Kerouac and the dharma bums. He imitated their attitude that "we're all ultimately enlightened already, so anything goes," a pseudo-Zen philosophy that allowed him to "shoplift being Buddha" (132). Reynolds realizes that his life on the road, with occasional partying, constant anxiety, and deception of Chinese authorities, does not lead to clarity and peace of mind. At this moment of recognition, he decides to become a monk:

Trekking and Tracking the Self in Tibet

> At the beginning of this trip, I wasn't sure I was ready to become a monk. In many ways, I think I needed one last, exciting journey in the outside world. But this trip has shown me that I'm more ready to make a spiritual commitment, to enter a monastery, and to devote my life to meditation, than I had ever imagined. As a monk, I can spend my time looking within, exploring the inner path. (132–133)

When Reynolds went to Tibet, it was not its distinctive forms of Buddhism that drew him. He was not attracted to esoteric practices and quests for supernatural power, preferring "the simple 'clean the toilet and be mindful' approach of Zen, of being aware of the present moment" (26–27). In the Theravada monastery, he appreciated its "nuts and bolts approach of developing the mind" (27). Reynolds was initially attracted to Buddhism because of the intellectual appeal of its worldview; he was convinced by its analysis of the causes of suffering and the path to freedom. As he travels through Tibet, he comes to respect and admire its people, whose way of life is imbued with Buddhist practices and beliefs. As he witnesses their resolute resistance to Chinese attempts to suppress their culture and religion, he sees the depth of their commitment: "The power of such faith has carried Tibetan Buddhism through years of vicious persecution" (158–159). In Tibet, Reynolds began to understand that Buddhism could and should be expressed not only in meditation and the insights that grow out of it but also in every daily activity. This enlarged sense of Buddhism as a living faith that encompasses but transcends intellectual ideas comes about through many encounters and interactions during his travels.

After his journey, Reynolds returned to his home in California. He was struck by "how modern society obsessively and neurotically attempts to eliminate any trace of physical or mental discomfort" (179). Efforts to avoid *dukkha* or suppress it with alcohol, distractions, or sensory stimulation only increase dissatisfaction. Traveling taught him an alternative; he learned to be content in unpleasant conditions and to develop equanimity and patient endurance. The continual uncertainties and deprivations of his trek forced him to be alert, aware, and flexible. When he finally decides that the outer path leads in circles, he turns inwards:

> The continual moving around, the constant hassles and excitement eventually became mere distractions. The road is a good teacher, but by the end of my journey I saw the limits of what I could learn from it.
>
> For a while I wasn't sure if the outer path was leading me somewhere or if I was just running in circles. But then I knew it was time to STOP. "Nothing to do, nowhere to go, no one to be." Just look and see. I was ready to devote myself to traveling the "inner path" and to turn all of my mind's attention inward to watch itself. (180)

In "About the Author," a brief note informs the reader that at the time of publication in 1992, Jim Reynolds was known as Chandako Bhikku and was a monk practicing at Wat Pah Nanachat. Since then, he has become Ajahn Chandako and the abbot of Vimutti Buddhist Monastery in New Zealand. He has not turned away entirely from the "outer path," as the ending of his book implies. His *Tales of Tudong* describes a period of wandering in 2008 in New Zealand when, like Ajahn Sucitto walking through India, he tries to live as a monk and practice mindfulness while on a long journey by foot, utterly dependent on the unpredictable generosity of whosoever he encounters.[10]

In *The Outer Path*, Reynolds explains the value of his Tibetan journey in two ways: it forced him to experience suffering and develop ways of enduring it and it led him to recognize his desire to practice Buddhism on an inner path without the distractions and stress of the physical journey. Twenty-five years after the publication of the book, Ajahn Chandako explained to me additional dimensions of his Tibetan journey.[11] He said that he went to Tibet partly because he knew that, once he became a Buddhist monk, China would not allow him to visit it. This comment suggests that his decision to become a monk had already been made or was further along in a long process of reflection and decision. Like Christian conversion narratives, Buddhist stories sometimes condense into a moment of insight a lengthy period of transition.

Ajahn Chandako added that an important value of his travels was seeing how differently another culture reacts to suffering. In Tibet and Thailand, for instance, a person's accident or injury sometimes provokes amused laughter, which may shock or anger a Western visitor. These differing reactions indicate that every response to suffering depends on many factors and could be otherwise. The relativizing effect of encountering another culture's attitudes to suffering can help dislodge one's immediate reaction and help a person imagine other possible ways to respond.

The Outer Path is a striking story of transformation that portrays the author just at the time of transition from lay to monastic life. Reynolds presents his Tibetan journey as the crucial turning point when he made that momentous decision.

*

[10] This undated document is available at Ajahn Chandako's website, vimutti.org.nz/teachings/writings.

[11] In conversation July 2, 2017, in Northfield, Minnesota.

In October 1995, Robert Thurman, the renowned scholar and professor of Buddhism at Columbia University, led a group of nine trekkers on a journey to and around Mount Kailash in remote western Tibet. This traditional pilgrimage route involves walking for several days to the revered mountain, circumnavigating its thirty-two-mile circuit of sacred sites, and visiting Lake Manasarovar. Along the way, Thurman gave dharma talks and guided meditations based on an advanced Tantric path to enlightenment. One member of the group was Tad Wise, a novelist, former student, and friend of Thurman. Wise was drawn to Tibetan Buddhism and to Thurman as a spiritual guide, yet he resists their teachings as he struggles with several personal issues. In 1999, Thurman and Wise published *Circling the Sacred Mountain*, an account of this pilgrimage.[12] The core of Thurman's dharma talks is teachings about the contrast between "addiction to self" and selflessness, and Wise's reactions reveal his difficulties and challenges in accepting and living out his mentor's understanding of Tibetan Buddhism.

Thurman and Wise take turns narrating the chapters of *Circling the Sacred Mountain*, so the reader gets two contrasting perspectives on the pilgrimage. Almost all of Thurman's words are transcribed from tape-recorded dharma talks explicating a dense and difficult ancient text, *The Blade Wheel of Mind Reform*. Although Thurman translates these abstruse ideas into a contemporary American idiom that makes them come alive, we learn little about his own spiritual journey. He speaks from a position of authority as an eminent scholar of Buddhism, the first American to be ordained as a Tibetan Buddhist monk, and a close friend of the XIV Dalai Lama. Thurman is a leading interpreter, practitioner, and advocate of Tibetan Buddhism in the West. Although he understands and describes the forms of delusion and suffering that make people miserable, in this book he no longer seems afflicted by ordinary human cares. Not only does he describe the ideal of selflessness as he understands it after many decades of practice and study; he demonstrates it, displaying no lingering attachments or uncertainties. In Wise's eyes, at least, Thurman is a contemporary bodhisattva devoted to bringing others to enlightenment.

Tad Wise, in, contrast, discloses several personal issues that worry him throughout the journey. He has fathered three children by three different women and engaged in numerous other sexual relationships. He wonders whether to marry the mother of his most recently born child and feels

---

[12] Robert Thurman and Tad Wise, *Circling the Sacred Mountain: A Spiritual Adventure Through the Himalayas* (New York: Bantam Books, 1999).

guilty for having left them behind so soon after the birth. Wise refers many times to past short-term affairs and his lust for Tibetan women he encounters, sounding like Augustine at the point when he felt enslaved by his own sexual desires yet unwilling to change. He also struggles with alcohol abuse. As significant as these outward behaviors is his flickering awareness of an underlying selfishness and narcissism that impedes his commitment to Buddhism: "I falter on the central tenet of 'selflessness' since, like many committed to the arts, I suffer from an enlarged sense of self-importance" (17). At times, both Wise's self-preoccupation and Thurman's lectures become tiresome, but the alternation and contrast between them illuminate the gap between the theory of no-self and human experience and the reality of both spiritual aspiration and all-too-human fallibility.

From Katmandu, the group drives into Tibet and through the Himalayas. When they arrive at Lake Manasarovar, in sight of Mount Kailash, Thurman addresses the central theme of the book, what Wise calls "my nemesis, the teaching of the wisdom of selflessness" (106). Thurman uses the term selflessness rather than no-self to describe the ideal and goal of Buddhist practice: "The teaching of selflessness is the Buddha's greatest gift to the world" (110). Understanding this crucial idea alleviates the cause of suffering: the delusion that one has a fixed and essential self.

This delusion is a real and inextricable part of human experience. Elaborating a basic Buddhist distinction, Thurman differentiates between the illusion of an "absolute self" that is timeless and independent and the "relative self" that must function in the world. Buddha did not recommend that his followers meditate upon selflessness; rather, they should meditate on the self, in order to discern its true nature. Watching every moment of consciousness, as well as the watcher of the self, becomes a dizzying, twirling effort that Tibetan sages liken to a diamond cutter: "The diamond is that sense of a unique, absolute, and sustained inner core, and when it spins around looking for itself it becomes a drill and it drills through itself" (113–114). This meditative exercise disrupts and disorients the ordinary sense of self, and "suddenly you feel like you're open as the sky" (114) or like water flowing into water, at one with the world. In the blissful dreamlike state of unbroken concentration (*samadhi*), there is no sense of separateness from other things.

This state of decentered oneness with the world, "the experiential understanding of selflessness," is Thurman's version of unselfing. It happens primarily during meditation, although something like it is triggered

Trekking and Tracking the Self in Tibet

by certain moments of awe or exhaustion during the pilgrimage. He is less interested in describing the experience than its consequences. A person returns from selflessness to the world and one's ordinary or relative sense of self but with a difference, having realized that one's usual sense of separateness from other things is a habitual and arbitrary viewpoint, not an absolute reality. Having known the boundaries of the self to melt away, a person can be more generous and compassionate. This state, too, is temporary: "You will become egocentric again" (116). When old habits reappear, however, a person can return to meditation practices that elicit and foster selflessness. The process of integrating the blissful wisdom of the selfless state with action in the world is never finished. For Thurman, recognition of selflessness does not eliminate consciousness of "I" nor mean that the ego disappears forever:

> This state should not be described as egolessness, because the ego is just the pronoun "I," which you get even better at deploying when you no longer mistake its referent as something absolute. When you're in the relative state—the aftermath state—you know who you are. You're "I," you're the person who just had the equipoised Samadhi. You don't think the equipoised Samadhi is your essence, any more than your alienated ignorance was your essence. You don't cling to that timeless feeling of infinity as if it were some sort of soul. Your mind and body ultimately maintain a calm unity of wisdom while fully engaging with the creative diversity of compassion. (116)

Guiding his group through advanced meditative practices, Thurman prepares them for an experience of selflessness that could help each of them to engage the world with a distinctive but not absolutized sense of self. His teachings about selflessness are the most developed theoretical account of no-self in Western Buddhist travel narratives.

It is significant that teachings about selflessness come before engaging in Tantric practices and circumambulating Mount Kailash, not after them. Thurman holds that one must first have a clear intellectual understanding of selflessness:

> You must be aware that any sense of self or reality is constructed, relative, interactive, and not absolute. If you have never dislodged the habitual absolutism of the ordinary self-habit and then begin to imagine: "Now I'm going to be the Superbliss Wheel Buddha," you will experience what Jung called inflation. You can become a megalomaniac, which soon leads to paranoia when you find the world does not agree with you. Selflessness is essential to ground the creation of the Buddha-self. (133)

Certain contrasting views of unselfing and mystical experience emphasize that interpretation comes after the crucial experience. For Thurman, however, proper understanding should precede an experience of self-transcendence and creates what that experience is: in this case, a distinctively Buddhist version of selflessness rather than Jung's inflation of the ego. For Thurman, language and conceptualization are constitutive of religious experience, not simply expressive of it.

In part II of the book, the group stops at each of eight sacred places on the circumambulation route around Mount Kailash: charnel grounds, monasteries, hermits' caves, secret paths, and other sites. At each spot, Thurman gives a lecture interpreting *The Blade Wheel of Mind Reform*, a spiritual treatise created a thousand years ago by Dharmarakshita and elaborated on in an eighteenth-century commentary by the fourth Panchen Lama. This teaching aims to transform the practitioner by "mind reform," a series of meditations that destroy the self's ingrained habits. The central metaphor of this spiritual alchemy involves turning the blade wheel, a fearsomely destructive weapon, against the self:

> A blade wheel is a weapon for doing battle with an enemy, like those little metal stars called *shaken* that ninjas use, with eight or twelve blades sticking out. This blade wheel hits our real enemy, which is our own inner habit of self-preoccupation. It causes damage—serious, blessed damage to narcissism, vanity, the self-habit. (126)

The ancient text addresses Yama taka, literally "Death Exterminator," a fierce and terrifying deity who attacks the greatest danger in human life, "the real devil": self-addiction. Preoccupation with self cuts us off from the rest of the world, killing "the source of our life and energy—our relationships with the rest of the world … Self-addiction is death because it is the essence of self-enclosure, the self-isolation that cuts off our living being from the interrelational weave of life" (127–128). A series of verses describes various negative habits of self-addiction, and each stanza ends by inviting Yamantaka to "Stomp! Stomp!" on a barrier to freedom and happiness.

The natural human reaction to the Blade Wheel's systematic assault on ego attachment is terror and defensiveness. Tad Wise's responses to Thurman's talks show both his attraction and resistance to the teachings. After a sermon about unsatisfying pleasures, Wise feels guilt and shame about his sexual addiction: "I swear it will be different but I know that after a few months I will get addicted to a certain woman. And it will go on a long time until I get addicted to another. Three children by three women and I'm only a good father to one" (157). He broods about harms he has caused, using images of the Blade Wheel slicing and cutting to describe how remorse tears at him.

Another form of resistance to the teachings is to discredit one's teacher. Wise identifies with Milarepa, who abandoned sorcery and became one of Tibet's most famous holy men. He compares Thurman to Marpa, the teacher who put Milarepa through ordeals before gradually giving him the deepest teachings. Although Thurman protests that "I'm no Marpa, and Tad's not Milarepa" (71), this archetypal teacher–student and guru–devotee relationship is frequently in Wise's mind as he describes his testy yet admiring relationship to Thurman. Whether or not Thurman consents, it is his face that flickers in and out of Wise's mind when he visualizes his mentors, along with Thomas Merton and the Dalai Lama. Wise understands why in Tibet the practice was to find a guru living three valleys distant, so that one wouldn't know his flaws and foibles. Along with a "clear case of hero-worship" (13) for Thurman, Wise reacts with prickly defensiveness to his mentor's teasing and occasional admonitions, which are a mild version of the attack on selfishness carried out by Tibetan Buddhism's wrathful deities. Wise's brooding, wounded vanity and moody dependence on his teacher's approval express the narcissism that mind reform is intended to correct.

Thurman's teachings are compelling yet somewhat disconnected from his own life. Although he teaches that the effort to integrate absolute truth with the relative reality of self goes on as part of every Buddhist's life, Thurman does not appear to struggle with his ego or the role of teacher and spiritual guide. He never reacts defensively, gets irritated by Wise or other participants, doubts himself, or worries about the journey. When he falls fifteen feet onto a boulder-strewn riverbank, narrowly avoiding serious accident, he laughs and discerns a lesson about respecting the powerful time of an eclipse. Throughout *Circling the Sacred Mountain*, Thurman acts like a bodhisattva devoted to helping others escape suffering. He will strike some readers as a classic absent-minded professor: verbose, pedantic, and immersed in abstruse teachings that sometimes seem remote from the practical realities of the world. Yet perhaps the reader, like Wise, is simply at a spiritual level that cannot recognize the relevance and applicability of the teachings or fully appreciate this teacher. We divert our attention to the messenger, away from a message we don't want to hear: the need to annihilate the sense of self that creates so much suffering.

The third and final section of *Circling the Sacred Mountain* shows what Thurman and Wise each learned from the pilgrimage, especially how teachings about selflessness can be expressed and lived out after the journey ends. For Thurman, the pilgrimage does not bring about a radical change but rather confirms and intensifies his prior understanding of

Buddhism. Wise's future commitment to Buddhist beliefs and practice remains in question, as does the effect of the journey on his character. Taking the bodhisattva vow to benefit all sentient beings "seems a very real option up here" (219), but he does not do so. Instead, he promises the universe "that it will be different. That I will be different, not so blind and self-centered and stupid" (218). This vow, although still focused on himself rather than others, seems a step in the right direction. Wise doesn't claim to have been transformed by the journey, but he expresses resolution and hope that his life will be different and points to lessons learned that may help him realize his intentions.

For instance, he may return to the Tibetan meditation practices that Thurman gave the group. One such exercise begins: "Imagine yourself as the chief Superbliss Buddha-deity in the center of the mandala in union with your consort, surrounded by sixty heroes and heroines" (281). This practice of visualizing oneself at a banquet with a community of deities and enlightened beings provides a glimpse of the oneness of all being and gives inspiration and feelings of bliss. When one simulates in meditation what it would feel like to be enlightened and compassionate, one is a step closer to realizing that condition in all of one's life. Memories of their trek may strengthen the returned travelers by giving them "a transcendent experience that is not apart from ordinary or relative experience" (287). Trekking in Tibet disclosed how the ordinary and extraordinary are intermingled, not two separate realities. Mount Kailash is an enormous mandala that reveals the nonduality of all of life.

Because self and selflessness are both real – or, better, both perspectives on the real – Thurman emphasizes being able to tolerate cognitive dissonance. That is, the absolute reality of selflessness and the relative reality of the ordinary self are equally valid perspectives, even though they appear contradictory. Thurman's last dharma talk takes place during a solar eclipse, when it is night and day at once. He interprets this uncanny astronomical event as an apocalyptic moment when the customary perception of the world ends and a new orientation becomes possible, one that perceives how habit and perspective influence what one takes to be the truth. During an eclipse the world "slips between realities" and cannot be comprehended in terms of ordinary dualities. The time when it is both day and night invites one to be open to nonduality and to appreciate opposed perspectives. For once, Tad Wise responds to Thurman's talk with silent appreciation, happy to enjoy the moment without questioning it.

Trekking and Tracking the Self in Tibet 165

In contrast to Western Buddhist travel narratives that end with the author eager to begin another pilgrimage, Thurman asserts that returning to Mount Kailash is not something that has to be repeated. Nor should the group yearn nostalgically for the place or the act of journeying. Unlike addictions, which because they aren't satisfying leave a person craving more, the Kailash pilgrimage is "a doorway to seeing the entire universe with axial centrality in every atom, feeling the bliss of male-female union in every cell, on the subtle plane of deepest reality experience" (336). We should not long to return to the mountain but rather "bring its blessings along with us and share them freely around the loving world. We will work within the nonduality of the extraordinary and the ordinary" (339). Thurman hopes the trek to Mount Kailash will transform each traveler so that he or she is energized to embrace and bless the world of jarring, conflicting perspectives. Returning pilgrims should neither reject nor absolutize the claims of the self, which contrast starkly with the ultimate truths of interdependence and selflessness.

A test of whether the pilgrims have benefited from their journey takes place as they leave Tibet and encounter Chinese border guards. Because Thurman had protested against Chinese atrocities and violations of human rights, there was initial uncertainty as to whether he would be allowed to enter Tibet, as well as lingering anxiety throughout the trek. When the travelers are stopped by surly border guards who want a bribe, everyone in Thurman's group is disturbed and frightened. This loss of equanimity makes Wise doubt that the pilgrimage accomplished anything. Yet unflappable Robert Thurman reframes the tense encounter and finds a lesson. To him, the border incident shows the importance of Buddhist practice in calm conditions, so that one knows what to strive for in tense ones. He acknowledges that their best insights seemed to dissolve when they encountered a small hassle. Their practice made a difference, however: "Did you watch yourself a little? Did you experiment with your spy-consciousness when you felt righteously innocent?" (298). As they load their truck to depart from Tibet, Thurman asks the group to pray for their drivers and the Chinese soldiers, to visualize them laughing, and to "push your heart into that joy with them" (307). Although prayer and meditation do not stop Tibet's current suffering, they contribute as causes and conditions to the spiritual evolution that Thurman believes is the only long-term hope for the Chinese and Tibetan peoples.

The final chapter, set in Katmandu, provides a chance to "test run the new Tad Wise" (345) without the presence of his teacher. His name seems significant: After his journey he is a little bit wiser yet well aware of the limitations of his tad of wisdom. He is a seeker of wisdom who recognizes that unruly desires and obsessions sometimes displace or undermine what he has learned. Wise meets a local man he calls Damon, the name Yeats used to describe his higher self. As Damon guides him through Katmandu, "the very last maze of my journey" (345), he presents Wise with several opportunities to practice selflessness, or at least to discipline his wayward desires. Attracted to a pretty young woman cleaning his hotel room, Wise considers seducing her. He doesn't, and this restraint may signify a change in his behavior, even as, like the converted Augustine, he recognizes and acknowledges continued feelings of lust. Damon guides Wise to an abbot who gives him a medicinal drink, assuring him "No booze" – perhaps both a description and an admonition to reform. Yet when Wise encounters a fortune-teller given to drink, he endorses Tantric excess rather than strict moral reform: "A drunken magician! Perfect. I've contributed a few days of sobriety to a Tantric master—which is a contradiction in terms, I know. Tantra does not recognize the word 'sober.' Everything is beyond belief always" (349). The oracle advises him to include a woman in his future spiritual practice and to seek as his guide a yogi or Tantra master rather than a monk.

In the final scene of *Circling the Sacred Mountain*, a beggar accosts Wise. Damon tells Wise to give the beggar the ceremonial shawl presented to him by the oracle. Later in the day, as Wise packs and is about to depart, Damon calls him down to the street, where the beggar returns the shawl. Wise and the beggar each bow and say "Namaste": "the divine being in me recognizes the divine being in you." Both the reality of individual selves and a spiritual truth that connects and encompasses them are joined in this choreography that acts out the meaning of Namaste. Like the ending of *The Snow Leopard*, when Peter Matthiessen realizes that Tukten is his true spiritual mentor, and as in many other Western Buddhist travel narratives, Wise concludes with a recognition scene in which he perceives his oneness or affinity with a very different person or foreign place. The sense of unity and belonging-together that – only for a moment – overcomes distinct and separate identities symbolizes the simultaneous nondual truths of selfhood and selflessness.

*

Ian Baker's *The Heart of the World* (2004) documents the author's fascination with the *beyul*, Tibet's "hidden lands" where revered scriptures are preserved for future generations. In journeying to these remote

Trekking and Tracking the Self in Tibet   167

Himalayan valleys, pilgrims may discover the interconnectedness of all life and experience a deepening of awareness similar to the Buddhist path to enlightenment.

Ian Baker first learned of the Tibetan hidden lands in 1977 as a student on a semester abroad program in Katmandu. *The Heart of the World* describes eight journeys between 1993 and 1998 to the forbidding Pemako region at the eastern edge of the Himalayas, centered on the Tsangpo River gorge. This enormous canyon, nearly 18,000 feet deep and 300 miles long, was rumored to contain a large waterfall, but its inaccessibility thwarted a succession of expeditions from the West and China. Baker's quest to find and measure this waterfall motivates several expeditions into Pemako from different directions, as well as a circumambulation of a remote mountain that a lama suggests will give him a mysterious key to unlock the secret of the gorge. *The Heart of the World* is an engrossing adventure story full of challenges and dangers: torrential rain, bitter cold, hunger, hordes of tormenting insects and leeches, avalanches, falls from steep cliffs, tigers, unpredictable porters, hostile tribal inhabitants, and the frustrating bureaucracy of the Chinese government. All of these threats and uncertainties make for a ripping good yarn. Adventure – being open to whatever happens – is also an essential ingredient in Buddhist pilgrimage:

> Tibetan tradition speaks of *Kha sher lamkhyer*—"whatever arises, carry it to the path"—a Buddhist injunction to abandon preferences and integrate all experience beyond accepting and rejecting. Without that dynamic openness to adventure (from the Latin *ad venio*, "whatever comes"), Tibetans say, pilgrimage devolves into ordinary travel and the hidden-lands—both physical and metaphysical—will never open. (104)[13]

Baker's journey is an opportunity to be open to the unexpected and to let go of his need to control experience. His expeditions require extensive logistical planning and complex coordination with other people, yet he must constantly adapt and improvise when things don't go according to plan.

In his introduction to Baker's narrative, the XIV Dali Lama asserts the value of travel to certain special places that elicit a deeper awareness of life and a sense of interconnection that is often hidden in daily life. "Visiting such places with a good motivation and appropriate merit, the pilgrim can learn to see the world differently from the way it commonly

---

[13] Ian Baker, *The Heart of the World: A Journey to Tibet's Lost Paradise* (New York: Penguin, 2004).

168 Trekking and Tracking the Self in Tibet

appears, developing and enhancing the Buddhist virtues of wisdom and compassion" (2). One of the many paradoxes of Buddhist pilgrimage (and journeys in other religious traditions) is that this travel seems to depend on the qualities of a particular location, yet its benefits are said to yield a kind of awareness that can be practiced anywhere. The Dalai Lama tells Baker that, although meditation is not dependent on place, "spiritually advanced beings leave imprints on the physical environment" (23). The effect of such a place is not automatic or certain, but for individuals who have prepared and practiced spiritual discipline, particular locations such as Tibet's *beyuls* are especially conducive for revealing the nature of the mind.

According to Tibetan Buddhist tradition, the primary thing that keeps our minds from recognizing the way things really are is the illusion of a separate, autonomous self. Baker is drawn to esoteric Tantric practices that overcome the sense of separation from the world: "The joyful awareness arising from the practice of Tantric yogas is never an end in itself, but a means for expanding deeper into the vast, open, nondual nature of *anatta*, or egolessness" (257). Like Tantric practices, a journey can dissolve consciousness of self and nurture a sense of connectedness to all things. Travel can bring experiential understanding of the Buddhist concept of emptiness, the lack of any enduring substance in both the self and the world.

Travel in the Pemako region has produced numerous vivid accounts that blend geographical description with depiction of exalted states of consciousness. Guidebooks by Tibetan lamas, accounts by Western explorers, and Baker's own self-analysis all portray moments when the writer feels as if he has transcended the limitations of ordinary awareness. These mind-boggling experiences are Baker's version of unselfing. A crucial passage interprets the moment when, in a circumambulation of Kundu Dorsempotrang, the mountain that Baker hopes will give him the "key" to reach the Tsangpo Gorge, a lama tells him that a rock wall covered with lichen is the place that can open a path to the heart of the *beyul*. Baker knows that the key is not simply getting to a place but perceiving it with a certain kind of awareness. Standing next to the cliff, he tries to still his mind and become receptive to whatever the rock will show him. He sees and feels with open hands the fungi, algae, and lichen beneath water flowing over the slab:

> The mist, the rain, the rock wall, the vegetal growth, the microorganisms veiled from sight, all entered through the pulsations and cuts in my scratched and torn hands, and where I could not go I could only yield

and be entered. The rain poured down my sleeves and neck and along my spine. The elements saturated me. All Pemako seemed to coalesce into the square foot of rock directly before me, and all its hidden depths were concealed only by my limited awareness and the mechanisms of mind itself.

The surface of the rock seemed to be turning to water beneath my touch and my vision began to waver and become porous, like a veil lifting. I felt at the edge of something just out of reach, but even as this thought intruded the feeling passed, and I was again standing against the rock, now aware that a small misstep would send me plummeting into empty space. (289–290)

In this moment of intense concentration on the present time and place, Baker's mind flickers between receptive openness and striving for something beyond what is present, just out of reach. As he tries to discern a message hidden in the cryptic script of lichen covering the enigmatic wet rock, "inner and outer experience had merged into a kind of dreamtime continuum in which familiar oppositions no longer pertained and anything seemed possible" (311). This event seems to be the key to the *beyul*; it shows that the significance of a place is linked to a state of mind. For a brief time, Baker encounters the world in a way that overcomes his sense of separation between inner self and external reality. He remains fully rooted in the world, not floating in a state of bliss, but fully aware of every detail and his perilous position on the rock.

Baker's final expedition into Pemako's hidden lands takes him into the depths of the Tsangpo Gorge. His account of this trek, too, weaves together a classic adventure story, scientific and historical accounts of the region, Tibet's Buddhist lore, and his own spiritual quest. Using ropes to descend from steep cliffs, his team discovers and measures the waterfall whose legend enticed Tibetan lamas as well as Western and Chinese pilgrims and explorers. In Buddhist thought, a waterfall has many symbolic meanings, pointing to the world as an entrancing spectacle and to the ephemerality of all things. In his introduction to the book, the Dalai Lama explains:

> Waterfalls serve an important role in Buddhist practice as symbols of impermanence and supports for certain kinds of meditation. Such places often have a power that we cannot easily describe or explain. When approached with an awareness of the emptiness and luminosity underlying all appearances, they can encourage us to expand our vision not only of ourselves, but of reality itself. I hope that Ian Baker's book about his journeys into one of the least explored regions of Tibet will inspire others not only to venture into unknown lands on a geographical level, but also to discover the inner realms within which our own deepest nature lies hidden. (2)

Waterfalls suggest the transitory nature of all things, including the individual self and its flashes of insight. They suggest a union of form and transformation, like Thomas Merton's description of the mountain Kanchenjunga. As Baker gazes in awe, the stupendous power of the Tsangpo River explodes into foam and frees itself of form. To behold this colossal wave of sunlight, water, and air is to be confronted with impermanence, a liquid image of constant becoming. Because the seething cascade of foam has no fixed boundaries, the group's scientific instruments can't measure its dimensions, and Baker realizes the absurdity of their mission.

As well as the self's insubstantiality, the waterfall symbolizes the unification of "above" and "below" in human nature, the active flow and circulation of power through the body and mind. The impossibility of grasping flowing water also suggests that one cannot hold on to any condition, sense of the self, or conceptualization of ultimate reality. Intense desires, including the longing for religious truth and experience, divide one from what is sought and estrange one from the present moment. The culmination of the Tsangpo Gorge expedition is this moment when Baker gives up his need to control experience and loses himself in wonder at the spectacle of the Falls. He surrenders to

> the incalculable reality that had enveloped us—without further thought of walls, doors, or keys. If there was any innermost secret to be revealed here in the configurations of cliffs, waters, and oval doorways, I felt no need for it: the inconceivable wonder that surrounded us was already more than enough, an intertwining world of snakes, orchids, lithe huntresses, and evanescent mist. I felt no yearning for more etheric realms. (405–406)

The Tsangpo waterfall is a tangible image of *anatta* that shows that what we believe has enduring and fixed nature is in constant flux, lacking permanent substance. "As the Buddha pointed out, waterfalls are in essence no thing at all, just shimmering displays of water, light, and air, their very features—like ourselves—an optical illusion of the senses" (436).

Baker asserts that what he discovered on his journeys is available everywhere. His quest for the perfect realm said to lie at the heart of Pemako finally leads to this affirmation: "There is no paradise beyond that which is already present, even if still hidden from our view. The gates of Yangsang pervade all space, and the portals are everywhere, as numerous, say the texts, as pores on the skin or blades of grass on the earth" (406). Hidden lands are revealed by finding a new mode of perception, whether or not this results from making a journey. Cultivating receptive awareness is the essence of both meditation practice and Buddhist pilgrimage. A journey to a special place may be helpful, but it will inevitably have ups and downs, moments of serenity, and periods of intense anxiety and striving. Brief epiphanies that reveal the meaning of no-self are quickly interrupted when Baker needs to act to stay warm, dry, fed, and safe on the dangerous ordeal and by tense and wary negotiations with his team, support staff, local Tibetans, and the Chinese.

In spite of the exalted mystical affirmations that Baker makes at several points, his return home entails the return of a restless and insecure ego. As the expedition makes its way back through Tibet, Pemako's sacred space becomes a distant memory, and Baker feels as if he crossed a threshold into profane space. His team reached the Tsangpo Falls just before a Chinese expedition that was exploring the Pemako region to investigate the possibility of building a huge hydroelectric dam twice the size of the Three Gorges Dam, which would flood the Tsangpo gorge and obliterate its unique environment and human cultures. Baker criticizes the Chinese lack of concern for the environment, calls for preservation of this threatened region, and hates the media frenzy that acclaims his team as the winner of an international competition to discover a real Shangri-La. When he reports to the National Geographic Society, which helped sponsor his expedition, Baker wonders whether he is betraying the deeper spiritual meanings of Pemako. The end of the narrative, which describes the uncertain fate of the Tsangpo Gorge and Baker's return to the United States, shows that the mystical moment when he felt at one with reality cannot be sustained. After the peak experience, one must descend the mountain. After unselfing comes the return to self.

The Heart of the World depicts striking moments of self-transcendence. Does it show self-transformation? Was Ian Baker changed by his journey? How is he different than the person who first heard about the Pemako region? Did he internalize the meaning of *anatta* in a way that changes how he perceives and experiences reality? These questions about an author's character are hard to answer with assurance. *The Heart of the World* covers several journeys and portrays Baker from 1977 until about 2000, when he wrote the book at a friend's house in New York. A lot of personal growth and religious learning and experience took place over these decades, much of it because of his journeys and research on Tibetan Buddhism and the Pemako region. Baker is recognizably the same person at the end of his travels as he was at the beginning. His voice as narrator gives a sense of continuity to all his adventures and thinking. He has not escaped from the self-consciousness about personal identity that is central in autobiographical writing. At the same time, Baker changed in two distinct ways. He experienced moments when ordinary self-consciousness dropped away and he felt identified or merged with his surroundings. Even though these moments do not last, they disclose a potential way of being that may again be realized, and to which he will try to remain receptive and open.

The second way in which Ian Baker seems to be a different person than when he started his travels is his new perspective on the question of the self's essential nature, which involves, paradoxically, a letting go or evading of the question. A lama points out to him that "not to find mind is to discover its true nature" (404). Empty space can open up within experience, allowing a glimpse or fresh perception of a reality not filtered or projected by the needy self. Buddhist ideas help Baker to articulate a conception of selfhood as a construction that is both real, in that a distinctive personal identity shapes what happens to one, and an illusion if one thinks the self has a permanent essence. At the end of *The Heart of the World*, Baker returns to the divisions of ordinary life with an ideal of openness and receptivity to the ever-changing present moment. He seeks to realign his consciousness with this ideal, just as in meditation consciousness wanders but comes back again and again to the breath. This travel memoir shows the continuity of the writer's character evident in any autobiography; it also portrays moments of self-transcendence when Baker embraces a new and different way of being in the world. Baker's depiction of how his Tibetan treks changed him is decisively shaped by his understanding of the Buddhist *dharma*, especially the concept of *anatta*.

*

In the Shadow of the Buddha (2011) recounts Matteo Pistono's several pilgrimages to Tibet to visit four sites associated with Tertön Sogyal Lerab Lingpa (1856–1926). This man was a revered "treasure revealer," mystic, teacher of the XIII Dalai Lama, and spiritual leader of his country at a time when its independence was threatened by China and the West. Pistono's several treks and journeys led to a growing understanding of and commitment to the bodhisattva's vow to free all beings from suffering. To bring this vow into the realm of politics involves Pistono in difficult and dangerous human rights work documenting Tibet's contemporary political ordeal. His journeys into Tibet have a strong political dimension that expresses his "socially engaged" Buddhism.

Before his pilgrimage, Pistono had worked in Wyoming on environmental politics. Although he had practiced meditation in Nepal with a Tibetan lama, what serenity he found soon dissipated. "In the face of

Trekking and Tracking the Self in Tibet

my political adversaries, a vindictive mind would arise with ferocity. The divide between my social activism and spiritual practice was vast because I didn't know how to take the insights and peace I experienced on the meditation cushion into the world" (4).[14] Disillusioned with politics, he went to London to study Indian philosophy. There, in 1996, he encountered Sogyal Rinpoche, one of two reincarnations of Tertön Sogyal, who exemplified the union of politics and spiritual wisdom to which Pistono aspired. (A tertön, or treasure revealer, discovers and makes known ritual objects and religious teachings that were hidden in Tibet by Padmasambhava, an eighth-century master considered a founder of Tibetan Buddhism.) Pistono went to India for a retreat with the Dalai Lama, who similarly embodies the ideal of the bodhisattva. Inspired by this encounter, Pistono took the bodhisattva vow to benefit others before attaining enlightenment.

At the suggestion of Sogyal Rinpoche, Pistono went to Tibet to meet another reincarnation of Tertön Sogyal, Khenpo Jikmé Dhuntsok. Encountering this man gives Pistono a glimpse into the possibility of a form of awareness free of self-consciousness: "Looking into his eyes, I felt Khenpo's thought-free awareness being poured into me. Only crystal-clear awareness remained. I was looking into the face of awareness itself, where the looker, the looking, and that which is being looked at dissolve of their own accord" (29). This prominent teacher tells Pistono to visit four places that figured in Tertön Sogyal's life: "Kalzang Monastery, where Tertön Sogyal met his first teacher; the Jokhang Cathedral in Lhasa, where Tertön Sogyal entered the Dalai Lama's court; the Cave That Delights the Senses near Palpung Monastery, where he revealed a powerful phurba practice; and Nyagar in Golok, where Tertön Sogyal passed away" (32). Later, Pistono realizes that these four places parallel the pilgrimage sites tied to the historical Buddha: where he was born, attained enlightenment, gave his first teachings, and passed into nirvana. Starting in 2000, Pistono worked as a journalist in Katmandu for eight years to fund frequent trips to Tibet to visit the places associated with Tertön Sogyal and to learn from contemporary masters, yogis, and hermits who pass on the oral traditions of this spiritual lineage. He rode buses, hitchhiked, and walked for weeks to visit every location in which the great master lived and taught. Interspersed with Pistono's narrative of his journeys are accounts of the lives and teachings of sages and tertöns and the history of Tibet's

---

[14] Matteo Pistono, *In the Shadow of the Buddha: One Man's Journey of Discovery in Tibet* (New York: Plume, 2011).

174   Trekking and Tracking the Self in Tibet

struggles to defend its political and spiritual heritage against internal and external threats.

As Pistono pursues this pilgrimage, it turns in an unexpected direction. Again and again, he encounters Tibetans who tell him about Chinese persecution, abuse, and torture. He learns of monasteries closed or destroyed and witnesses the scars and burns of ordinary Tibetans punished for carrying symbols of their religion. Pistono sees the Tibetan people's deep love for the Dalai Lama and their frustration and pain because of his exile and vilification by the Chinese government. Tibetans ask him to provide evidence of these human rights abuses to international advocacy groups and Western governments. Pistono's pilgrimage develops a political dimension when he turns to documenting graphic accounts of persecution. He photographs demolished monasteries and secret prisons where Buddhists are incarcerated. He smuggles out of Tibet written testimony about the situation there. To get this evidence to the West, he must evade the huge Chinese security network that includes internet surveillance and undercover agents wearing plain clothes or monastic robes. Issues of trust and mistrust arise constantly as he interacts with Tibetans and tries to protect those who might be harmed by his actions. His extremely dangerous journeys are frustrated or discouraged by many obstacles. However, Pistono continues his efforts to bear witness to what he has seen, fulfilling requests by numerous Tibetans including his mentors and the Dalai Lama. He also becomes an intermediary, bearing messages between spiritual leaders inside and outside Tibet.

Throughout his sojourns in Tibet, Pistono feels angry at China. At moments, he blames all Chinese people for their government's brutal actions. He is also bitter that the US government became less willing to confront China's violations of human rights after 9/11 because of "the Bush-Cheney doctrine of rendition, secret prisons, and use of torture" (171). He criticizes the Obama administration for downplaying its concerns about Tibet in order to prioritize economic and security issues.

In Pistono's search for a better way to participate in political action, he discovers an unexpected resource in Tibet's phurba ritual. A phurba is a three-bladed dagger used ceremonially. In his first encounter with this practice, Pistono sees Uncle Apu, an elderly sage, plunge the phurba into an effigy. Pistono is shocked at this violent action, which seems to contradict all that he has learned about the need for compassion. He is told that the phurba ritual symbolizes an expression of compassion. It is one of a bodhisattva's skillful means, uniting compassion with fierce assault on what obstructs the enlightenment of others. The phurba ritual can only be performed by a

Trekking and Tracking the Self in Tibet   175

person who has overcome negativity in his heart and mind. Like other practices of Vajrayana Buddhism such as chanting a mantra or contemplating a mandala, this ritual helps an adept to internalize a spiritual ideal. Shocking imagery is used – in some cases, sexual imagery or practices, in this case, stabbing an enemy – to reveal a truth about the reality that humans split into what is acceptable and what is rejected. Although Pistono grew up as a Roman Catholic, he left the Church when he was in college. Yet he realizes that the ritual and ceremonial aspects of Tibetan Buddhism speak deeply to him partly because of his Christian background.

Identifying with a deity can change a person's sense of self, as we saw in Robert Thurman's explanation of Tantric visualization practices. Sogyal Rinpoche teaches that the phurba is a "weapon of compassion" wielded by the deity Vajrakilaya. By identifying with a divine figure while in a state of contemplation, "we can change the way we react to what arises in our minds and the challenges in life" (98). The crucial issue for Pistono is how to understand and express his own anger. According to Sogyal Rinpoche, compassionate wrath is different from destructive anger:

> While the intention behind ordinary hatred and anger is to inflict pain and do harm, the intention behind Vajrakilaya's wrath is quickly and decisively to remove the obstacles and delusions that hinder spiritual progress and cause suffering. Wrathful enlightened activity may appear in some ways akin to anger, but its motivation is the opposite, as it is driven by compassion. (99)

This kind of energy empowers compassion and can fuel the right kind of participation in politics.

In the final section of the book, Pistono has a breakthrough when a Tertön named Wangchen helps him to experience anger in a new way. This sage advises him: "Should you wish to look into the essential nature of mind, do not fabricate or transform anything, and do not 'meditate,' but rather, allow whatever arises to be liberated by itself, without inviting or following after thoughts" (191). The trouble comes from thinking about thoughts, grasping for and being distracted by them. Rather than focusing on it, he must "liberate his anger" by allowing it to pass: "Instead of acting from that swirling rage that is within you at this moment, recognize it just for what it is—a powerful force of energy—and let that force blaze your awareness, not your anger" (192). Instead of resisting anger and brooding about his inability to overcome it, Pistono learns to observe anger with equanimity. His resentful thoughts dissipate, leaving him free, at rest in lucid awareness. This incident, when Pistono perceives anger dissolving, is a form of unselfing: he becomes able to see as other than himself an emotion that had seemed to consume him and take over his identity. The experience suggests that a new way of being is possible if he does not identify with the anger that had dominated and defined him. For many years, Pistono had occasionally known in meditation the clarity and freedom from distraction that foster vivid awareness of the constantly changing moment. Now, he glimpses the possibility of bringing this kind of awareness into political action, thereby calming turbulent emotions. It is not as if he is completely changed by this experience or will never feel anger again; he knows that he will continue to be challenged by the frustrating limitations of what can be achieved politically, as well as his own weaknesses. Yet now he knows what is possible and the path he must try to follow, and he forms the intention to do so.

Pistono thus describes two new understandings of anger that seem contradictory. The phurba ritual involves transforming anger into a tool of compassion and accepting it as a part of oneself. This is similar to other deity yoga practices of Vajrayana, which are intended to "transform our perception to reveal directly our enlightened nature. Once this enlightened potential fully manifests, we can truly benefit others" (14). The second new perspective on anger that Pistono learns is the possibility of "liberating" it through detachment so that it passes away and is no longer part of one. These two perspectives suggest contrasting views of a person's relationship to anger, based on identifying with it or dissociating oneself from it. These strategies are both skillful means intended to transform what was experienced as destructive and paralyzing anger that dominates the self. Each of these methods involves a form of unselfing that reveals the potential for a different kind of relationship to anger. Both strategies attempt to transform anger from being only a destructive weapon of the ego; they liberate the self from being dominated by rage. Although the two practices seem so different or even contradictory, Pistono's teacher, Wangchen, links them: "The physical phurba is only a reminder for the sublime practice of liberating anger upon arising—this is now your practice, so persevere" (198). One must both recognize anger and let it go, accept what has been rejected yet not identify it with one's essential selfhood.

Pistono's pilgrimage comes to a climax when he reaches the Nyagar encampment, the fourth site associated with Tertön Sogyal, where he made his final home and "passed into nirvana" (204). The rock houses, temple, and stupa lie in ruins, torn down after the Communist takeover of Tibet. As he sits on the rubble that remains from the tertön's home, Pistono is

Trekking and Tracking the Self in Tibet 177

forcefully struck by the truth of impermanence and the knowledge that all he ever has is the present moment. He sees, too, another truth: every moment contains the seeds out of which will grow the future. He links the bodhisattva's commitment to benefit others to full consciousness of the present:

> The spiritual path of the bodhisattva is about integrating whatever circumstances arise right now, whatever presents itself, not only the inspiring moments but the painful situations as well. The path of living in the world is about working to bring about the conditions for others to find security and contentment—and this can only occur when we are fully cognizant of reality as it presents itself, situation by situation. Both the spiritual and political paths are accomplished by maintaining clear awareness of what is clearly before us. (207)

He feels that the peace he experiences at the ruined stupa, when he finished his pilgrimage and had no more to accomplish, is what he has been striving for.

Before Pistono departs from Nyagar, he vows to build a new stupa to honor the life and teachings of Tertön Sogyal. After arranging with local leaders for the new construction, Pistono journeys back to Nyagar to install sacred relics given for this purpose by the Dalai Lama. Like the lotus that blooms in a dirty pond, the occasion that honors the Tertön rises above the bitter anger and aggression befouling Tibet. The stupa symbolizes the hope that all may transcend violent impulses and ignorance and act with compassion for others. Pistono's outer pilgrimage ends at the Enlightenment Stupa of Tertön Sogyal, and his inner pilgrimage culminates in a reaffirmation of the bodhisattva's commitment to dispel the misery of others. The spiritual path merges with political and social engagement in the vow to bring all beings from illusion and suffering to true and lasting contentment.

Pistono's self-transformation is not a conversion to Buddhism but rather a new understanding and commitment to a particular form of Buddhism. His movement to what is often called "engaged Buddhism" can be compared to Dorothy Day's transition from a form of Catholicism that seemed to her disconnected from the urgent political questions of the 1930s to the form of commitment expressed in the organization she founded with Peter Maurin, the Catholic Worker Movement. Using Lewis Rambo's typology of conversion, these transformations are not "tradition transitions" from one major religious tradition to another but rather involve both intensification, that is, revitalized commitment to a tradition, and affiliation, a change from minimal involvement with an institution or community to full commitment.[15] The experiences that precipitated the change in Pistono's way of being a Buddhist were several. He confronted the pain and frustration of Tibetans and was moved to compassion. He met exemplars – both living teachers and stories about earlier sages – who showed the possibility of uniting political action and religious devotion, expressing in a new way the ideal of the bodhisattva. His response to their charisma and the power of the sacred places where they lived moved Pistono to try to make their way of being his own. He found two new ways to view his anger in the phurba ritual and the practice of liberating his anger through detachment and observation. These experiences of unselfing facilitated Pistono's gradual transformation into a different kind of person by extending his sense of what was possible. After being dislodged from old habits by these encounters, he begins to think of himself as a potential bodhisattva.

Pistono's travel narrative is one of the most convincing portrayals of a writer's Buddhist transformation. The book's epilogue describes work he has undertaken since his journeys, including founding Nekorpa, a nonprofit organization dedicated to protecting pilgrimage sites throughout the world. He continues to study Tibetan Buddhism and works to conserve its threatened heritage. He has written a biography of Tertön Sogyal and several other books about meditation and socially engaged Buddhism.[16] He advocates for Tibet's political and human rights and insists that Tibetan and Chinese people must find a way toward peaceful coexistence. Pistono does not claim that he no longer struggles with anger or feels discouraged by Tibet's political situation, but he has come a long way from the beginning of the narrative a decade earlier, when his religious and political commitments seemed unrelated and he alternated between vindictive rage and a detachment disconnected from the world. If he has not yet fully realized the bodhisattva ideal in his life, he now knows the path and follows it with confidence.

In diverse ways, these Western Buddhists describe how treks in Tibet led to experiences of unselfing that decisively changed their lives. Reynolds, Thurman and Wise, Baker, and Pistono understand no-self in various ways and correlate it with rather different experiences, yet they all find this concept to be crucial in understanding and explaining the transformations that were initiated in Tibet.

---

[15] Lewis Rambo, *Understanding Religious Conversion* (New Haven: Yale University Press, 1995), 13–14.

[16] Matteo Pistono, *Fearless in Tibet: The Life of Mystic Terton Sogyal* (Carlsbad, CA: Hay House, 2014). Pistono has written essays and articles about socially engaged Buddhism and a study of a Thai thinker and activist: *Roar: Sulak Sivaraksa and the Path of Socially Engaged Buddhism* (Berkeley, CA: North Atlantic Books, 2019).

CHAPTER 7

Life-Changing Travels in the Tibetan Diaspora

Because it has been difficult for Western travelers to visit Tibet since the 1950 Chinese invasion, many encounters with Tibetan Buddhism have taken place in the Tibetan diaspora, the diffusion of this distinctive form of Buddhism to adjoining areas and beyond. In this chapter, I consider several travel narratives that, like John Blofeld's *The Wheel of Life*, portray a major life transition that takes place when the author encounters Tibetan Buddhism beyond the borders of Tibet: in Ladakh, Bhutan, Nepal, Sikkim, India, and Switzerland.

*

In 1981, Andrew Harvey, a twenty-nine-year-old Englishman, went to Ladakh, a sparsely populated mountainous region that is part of Kashmir, nestled between India, Pakistan, and Tibet. The culture and people of Ladakh are closely linked to Tibet, although Kashmir's predominantly Muslim population dominates in this region. At that time, Harvey, a fellow at Oxford's All Souls College, felt "frustrated by my life and the limitations of my poetry, its obsession with irony and suffering, its largely unremitting anger and hopelessness" (5).[1] In contrast to his life's turbulence and anxiety about finding a voice as a poet, he admired Buddhism's "exacting and un-self-flattering" philosophy but lacked the discipline and guidance to practice it. He traveled to Buddhist sites in India, Sri Lanka, and Nepal, and then, with Tibet largely off-limits to Western travelers, to Ladakh, "one of the last places on earth, with Sikkim and Bhutan, where a Tibetan Buddhist society can be experienced" (5). Soon after his travels, Harvey published *A Journey in Ladakh* (1983), an account of how he was affected by his sojourn in this Tibetan Buddhist region, especially his relationship with a Rinpoche.

---

[1] Andrew Harvey, *A Journey to Ladakh: Encounters with Buddhism* (New York: Houghton Mifflin, 1983).

In the first two of the memoir's three parts, Harvey writes lyrically and enthusiastically about the beauty of the mountain setting and the Ladakhi people and way of life. He doubts that this traditional culture can survive the challenges of modernization. The influx of consumer goods, a more individualistic desire for self-fulfillment, and increased contacts with the rest of the world lead children to become beggars, monks to become tour guides, and young men to seek Western lovers and foreign jobs. Harvey's tone of lament is familiar in travel narratives to Tibet and other parts of the non-Western world, but he is more self-critical than many writers and questions whether his literary portrait of Ladakh will contribute to the destruction of its traditional way of life. A German friend, Hans, challenges him: "That's only another kind of exploitation, isn't it? I mean, if you 'bear witness' eloquently, and, as you say, 'clearly,' who else will get the reward but you? And your readers, of course, a little … but aren't you inviting them to a rather corrupt party? 'Another moving study of a doomed culture,' 'Another poetic rendering of the East'" (96). Harvey addresses this question by presenting the view of several Ladakhis, including the Rinpoche he follows, that his writing will preserve a fragment of the vanishing culture. Nawang, a young scholar, urges him to write about Ladakhi culture in spite of the risks of appropriation and exploitation: "I think that it is almost certain that we will be destroyed as a culture, and that nothing, now, can save us from that destruction. Our only chance of being remembered at all may be through being 'appropriated' and 'consumed,' as you say, by the West" (97). This young man hopes that preserving a record of traditional life will help Ladakhis to remember their origins and Westerners to value this culture. Although fatalistic about the demise of his culture, he translates and publishes traditional folk songs, and he urges Harvey, too, to make "a gesture against death" (99).

Harvey's passionate response to Ladakh shakes him out of his cold, egotistical, and ambitious self-absorption as a poet. This region and its Tibetan Buddhist culture are at once a way out of selfish preoccupation and the place where he discovers his true self. Harvey uses the rhetoric of false and true self, rather than no-self, to interpret his transformation. Like other authors commonly labeled as New Age, Harvey understands religious traditions primarily in psychological terms as vehicles for self-development. When he encounters a female oracle whose trance becomes terrifyingly violent, he realizes that she revived his old fears of his mother and grandmother, as well as "buried male fears of a female cruelty that no reason could restrain" (82). His attraction to Buddhism as a path to harmless serenity, he now sees, repressed a violent part of himself. Because "no

Life-Changing Travels in the Tibetan Diaspora
181

true transformation can be achieved by a neurotic refusal of a whole side of the psyche" (82), the wrathful deities of Tantric Buddhism have psychological value; they give the adept an opportunity to recognize anger, desire, greed, and other repressed energies and "to confront, understand, and master them, to turn them, as the oracle had turned her hysteria, into a power to heal" (83). Like Matteo Pistono's experience as described in *In the Shadow of the Buddha*, Harvey's encounter with Tantric aspects of Tibetan Buddhism leads to a transformed sense of self that encompasses the dark side he had rejected as not himself. Harvey's New Age version of transformation, however, seems less grounded than Pistono in Buddhist ideas about no-self. He sees all religions as expressions of a universal spiritual wisdom, a perennial tradition whose core is mysticism, the individual's sense of oneness with the universe.

A similar de-emphasis of no-self in favor of recognizing an enlarged, deeper, or more complex sense of self takes place when Harvey realizes that one source of his exhilaration in Ladakh is the way it triggers childhood memories. Smelling the smoke of eucalyptus, drinking thick Tibetan tea, and other sensations and images remind him of the first decade of his life in southern India:

> For years that part of my childhood had been lost to me, buried under England; drinking that tea, in that silence, in the thick of that fragrance, I had found it again and felt I could never again lose it. The images that came to me so intensely came from a quiet light and returned to it; they were mine and not mine; I did not own them or want to possess them; they burned and faded and I was not afraid of their fading, because I had seen and known them again, because I felt that, at last, after so many years, the road between me and them had been opened again and they would return. (113–114)

Harvey's journey to Ladakh releases a flood of forgotten memories that are not possessions but at once "mine and not mine." His renewed access to this storehouse of memories and source of personal identity is a crucial breakthrough that he interprets with the psychological language of the self's lifelong process of gaining fuller consciousness.

The tension between New Age rhetoric of finding a true self (or Self) and Buddhist rhetoric of no-self or empty self influences Harvey's presentation of his relationship to his spiritual mentor in the third and final section of the narrative, "To the Rinpoche." Sometimes he says the self must be left behind, and sometimes its realization is the goal of spiritual development. Harvey does not explain the contradictions or resolve the paradoxes involved in these two perspectives. In a discussion with his friend Dilip, Harvey interprets the Rinpoche as "the highest part of yourself, come at last to its expression" (138). Dilip responds that the spiritual life is a matter of "letting yourself be yourself, of letting everything that is not yourself fall away." What remains then is "Nothing. Emptiness. Sunyata. There is no real Self ... To be freed from a false perception of the Self is the end of Buddhism" (138). Harvey presents Buddhism as both a path to self-realization and a way to transcend concern with self. Perhaps he would reconcile these differing emphases by distinguishing between the self that is always changing and a Self understood as an eternal essence. Or he might contrast the false self with which ego identifies and a true self that knows its interconnections or mystical oneness with the world. Like most authors of travel narratives, Harvey does not analyze these distinctions and philosophical issues in depth. Rather, he suggests that two contrasting perspectives on the self may each have a value and therapeutic use, like the "two ways of saying Sunyata": harshly or gently, bringing either terror at dissolution or a joyful sense of freedom.

The intense relationship with a Rinpoche that is so important in Tibetan Buddhism is a daunting challenge to anyone who believes in an independent self in charge of its own fate. A form of unselfing is required to trust so much in the guidance of a guru that one feels one's identity merging with him. Harvey has many doubts about Thuksey Rinpoche (1916–1983), the Tibetan master with whom he forms a close bond. He wrestles with whether his yearning to devote himself to a guru simply disguises unrecognized selfish needs. He takes a psychological perspective on his attraction to the Rinpoche, wondering whether he is "inventing" him, projecting or imagining an ideal figure rather than responding to his genuine qualities. He imagines how a skeptical German friend would view his attraction to Thuksey Rinpoche:

> This man is in search of the Good Father and has found him. He has found him in an old man from a culture so strange to him that he cannot understand it and so is relieved of the burden of irony, of criticism, of detached judgement. He can therefore indulge his fantasy to the full, elaborate it to the most absurd (and possibly dangerous) lengths. The Rinpoche is not only the Good Father; he is also an idealized portrait of the writer himself ... In this old man from another, unknowable world the writer has found the perfect way to aggrandize himself, advertise his own spirituality. (150)

Harvey acknowledges this possible objection to his devotion, but rather than trying to refute it with arguments, he continues to pursue his relationship to Thuksey Rinpoche.

Life-Changing Travels in the Tibetan Diaspora   183

A Journey in Ladakh records many conversations between the Rinpoche, Harvey, and his friends and fellow devotees. It describes the landscape and people in glowing, tender, and affectionate terms and shows little interest in conflict, suffering, or the darker side of the world. There is not much outward action or adventure, and the plot or arc of the narrative follows Harvey's internal struggle between skepticism and enthusiastic giving of his heart to Thuksey Rinpoche.

A turning point comes in a dramatic experience of unselfing that takes place as Harvey sits in the presence of the Rinpoche during a performance by a group of drummers. He notices his mind "detaching itself slowly and gently" from his body, hovering outside it and observing in every object the meaning of emptiness:

> I saw for the first time, not intellectually, not with my mind only, but with the eyes of my whole body and spirit what is meant by "Emptiness," by Sunyata. Each object looked at once startlingly, intensely real—and completely fabricated, an invention, as if painted, or made out of ricepaper and balsa wood. Even the Rinpoche looked at once imposing and a doll, a sage and a structure of wood and paper, the paper tightest in the severe lines of his face, where the wood almost peeped through. The fruit in front of him seemed at once solid and so fragile that a breath could blow it away or break it. I felt that for all their strength I could put my hands through the stone walls, lean back through them, and through the garden behind them, through the stream, the mountains. I did not feel separated from any of the people or objects I was looking at, I did not feel any more "real" than they, with any greater right to be taken as solid or absolute. I realized that even the self that was watching all this, reveling in all this, was itself as insubstantial as wind. (204)

In this passage, the rhetoric of no-self is prominent. Harvey feels intense love for the Rinpoche even as he views him as not inherently real but, like himself, "a transitory fiction." When the drumming stopped, Harvey "re-entered my body, and my mind grew dull again" (205). This version of unselfing takes the form of love and devotion to a guru, a merging of identities that reveals the limits of his usual self and the possibility of feelings of joy, spaciousness, and identification with all of reality, even though every object is seen as fragile and temporary.

The ending of this travel narrative suggests that Harvey was changed in two ways. First, he makes the vow of Avalokiteshvara, the Bodhisatva of Compassion, dedicating his meditation practice not to his own enlightenment but to the welfare of all beings. Thuksey Rinpoche teaches him a way to meditate by visualizing and identifying with this bodhisatva: "You offer him your senses, your body, your heart, your spirit. You make a

184 Life-Changing Travels in the Tibetan Diaspora

sacrifice to him of everything that you are and then you merge with him, you melt into him. You become your highest self, which is He" (235). In a final stage, to free himself from any vanity or egotism involved in "merging with the God that you have projected out of yourself," Harvey learns to dissolve the meditation and rest in formless Emptiness:

> You must enter in this last stage into the Sunyata that is the mother of all projections, the Emptiness from which all forms are born, yours, mine, and all the imaginations of our minds and hearts. There must be nothing left of yourself or of the experience of the Bodhisatva or your delight in his splendour, and in your own, nothing but Sunyata, and the clear radiance of the Void. (235)

That Harvey was able to make this commitment to Buddhism is a significant step, although he did not join a sangha or stop exploring other religious pathways. His joyful offering of all of himself, especially his heart, shows a striking change from the self-contained, cold, unhappy young man he was in England.

As so often in Western Buddhist travel narratives, the ending both affirms the reality of personal change and acknowledges the author's ongoing struggle with old habits of character. After the Rinpoche's final guided meditation, he asks Harvey whether his visualization was good. Harvey responds: "I could hardly visualize anything. I feel a fool. In my mind is a dark stone" (236). The final line in the book is the Rinpoche's counsel to "practice and wear it down" (236), indicating how slowly the process of transformation goes, and that it does not depend on a momentary gush of enthusiasm. Harvey's bodhisattva vow is a statement of intention, not achievement.

A second way in which Harvey depicts his transformation is his new understanding of his future task as a writer. His spiritual search was motivated in large part by awareness that his work and identity as a poet were dominated by vanity and ambition. He confesses to a friend: "To be absorbed by language, by art, can be as selfish as making money, and as cruel. I am tired of the way I have lived, enclosed in my words, my past, my griefs, my relationships" (126). He tells Thuksey Rinpoche that, although his writing interferes with spiritual awareness, he is afraid that religious commitment would pull him away from writing. The guru's response to this dilemma, he hopes, might give "a whole direction for my life" (173). The Rinpoche tells Harvey that he must find a way to work that does not tempt him to vanity but rather expresses his spirituality. He asks the young Englishman to use his writing to convey the wisdom of Buddhism to the West and to help others understand and appreciate

Tibetan culture and people. Harvey must bear witness to what he has seen in Ladakh and connect it to the spiritual crisis of Westerners disillusioned with materialism and individualism. This commissioning scene authorizes Harvey's subsequent career as a popular writer on spirituality. It justifies the reinterpretation of Buddhism into terms that will make sense in the West. Harvey apparently shares the view of one of his Indian friends that the land and people of Tibet are less important than "the philosophy of Tibetan Buddhism," which "belongs to the world" (166). Tibet's loss is the world's gain: "It may be a good thing that Tibet has fallen, has passed away. Now the philosophy that was confined to Tibet can be shared with others" (166). This view is remarkably free of the grief and anger expressed by most Western writers who have witnessed Tibet's trials since it was invaded by China in 1950. Harvey depoliticizes the contemporary situation of Tibet and reduces its future to being a museum of the birthplace of a world philosophy that has moved beyond it.

Harvey's outlook is extremely optimistic, and perhaps naïve, about how well Westernized forms of Buddhism transmit the authentic Dharma. The traditional forms of Tibetan culture and religion are very casually disposed of, even though his guru approves: Thuksey Rinpoche advises him not to go on staring at the finger that points at the moon (219). Another Rinpoche states: "A true Buddhist does not remain attached to one particular tradition or another ... Buddhism will change, it must change, it is good if it changes" (182). Whatever is not useful for the next transformation of Buddhism must be discarded. This emphasis on change as inherently good is too quick to cast off traditional forms of Buddhism. Instead, specific changes should be evaluated in terms of a religious tradition's most important norms and values. Harvey's view of Tibetan Buddhism's fate in the West, which is closely linked to his own career as a spiritual writer, exhibits the problem when Western writers see Buddhism as only a philosophy that addresses their own spiritual preoccupations rather than having an inherent worth and very different meaning for other Buddhists. A cynical perspective would say that the main value for Harvey of his encounter with Thuksey Rinpoche and Tibetan Buddhism is simply to justify his new vocational direction, which begins with writing a travel narrative that he admits will contribute to the loss of the very qualities about Ladakh that he appreciates and admires.

Tibetan Buddhism and the culture and people of Tibet, wherever they are located, are not only valuable because they provide qualities that Westerners feel are lacking in their own lives. In his final remarks, Thuksey Rinpoche warns about this danger:

> So many Westerners who find solace in the East are coming to have their Egos healed, their shattered personalities reassembled in some way. But the East is not a large convalescent home for the West, a sort of enormous recreation room where Westerners can play at being spiritual, at 'exploring themselves'; it is a place of power, of new power, a new kind of strength which must be used in the world. (227)

To his credit, Harvey acknowledges this risk, but the Rinpoche's cautionary words challenge Harvey's account of how he found a new vocational purpose in Ladakh.

Since the publication of *A Journey to Ladakh*, Andrew Harvey has become a popular writer who lectures, conducts workshops, and leads travel groups to sacred sites around the world. He founded Sacred Activism, a movement that links spiritual growth to concerns for social justice. He has explored the teachings of Rumi, yoga as a philosophy and practice, female imagery for the divine, and the common core of mysticism he sees in the world's religious traditions. In many of these various interests and pursuits, Buddhism has been an important although secondary concern. In 1999, Harvey added an afterword to *A Journey to Ladakh* that sheds light on his development after that early work, which remains his most popular book. He describes how overcoming his initial doubts about this travel narrative helped him become his true self: "I would have to write *A Journey in Ladakh* or permanently stifle something essential in my true nature" (237). He realized that his personal and artistic destiny was to help others pursue "the mystical search" (238). Two years after the book was published, he returned to Ladakh, where he encountered Thuksey Rinpoche, who now suffered the effects of severe diabetes, shortly before he died. The Rinpoche blessed Harvey's career as a writer, but he also warned him not to abandon spiritual practice: "You may write a hundred wonderful books, but what will they matter if you never find out who you are?" (239). Two extraordinary events, a loud clap like mountain thunder and a mysterious sound of sacred chanting, apparently confirm that Thuksey Rinpoche is dying as an enlightened being. His final words to Harvey suggest that there is no inherent contradiction between Harvey's work as a popular spiritual writer and Buddhist values, nor between a successful career and the search for self-transcendence.

In Andrew Harvey's view, the mantle of leadership should be passed on to a new kind of Buddhist teacher. He is critical of Tibetan Buddhist teachers in the West, most of whom he thinks have succumbed to temptation and corruption: "The Dalai Lama himself, marvelous sweet being though he undoubtedly is, has himself delivered depressingly regressive teachings

Life-Changing Travels in the Tibetan Diaspora

on sex, made homophobic remarks, and espoused an anti-contraception stance in India; the apostle of nonviolence has even saluted India's development of a nuclear bomb!" (241). Harvey challenges traditional authority figures and suggests the need for new teachers who can pass on the essential truths of Tibetan Buddhism to contemporary Westerners. Like most New Age writers, he is suspicious of the traditional institutions of religion, including Buddhist ones, and prefers a freelance and improvisational spreading of what he calls "the sacred technology":

> What will never die ... is the brilliance and importance of the sacred technology—the great treasury of visionary practices and philosophies—that the Tibetan mystical schools developed and preserved. The social and religious systems that formed around these teachings will die; the teachings themselves will go on living and will inspire and shape and awaken seekers of all paths and persuasions. (242)

The term "sacred technology" suggests a view of religion as a collection of techniques for enhancing an individual's capacity for spiritual experience.

A contemporary Western seeker may learn a great deal from a guide like Thuksey Rinpoche or Andrew Harvey without being bound by loyalty, identity, or commitment to any ongoing community. There is much to appreciate about Harvey's serious encounter with Tibetan Buddhism and much to admire about his travel writing. Yet I think that in his work the distinctively Buddhist understanding of no-self has been displaced by an amorphous blending of traditions that are taken to represent a supposedly universal mystical quest and by the therapeutic impulse to evaluate religious ideas only in terms of how well they enhance the individual self's development and mental health. This is a legitimate concern, but it needs to be balanced by an appreciation of what traditional Buddhist ideas mean in their original context. Teachings about no-self should provide a more incisive critical challenge to deeply engrained Western habits of thought about the self.

*

Jamie Zeppa's *Beyond the Sky and the Earth* (1999) stretches beyond the usual time frame of travel narratives in that it describes a period of more than three years that she spent in Bhutan. She wasn't just passing through. In 1988, Zeppa went to this country, whose people are predominantly Tibetan Buddhist, to teach English in a junior high school and then at Sherubtse College. Living in Bhutan transformed her in many ways, including a conversion to Buddhism. *Beyond the Sky and the Earth* builds to a climax centered on Zeppa's decisions about whether to marry a Bhutanese man and whether to return to her home in Canada or stay in the land and culture she has come to love. These are also choices about what kind of person she wants to be. In wrestling with these questions, Zeppa brings Buddhist ideas about impermanence and no-self into dialogue and sometimes conflict with deeply rooted Western values related to selfhood, including moral integrity, romantic love, self-expression, and individuality. She must resolve these conflicts not in theoretical terms but in life-determining commitments. Throughout her memoir, she reflects on the interdependence of her sense of "home" and the kind of person she is becoming.

When she arrived in Bhutan at the age of twenty-four, Zeppa had never been outside of Canada. She felt profoundly disoriented. The only connection between her former life and the present was a sense of self that felt increasingly fragmented: "I myself must bridge the gap, I am the bridge—although I feel more like the gap. All the experiences and achievements that defined me at home are irrelevant and insignificant here. There is just me, here, now. *Wherever you go, there you are*" (28).[2] As her identity becomes harder to define, Zeppa begins to understand the concept of no-self as directly applicable to her uncertainty: "The Buddhist view that there is no real self seems completely accurate. I have crossed a threshold of exhaustion and strangeness and am suspended in a new inner place" (45). She feels the culture shock of adapting to life in a remote village in one of the most isolated countries in the world, a kingdom that severely restricted visits by outsiders and banned television. Zeppa learns the local language (Sharchhop), puts up with rats, fleas, and vicious dogs, eats food that she does not recognize or like, and puzzles over strict rules of etiquette. Living in a society that believes in ghosts and magic, she can no longer say that she does not believe in them: "If, as Buddhism teaches, separateness is an illusion, if we all partake in and help create a much vaster reality than we can know, then everything is interdependent, and anything is possible" (148). She gradually comes to feel at home in Bhutan as she cooks on a dangerous kerosene stove, explores nearby villages and hills, admires stunning natural beauty, and develops deep bonds with trusting schoolchildren. She wonders who she would have been had she grown up in Bhutan:

> I try to imagine who I would be if I had lived all my life here at this temple by the river. I wonder what I would want if I had grown up without ads telling me my heart's desires: to be thinner, richer, sexier, look better, smell

---

[2] Jamie Zeppa, *Beyond the Sky and the Earth: A Journey into Bhutan* (New York: Penguin, 1999).

Life-Changing Travels in the Tibetan Diaspora

189

> better, be all that I can be, have a faster car, a brighter smile, lighter hair, whiter whites, hurry now, don't miss out, take advantage of this special offer. If instead I had spent twenty-four years absorbing the silent weight of the mountains, the constant pull of the river, the sound of hot white light burning into black rocks. (112)

In countless jarring encounters, Zeppa learns how her sense of selfhood has been constructed by a particular culture, and she finds that Buddhist ideas help her understand these incidents. The interdependence of the self and its environment means that, if she finds a new home, she will form a new identity.

Although Zeppa learns to appreciate Bhutanese values, she cannot simply discard all Western standards and norms. From a detached intellectual perspective, she can understand that all values are constructed, but at certain points, she must take a stand and assert her own convictions. For instance, she is disturbed by the common practice of beating schoolchildren, which often becomes abusive. Zeppa argues with herself about whether her negative judgment about beating is an inappropriate imposition of foreign values or rightly expresses a strong moral conviction about a universal human value. When she decides not to intervene in another teacher's classroom, she doesn't know whether this reflects cultural sensitivity or cowardice.

Zeppa becomes deeply concerned about "the Situation": the worsening political tensions between students from the north of Bhutan and the southern students of Nepalese background. When she tries to get students to talk openly about politics and to accept a multicultural Bhutan, they tell her politely that foreigners cannot possibly understand their world. She must reconcile the aspects of Bhutan she loves with the grim reality that students disappear or are found beheaded. The Buddhist belief that all is connected helps her to confront the painful political situation and to feel compassion for all who suffer. At the same time, she evaluates the Situation in terms of Western ideas and moral concepts such as human rights, the ideals of democracy, and respect for other ways of life in a multicultural society. These values depend on the idea of an independent and responsible self.

Zeppa reflects on challenges in teaching writing in a culture that does not value individual self-expression in the same ways as the West. The students all seem to her to write in the same way, with clichés, hackneyed advice, and bland avoidance of controversy. She wants to teach each student to find an individual voice and to criticize received opinions. This violates traditional Bhutanese values of respect for elders, obedience to authority, and conserving the status quo. She encourages her students to develop a strong sense of individuality yet recognizes that this goal threatens a communal and traditional society. In depicting these ambiguous situations, Zeppa provides no simple answers to quandaries about how to act or to the theoretical issue of whether the ideal of articulate individual selfhood that guides her teaching practices is justifiable in Bhutan or coheres with the concept of no-self. Although she tries to integrate the values of two very different cultures, sometimes she cannot affirm Bhutanese culture alongside her Western values. At certain points, she must decide what kind of person she wants to be: what kind of self.

Two relationships to lovers each force this kind of choice. When Zeppa departs for Bhutan, she is engaged to a fellow Canadian, Robert, and plans to return to marry him and enter graduate school. As she becomes immersed in her new life in Bhutan, it becomes difficult to explain to him how she is changing. Her letters feel forced and false. Her commitment to Robert and her former plans no longer express what she wants for her life. Although the idea of no-self helps her to accept her dawning awareness of new possibilities, she can't see herself as infinitely malleable. Matters of integrity and of affirming what she values most are at stake. The question of whether or not to marry Robert and return to Canada is a question about who she really is and wants to become:

> Everything about my relationship with Robert, in fact everything about the life I left behind, seems small and narrow in comparison with where I am now. Everything I imagine in that life is repulsive to me: a house in an affordable suburb, a car that I will hate because it is too big, sprinklers keeping the lawn green in the summer while we sit in air-conditioned rooms inside, sealed off from the elements, safe and smug. Part of me knows this is unfair to Robert but the rest of me doesn't want to hear it. I can see only what I have now, this view, and the dark, bright world below, with its stories of kings and curses and guardian deities, flying tigers and thunder dragons, religious scrolls hidden in rocks and valleys hidden in mountains by magic or Buddhism or both, and yetis and ghosts and the levitating lama in the temple on the ridge the sun rises over each morning, and all the places I haven't been to, and the stories I haven't yet heard, all the things I haven't figured out. (198)

She writes to Robert that she cannot marry him because "Bhutan has changed me, and I don't want the same things any more" (199). Zeppa's appreciation of the idea of no-self helps her see that her personal identity could be different and depends partly on her relationships and cultural environment. Yet she has a say in what she will become, and her choices are influenced by the Western ideal of a true and authentic self that is responsible for, grounds, and justifies pivotal decisions. The self is dependent on its environment but not simply determined; it has desires, needs, and aspirations that can be thwarted or expressed. In describing crucial choices such as whom she will marry and where she will live, Zeppa seeks to integrate the Buddhist idea of no-self with her Western sense of selfhood.

In the last third of Zeppa's memoir, she falls in love with and marries a Bhutanese man named Tshewang at the same time that she starts to see herself as a Buddhist. These simultaneous commitments present some striking tensions. There are enormous obstacles to the relationship with Tshewang, beginning with the fact that he is her student. The need for secrecy, ethical scruples, cultural differences, and their uncertain future all make understanding each other a constant challenge. Zeppa tries to deny her feelings for Tshewang by viewing them in Buddhist terms as desires that can only lead to suffering. Yet this suppression makes her miserable. She is as drawn to the worldview of the Romantic poets as she is to Buddhism: "I wonder what is wrong with attachment anyway, and what poetry could be born out of nonattachment. Why shouldn't we throw ourselves into our lives and love the world deeply and break our hearts when it changes, fades and dies? I paddle back and forth between the Four Noble Truths and Wordsworth, Coleridge, Shelley and Keats" (175). Zeppa shows how Buddhist ideas, or at least a certain understanding of them, could thwart a crucial life transition when a person becomes aware of new values and possibilities. The way she portrays her dilemma suggests that an appeal to the concept of no-self, or to how desire leads inevitably to suffering, should not be used to shut down vital questioning of what one wants to become as a person. How a person imagines a future self is based on values and attachment to a particular conception of the good. As she focuses on key moments of crisis and development, Zeppa explores both helpful Buddhist insights and ways that, like other religious worldviews, it can also be used to suppress full awareness of alternative "goods" that a person is drawn to as admirable or worthy ends in life and which orient one as a self in moral space.[3] At certain moments, Zeppa tried to use Buddhist ideas to protect herself, shut down awareness, and avoid having to make a difficult choice about whether to pursue that for which she yearns.

Zeppa had read books about Buddhism and was attracted to its ideas, in particular the emphasis on the mind as at once the source of problems and

---

[3] On the ways in which life narratives explore what philosopher Charles Taylor calls "the full range of goods," see David Parker, *The Self in Moral Space: Life Narrative and the Good* (Ithaca: Cornell University Press, 2007).

the key to liberation from them: "Buddhism requires that I take on the terrifying responsibility for myself: I am the author of my own suffering, and my own deliverance" (240–241). She tries to practice teachings about mindfulness and compassion. A pivotal event takes place when, after a student dies, another student explains to Zeppa how her suffering demonstrates attachment to the world through endless rebirths. Remembering the student's words while meditating, Zeppa has a crucial experience of insight that brings home to her the truth of an idea that she had been pondering as an interesting theory:

> Later, in meditation, these words come back to me. It is like something opening in my head, too fast for words. *I must have experienced everything by now, but I am still here, so I have not learned anything.* In a moment, I grasp it. Not the Buddhist theory of the self, how there is no essential Jamie Zeppa, how she is only a collection of changing conditions, attributes and desires common to all sentient beings, but the experience of that fact. Everything falls away. It is the experience of pure freedom, a momentary glimpse of how it would be—to be in the world and not be attached to it, to move through it, experiencing it and letting it go. It is impossible to put the feeling, the certainty, into words, but later, I know that this is the moment I became a Buddhist. (252–253)

Zeppa's powerful feelings soon dissipate, leaving her with "only the shell of the experience, the words," and a yearning to return to the moment's intense feeling and clear understanding. She realizes that she now knows the goal of practice and is ready to commit herself to the Buddhist path. This pivotal event, Zeppa's version of unselfing, shows her what it would mean to live without grasping and attachment. Her momentary insight into the meaning of no-self motivates and guides her as she returns to the struggles and uncertainties of daily life. Soon she takes the refuge vows with a visiting lama and commits herself to the Buddha, the Dharma, and the Sangha.

As she describes her conversion and the surge of passion she feels for Tshewang, Zeppa expresses Western ideas about self-fulfillment. At first glance, her story illustrates the romantic belief that love conquers all. At the same time, she confirms the truth of the Buddhist insight that desire creates more desire: in her case, for a life with her spouse, a stable home, and a baby. A friend invokes Buddhism to tell her that she shouldn't try to grasp these things but just enjoy Bhutan and an affair with Tshewang and then let them go when she returns to Canada. The friend's skepticism about the couple's long-term prospects may be good advice, but Zeppa can't take it. She forces herself to meditate on the endless cycle of desire and grasping, the decay of the body, and the inevitability of death. Yet

Life-Changing Travels in the Tibetan Diaspora

she recognizes that she is using the Buddhist ideal of detachment to cope with her fear of a radically different kind of life full of possibility and risks.

On a trip "back home" to Canada, she realizes that Bhutan has become the place in which she feels most at home, most herself: if not her "true" self, then the self she wants to become. She feels slower and more mindful as she encounters the impatient, aggressive, and cynical attitudes of friends and family. When they complain and whine about inconveniences, Zeppa muses that "a small dose of Buddhism would go a long way" (265). In contrast to Bhutan, Canada is a place of extraordinary wealth and comfort yet where no one seems happy. They idealize Bhutan as Shangri-La while clinging to lives with which they are discontented: "Everyone wants a cleaner, simpler, saner world but no one wants to give up anything. No one wants to take the bus" (265). Returning to Bhutan, Zeppa feels relieved to be home and realizes how much she has changed. Her true home is not only Bhutan as a physical place but the person she is there, the self that thrives in that particular environment: "It is not just this or that, the mountains the people, it is me and the way I can be here, the freedom to walk unafraid into the great dark night. It is a hundred thousand things and I could never trace or tell all the connections and reflections, the shadows and echoes and secret relations between them" (268).

In most of the memoirs discussed in this book, the writer travels through a foreign land, encountering Asia's otherness as an outsider and planning to return to a home in the West. Jamie Zeppa is not a visitor passing through but rather a sojourner dwelling in Bhutan who slowly realizes that she might make her home there. In making her momentous decision, she finds support in a Buddhist prayer that also furnishes her memoir's epigraph: "You must leave your home and go forth from your country. The children of Buddha all practice this way." This conception of travel emphasizes renunciation, exile, and leaving home rather than bringing new knowledge home. Like a religious transformation that can be viewed as either a conversion or a deconversion, Zeppa's narrative is at once a story of finding a new home and of leaving an old one as she "goes forth" on the path.

In the final pages of the book, Zeppa, now pregnant, wrestles with choices about whether to live in Bhutan and marry Tshewang. Making these decisions about what kind of self she wants to be feels like standing on the brink of a cliff:

> I came to Bhutan to find out if the careful life I had planned, the life of waiting, watching, counting, planning, putting into place, was the life I really wanted. I can still go back to that life, even now, even after everything.

194 Life-Changing Travels in the Tibetan Diaspora

> Here I am, in another high place, the highest edge I have come to so far. I can still say goodbye to Tshewang, go home, find an apartment, have the child, go back to school. In some ways, it is the least risky, most sensible option. I can turn these last three and a half years into a neatly packaged memory, pruned by caution, sealed by prudence. I can still turn back. But I will not. I will go over the edge and step into whatever is beyond. (295–296)

Although it sounds suicidal, her desire to leap from a cliff expresses Zeppa's exhilaration and terror in choosing to become a different person, another self. The Buddhist idea of no-self does not diminish her desire to find a more authentic self and a richer, freer life. Rather, the lesson of nonattachment means throwing caution to the wind; it makes it possible to choose an alternative self by embracing the unknown and taking risks that feel like jumping off a cliff.

A brief postscript summarizes what came after her decision and raises new questions. Zeppa lived with her husband and young son in Bhutan for several years. During this time, "Tshewang and I found some of the cultural differences between us to be even greater than we had expected, and had to make some difficult decisions about the future. Eventually, I decided to return to Canada, at least 'for some time,' as the Bhutanese say, and the future, well, we will see what it brings" (303). She does not describe what happened to their relationship and how a Buddhist perspective would interpret further developments. (Zeppa's website reveals that she now lives in Canada, is separated from Tshewang, and has become a professor and novelist.) The final paragraph of the book turns away from her marriage and religious orientation to the question of whether Bhutan now feels like home to her. In many ways, it does, she asserts, but she also uses the word "home" to refer to Canada. When she receives news of the death of her grandfather, who had opposed her desire to stay in Bhutan, she utters a traditional Bhutanese expression of gratitude: "Beyond the sky and the earth, thank you." The ending suggests a reconciliation or happy joining of aspects of the two homes and cultures that she has felt torn between and that still stand in tension.

Zeppa's moving account of her life in Bhutan is a blend of several traditional Western genres: a romantic love story, a conversion narrative, and a *Bildungsroman* portraying the education and formation of an artistic sensibility and adult identity. Along with explaining these aspects of self-development, the book also reflects her understanding of the Buddhist idea of no-self, which helps her to let go of her old conception of herself and choose a life and identity in keeping with the many good things she

Life-Changing Travels in the Tibetan Diaspora

came to appreciate in Bhutan, including the compassion and generosity of its people, soaring mountain vistas that create a sense of vertigo, and the possibility of a life that embraces risky freedom. More than most of the books treated in this study, *Beyond the Sky and the Earth* depicts a significant transformation as a consequence of the author's travels and life in a Buddhist culture. For Zeppa, self-realization and no-self are not irreconcilably opposed but rather contrasting perspectives on her life. Both are necessary to understand moments of unselfing and the difficult choices she made as she journeyed, married, dwelled in a new culture, and committed herself to a Buddhist path.

*

In *Dreaming Me: An African American Woman's Spiritual Journey* (2001), Jan Willis raises profound questions about the relevance of no-self to people who have been denied selfhood.[4] Although this book is an autobiography rather than an account of a single journey, an encounter with Tibetan Buddhism was a crucial event in Willis's lifelong "journey" of transformation. She was born in a mining camp in Docena, Alabama, in 1948 and became a scholar, teacher, and practitioner of Tibetan Buddhism at Wesleyan University. As a child, she encountered terrifying violence from the Ku Klux Klan and mocking derision from African Americans who called her "white girl" because of her light skin. The history of black people in the United States and her ambivalent relationships to her family engender a search for acceptance, love, and a sense of self-worth:

> To get beyond the pervasive sense of pain and suffering I carried, I knew I would have to find healing, to find that place of belonging that is so basic for us all: feeling at home in our own skins. And so, from my earliest days, my solitary quest became to find a way to accept myself, and to love *me*. (13)

After initial mistrust and resistance, Willis felt welcomed into the Baptist Church and had a powerful experience of baptism. She now declares herself to be a "Baptist Buddhist" and affirms that the two religious traditions have much in common. Participation in civil rights struggles, including marching with Martin Luther King in Birmingham, was a crucial event when she "*stood with*, and, therefore, *stood up for* myself and for my people" (61). Doing well in school and earning degrees at Cornell University and

---

[4] Jan Willis, *Dreaming Me: An African American Woman's Spiritual Journey* (New York: Riverhead Books, 2001).

196 Life-Changing Travels in the Tibetan Diaspora

Columbia University instilled growing confidence. Yet for many years, she suffered from deep feelings of insecurity and self-doubt.

Willis first became interested in Buddhism when she learned of Buddhist protests against the war in Vietnam. Studying in India during her junior year at Banaras Hindu University, she met Tibetans living in exile and was moved by their capacities for warm acceptance and compassion. They had endured terrible trauma yet found spiritual resources enabling them to be resilient and even joyful. Could Buddhism also help African Americans? A Gelugpa monk invited Willis to stay at a monastery in Nepal and study his tradition, but she returned to Cornell. In 1969, she became involved with the Black Panther movement when its members were arming themselves with guns. She made "the most important decision of my life" (124) when, following graduation, she chose to return to the Tibetan Buddhist monastery in Nepal rather than become further involved with the Panthers. This choice may well have saved her life, in contrast to several people she knew.

In Nepal, Willis had a life-changing encounter with Lama Thubten Yeshe, who would become her spiritual teacher.[5] Like Matteo Pistono, Willis found relief and comfort in learning to accept painful emotions that had plagued her. When she is furious at friends, Lama Yeshe tells her to say to herself: "Buddha's mind is angry today" (158). Although not referring to no-self, Lama Yeshe's words help Willis to take another perspective on what she thought was herself: "The suggestion that *my* mind, even filled with anger, was also the Buddha's mind brought a big smile to my face. My body began to release its tension … I was never able to look at myself the same way again" (158). Her identification with these negative feelings – anger, guilt, shame, doubt, and a sense of helplessness – dissolves when her teacher helps her to see them as an aspect of the Buddha's mind and an impersonal process always in flux. Willis realizes that her suffering had been linked to a form of pride rooted in a false sense of self: "Wounds like mine had a flip side too, a false and a prideful view of entitlement: Look at all that I've endured. I'm great. In time, Lama Yeshe would find a way to pull the rug out from under this pride" (158). Letting go of that false self brings release and relief.

Yet although undercutting the self's presumptions is liberating for her, it would be simplistic and dangerous to say that denying the self is a spiritual

---

[5] Jeffrey Paine devotes a chapter to Lama Yeshe's career, including several pages summarizing Willis's memoir, in *Re-enchantment: Tibetan Buddhism Comes to the West* (New York: Norton, 2004).

Life-Changing Travels in the Tibetan Diaspora

panacea for the suffering of African Americans. This is probably why no-self plays a secondary role in Willis's narrative. For people whose humanity was degraded and denied for centuries, it is necessary to affirm the worth of one's being, to struggle for the right kind of selfhood, and to insist that one be treated with dignity and respect. The marchers in civil rights demonstrations carried signs that declared, "I am a man" and "I am somebody." When people freed from slavery took new names to replace those of their former masters, they sometimes chose "Self," "Person," or "Worthy." If no-self is taken to mean the denial of personhood, it is a pernicious doctrine rather than an insight that brings liberation from suffering. This is an issue that other African-American Buddhists have addressed in various ways.[6]

Lama Yeshe becomes an indispensable guide for Willis as, in a delicate balancing act, he sometimes challenges her arrogance or selfishness and at other moments affirms her dignity and worth. In one memorable interaction, he formulates Willis's essential task: "Living with pride and humility in equal proportion is very difficult, isn't it? Very difficult!" (160). Lama Yeshe has an uncanny ability to provide just the gentle reassurance or stern challenge that will bring his student back to a calm, steady groundedness. He diagnoses the source of Willis's suffering as attachment to a particular self-image: "Whether our suffering takes the guise of self-pity or self-absorption, its source is the same: holding too tightly to our projected images of ourselves" (167). His form of therapy for this misery is to deny these false images while affirming Willis's worth and value: "Apart from the one instance when Lama Yeshe yelled at me to teach me a lesson about my own judging mind, he used gentleness, encouragement, and respect for my intelligence to help me build up my confidence and regain self-worth" (167). Willis compares her relationship with her teacher to that between Milarepa and Marpa, Tibetan tradition's paradigm for the teacher–student relationship that is the proper context for spiritual transformation.[7]

---

[6] See Angel Kyodo Williams, *Being Black: Zen and the Art of Living with Fearlessness and Grace* (New York: Penguin, 2002); Hilda Gutierez Baldoquin (ed.), *Dharma Color and Culture: New Voices in Western Buddhism* (Berkeley: Parallex Press, 2004); and Angel Kyodo Williams, Lama Rod Owens, and Jasmine Syedullah, *Radical Dharma: Talking Race, Love, and Liberation* (Berkeley: North Atlantic Books, 2016).

[7] In an essay on teaching Buddhism to American undergraduate students, Willis reflects on the challenge of presenting a tradition that assumes a close relationship between a student and an esteemed living teacher. This model of learning conflicts with the suspicion in Western academia that such a relationship – and indeed, any religious practice by a "scholar-practitioner" – prevents the necessary objectivity and detachment required in the academic world. See Jan Willis, "Teaching Buddhism in the Western Academy," in *Teaching Buddhism: New Insights on Understanding and Presenting the Traditions*, ed. Todd Lewis and Gary DeAngelis (New York: Oxford University Press, 2017), 151–165.

198 Life-Changing Travels in the Tibetan Diaspora

Her relationship to Lama Yeshe was the catalyst for a transformation that didn't happen all at once. In later years, Willis had periods of joy and blissful awareness that resemble the form of consciousness that some people equate with no-self. During a silent meditation retreat, she notices individual birds with delight and a sense of identification. She loses awareness of her distinct individuality and feels merged with the world:

> Thinking about nothing in particular, I noticed that I could see myself standing on the roof of a house some distance away. I had the strange sensation that I was not only standing there but that I could also look back toward the house I was actually in and see myself sitting there. My mind and body felt completely free and unhindered. My normal seeing orientation just suddenly, and subtly, shifted. It was no longer anchored to my physical eyes. I could see myself anywhere I chose, and I could see anywhere. It felt as though my mind suddenly became immeasurably vast. It encompassed everything, the very universe, itself. There was no longer any separation between me and everything else in the universe. The duality of "subject" and "object" simply dropped away and disappeared. The birds and I were of one essence. (221)

Here and elsewhere, Willis describes an experience of unselfing without referring to the concept of no-self. Other moments of great significance on her spiritual journey include taking Buddhist vows, meeting the Dalai Lama, and finding fulfillment and respect as a scholar, professor of Religious Studies, and teaching practitioner of Buddhism. She found enhanced self-confidence through the practice of deity yoga. Meditation training to see oneself as having divine attributes such as wisdom, compassion, and courage can dissolve ordinary conceptions of the self and nurture the qualities of an enlightened being: "The heart of tantric Buddhism is transformation, the idea that we can change our ordinary negative patterns of seeing and feeling into positive ones. And the method employed to bring about such a transformation is nothing other than visualization, in this case, deity-yoga" (207). Just as great athletes enhance their performance by visualization exercises, tantric meditation focuses on positive qualities of deities that are potentialities within all humans but obscured by negative habits and vices.

In the final section of *Dreaming Me*, Willis describes several situations that challenged her Buddhist commitments. A chapter on "Little Things" portrays the toll taken on African Americans by the countless indignities and insults that are often invisible to white people: what have come to be called "microaggressions." Not to respond to them with hatred takes "commitment, prayer, and practice. It also requires that one know how to love oneself" (240). Willis is inspired by others who responded with love

Life-Changing Travels in the Tibetan Diaspora   199

to oppressive situations, such as Martin Luther King, Jr., Nelson Mandela, the Dalai Lama, and Lama Yeshe. Their example helps her when, in the course of genealogical research on her family, she discovers that a white racist who belittled her is a distant relative, another descendant of the slaveholder who raped her great-grandmother. Here, as in many other perplexing situations, Willis must find an inner strength and dignity that is neither intimidated by nor impulsively reactive to threats and humiliations. She asserts that Buddhism and her Baptist roots have much in common as they try to overcome suffering through patience, strength, and compassion. In going to church with her father, being present with her mother as she died, and reflecting on women's liberation and her practice as a teacher, Willis combines Christian and Buddhist ideas and practices. Confronted with a terrifying near disaster on an airplane flight, she calls on both Jesus and Lama Yeshe. Although she refers to herself as a Baptist-Buddhist and an African-American Buddhist, Willis is less concerned with any particular label than with "the eternal truths espoused both by Baptists and by Buddhists" (311).

The title *Dreaming Me* suggests at once the dreamlike, ephemeral, and fictive nature of the "me" of selfhood and the crucial importance of the author's lifelong task of identity construction, which is not only a matter of psychological development but also the goal and the path followed in this "African American Woman's Spiritual Journey." Dreaming both happens to her and is a matter of intention and agency. At five points in the book, Willis describes a dream about lions. The first one expresses terror as these beasts chase her. Later dreams express feelings of anxiety about a lion's presence but also her intuition that it is related to "something deep and mysteriously powerful inside of me" (134). In the final dream, Willis identifies with a lioness and claims its strength as her own: "As I come nearer to the lioness I see reflected in her eyes, my own. My hand goes out to touch her. Reaching for her I seem, suddenly, to see the world as though through her eyes. I feel a deep rumble building in my chest, and rearing my head, I roar" (313). The lion's roar is a traditional Buddhist metaphor for the power of the Buddha's speech. For Willis, it is also a symbol of her own inner strength that she had tried to repress because of shaming experiences. Recurring dreams about lions connect Willis with her African roots and call forth an emerging self: "They are the 'me' that I have battled ever since leaving Docena and venturing forth into a mostly white world. I believe it is time to let the lions come to the fore and to make peace with them. For making peace with them is making peace with myself, allowing me to be me, authentically" (317).

As much as any Western Buddhist writer, Jan Willis uses the ideal and rhetoric of authentic selfhood to convey how Buddhism transformed her. What she learned on her journeys to India and Nepal was a crucial resource as she struggled to create a strong identity throughout the rest of her life. Writing her memoir was also a crucial step: "In discovering and retracing early memories from my life, I found my true self."[8] Although she doesn't discuss the concept of no-self, it shapes her criticism of false ideas about herself that brought suffering. In the end, the title and theme of *Dreaming Me* suggest the need for a critical perspective on every particular idea of self as well as a rejection of any wrongheaded version of no-self that would hinder Black Americans' historic struggle for dignity and a sense of self-worth. Willis suggests that every version of "me" is like a dream: a metaphorical and imaginative projection. Like a dream, it can be significant and real in its effects; it also needs to be recognized as a dream, correlated with other perspectives, and evaluated. The lioness that Willis dreams is neither an identity to be desperately clung to nor an illusion to be rejected or cast off. It is neither self nor nothing but a metaphor of self. Willis's memoir emphasizes the healing power of her identification with this metaphor and her hope that her life story will benefit others, especially those whose selfhood has been systematically denied. In this way, no-self plays a distinctive role in her thinking about the experiences of African Americans searching for healing of wounds to their selfhood.

*

Another traveler who encounters Tibetan Buddhism in its diaspora is Stephen Schettini, whose memoir *The Novice* (2009) describes, as the subtitle puts it, "Why I Became a Buddhist Monk, Why I Quit, and What I Learned."[9] The first of the book's three parts, "Home," describes an unhappy boyhood and adolescence in Gloucester, England, a springboard that propels him on a far-flung journey with little sense of purpose or destination. Schettini grew up in a Roman Catholic family but was never comfortable in the church. He did not do well in school or university. Throughout his life, he was alienated from institutions and communities, including, in the end, Buddhism. He was filled with feelings of inadequacy and guilt, awkward around women, often high on drugs, and a compulsive shoplifter.

[8] Ibid., 160.
[9] Stephen Schettini, *The Novice: Why I Became a Buddhist Monk, Why I Quit, and What I Learned* (Austin, TX: Greenleaf Book Group Press, 2009).

After being arrested for petty larceny, almost on a whim, he departs for India in 1974, at the age of twenty-two. His vague purpose and internal turmoil are suggested by the epigraph of the second part of the memoir, "Away," which recounts the beginning of a life-changing journey. Byron's *Childe Harold's Pilgrimage* describes travel motivated less by a desirable destination than by the impulse to escape misery and self-destructive habits:

> Apart he stalk'd in joyless reverie,
> And from his native land resolved to go,
> And visit scorching climes beyond the sea;
> With pleasure drugg'd, he almost long'd for woe,
> And e'en for change of scene would seek the shades below.　　　(65)[10]

Schettini suffers from many ailments, uses several forms of drugs, and shoplifts compulsively en route to India. Thoroughly disgusted with himself, he realizes that this kind of travel would not liberate him from self-loathing and lack of control: "This journey wouldn't free me from anything. I'd dragged along all I hated and feared about myself like a ball and chain" (91). Debilitated from hepatitis and injections of morphine, he nearly dies in Pakistan, but a Dutch girl confronts him and puts him on a bus to India.

The third section of *The Novice*, "Community," covers the rest of Schettini's life, focusing on the period when he was a Tibetan Buddhist monk. He first encounters Buddhism in Dharamsala, the center of the Tibetan exile community. Buddhist teachings helped him understand his self-destructive actions, loneliness, and lack of control:

> I credited Buddhism for this new perspective. It confirmed that my sense of isolation and entrapment were self-imposed. I was no longer the odd one out. Uncertainty was normal. Life was unpredictable. Denial is rooted in the pretense that we know what's going on, and only when things get desperate do we break down and admit otherwise. (148)

He learns to meditate and responds enthusiastically to the teachings and personalities of several lamas. He decides to study and practice as a monk at the Rikon Institute, a monastery in Switzerland. There he becomes close to several Westerners who were among the first to become Buddhist monks, including Alan Wallace, now a writer on Buddhism and science, and Stephen Batchelor, who would later conceptualize a "secular

---

[10] George Gordon Lord Byron, *Childe Harold's Pilgrimage*, Canto the First, verse VI.

Buddhism" that is much like Schettini's final orientation.[11] Financially supported by an elderly Swiss patron, Schettini commits himself at the age of twenty-two to live as a Tibetan monk in the Gelug tradition.

For much of the eight years of his monkhood, Schettini finds meaning and purpose in learning Tibetan, interpreting, and teaching. He helps found Tharpa Chöeling, a center for Tibetan studies in Switzerland. As time goes by, he becomes skeptical of many aspects of Tibetan Buddhism. Schettini is temperamentally and intellectually more inclined to doubt than he is to believe. In spite of his gratitude to his teachers, he finds it impossible to be devoted to a guru. He feels inadequate and false as he races through chanting and recitations. Although he sometimes longs to have faith, his strong analytical bent and skepticism of authority hold him back:

> Analytically, skepticism was my yardstick. Emotionally, I kept the faith. The two formed a dialectic that spurred me with sufficient focus to stay on track and enough doubt to remain alert. The fact that it left me vaguely uncomfortable was actually reassuring. To this day, the deadening weight of comfort, security and certainty makes me nervous. (224)

He seems most at home in a state of anxious uncertainty, most himself when torn by internal conflict.

As well as taking him to India, travel plays a role in Schettini's transformation as, for a decade, he moves around between various Tibetan Buddhist teachers and centers in India and Europe, teaches at Sera Monastic University in south India, and makes a long retreat at Kanduboda Meditation Center, a Theravada monastery in Sri Lanka. Shuttling between many Buddhist centers and teachers, he compares various understandings of the Dharma. This helps him in "identifying and separating the 'Tibetan' from the 'Buddhism'" (239). He realizes that Buddhism must be translated into the vernacular of every culture and that he could participate in the formulation of a distinctively Western version of the Dharma.

Given his highly individualistic understanding of Buddhism, Schettini sees belonging to a community as a threat to autonomy and integrity. He resists the stretching of the sense of self that can come with participation in a group, which is one way that many Western Buddhists experience unselfing. Ideas about no-self are not important to him; in contrast, he asserts the need for a strong sense of individual selfhood:

---

[11] Stephen Batchelor, *Buddhism without Beliefs* (New York: Riverhead, 1997) and *After Buddhism: Rethinking the Dharma for a Secular Age* (New Haven: Yale University Press, 2015).

My own inability to identify with family, religion and country began to look like an advantage, albeit an uncomfortable one. For a brief respite I thought I'd found my place at Tharpa Chöeling; Now, I was pushing away such feelings again, this time more deliberately than ever. The yearning to belong had led me astray. My path lay in the resolution of my own insecurities, not indulgence in those of a commiserating group. My loyalty should be to my own integrity, without regard for comfort. (262)

Schettini's deconversion from Buddhism is based on ethical scruples shared by many Western writers who recount a loss of faith.[12] Convictions about the ethics of justifiable belief and the primacy of individual conscience require him to leave a religious tradition that he sees as based on uncritical faith that suppresses questions, doubt, and independent thinking. This issue comes up, for example, when he sees instances of male chauvinism among the monks. When he and other monks ask their Tibetan teacher about this issue, Geshe Rabten retorts that it is none of their business. Some monks assert that Geshe has wisdom beyond what they can understand and that proper "guru devotion" means accepting his views as justified. Schettini, however, is amazed and appalled by the "self-imposed blinkers" of these Western adherents: "Here were people claiming to be Buddhists, but so dazzled by exotic thinking and ritual as to be unable to exercise their own critical judgment" (305). After eight years as a monk, he decides that he must leave Buddhist institutions behind in order to explore Buddhist ideas on his own terms.

In the epilogue, Schettini explains his present views, which resemble Stephen Batchelor's "secular Buddhism": "The Buddha's claim to Awakening still charged my imagination, but I saw Buddh*ism* as another matter" (318). He calls for a winnowing or distillation of what is most important and valuable about the Buddha's teaching, separating this from other features "dressed up in the cloak of Tibetan mysticism" (318). What is left of Buddhism after this winnowing process is the Western psychological view of the self. The self's coherence, autonomy, and integrity are the goal of individual development and the definition of psychological well-being, rather than an attachment that causes suffering. This perspective shapes his summary of his past: "In time I came to see myself as a relatively average, partially adjusted individual with the rather typical neuroses of an incompletely outgrown childhood" (322). Like Andrew Harvey, and in contrast with the memoirs of Jamie Zeppa and Jan Willis, Schettini's final stance seems to reduce Buddhism to Western terms, rather than leaving it in unresolved but fruitful dialogue with Western ideas about the self.

---

[12] See the chapter "Hypocrisy and the Ethics of Disbelief," in Barbour, *Versions of Deconversion*.

In one important way, Schettini does rely on an idea related to no-self. At several points, he highlights his conviction that the central theme of the Buddha's teaching is "the end of views." In the Preface, he praises people who can "face their weaknesses or do good, without having to resort to some proprietary belief system" (xiii). He recommends the psychological wisdom of letting go of fixed convictions: "Of all roads to sanity, the quiet good sense of the Buddha's *end to views* may be just what we need to regain our balance" (xiv). Insofar as a person clings to a system of beliefs and identifies it with her very being, she will suffer. The end to (or of) views means not defining one's selfhood and happiness as bound up with ideas, doctrines, or theories. Since leaving monastic life, Schettini has become a teacher of meditation and mindfulness, but he doesn't call himself as a Buddhist, "mainly because I don't identify with any establishment, and don't want to" (329). What he now teaches is how to let go of fixed beliefs and live with uncertainty. The final lines of the book define his goal as a teacher as helping people "question the very things they believe in most earnestly. After all, if I've learned one thing it's that the pursuit of truth has more to do with letting go of certainty than finding it" (332). There is an analogy to no-self in his emphasis on "no-views," the agnostic letting go of beliefs. The end of views means that a person must relinquish any fixed ideas believed to define his selfhood. The title of the memoir, *The Novice*, applies not only to the unformed student who trained to be a monk but also to Schettini throughout his life as he tries to approach every new situation with the openness and freshness of what some Buddhists call "beginner's mind," rather than as a person who has all the answers.

This is a paradoxical, if not inconsistent, place to end up: the view that one must let go of all views. There are plenty of convictions, beliefs, and views involved in Schettini's understanding of Buddhism and the road to psychological health: for instance, ideas about human nature, the basic causes of suffering, and the path to freedom from self-inflicted misery. As he acknowledges, it is not enough to simply empty the mind or be mindful of what passes through it. Correct understanding and an adequate conceptual framework are needed to reorient as well as free a burdened psyche; for instance, one must understand "the cyclic and short-term nature of temporal happiness" (330). Like many other Westerners trying to understand Buddhism, Schettini alternates between formulating this tradition's crucial and enduring core ideas and insisting that every view is tentative, limited, and disposable. In particular, there is a tension between his skepticism about all ethical convictions – since "ethical codes

Life-Changing Travels in the Tibetan Diaspora 205

are as likely to produce hypocrisy as goodness" (329) – and his insistence on certain moral virtues and values: "I tell my students that if they don't cultivate integrity they'll end up grumpy old men and women, and that there's no third option" (332). Some readers will view these inconsistencies as a fatal flaw, others as revealing contrasting perspectives on life that can't be formulated in a logical system (or that, as in the Madhyamika school of thought, require a distinction between ultimate and relative levels of truth).

The Novice contrasts with most Western Buddhist travel narratives in several ways. As much as transformation, Schettini emphasizes a "lifelong attempt to live by my convictions" (321). He locates the source of change not in the impact of Buddhist ideas such as no-self but rather in long-standing qualities of his own character: "What liberation I've found can certainly be explained in Buddhist terms, but it's the product of the soul-searching that started well before, and continued well after, my monkhood. My purpose is not to be Buddhist but to be true" (332). A second difference is that Schettini's story describes both becoming a Buddhist and leaving Buddhism. He views his period of commitment through the lens of later disenchantment, like Malcolm X's perspective on his Black Muslim phase. Although other narratives often show the author abandoning another worldview, *The Novice* is one of the few that portrays a deconversion and loss of commitment to Buddhism.

Schettini's memoir covers all of his life; its genre is religious autobiography, not an account of a single journey. Travel plays a huge role in that his long and miserable trip from England to India as a young man culminates in a period of drug-addicted *duhkha* that opens him up to Buddhist teachings about liberation from suffering. In Schettini's account of travel and transformation, Buddhism played a decisive role in his movement from guilty, anxious self-loathing to a relative contentment that, in his third marriage, includes a happy family life. In addition, Schettini's many movements among Buddhist centers and teachers allowed him to compare and evaluate their merits and flaws. A restless, drifting life turned out to have this crucial advantage. Seeing the dependence of every form of Buddhism on a particular culture, Schettini tried to separate extraneous Tibetan elements from the essential Buddhist ones and devise a new language to interpret these core truths to a secular Western audience resistant to appeals to faith or belief and unaffiliated with any religious community. Although the psychological language he finally adopts does not invoke the idea of no-self, Schettini makes use of a related Buddhist ideal: the end of views.

Harvey, Zeppa, Willis, and Schettini are more assertive than most other Western Buddhist writers about the need to define and claim an autonomous sense of selfhood. It may be that they don't explicitly rely on the concept of no-self because they fear that its interpretation in the West would deny the legitimate place of selfhood when rightly understood. They describe moments of dispossession or detachment from the self's insistent demands, yet in the end they are all very much concerned with the achievement of an adult identity, which did not come easily for any of them. Each writer shows the decisive impact of travels in regions of the Tibetan diaspora and seeks to translate Buddhism into a new idiom in the West. This is especially the case for Harvey and Schettini, both of whom now have careers based on their interpretation of Buddhism. Harvey is a teacher of an eclectic spiritual path among the world's religions, while Schettini gives nonsectarian instruction in meditation. Their memoirs raise the complex question of whether their versions of Buddhism are admirable attempts to learn from and translate insights from another culture or examples of appropriation, exploitation, or the transformation of Buddhism into something else. Zeppa integrates Buddhist concepts with Western ideas of romantic love, personal integrity, a woman's agency, education, and self-fulfillment. Willis combines her critique of false notions of the self with the rhetoric of an authentic selfhood that will help liberate African Americans from racism and internalized denials of their full humanity.

In diverse ways, then, these four narratives downplay no-self or put it in uneasy tension with Western ideals of selfhood. This testing of discrepancies between the norms of a religious tradition and an individual's doubts, other values, and personal experience is a crucial aspect of autobiographical writing and one reason for its significance in understanding religion. Yet if Harvey, Zeppa, Willis, and Schettini do not discuss no-self explicitly as a theory or affirm it as an essential Buddhist truth, experiences of unselfing were for each of them an important turning point or moment of recognition when they glimpsed the possibility of a new way of being in the world. Their alertness for these moments and the ways they interpret their significance show how much they were influenced by the Buddhist view of the self as always in flux, arising and passing away, insubstantial, and as real in its effects as a dream.

CHAPTER 8

Encounters with Theravada Buddhism

Theravada is the name of the Buddhist traditions now dominant in Sri Lanka and Southeast Asia (except for Vietnam, which is Mahayana). The name Theravada in Pali means "the way of the elders." This branch of Buddhism sees itself as preserving the most ancient teachings of the Buddha and uses Pali, the language he spoke, for liturgy and study. Without explaining the history and distinctive qualities of Theravada, I would highlight two characteristics of this tradition that have a strong influence on Western travel narratives. First, monastic life is the preeminent context for Buddhist practice, and the role of monasteries in contemporary life in Southeast Asia is pervasive. The so-called Thai Forest Tradition is a modern revival movement centered in rural monasteries that shaped the development of Vipassana ("insight") meditation and the many permutations of "mindfulness" in the West.[1] I discuss two Western Buddhist travel narratives that dramatize experiences in Thai monasteries: Tim Ward's *What the Buddha Never Taught* and *Phra Farang: An English Monk in Thailand*, by Phra Peter Pannapadipo, who is now called Peter Robinson.

A second distinctive quality of Theravada Buddhism in Southeast Asia is that in this region it is by far the dominant religion. In Thailand, for instance, about 95 percent of the population is Buddhist, and Buddhism is closely aligned with national identity and the monarchy. In contrast to some countries in Asia that are more religiously pluralistic or secular, the nations of Myanmar (formerly Burma), Cambodia, and Thailand appear to Western visitors to be societies where Buddhist values and beliefs play a decisive and pervasive role in all aspects of life. I explore two narratives by Westerners recounting travels and residence in Theravada societies, especially dense urban centers: Rudolph Wurlitzer's *Hard Travel to Sacred Places* and Stephen Asma's *The Gods Drink Whiskey: Stumbling Toward*

---

[1] See Eric Braun, *The Birth of Insight: Meditation, Modern Buddhism, and the Burmese Monk Ledi Sayadaw* (Chicago: University of Chicago Press, 2013).

207

Enlightenment in the Land of the Tattered Buddha. These works portray encounters with contemporary Asian Buddhism, which sometimes contrasts with traditional teachings and is at once influenced by and in tension with the impacts of modernity and globalization. The doctrine of no-self plays a crucial role in all four of these travel narratives, yet it takes on contrasting meanings that reflect each writer's distinctive experiences of unselfing.

*

Westerners began visiting Southeast Asia to understand Theravada forms of meditation as early as the late 1950s. Three groundbreaking books about experiences of Vipassana meditation paved the way for the genre of Western Buddhist travel narratives. In 1958, British Rear Admiral Ernest Henry Shattock published *An Experiment in Mindfulness*, an account of his training with Mahasi Sayadaw in Burma.[2] Marie Beuzeville Byles was an Australian lawyer with a Quaker and Unitarian background; her *Journey into Burmese Silence* (1962) portrays experiences while practicing Vipassana meditation as taught by Ledi Sayadaw.[3] John Earl Coleman was an American CIA agent who, while advising the Thai government on security matters in the 1950s and 1960s, traveled widely in Asia to investigate many religious traditions. In *The Quiet Mind* (1971), Coleman describes a continuing search for relief from the anxiety and stress of modern life, although ironically he says little about his dangerous and deceptive life as a spy.[4] Coleman experimented with nearly every form of meditation in Asia and encountered many remarkable teachers; he especially admired D. T. Suzuki, Krishnamurti, and U Ba Khin, a Burmese teacher following the methods of Ledi Sayadaw. After many years of frustration, Coleman found peace of mind at U Ba Khin's meditation center in Rangoon. He later became an influential instructor in this tradition and lived in England.

These three books share certain characteristics and emphases with Western Buddhist travel narratives. I pass over them quickly for several reasons. While all of them are greatly indebted to Buddhist ideas and discuss *anatta*, they present mindfulness as a method of therapy that can be extracted from its religious context. Coleman, for instance, asserts that

---

[2] Ernest Henry Shattock, *An Experiment in Mindfulness: An English Admiral's Experiences in a Buddhist Monastery* (New York: E. P. Dutton, 1960).

[3] Marie Beuzeville Byles, *Journey into Burmese Silence* (London: George Allen & Unwin Ltd., 1962).

[4] John E. Coleman, *The Quiet Mind* (New York: Harper and Row, 1971).

Encounters with Theravada Buddhism 209

"although Eastern religious thoughts and teachings are spotlighted more than others in this account it does not follow that a person seeking the quiet mind state for himself must abandon his existing religious convictions and turn to Buddhism. The goal is to transcend the teachings of others and experience directly the liberation which can only come from within."[5] Like many Westerners who would follow him, Coleman believes that the original teachings of Buddha were corrupted by his followers, and that an individual can have a direct experience of the state of mind Buddha attained that is free from faith or belief in doctrines.

Although they all traveled widely in Asia, these writers focus on what happened to them during meditation. Much of each book is a "how-to" manual devoted to explaining meditation techniques and an introduction of basic Buddhist ideas to a largely uninformed reading audience. They provide detailed records of what Byles calls "progress and distractions" in meditation with a tightly introspective focus that differs from later travel narratives that balance and connect inner and outer journeys. These memoirs about mindfulness lack the narrative arc provided by the story of a journey, and their authors do not pursue experiences of unselfing away from the meditation cushion. In comparison with the memoirs of Zen monastic life discussed in Chapter 3, Shattuck, Byles, and Coleman do not integrate their analysis of meditation with their encounters with other people and the cultures of Asia. To qualify this assertion: Marie Byles, an outspoken early feminist, exposes the discrepancy between the theory and preaching of no-self and the gender dynamics of monastic practice. That is, she criticizes the hypocrisy of monks who speak of no-self but insist that women serve them. In contrast, "as if to compensate for the self-satisfied superiority of the monks, the nuns were charming, humble, and alive with love and kindness."[6] Byles reminds the reader that meditation is only one of the eight steps in the Buddha's Eightfold Way and that some people who are proficient in meditation "are nonetheless bubbling over with egoism and get angry, possessive, afraid, jealous, and upset over trifles."[7] She is a forerunner of later women who are both drawn to ideas about no-self and wary of how this ideal is used to keep women in a place of subservience.

The memoirs of mindfulness by Shattock, Byles, and Coleman inspired other Westerners to go to Southeast Asia to study Vipassana traditions.

---

[5] Ibid., 20.
[6] Byles, *Journey into Burmese Silence*, 111.
[7] Ibid., 192.

They contributed to the emergence of the contemporary mindfulness movement that advocates this practice as the cure for innumerable problems of daily life, sometimes while maintaining distinctively Buddhist elements and sometimes turning it into a secular therapy or commercial product. These three books were important predecessors of the Western Buddhist travel narratives at the heart of this study, which probe more deeply into how the experience of travel transformed the author in the long term, usually in circumstances influenced by but distinct from the practice of meditation.

Two later books contrast with mindfulness memoirs by focusing on the daily challenges of living as a Theravada monk. The "forest tradition" of Theravada Buddhism began as a reform movement in the late nineteenth century; it emphasized strict observance of monastic codes and existed alongside the urban and village Buddhist temples of Thai society. *What the Buddha Never Taught* (1990) describes a period of two months that Tim Ward spent at Wat Pah Nanachat (International Forest Monastery), an institution in northeast Thailand founded in 1975 by the charismatic teacher Ajahn Chah as a training ground for non-Thais drawn to Buddhism. In this setting, Westerners could practice a strict form of Theravada monastic life while communicating in English. Leading interpreters of Buddhism who were formed in this environment include some who took monastic vows and founded Buddhist centers in the West, such as Ajahn Sumedho, and other teachers who lived a secular life as they adapted Buddhism to Western society, such as Jack Kornfield.

When Tim Ward arrived at Wat Pah Nanachat in 1985, the twenty-six-year-old Canadian had been traveling through Asia for more than a year, including spending three months the previous summer at a Tibetan monastery in Ladakh. In Thailand, he discovered Ajahn Chah's books on meditation and heard that Wat Pah Nanachat was the best place for foreigners to practice Buddhism. Ward planned to stay for three months at the forest monastery as a *pahkow*, a status below that of a novice or an ordained monk. He left earlier than planned with a mixed assessment of the Buddhist life he experienced there. Although strongly attracted to the Buddha's teaching, he was highly critical of the institutions of Buddhist monasticism, especially the ways in which the rules of the *Vinaya*, the monastic code, are interpreted. Among several meanings of the title, *What the Buddha Never Taught*, the most central is that much of institutionalized Buddhism departs from the Buddha's original teaching. In making this critique, Ward is a forerunner of Stephen Batchelor's "secular Buddhism" and other Westerners who want to retain certain key insights of the Buddha but shed as unnecessary baggage most of the doctrinal

Encounters with Theravada Buddhism

elaborations and established structures of historic Buddhist tradition. This orientation resembles the "spiritual but not religious" self-identification of many contemporary seekers of wisdom and transformative experience, who are skeptical about all religious institutions because they wield hierarchical power, define correct beliefs and practices, police boundaries of membership, and insist on observance of particular cultural forms.

Rather than simply dismissing the monastic system as corrupt, Ward explains how he discovered flaws and inconsistencies in the way of life that he sincerely attempted to practice. In formulating his intentions for living at the wat, he roots himself in one of the Buddha's teachings that strongly appeals to Westerners skeptical of appeals to the need for faith or obedience to authority:

> I wanted to place myself within the ancient Theravada tradition in order to judge the fruits of Buddhist philosophy in a living community of monks. The Buddha told his disciples not to accept his words but to practice them and believe only what personal experience revealed. It was an experiment I could not resist. I was not here to seek enlightenment, I reminded myself, not even to demand the truth. I was here only to open myself to experiencing what the Buddha taught. (24)[8]

When he finally leaves the monastery, Ward explains his decision in terms of trying to live in better accord with "what the Buddha really taught," including ideas about no-self.

The greatest challenge for Ward is observing the *Vinaya*, the Pali codebook of 227 regulations governing monastic life. An ajahn (teacher) tells him when he arrives that every rule is a teaching, in that one's resistance to following it reveals that to which one is attached. One's personal preference for less sugar in one's coffee or one's reluctance to bow to a particular senior monk discloses "defilements" based on greed and aversion. Mindfulness is taught at Wat Pah Nanachat less by means of formal instruction or meditation practice than by carefully attending to scrupulous performance of the rules. When he asks the head monk for a teaching, he is told:

> Persevere with the discipline and the defilements will gradually drop away, leaving your mind clear and peaceful. Establish the rules in your heart, follow them with mindfulness and you will stop your craving and thirsting, even for meditation. Here we teach renunciation. Here you can learn to give up cherished ideas of self. Once they are given up to the *Vinaya*, you will see they were only burdens after all. (66–67)

---

[8] Tim Ward, *What the Buddha Never Taught* (Toronto: Somerville House Publishing, 1990).

The ultimate purpose of following the rules of monastic practice is release from suffering; a monk who can transcend personal desires and dislikes in this way will attain liberation. Behind repeated admonitions to just follow the rules lies a theory of how to displace the self.

In practice, Ward encounters many problems in following the *Vinaya*. To observe all the rules requires great effort and what often seems to Ward wasted energy. For instance, as a *pahkow* training to become a novice, he wears white robes rather than the brownish-ochre ones of an ordained monk. Every time he washes his bowl, he is required to squat on the ground, which means that his robes get dirty and have to be washed. Some rules seem anachronistic, such as the ones prescribing careful treatment of begging bowls, which were originally clay but are now made of metal. More troubling than these tiresome regulations are what he views as temptations to moral compromises. Even though he wants to bend the strict requirements of certain rules in his own favor, he criticizes monks who do this, especially the ways in which they think about compromises with the ideal. Although accommodations in implementing rules are sometimes necessary for communal residence in a jungle environment, Ward detects a good deal of hypocrisy about what is really going on. For instance, monks are not allowed to cut down any living plant or even ask another person to do so. This leads to various forms of circumlocution whereby a monk suggests to a *pahkow* which plants are intruding into the monastery's work spaces. Through indirect permission, a way is found to avoid burdensome regulations: "It's just a convenient way of getting around an inconvenient rule" (70). Similarly, because a monk should not harm any living creature, he may not empty a water barrel or cistern that might contain mosquito larvae. Yet measures need to be taken to suppress the mosquito population. So, a monk suggests to Ward: "I suppose you could dump that wash jar over if you wanted to" (68). Ward thinks the whole system produces hypocrisy and self-deception about the covert ways that desires are expressed.

What the Buddha Never Taught recreates extended conversations about the justification and implementation of particular rules, as well as the theory behind this way of life. Ward seems to spend more time engaged in such debates than doing anything else. He admits that he was sometimes arrogant and preachy as he condemned what he didn't approve of. His arguments and judgmental attitude illustrate Ajahn Chah's claim that resistance to a rule discloses attachments, as well as the mind's distraction by idle intellectual controversy. Yet he also shows how manipulating the rules allows monks to gratify their desires, and how their attention becomes directed at getting what they want without causing offense. In this devious way, the teaching of selflessness is violated while monks believe they are rigorously following the prescribed path to realize it.

In this travel memoir, Ward does not explicitly describe any events as illustrating the meaning of no-self. The most intriguing if debatable moment of unselfing is a vivid description of a visit to a local village market. On the way there, Ward debates whether or not the effect of carefully observing the *Vinaya*'s rules is mindfulness. He asserts that an enlightened being should be focused on being mindful rather than obedient and that this kind of consciousness can be practiced anywhere. The market scene follows: a thick description of sights, sounds, and smells as he wanders through a bustling Thai village stocked with enticing delicacies. For once, Ward stops his philosophizing chatter and querulous arguing as he is absorbed in a kaleidoscope of colorful vegetables, clucking hens, piles of animal organs, and dripping meat roasting on spits. When he returns to Pah Nanachat, he falls into a deep meditation, the most focused and energetic session he has experienced. "It was the reason for which I had been sitting and trying to focus for near to a month. Perhaps something was grasped, or something shaken free by the marketplace. I did not know. What I cherished was the feeling of ease. I thought I could recall it at will" (150–151). Yet this state is not something a person can reproduce voluntarily. These two experiences of immersion in the present moment, in a busy marketplace and in quiet meditation, seem to have nothing to do with observing the rules of the *Vinaya*. They seem to be evidence proving Ward's assertions that mindfulness can be practiced anywhere and is more likely to arise without the distractions and resistances created by trying to observe monastic codes. He does not consider what this narrative sequence suggests: that a persistent struggle with the rules may have been a condition for the sense of release that finally comes to him, bringing relief and pleasure. In other words, unselfing came about only after giving up efforts to escape the self that only tightened its determined grasp.

Many Western travelers to Buddhist lands are disturbed by customs linked to "making merit." Ward's closest friend, Jim, leaves the monastery after only a month because he thinks the monastic system exploits local Thai people who render pious devotion and donations in order to earn a more auspicious rebirth. This practice makes sense within Thai society, but Jim is angered when Western monks benefit from these practices; they are not denying the ego but building it up: "These *farang* monks, Tim, they aren't suffocating. They just use the monastery and the rules to make points. They call themselves blessed disciples and allow the Thais to bow down to them. All I see here is ego" (165). Tim and Jim, who most Thais cannot distinguish from each other, are skeptical about whether it is possible to escape ego and doubt that monastic discipline and meditation have any effect. Self pops up everywhere, even wanting to score points out of the "pointlessness" of meditation practice: "My ego still wants to think it's getting enlightened" (167). Like Janwillem van de Wetering in a Zen monastery, these young men all come to recognize the inevitability of egoistic desire in human life, including the quest for self-transcendence expressed in ascetic renunciation. In contrast to monks who assimilate this insight into their practice, Tim Ward and his friend decide to leave the monastery rather than feel that they are acting deceitfully. They are motivated more by an ethical concern about integrity than Van de Wetering, who simply wearies of the futile struggle to escape self.

To Ward, Buddhism as practiced in this Theravada monastery seems joyless and uninspiring, and the dharma talks of the senior ajahns bore him. He is not alone in this view, he asserts, reporting the widespread belief that the Dharma is in decline in contemporary Thailand. After Ajahn Chah was crippled by a stroke, discipline and spirit began to break down, and the current ajahns fail to bring his teachings to life. Looking for inspiration, Ward decides to visit the venerable teacher who for so many embodied the Buddhist way. "Ajahn Chah Gives a Teaching," the memoir's final chapter, portrays his encounter with the aged master as the pivotal event that crystallizes his understanding of Buddhism and impels him to leave the monastery.

Ward sees Ajahn Chah in a wheelchair, completely paralyzed, being pushed around the grounds of his home monastery, Wat Pah Pong:

> Ajahn Chah's eyes are closed, his head fallen to the side. It leans against the back of the wheelchair. The lower jaw is slack. The mouth hangs open at an unnatural angle, forming a triangle from which a pale tongue protrudes. White spittle covers the corners of the lips. The attendant keeps a cloth ready which he uses to wipe away the drool from the master's chin. The old hands are folded one on top of the other. They are mottled and pale for a Thai. The right one twitches occasionally like a dying fish. This is the only movement other than the gentle heaving of the great and collapsing chest buried beneath the robes. I hear him groan, a faint rumble within the sunken frame. (232–233)

In spite of Ajahn Chah's earlier instructions that his followers should not prolong his life by artificial means, for years he was given intravenous feeding, lived in an air-conditioned building, and was lovingly nursed. A mausoleum was under construction so that he could be venerated forever. The

Thai people saw in his final condition a lesson about the impermanence and suffering of human existence. For Ward, though, the spectacle of Ajahn Chah trapped between life and death as a "living corpse" is shocking. He thinks that keeping the Ajahn alive in this manner violates all his teachings about not clinging to what must pass. He sees the tender compassion of monks who tend the Ajahn as a means of scoring merit points, when true compassion would allow him to die. Ward makes a cynical interpretation of plans to build statues and temples in honor of Ajahn Chah, saying that the Sangha will use him to exploit the Thai people so that donations pour in. The "merit industry" must continue to thrive, even if the most important Buddhist truths are subordinated to it: "This is a body, I think, a living corpse. The personality—whether ego or inner spirit, whatever it is that gives life—is gone. It was only illusion to begin with" (234). According to Ward, Ajahn Chah's followers fail to grasp the most basic implication of the truths of impermanence and no-self.

Ward bows to acknowledge his deep reverence for the teacher who introduced him and so many Westerners to a compelling experience of Buddhist life. Then he walks back to Wat Pah Nanachat with Ruk, a German monk who plans eventually to return to the Black Forest and wander from village to village. Ward tells Ruk that his ideal of a monk is "laughter in the villages" and views the German as "an example to carry on the master's teaching" (237). As it begins to rain, Ward suddenly decides that the next day he will leave Pah Nanachat. The book concludes with these lines: "And suddenly, there's laughter in the rain. After so much searching for a teaching—in the texts, the practice, the Ajahn's eyes—it makes me laugh to feel, just for the moment, what the Buddha never taught" (237). This ending conveys several aspects of Ward's ambivalent encounter with Buddhism. The laughter in the rain and in his heart contrast with his bleak portrayal of monastic life as dour, joyless, and grimly obsessed with rules. Leaving the monastery lifts his spirits and liberates him from scrupulous observance of trivial requirements and calculation of ways to get around them. The monastery's focus on strictly following the *Vinaya* did not help him to practice mindfulness but brought only boredom and frustration. Yet although Ward rejects monastic life, he continues to revere the teachings of Buddha and Ajahn Chah, and one senses that they will influence his future life outside it. The title of *What the Buddha Never Taught* takes on a second meaning: it refers not only to the institutional Buddhism that Ward rejects but also to a way of living in the secular world according to the Buddha's wisdom, which Ward was not taught and must imagine and realize on his own.

216 Encounters with Theravada Buddhism

Tim Ward does not portray dramatic moments of unselfing as turning points in a process of transformation. Compared with most of the other authors of Western Buddhist travel narratives, he does not change much during his two months in Wat Pah Nanachat. His cynical judgment of other people's motives does not mellow into a more sympathetic sense of the common human predicament. Yet if self-transformation remains elusive, ideas about no-self were crucial in Ward's assessment of what he learned. He adopts from the outset the ideal of overcoming egoism, and this is the standard he employs to criticize how individual monks and the forms of institutional Buddhist monasticism succumb to hypocrisy and self-deception about how to get what they want. For Ward, that they fail to practice what they preach about selflessness is sufficient grounds for him to reject monastic life. He often seems self-righteous and judgmental, like an adolescent who delights in pointing out the flaws of the adult world. A more mature perspective might see awareness of tensions between the ideal of selflessness and the reality of selfishness as a crucial aspect of spiritual and ethical consciousness, and perhaps as occasions for irony or humor.

Although Ward adopts the ideal of no-self as the standard by which to judge Buddhist monastic practice, *What the Buddha Never Taught* also shows him to be highly ambivalent about this idea. Sometimes he affirms or assumes the ideal of no-self; at other moments, he is skeptical about it or tries to reconcile it with his Western sense of self. This travel memoir, written soon after Ward left the monastery, shows him trying to integrate what he learned there with his plans to return to the West, live a secular life, and become a writer. In an interview in 2011, Tim Ward says that his later writing tries to balance his sense of the ego as a curse with awareness of its blessings:

> One of the things that came out to me as a paradox in Buddhism is the idea that you should strive with all your might to become enlightened. But then when you are enlightened, the "I am" disappears. So what is it that's enlightened? Why would the "I am" strive toward its own destruction? I've never been able to get away from that thought. What is the nature of the self? Is it an illusion? Why is it such a powerful illusion? I don't buy the Buddhist explanation of where this powerful illusion came from. Is it something real, like a soul? I don't buy that mythology either. So who is this self that I am? I'm finishing up a book which tries to grapple with this, by having one Buddhist eye and one scientific eye open.[9]

---

[9] This podcast is episode 49 of "The Secular Buddhist" website, accessed June 2, 2021, at secular-buddhism.org.

Ward's conflicts about the self in his travel narrative later led him to affirm the need for two perspectives based on no-self and self. He takes the concept of no-self seriously as a framework for viewing with detachment the chattering of one's monkey-mind, feelings of dissatisfaction with life, and the endless arising of new cravings. At the same time, *What the Buddha Never Taught* reveals that he could not escape these sometimes unsavory expressions of self. He could not take permanent refuge in no-self to avoid the insistent questions and ambitions of a young Westerner wanting to create an adult identity in his homeland. Like most memoirs about young adulthood, *What the Buddha Never Taught* is not a story about renouncing the self but rather one about finding it, as the author emerges from an oppressive community and claims an individual identity focused on the work of a writer.

The idea of no-self figures prominently in Ward's critique of institutional Buddhism. Yet in his travel memoir it is not experiences of unselfing that are most vivid and transformative but rather the moment of decision when he determines what he wants for his future self.

*

A contrasting perspective on Theravada monastic tradition is *Phra Farang*, which means "foreign monk" in Thai. This memoir was published in 1997 by Phra Peter Pannapadipo, which translates as a monk named "Light, or Lamp, of Wisdom" (33).[10] The book describes the first five years of a decade that Peter Robinson spent as a Theravada Buddhist monk. (I will refer to him with this name, the one he used before and after he was a monk.) *Phra Farang: An English Monk in Thailand* describes the metamorphosis of a successful London businessman into a practicing Buddhist monk. This story contrasts with *What the Buddha Never Taught* in that Robinson changes significantly in many ways during his years as a monk, and he dramatizes certain crucial breakthroughs when he recognizes that he has become a very different person. Like Tim Ward, he attempts to integrate ideas about no-self with key aspects of Western selfhood. For example, he depicts how certain enduring aspects of his character continued to affect him as a monk. The ending of the book, written when he is no longer a monk, raises questions about what changes and what remains the same through his transformations. When Robinson addresses certain ethical issues, he has to reconcile Buddhist ideas about impermanence and

---

[10] Phra Peter Pannapadipo, *Phra Farang: An English Monk in Thailand* (London: Arrow Books, 1997).

no-self with Western moral values linked to a conception of a stable and enduring self.

Peter Robinson does not say much about what drew him to Buddhism. He had a "vaguely Christian" background but found religion irrelevant to his life until he was about forty. As he pursued a business career and pleasure, he began to question whether living a life devoted to good times was enough. His brother, who was also a successful businessman, suddenly died at forty-two. Very much like the initial spiritual crisis recounted by Leo Tolstoy in his *Confessions*, a brother's death brought home "the apparent futility of everything he had achieved, experienced, and acquired. All his success, material gains and future plans were suddenly without an iota of importance. Nor were mine" (7). Having achieved material success and recognition, Robinson started to ask: "Is this all there is?" On a vacation in Thailand, he visited Buddhist monasteries and was impressed by "the feeling of tranquil purpose" (8) there. On returning to England, he began to study and meditate at Wat Buddhapadipa, a Thai monastery in Wimbledon. He soon decided to ordain as a Thai Buddhist monk. (Robinson refers to his tradition in this way rather than to Theravada Buddhism.) It took nearly five years for him to slowly withdraw from his old way of life. His transformation reflects both a perduring character and a determination to discard as much of his past self as he could:

> I've always been one for throwing myself totally into everything I do. In this case, it wasn't just a matter of throwing myself into something but also of throwing something else out. All of it, all the garbage of my life: all my delusions, cravings and aversions, my stupid fixed ideas and all the conditioning that had built up in my head over so many years. (11)

He gives away wealth and possessions, becomes celibate, eats according to strict monastic rules (e.g. not after noon), and resides full-time at the monastery for six months. He realizes that his old lifestyle gave only superficial pleasure and was based on habits acquired thoughtlessly.

Robinson links his renunciation of his former English life to the practice of Vipassana (Insight) meditation, the tradition cultivated in Theravada forest monasteries since the early twentieth century. Robinson has written a manual on Insight meditation practice, *One Step at a Time*.[11] In *Phra Farang*, his brief account of Vipassana focuses on simply observing whatever is going on in one's mind and body and discerning the causes of stress

---

[11] Phra Peter Pannapadipo, *One Step at a Time: Buddhist Meditation for Absolute Beginners* (Bangkok: BangkokWriters, 1999).

and suffering. A standard Theravada understanding of no-self underlies this view of meditation:

> The meditator does not attach to, or try to hold on to, any thought or emotion, even happy ones, but instead observes objectively and dispassionately without any sense of "I" or "my" or "self" being involved. Freed of the I-concept, the mind in its pure state is not disturbed by feelings such as anger, jealousy or unhappiness. It is only the I-concept which gives these feelings life and makes them into "*my* anger," "*my* unhappiness." (19)

When a meditator learns to view thoughts and feelings without attachment, equanimity can arise. The letting go practiced moment by moment in meditation is the model for Robinson's renunciation of his prior way of life when he departs for Thailand.

At the time when Robinson sought ordination, it was not possible to do this in England. He went to Wat Mahadhatu in Bangkok, the "home temple" of his English monastery, where he went through the ordination ceremony and lived as a monk. It took many years to recondition himself to not simply go through the motions but actually become a monk "on the inside":

> With my shaven head and saffron robes, I certainly looked like a monk, but now I had to learn how to *be* a monk. More importantly, I had to begin ditching many of the concepts, delusions, opinions and ways of behavior that I had accumulated over the previous forty years or so on my way to this new starting point. (36)

Compared to most other Western Buddhist travel narratives, Robinson's version of unselfing emphasizes a much longer period of time and a deliberate attempt to transform himself. It doesn't just happen but comes about through prolonged effort. His narrative depicts many awkward moments when he could not understand his Thai context and continued to act and think like a Western person, to the great amusement of Thai monks. Even as he shows how difficult and inconclusive was his attempt to become a Buddhist monk, Robinson also depicts certain pivotal moments when he discerns how he is changing and gains insight into the insubstantial nature of the self.

Living as a Thai monk requires Robinson to radically change his beliefs about what he needs, for instance with regard to living space. Long accustomed to having plenty of space, comfort, and privacy, he now lives in close proximity to other monks in a tiny room without a window or any furniture but a plastic sleeping mat. He adjusts remarkably well to what most Westerners would consider wretched living conditions. His mind develops a new sense of space and freedom: "Where I am is home and I carry my space with me wherever I go" (44). Wearing monastic robes requires a more demanding adjustment, not only to the physical challenges but also to other people's reactions. At first, his vanity and ego are inflated by wearing robes. This quickly dissipates when he realizes that both Thai monks and Westerners think that the tall, pale, and awkward *farang* looks ridiculous. One day at Bangkok's Temple of the Emerald Buddha, he feels humiliated when two young Englishmen mock him: "You look like a bloody idiot" (63). Talking this over with a Thai monk, Robinson has his "first real lesson about the false nature of ego and pride" (65). An insult is only someone's opinion, usually based on ignorance or prejudice. Why should one's equanimity be disturbed by a superficial judgment? In interpreting this incident, Robinson criticizes himself for taking offense at the insult and appeals to the idea of a true self that others do not know. Thai people who bowed to him and tourists who mocked him "knew nothing about *me*" (65) and judged by appearances. The experience of humiliation, rightly understood, was a wake-up call leading to a breakthrough moment when he recognizes his attachment to a particular conception of himself.

Going on early morning alms rounds reinforces monastic training to overcome preferences and aversions. A monk does not "beg" but receives a gift of food from laypeople. He cannot request or reject specific foods or target preferred households. Strict rules regulate the way food is to be accepted. The ritual actions of lay donors and monks symbolize the merit of generous giving and the meaning of food as a support and necessity for the body. Yet Robinson is troubled by ethical questions about alms rounds. For instance, when he sees large amounts of food being wasted, he wonders whether monks should stop accepting more food than they can eat. In response to his scruples, his teachers say that a monk should accept as much food as people offer, even if it will be thrown away. Because the meaning of this practice is the giving, not the receiving, his questions about better efficiency and distribution miss the point. Robinson accepts this view and, his social conscience set at rest, continues to participate in alms rounds. However, like Tim Ward, he is troubled by the way almsgiving is a way of "making merit" that can degenerate into a superstitious and mechanical routine.

In interpreting the transformations he senses are taking place, Robinson relies on the rhetorics of both self and no-self. For instance, take this early moment of amazed self-recognition: "I was a forty-five-year-old former businessman from London, who now found himself walking bald and barefooted in an exotic city at dawn, wearing a robe and accepting food from complete strangers in total silence. And the oddest thing was, it felt *right*" (77). That last phrase suggests an appropriate fit between his new identity as a monk and an underlying nature or character. Yet after only a few weeks in the monastery, he finds his sense of self altering:

> I found I was beginning to forget the businessman that I once had been and it became increasingly difficult, and unnecessary, to relate to his hedonistic pleasures and desires. He was someone who lived a very different lifestyle in a distant land and a seemingly distant past. I was beginning to find a new and hitherto unknown satisfaction in my life; a spiritual satisfaction that I had never experienced before. Slowly, I was becoming a monk, on the *inside* as well as the outside. (78)

In this passage, his former identity becomes "he," while the present-moment monk is "I." Yet when this "I" compares his current satisfaction to past experiences, he makes the assessment that the outer change not only is a matter of appearance but corresponds to a deeper reality, an "inner" character, as well. Robinson assumes that there is a core of identity that underlies shifting social roles and guises: a true self.

Transformation is a gradual process with many aspects, not an instantaneous and total metamorphosis. To render this complex process, Robinson depicts both continuities in his character over many years and moments that crystallize his recognition of significant change. For instance, he notices that he is becoming more of an observer and is less inclined to react in a conditioned and habitual way. He feels more at peace with himself and his environment: what the Thai people call *sabbai*. He is less attached to desires and realizes that past clinging to pleasures led to disappointment and dissatisfaction. These insights affect him at a deep level: "As I could see and experience for myself that the Buddha's teaching worked, even in the smallest of ways, each day brought a strengthening of purpose and a new commitment, not only to my life as a monk but to my life as a *person*" (144). Being a person means having a continuing identity, a character that is partly his/her given nature and also a matter of choice for which he/she is responsible.

The core of his selfhood is called into radical doubt in a central moment of unselfing. Robinson was disturbed by the mixture of Buddhist practices with what he calls Animism and Thais call local custom. In particular, he feels uneasy when asked to participate in ceremonies involving blessing a tree, a cattle truck, or a new washing machine. Exorcisms, which do make some people feel better, also disturb him. Are these practices Buddhist or "just superstitious rubbish" (223)? Because Robinson, like Tim Ward, wants to adhere to what the Buddha actually taught, his belief that contemporary Thai Buddhism has deviated from authentic tradition disturbs his sense of *sabbai*, and he feels cynical and unhappy. He tries to push his doubts aside, but they erupt in a dramatic outburst that leads to a pivotal experience of unselfing and a transition that contrasts with Ward's decision to leave the monastery.

Another monk expresses a vicious streak of cruelty to animals. Robinson attempts to ignore disturbing incidents, telling himself that his Western values are simply different from local ones and that he should not be judgmental. One day, hearing a dog howling in pain, he discovers the other monk castrating it with a machete. Although Robinson rarely felt anger, this time he exploded with rage: "Any ideas I might have had about remaining aloof and non-judgmental disappeared in an instant" (230). He beats the monk furiously, wanting to show him what pain and humiliation feel like. A minute later, he is horrified at his total loss of control: "I watched my faith and belief in myself as a monk, as a *meditative* monk and a strict follower of the Buddha's teaching, evaporate" (231). He becomes bitter and depressed and thinks about leaving the monkhood.

A week after this incident, in despair, Robinson spends a night meditating in the presence of an image of the Buddha. He focuses on his teachers' admonition: "let go … let go … let go." He realizes that his angry outburst has a deeper cause: he resents Thai Buddhism because the monks' superstition, greed, and ignorance allow the original purity of the Buddha's teaching to become corrupted. Magic charms, the constant emphasis on making merit by donating to temples, empty blessings, and the monks' moral lapses all seem to betray that to which Robinson has given his life. He wants monastic practice to measure up to the standard set by the Buddha. At the same time, he is aware that this view, including his sense of aggrieved suffering, reflects clinging to his own ideas: "I wanted everything to be perfect in my little world. I wanted everybody to practice the way I thought they should practice. I wanted perfect monks in perfect monasteries practicing the perfect teaching in a perfect way. And wasn't there some ego here as well?" (238). He tries even harder to let go of resentments, only to realize that he is clinging desperately to the idea of letting go. There is no method of letting go, no teaching that can help him to do so. Suddenly he feels as if he has learned nothing from many years of effort. Exhausted, he tries to get up to do his duty as the morning bell-ringer, and at last what he has been striving for simply happens to him as his mind lets go:

> I actually fell back to my knees. It felt as though someone had thrown a bucket of clean, cold water over me. Not over my physical body, but over my mind. For just a few moments, my mind seemed to empty itself of all

Encounters with Theravada Buddhism

the conflicts and rubbish that was in there. Not just from the past week, but all of it, all forty-odd years of it.

I cannot adequately describe the feeling, but in those few moments my mind had seemed to be totally silent, totally still, totally *pure* and I had an overwhelming Insight into how things could be, how they were meant to be. This was not a spiritual or religious experience, nor any sort of enlightenment, at least not with a capital E; it was just a natural result of my practice. But, for the briefest moment and for the first time, I saw the potential goal. For the first time I knew what meditation was about. (241–242)

Robinson's version of unselfing takes the form of a loss of agency, an effortless doing of what exertion could not accomplish. What takes place is the "letting go" that he has strived for but cannot accomplish by an act of will, a slipping into another way of being that feels as if it happens by itself, without his own agency. Although Robinson is modest about this event and does not call it enlightenment or even a spiritual experience, it resembles what Japanese Zen tradition calls *kensho*, the initial momentary glimpse of one's true nature that must be developed and deepened.

This incident marks a turning point that dissolves his resentment and anger at Thai Buddhism. He stops fretting about the activities of other monks. Rather than be self-righteous, he decides to simply practice in the way he thinks best, leaving others to do what they will. "How others chose to practice needn't affect the way I practiced. Each of us must follow his own path. Let it be ..." (242). After this crucial experience, he accepts what is going on around him, including Animist ceremonies that he has to be involved in. He distinguishes his duties as a monk from his personal practice and beliefs. This accommodation to local practices seems a dubious compromise with both his ideal of Buddhism and his ethical standard of correspondence between outer appearance and "inner" reality. For Robinson, however, the fundamental issue at this point was the need to let go of resentment. His transition from high-minded and demanding judgmentalism to a more accepting equanimity in relation to other monks came to him, after the failure of desperate efforts to stifle his resentments, in a moment of unselfing when his moral demands on himself and others dropped away.

Although he stops condemning other monks, Robinson continues to think about his moral obligations to others in larger terms and wonders "how far the monk's social responsibilities should go in modern times" (296). The ending of *Phra Farang* focuses on how he resolves this issue for himself. He teaches English in several of the wats where he resides, sometimes in formal classes and sometimes through informal conversations. When this activity starts to consume so much time that it impedes his

224 Encounters with Theravada Buddhism

duties as a monk, he asks various abbots for permission to continue and for instruction about a monk's responsibilities to the world outside the monastery. One abbot refuses to allow him to teach English because "a monk should be above the world and the problems of the laity, whilst remaining compassionate for them" (295). The abbot does not object to laypeople visiting a monk, however, so Robinson goes on teaching informally. This activity eventually led him to establish a small fund to help impoverished Thai students to finance their studies. The Students' Education Trust is now a successful nonprofit charity that has benefited more than a thousand students, and Robinson is the director.

Robinson portrays his growing involvement in this work not as an expression of his Buddhist beliefs but as an ethical commitment that reflects his personal standards and a more general human duty:

> I don't do that work because I am a Buddhist monk, nor even because I am Buddhist; I do it because I believe it is the *right* thing to do, the compassionate thing to do. I am in a position to help and I consider it my social responsibility and my duty—not as a member of the Thai Sangha but as a member of the human family—to give what help I can. (297)

When he encounters an abbot who turned his monastery into an AIDS hospice, Robinson is impressed with this work, "but I couldn't honestly say if it is right or wrong of him to be doing it *as a monk*" (298). It is surprising that Robinson does not consider an alternative way of viewing compassionate activities of monks as an expression of "socially engaged Buddhism."[12] He roots his ethical responsibilities in personal moral capacity and universal human obligations but not in specifically Buddhist terms.

Phra Farang concludes in 1997, when Robinson, still known as Phra Peter Pannapadipo, had been a monk for about five years. This conclusion focuses on two distinct topics that are more closely related than is obvious: his practice of meditating inside a crematorium and his recent attraction to Zen. Meditating inside an oven where bodies are burned was an attempt to experience at intuitive and physical levels what he knew as an intellectual truth: that there is no escape from the dissolution of the body. He was also reacting against what he saw as a wrong-headed attitude to the decaying body: one that attempted to stifle desire by creating horror, repulsion, and disgust. This dualistic perspective is very different

---

[12] Sallie King, *Socially Engaged Buddhism* (Honolulu: University of Hawaii Press, 2008) and Donald Swearer, *Conflict, Culture, Change: Engaged Buddhism in a Globalizing World* (Somerville, MA: Wisdom Publications, 2015).

from Robinson's desire to foster recognition of things just as they are, independent of human aversion and attraction.

As he struggled to escape dualism, Robinson found a spiritual guide in the Zen teaching of Huang Po, a ninth-century Chinese master. His attraction to Huang Po's use of paradox and his rejection of dualistic thinking grew out of Robinson's frustration with his meditation practice. He wanted to go beyond cultivating "good" qualities of mind and eliminating "bad" ones, an orientation that remains rooted in attachment and aversion. Robinson's social conscience and sense of moral responsibility stand in uneasy tension – or perhaps in paradoxical relationship to – his assertion that concepts of good and bad reflect a dualistic splitting up of the world into what we want and reject. In contrast, Huang Po said: "Away with your likes and dislikes, every single thing is just the one mind" (367). As is the case with most Westerners drawn to Buddhism, Robinson wants to have his moral cake and eat it (i.e. have it disappear), too. He wants to affirm certain ethical values, such as compassion for suffering and responsibility to help others, yet also acknowledge the limitations of personal moral beliefs and judgments. Zen seems to understand this paradox better, or at least to express it more compellingly, than does Theravada Buddhism. Yet Robinson affirms that every form of Buddhism is valuable. The color of one's robes, the location in which one practices, or the label for one's tradition don't matter compared to the common vocation of all monks: commitment to "mind work" or "mental cultivation" in pursuit of "the personal realization of Ultimate Truth" (369). Every day he takes another step on that path: "I am happy, I am sabbai, to continue the journey" (370). Robinson's calm, ironic, and wise voice, along with his lack of pride, defensiveness, or desire to set others straight, is convincing evidence for this claim.

A second ending of *Phra Farang* is an afterword dated two days before October 11, 2003, when he disrobed as a monk. After ten years, his work directing the Students' Education Trust had become so demanding that he could no longer fulfill his duties as a monk. "Instead of being a full-time monk doing a little social work in my free time, I became a full-time social worker dressed in robes" (374). In addition, after he published *Phra Farang* and three other books about Buddhism, Robinson began counseling people by email, receiving Western visitors drawn to Buddhism, teaching, giving talks, leading meditation retreats, and helping disadvantaged persons. These demands forced him to rethink his priorities. Again Robinson does not justify his work with specifically Buddhist principles, but instead invokes a more general human ethical responsibility: "I consider I would be failing in my moral duty as a *person*—as a member of the human family—if I didn't offer that help" (374). The work of the Students' Education Trust is "more satisfying than anything I have ever done before" (376), so it is not only a moral duty but also the primary source of meaning and happiness in his post-monastic life.

As he anticipates the imminent ceremony of disrobing, Robinson interprets his next transformation both in terms of no-self and as the expression of an enduring self with abiding values and commitments. On one hand, change is the way of all beings: "No phenomenon remains the same for two consecutive moments, including the working of our own minds" (372). At the same time, Robinson uses the traditional language of Western selfhood to interpret the continuity of his life as a whole:

> *Nothing whatsoever should be clung to.* Anyway, saying those Pali words can't change what I am *inside.* I will exchange my robes for a shirt and trousers, but that will be the only difference. For me, it will be a superficial one. Whether I am Phra Peter or Mr. Peter, I will be the same person and I will try to live my life by the same code of ethics that has sustained and guided me for the past ten years. (377)

The idea of an "inside," the reference to being a person, and the ideal of conforming one's life to a code of ethics are deeply rooted in Western ideals of selfhood and moral character such as integrity, the wholeness and coherence of a person's entire life. Two perspectives on transformation, based on Buddhist ideas about no-self and Western ideals of ethical selfhood, stand in tension, and perhaps in contradiction. Yet there is wisdom in affirming both these perspectives as frameworks for understanding the experience of transformation, in contrast to a theoretical scheme that would be simpler. This kind of complex truth is best rendered in narrative, even as it elicits our reflective thinking about how to reconcile and integrate the apparent tensions between the rhetorics of self and no-self.

*

The concept of no-self plays a different role in two travel narratives by individuals who traveled in Southeast Asia, one for a few weeks as a tourist and one for a year as a teacher. Rudolph Wurlitzer's *Hard Travel to Sacred Places* (1995) must be the most depressing Western Buddhist travel narrative ever written; it might have been titled "Miserable Travel to Disappointing Places." This memoir fathoms the depths of *dukkha*, the multiple forms of suffering and dissatisfaction that afflict human life. The book's bleak, exhausted, hopeless perspective denies the reader's desire for an uplifting story of transformation or even a bit of learning or wisdom. Yet *Hard Travel* also challenges the reader to recognize that the desire for transformation may disguise the self's desire to perpetuate itself, control its experience, and exploit the resources of Buddhist tradition for personal gain.

Wurlitzer recounts a journey of several weeks in 1993 through Thailand, Burma, and Cambodia. He was accompanying his wife, Lynn Davis, a photographer who was on assignment from a New York magazine to portray sacred sites in these three countries, in all of which Theravada Buddhism is the dominant religious tradition. Wurlitzer, a novelist, essayist, and screenwriter for movies including *Little Buddha* (1993), was also scouting locations and discussing ideas for several possible film projects. Yet the "real reason we have come," he says, is to further the process of grieving for Davis's twenty-one-year-old son Ayrev, who had died six months earlier in a car accident. The couple hoped that travel would move them beyond numbness and agony, both distracting them and helping them mourn: "After long weeks of solitude, we finally needed to break out, to become part of life again, to be far away from everyone and everything in order to be closer to what, in any case, we are going through" (2).[13] His hopes are disappointed, however, as travel only reinforces the vices that cause suffering:

> The outside has taken over from the inside, and we don't have enough spiritual muscle to resist. We bounce back and forth from paralysis to gathering information to compulsive distraction. Too many thoughts. Too many plans, or, as the Buddhists might say, too many attachments to the three poisons of addiction, aversion, and delusion. (2)

Wurlitzer compares the journey to "an endless *bardo* tunnel, that strange in-between state that the Buddhists believe exists between life and death" (1). At the outset of the journey, he predicts failure to escape from the *bardo*:

> Grief, as I have been learning, along with everything else it brings, can sometimes shatter ordinary self-absorption and vanity with such force that, for a moment, it seems to set one free. Until, that is, the tonic of self-congratulation sets in and one is reduced once again to the old encrusted and habitual patterns of personality. (3)

The cycle of expectation followed by disappointment is repeated throughout *Hard Travel*, crushing any hope of exit from the *bardo* state. Grief can move a person beyond self-concern if one recognizes the universality of loss and is moved to compassion for others. Yet Wurlitzer's grieving, like *bardo* travel, is an endless repetition of selfish preoccupations.

---

[13] Rudolph Wurlitzer, *Hard Travel to Sacred Places* (Boston: Shambala, 1995).

The journey through Southeast Asia involves many forms of suffering (*dukkha*), and the need to come to terms with Ayrev's death is a radical confrontation with impermanence (*anicca*). The third of Buddhism's three marks of conditioned existence, no self (*anatta*), is a concept that Wurlitzer understands but struggles to experience and apply to his life. He searches desperately for a different kind of self and to escape entirely from the burdens of identity. He had studied and practiced Buddhism for many years, and this background shapes what he sees and hopes for in his journey. Both he and Davis are seriously ill for much of the journey, with physical symptoms including bronchitis, fever, nausea, diarrhea, dehydration, sunstroke, and convulsions. In addition, a spiritual malaise haunts each of them. Thai folk medicine describes a loss of "life spirit" (*khwan*) that Wurlitzer compares to what the West calls depression or melancholia. This diagnosis has roots in his professional work and is a "common enough complaint from middle-aged writers who have spent too much time on the celluloid trail, giving away their language to directors and producers, sublimating their 'self' to the outside, betraying their own signature, becoming, in a sense, a slave to others" (55). He expresses the pain of a creative writer whose work disappears into someone else's art. Like a neglected Thai ghost, he demands recognition and acknowledgment. At the same time, Wurlitzer surmises that his misery originates in breaking Buddhist vows and not practicing the teachings he received from a Tibetan lama twenty years earlier. He has indulged in a distracted life without mindfulness. The Thai remedy for the loss of *khwan* includes saying "no" with discrimination and "abandoning superficial ambitions which are full of aggression and ego enhancements" (55). To truly live out the meaning of no-self would require that Wurlitzer renounce his desire for credit and fame.

Much of Wurlitzer's nausea and self-disgust throughout *Hard Travel* focuses on his artistic work as a screenwriter. At the time of the journey, he had recently completed the script for Bernardo Bertolucci's *Little Buddha*. He says that making a Hollywood film for a mass audience, with a huge budget and manipulative effects, betrayed both his artistic intentions and the substantive content of Buddhist ideas. The film reflected his self-consciousness as a Buddhist and was pious, politically correct, and trivial: "Even a film on the life of the Buddha can become another quick fix, another reductive distraction for a passive audience, another hors d'oeuvre for hungry ghosts, and, of course, ultimately nothing more substantial than yesterday's newspaper-magazine-film-TV entertainment" (28). He does not discuss specific details of *Little Buddha*, and his criticisms are directed at the film industry itself; writing a script involves "cherishing and exploiting the illusions of the nonexistent self" (29). Yet even as Wurlitzer condemns his past artistic compromises and failures, he indulges in fantastic plans for future films that will make him and his collaborators rich. At a drunken dinner with expatriates from Hollywood, a book falls out of his pocket: Joseph Goldstein's guide to Buddhist meditation, *The Experience of Insight*. Wurlitzer quotes a passage that culminates in the ideal of getting free of the concept of self. In contrast, he and his cronies, "each in our own way, [are] promoting and toasting the 'concept of self'" (35). His personal hell is partly of his own making. He hopes to pass through this artistic *bardo* – the transitional zone between his previous work and what would come next. What came out of this liminal period is *Hard Travel to Sacred Places*, the antithesis of a feel-good Hollywood movie.

Wurlitzer encounters many instances of Western exploitation of Southeast Asia's resources and traditions, such as a thriving market of stolen Khmer sculpture. As Buddhists, he and his wife bear an even heavier burden of guilt. Her photography and his film script for *Little Buddha* profit from the religious tradition to which they are committed: "Lynn and I, each in our own way, are ripping off images and Dharma experiences and bringing them back to the reductive shredder of our own culture. It is up to us to assimilate and transform these experiences, not to exploit or showcase them" (151). Yet while he reproaches his past work, he is considering a proposal to make a film about André Malraux's youthful participation in pillaging Buddhist sculpture from Angkor Wat: "a contemporary caper picture ravaging and exploiting the soul of religion, with inevitable karmic results" (150). Wurlitzer's constant self-recrimination and guilt for his continuing temptation to make this kind of film contribute to the mordant tone and self-loathing in *Hard Travel to Sacred Places*, almost repelling the reader by showing unattractive aspects of the author and of Buddhism. The memoir seems an act of penance and expiation for his participation in Western exploitation, neocolonialism, and Orientalism. Although Wurlitzer wants to atone for previous acts of appropriation, he fears he is repeating the pattern.

Wurlitzer asserts that the three poisons of greed, hatred, and delusion dominate contemporary life in Southeast Asia: "The gods of consumerism are in the ascendency" (66). Bangkok is full of glitzy hotels, department stores stocked with Western goods, strip shows for tourists, and drug abuse. He condemns the effects of commercialism and capitalism on traditional Thai virtues: "In Bangkok we see traffic jams and pollution, but we cannot see human values" (43). Because in Thailand Buddhism is tightly aligned with nationalism and the monarchy, it has been corrupted and compromised. Wats and archeological sites have become nothing but tourist stops: "There are no pilgrims there, however, and everything seems too arranged, too protected and overrestored, too much of an archeological museum without any real spiritual substance" (59). *Hard Travel* undermines Western visions of Buddhism as a desirable or transformative spiritual tradition, at least in the contemporary world.

When Wurlitzer and Davis move on to Burma (now Myanmar), a much more isolated part of the Buddhist world, they "almost weep with nostalgia" (74), for they find no noise, commerce, or other tourists and few signs of Westernization. The Shwedagon Pagoda seems a magical place full of childlike, innocent people. For the first time on the journey, Wurlitzer feels that he is "inside a living refuge, a place of the spirit where every thought, every passion, every emotion becomes an offering" (87). Pausing for a moment, he experiences the "bare attention" he has longed for, but he quickly returns to the anxious consciousness of a tourist rushing between must-see distractions. Unlike most Western Buddhist travel narratives, in which the author usually claims that a moment of unselfing made at least a small difference in what came next, for Wurlitzer any moments of insight or absorption in something beyond himself quickly dissipate and leave no trace.

His initial delight in Burma quickly turns sour when Wurlitzer tours several temples and archeological sites. When he views the ancient ruins of Pagan, where 70,000 monks lived among 13,000 stupas and temples, he is intensely aware of his dissatisfaction with the present. He imagines an ancient golden age of Buddhism utterly different from contemporary Burma:

> What must it have been like to be totally surrounded by Buddha Dharma, to live in a community that was, for the most part, dedicated toward the evolution of the human psyche? Perhaps there were hundreds, even thousands of realized beings living here, teaching, meditating, transmitting. Is it possible that at one time a culture could exist without consumerism, without worldly manipulations, without even the idea of progress? (108)

Wurlitzer knows full well that the three poisons are present in every time and place. Yet his travel memoir demonstrates the persistent Orientalist tendency to see authentic Buddhism only in the distant past and to condemn contemporary Buddhist practice for falling short of the author's ideal.

When Wurlitzer visited Cambodia, it was still embroiled in conflict between the Khmer Rouge and the official government. He sees constant reminders of the Khmer Rouge's slaughter of more than a million Cambodians between 1975 and 1979. Wurlitzer identifies each of the countries he visits with one of the three poisons: Thailand with greed, Burma with delusion, and Cambodia with hatred: it seems to him "a hell world" (124). Touring Angkor Wat's magnificent temples, he is overwhelmed by their scale and abundant imagery, as well as disoriented and crushed by his inability to respond to this spectacle. He explains this failure in terms of grief's numbing effect, which leads to nihilism:

> Grief will do that to you. It will embrace you with despair, it will crystal-lize suffering as if suffering is somehow a more honest state of mind than transcendence or equanimity... In the twilight of fading grief, the seductive pimp of nihilism will once again appear, smiling from the doorway like an old friend who knows the power of negation and spiritual narcissism, the greatest trap of all. Hooked on pain, on the terror of impermanence, on nothingness, hooked on the demolition of loss. (137–138)

Overwhelming suffering such as grief can become an addiction that fills a person's consciousness so that *dukkha* dominates one's sense of self and what is possible.

In undertaking this pilgrimage, Wurlitzer had hoped to merge personal grief for Ayrev's death with awareness of other people's suffering. He and Davis wanted

> to raise our view, to surrender all these lingering attachments and join our personal suffering to a larger grief: the grief of the world, where millions of children die every day, where someone is killed in a car crash in the U. S. every twelve minutes, and finally, unalterably, where one lives at ease with the truth that "everything born is impermanent and bound to die." (85)

Yet there is very little compassion for others expressed in *Hard Travel*; the couple remains consumed by their own sorrow. Nor does Wurlitzer show much interest in possibilities for constructive activities that express concern for others. Once he mentions Thich Nhat Hanh's "engaged Buddhism" as a possible way to reenter society. While they are in Burma, with signs of military control everywhere, Aung San Suu Kyi, the leader of a movement to restore democracy, is under house arrest. Wurlitzer predicts that, if her reforms were to succeed, Western poisons would pour into Burma. In his personal interactions with others and his fatalism about political or social changes, he expresses dismay and disgust while dismissing any sort of compassionate or ameliorating response to suffering. He rejects the mere wish that things might be different as a temptation of Mara, the Lord of the Desire Realm: "Mara is present on this pilgrimage, lurking around, asking for a profound experience, a release from the pain of Ayrev's death,

232   Encounters with Theravada Buddhism

hope for Lynn, even an affirmation of life. Anything but the truth of the present moment" (62–63). In this prolonged *bardo* experience, grief and sorrow do not lead to a melting of the boundaries that keep each suffering person feeling isolated and estranged.

Depressing as it may be to read this book, by writing it Wurlitzer was trying to become a different kind of artist, even a different self, than he was in the past. Did he succeed? In comparison with other Western Buddhist travel narratives, the ending of *Hard Travel* offers little evidence that the author was transformed by travel. The waiting room at Siem Reap is another *bardo* passage just like the one in Bangkok where the memoir begins. Their physical journey ends with the couple no closer to relief from grief: "Our pilgrimage is over. But we have not yet been delivered back to anything resembling a life that we can recognize" (157). Wurlitzer suggests that his future life might go on with greater acceptance of the inevitability of suffering. Perhaps daily life could be based on different priorities "beyond the usual distinctions, beyond entertainment, beyond the material, beyond the sick addictions of our own culture" (159). Yet he has no idea what such a future life would look like.

Even moments of tentative openness to an alternative way of being are ephemeral. When the couple encounters a traffic jam on the way to the Phnom Penh airport, they panic, forgetting everything they thought they had learned about mindfulness and equanimity. On two motorcycles, they race to the airport:

> And then, for a moment, I let go. No more Lynn, no more Ayrev, no more grief, no more fear, no more hope, no more happiness, no more suffering. No more letting go. There is just the wind and the shifting, leaning exhilaration of the motorcycle as it maneuvers past obstacle after obstacle looming up on all sides of us, life arising and passing and arising once again. (160–161)

For an instant, he forgets his anxiety and unhappiness, aware only of dangerous speed. This moment of exuberant unselfing arises and passes, leaving no trace.

Wurlitzer doesn't change in the course of his journey but finishes it in the same condition as he began: exhausted, dispirited, and dissatisfied with both himself and the Buddhism he encountered in Southeast Asia. The only sign that he was affected by the journey is the memoir that he wrote about it, which is so different from the upbeat commercial Hollywood film *Little Buddha*. I found myself disappointed that Wurlitzer doesn't get anything out of his journey, much less self-transformation. Then, I considered this reaction. Perhaps my wish for a more cheerful tone and a happier ending simply reflects a desire for the familiar conventions of a Western redemption narrative. I want a travel narrative to culminate in the adventurer's triumphant return home. I expect a spiritual memoir to involve, if not conversion, at least some affirmation of whatever wisdom the author has learned. I would like hard travel to earn something, so that the ordeal leads to profit. I want to see a contrast between the author before and after the journey, a story of meaningful change: a transformation. Wurlitzer's grim and melancholy story, which offers no compensating and consoling lessons learned, denies this yearning.

Yet Wurlitzer's version of Buddhism may be closer to the meaning of nonself than stories that present the Dharma as a tool to improve, enhance, or aggrandize the self. *Hard Travel* reflects more than just the author's exhaustion and continued grief. It shows him trying to escape the ways that the egotistical self tries to turn everything, even an experience of noself, into a story of its own triumph. His passing glimpses of unselfing do not bring transformative long-term consequences; they do not fuel a project of heroic self-transcendence and spiritual ambition. Instead, they arise and pass endlessly, like everything else. With this unsavory presentation of Buddhism in Southeast Asia, Wurlitzer tries to avoid profiting from that spiritual tradition and renounces the artistic temptation to provide a Western audience with an idealized but false version of Buddhism.

In another of the many paradoxes related to no-self, Wurlitzer's portrayal of himself as essentially unchanged by his travels shows his detachment from the usual Western preoccupation with how Buddhism can help, benefit, or improve the author and reader, an orientation that risks turning this spiritual tradition into a means of self-enhancement. His narrative evinces an unusually gloomy version of a theme we have seen in other narratives that end with the author giving up hope for enlightenment yet perhaps also letting go of some of the ego's demands. This weary and disillusioned memoir expresses another interpretation of no-self as it renounces any spiritual gains and other typical appropriations of a globe-trotting tourist.

*

In *The Gods Drink Whiskey: Stumbling Toward Enlightenment in the Land of the Tattered Buddha* (2005), Stephen Asma explores various dimensions of Theravada Buddhism in a genre that he calls "philosophical journalism" (241), seven essays that interpret ideas and cultural practices that he encountered during the year he spent in Cambodia in 2003. Asma taught Buddhist philosophy to Cambodian students at Phnom Penh's Buddhist Institute in a program attempting to reconnect young Khmer

234 Encounters with Theravada Buddhism

students with their religious heritage. Cambodia had been devastated by the horrific events of the 1970s Khmer Rouge regime and, in the 1980s, prolonged civil war and fighting with the Vietnamese. Asma also visited Thailand and Vietnam. In the tradition of Montaigne's essays, his writing is autobiographical as it explores large philosophical and religious questions from the perspective of his own experience. He mixes narrative exposition with analysis and evaluation of Buddhist ideas:

> Following the essay method, I have generally avoided theories and tried instead to offer stories that may contain larger truths. I have tried to study simultaneously the ideas and beliefs of the people I met and the original ideas and arguments of the Buddha. My narrative here is personal, but it is also a narrative steeped in the wider issues of Buddhist philosophy. I hope that it has the detail to avoid the abstractions of pure theory while remaining theory-conscious enough to have some modest normative value as well. (xii)[14]

A committed Buddhist himself, Asma is confident and forthright about his assessments of Buddhist thought and practice in Southeast Asia. He affirms the rationality and value of certain Buddhist ideas and criticizes what he sees as superstition, incoherence, or inconsistency with what he sees as one of the Buddha's central insights: the truth of no-self.

The book's title refers to the practice in Southeast Asia of making offerings to local spirits that inhabit the natural world. Local people build miniature wooden spirit houses near homes, farms, and businesses, and they cajole spirits who take up residence there with incense, flowers, fruit, and whiskey. Many Western observers dismiss this animistic practice as completely inconsistent with Buddhism, as did Tim Ward. Asma, in contrast, is interested in the ways that Buddhism takes a specific form in any particular cultural context, and he tends to find value in most religious practices, even those he criticizes. In Southeast Asia, Buddhism is entangled with animistic beliefs and practices and with Hindu myths and ideas, including belief in karma and reincarnation. Moreover, Buddhism's early formulations ("what the Buddha really taught") often stand in tension with later developments such as worship of the Buddha as a deity. Asma appreciates these rich and sometimes contradictory dimensions of Buddhism as it mixes with other cultures in Southeast Asia. At the same time, he makes normative judgments about what he thinks is helpful or harmful for himself and for Asian Buddhists. In particular, he criticizes aspects of Buddhism in Cambodia that are inconsistent with the crucial doctrine of no-self.

---

[14] Stephen T. Asma, *The Gods Drink Whiskey: Stumbling Toward Enlightenment in the Land of the Tattered Buddha* (San Francisco: HarperCollins, 2005).

Encountering Theravada Buddhism "on the ground" in Cambodia and Thailand contrasts markedly with the forms of Zen and Tibetan Buddhism that have been influential in the West. Zen has often been introduced as a meditation practice without a history or cultural context:

> This neutered Zen Buddhism has no baggage whatsoever, so Americans felt that they could drape it over whatever beliefs they already enjoyed. That seems like a virtue at first ('Look, I'm a Christian *and* a Zen practitioner!'), but it lulled Americans into thinking that Buddhism is the Silly Putty of religions—infinitely malleable and conveniently fashionable. Buddhism becomes another accessory. Living in Southeast Asia, however, rids you of this confusion very quickly. (xv)

In contrast to Zen, Theravada Buddhism is "the whole enchilada": cluttered, messy, and irreducible to our utilitarian plans to improve our lives. Travel in Asia helps Asma see how Buddhism is expressed not only in meditation practices but also in metaphysical and epistemological speculations, moral traditions, rituals, and popular culture. He challenges Americans who take as normative Tibetan Buddhism (6 percent of the worldwide total of Buddhists), pointing out the distinctive character of its speculations about afterlives in the *bardo* and worship of lamas, including the Dalai Lama. American understandings of Buddhism are corrected and enriched by direct encounter with Theravada traditions, which, even in modern reform movements, are arguably closer to the Buddha's original teaching.

When he criticizes Buddhism in Southeast Asia, Asma's normative standard is the idea of no-self. In the chapter "Karma and the Killing Fields," he describes a visit to the notorious Security Prison 21, where 17,000 people were tortured to death by the Khmer Rouge. His guide at the prison, whose family was murdered, tells Asma that karma will eventually catch up with the killers even if a tribunal does not. The idea of karma gives this grieving woman comfort and is a deep part of Cambodian culture. Yet, in Asma's view, it is inconsistent with the most important insights of Buddhism. He recoils from the use of karma to explain why people suffer, for instance when the patriarch of one Buddhist sect says that, because of their previous sins, the Cambodian people deserved the atrocities inflicted by the Khmer Rouge. This patriarch, Tep Vong, argued that the sangha should not work to prevent HIV infections or care for people who get AIDS because they are being punished for immoral behavior. Because this way of thinking blames the victims of atrocity and disease and lacks compassion for them, it is morally abhorrent. Asma analyzes the contradiction between ideas about karma and the Buddha's avoidance of speculation about the unknown, as well as a fundamental inconsistency with teaching about *anatta*. Since the

236 Encounters with Theravada Buddhism

Buddha rejected the Hindu doctrine of atman, the eternal presence of the divine within a person, it makes no sense to assert that an individual's misdeeds will be punished in a later reincarnation. If there is no soul or indestructible self, what is it that would be punished in a later rebirth?

In criticizing the way karma gets linked to samsara, the doctrine of rebirth, Asma relies heavily on the teachings of a modern reformer of Theravada Buddhism, Buddhadasa Bhikku (1906–1993). Buddhadasa's crucial work *Me and Mine* describes the central teaching of Buddhism as the discovery that there is no person or self, no me or mine.[15] Enlightenment brings about the end of ego-consciousness, including self-interested preoccupation with accumulating merit to ensure a better rebirth. Following Buddhadasa, Asma uses *anatta* as the normative criterion by which other beliefs, including karma and samsara, are rejected as inconsistent with the fundamental truths taught by the Buddha. Karma and samsara are basically attempts to make people moral by appealing to their self-interest. Although these ideas may also provide comfort to people suffering, they are incompatible with anatta.

So argues Asma's friend Chaminda, a Sri Lankan who sees much of worldwide Buddhism as falling away from the Theravada orthodoxy preserved in his homeland. Asma, however, considers another possible interpretation. He does not completely reject karma, samsara, and certain developments in Tibetan and Mahayana Buddhism but rather discerns in them a symbolic meaning. When Tibetan Buddhists invoke deities and bodhisattvas, Asma suggests that such practices should not be understood as a way to engineer one's fate in a future life but rather as a technique for overcoming selfishness:

> Some Tantric Buddhists use the vital imagery of bodhisattvas not as *wish-granting beings* for prayer, but as *meditational devices* designed to bring the practitioner to greater ego annihilation. The practitioner doesn't think of the Buddha image as a deity but as a tool for focusing meditation, and the point of the meditation, residing squarely inside the heartwood of dhamma, is to overcome the self. (178)

He takes speculations about the soul's journey through *bardo* planes as a metaphorical way of describing what must happen psychologically for a person to overcome egotism in this lifetime. In this way, Asma appreciates aspects of Buddhist practice that other Westerners reject as not what the Buddha really taught, even as he continues to depend on the central

---

[15] Buddhadasa Bhikkhu, *Me and Mine: Selected Essays of Bhikkhu Buddhadasa*, edited with an Introduction by Donald K. Swearer (Albany: State University of New York, 1989).

criterion of consistency with no-self. Some later developments in Buddhist history are faithful to the Buddha's central concern.

This discussion with Chaminda, which spirals into increasing complexity and uncertainty as the two friends devour a large "happy pizza" laced with marijuana, ends without resolving the question of whether the austere philosophy of Buddhism that makes rational sense to Asma is fully compatible with the cultural forms that provide meaning to many Asian Buddhists. Asma is a philosopher who recognizes that the stripped-down Buddhism that a Western thinker approves of is not the same thing as the living culture of Buddhism that blends with Hindu, ancestral, and animistic practices and beliefs. He recognizes that the logical consistency and ethical ideals that he prizes, as well as his symbolic and psychological interpretations of Cambodian folk beliefs, will not appeal to most Buddhists. Asma doubts that terrible atrocities, such as what took place in the Killing Fields, can be explained by the Buddhist idea that people suffer because they are attached: tell that to the torture victims or the families of those murdered. Just as some Christian theologians have argued against the project of theodicy, the best Buddhist response to evil is not an explanation of why it happens but a response of compassion and care for victims, as well as using the dhamma to construct a society where such events will not take place. In sum, in the chapter "Karma and the Killing Fields" Asma weaves together Cambodia's traumatic history, philosophical analysis of Buddhist thought, and incidents and conversations during his sojourn in Phnom Penh, using the concept of no-self to understand his experiences and to assess various expressions and accretions of Buddhism.

Another way in which Asma's interpretation of no-self frames his account of his travels is his focus on pleasures that tempt a Western visitor. In the first chapter of the book, "The Ring of Gyges," he compares travel in Southeast Asia to Plato's famous myth about a magical ring that makes its wearer invisible and therefore free to indulge in any vice without being detected. "The general culture of impunity" allows an expatriate to escape the legal and ethical constraints of his home culture as he pursues countless invitations to hedonism: "For approximately sixty dollars, one can, in Cambodia, buy an ounce of marijuana, a half-gram of heroin, a handgun, and a full day at the brothel, finished off by a relatively decadent meal. After that full day, you can, for just a little more money, kill one of your enemies and bribe your way to safety" (47). A range of temptations appeal to his own cravings, from relatively benign pleasures such as tantalizing food and soothing massage to more dangerous desires for drugs or sex.

When he considers the Buddhist perspective on the ethics of sex, Asma agrees with its view that there are no absolutely good or bad activities. With no God to give commandments, ethical norms are justified in terms of the Buddhist path from suffering to enlightenment: "Ethics is couched within the wider framework of the pursuit of freedom or nibbana. Activities and life choices are always weighed pragmatically as to whether they contribute to or detract from *dukkha* (suffering), and the answer to that evaluation largely depends on who is asking" (43). Applying this view to activities involving sex or drugs, Asma argues that they are not inherently wrong but become problematic when they are addictive or harm other people: "So philosophically speaking, one could both *be* a prostitute and *employ* a prostitute, and as long as one remained egoless and detached about the whole business, one could continue as a good Buddhist" (43). While particular cases and circumstances (such as deceiving a spouse) call for further distinctions, the basic structure of Buddhist ethical thinking is consequentialist: actions are evaluated in terms of whether they lead to equanimity or unrestrained craving. Therefore, it makes sense to say that a person is punished not *for* his "sins" but *by* them, in the form of tormenting and unrelenting desire. Living as a Buddhist does not require one to abstain from ordinary human pleasures and emotions. Instead, we should follow the middle path of the Buddha, whose "liberation was not freedom from these experiences but freedom from the ego-consciousness that jumps in after these feelings and tries to hold on to them" (45). After learning about the moral complexity of the sex industry from local Cambodian women, Asma criticizes simplistic denunciations of it by Westerners. He portrays sympathetically the efforts of sex workers to make prostitution legal and safe while eliminating violence and the abuse of children.

Thus, Asma depends on an idea closely related to anatta – the ideal of overcoming "ego attachment" – to frame a Buddhist perspective on ethical questions related to sense pleasures. Buddhism offers invaluable guidance in negotiating the many temptations that lure a Western traveler in Cambodia:

> This is a dodgy world where passions can easily consume you, but Buddhism is powerful medicine. After all, what good is your Buddhism if it's never put to the test—if it's never tempted? If you can only be spiritual when women are covering themselves up, or when you're living in a monastery or a nunnery, or when you're prosperous, or when you're otherwise "protected" from the myriad causes of craving, then it's a pretty flimsy spirituality. There's nothing flimsy about Theravadan Buddhism, a spirituality that acts like an eye of tranquility in a hurricane of vice and suffering. (47–48)

Encounters with Theravada Buddhism 239

His own navigation of the streets of Phnom Penh was oriented by his understanding of the link between craving and suffering. It takes discipline and training to enjoy sense pleasures without becoming enslaved by them. Asma argues that Buddhism helps a privileged Western traveler to gain perspective on desires and attachments so that this simulation of wearing the ring of Gyges does not lead to harm. Although in this chapter Asma does not worry much about the danger of one's pleasures harming other people, at other points he addresses this issue. No-self is crucial in this case, too, in that not harming others and having compassion for them depend on overcoming egotism.

Asma describes several experiences of unselfing: incidents when his ordinary sense of selfhood was transcended as he discovered a new way of being in the world. In the chapter "Seeing a Man Get Shot to Death," he depicts three such moments. The first occurs when he encounters the most revered Buddhist leader in Cambodia, Venerable Maha Ghosananda. As a lapsed Catholic and an American committed to egalitarian ideals, Asma is deeply suspicious of all hierarchies and claims of authority. Yet he is moved to unfamiliar feelings of humility and reverence when he encounters the man often referred to as "the Ghandi of Cambodia," who responded to his country's political turmoil and suffering in ways that renewed his people's commitment to Buddhism. When Maha Ghosananda comes to his class on Buddhism, Asma sees his students' authentic respect and loving devotion, and he is overwhelmed and inspired by the patriarch's courage and compassion. His feeling of humility is an experience of unselfing:

> Humility, something most Americans have in short supply, is close to the heart of Buddhist dhamma. It is an experience of self-effacement, an act of ego transcendence. It is a shrinking of self-importance, and as such it expresses a *felt sense* of the anatta (no-self) philosophy. I felt small in Maha's presence, and I felt that my problems were relatively trivial by comparison with what he had seen. I felt compelled to let go of the grudging slights and minor ego injuries that fed and grew in the nursery of my bloated self-regard. But self-loathing was not the final result of this experience of humility; that would just be more self-regard. Rather, a sense of true inspiration followed from my experience with Maha Ghosananda. (190)

Asma hopes that his unprecedented experience of humility will help him to respond with more compassion and equanimity to forms of suffering he encounters henceforth.

A second moment of unselfing takes place when Asma witnesses a political assassination. He compares this shock to the Buddha's wake-up call when, as a young prince, Siddhartha Gautama first saw a dead man outside his palace and was moved to a sense of oneness with the dead man and compassion for all who suffer. Asma usually ate lunch every day at the same table in an outdoor street market in Phnom Penh. One day he happens to eat on the balcony and from this vantage point watches as a well-dressed Khmer man is gunned down right where he usually sat. The market disperses in pandemonium, and after a few minutes ordinary life resumes as if nothing had happened. Upset for days after this incident, Asma is struck by how intimacy with death is part of the worldview of Cambodians, who are resilient in spite of waves of violence that far exceed the experience and imagination of most Westerners. This confrontation with violent death stirs a response of compassion that Asma sees as closely linked to the teachings of impermanence and no-self: "I knew intellectually about my own impermanence, but I didn't really understand it in my belly, so to speak, until after the assassination. I slowly began to grasp how the most obscure doctrine in Buddhism, the teaching of anatta, is really just a rarefied expression of the human emotion of compassion" (196). Seeing a man get shot to death elicited a turmoil of emotions that helped Asma to understand in a direct and embodied way – that is, in an event of unselfing – a doctrine that sometimes seems only a matter for metaphysical speculation. His reaction to this death showed him that "compassion and anatta (no-self) are two sides of the same coin" (196).

A third form of unselfing comes about through his philosophical engagement with the Abhidhamma ("higher teaching"). He explains how the Abhidhamma analyses what humans think of as the self and breaks it down into many elements such as conditions of the body, mental factors, and forms of consciousness, all of which are not permanent substances but convenient names for a stream of changes. By means of this analysis, Buddhist philosophers arrived at the same perspective as can come through meditation: a decentered view of things that discerns in a moment of experience many chains of dependent relations. For a philosopher like Stephen Asma, this train of thinking is not simply an intellectual game but rather a form of unselfing, a transformative experience that moves him to a radically different place. Through the Abhidhamma, he arrives at a new perspective that changes how he interprets his life and understands the self.

In this way, Asma uses his head to arrive at the heart of Buddhism, compassion: "In the end, what matters most is compassion. All the theory and heavy philosophy of anatta is great if you've got that kind of twisted disposition (alas, I do), but one can certainly find the heart of Buddhism independently of its head" (213). Like William James, he affirms that the deepest source of religion is feeling, while philosophy and theology are secondary interpretations of powerful emotional experiences. Yet, more than

Encounters with Theravada Buddhism 241

James acknowledges, secondary intellectual constructions play a large role in shaping supposedly "primary" experiences. Experience and interpretation inform and influence each other. Asma's assertion that the most important feeling is compassion comes about not only because of the shock of the assassination but also as a result of a philosophical paradigm shift that discerns the interdependence of the world rather than independent, self-contained substances. "Seeing a Man Get Shot to Death" describes and correlates three interrelated experiences of unselfing: his sense of profound humility before Maha Ghosananda, the wave of compassion he feels for a murdered man, and his acceptance of the new philosophical framework he finds in the Abhidhamma.

Of the new perspective that results from his sojourn in Cambodia, Asma says: "If I could summarize the complex transformation that I felt, I would have to characterize my new viewpoint as 'transcendental every-dayness'" (223). "Transcendental" means going beyond a limit, which for Asma does not mean attaining or contacting some supernatural realm but rather self-transformation: "If I have an ecstatic experience (from the Latin *ex stasis*, to go out of one's place), I do not transcend to an unworldly divine realm. I transcend my usual egoistic perspective and see things in a fresh way" (224). One form self-transcendence can take is beholding one's mundane environment with attentiveness and wonder. Travel in Southeast Asia involves continual encounters with startling events that elicit surprise and awe:

> The atmosphere is so thick with unfamiliarity that I couldn't help but be rapt in infantlike wonder all the time. I'd sit down at a sidewalk food stand, and the proprietor might come sit next to me smiling and introducing family members, while an elephant lumbered by slowly, and a man with no legs or lower torso rolled up on a cart and took my shoes off for shining, and a snack plate of barbecued insects appeared on the table, followed by an amazing fish dish served inside a halved coconut, and then the streets might literally flood in minutes with monsoon rains, leaving motos and cyclos to wobble slowly through the muddy streets. I was forced to focus on everything because everything seemed to require it—I had to practice mindfulness by necessity. But even though my mindfulness was almost coerced by the exotic environment of Southeast Asia, I did carry some of that appreciation back to my less exotic life in Chicago. (226)

Asian travel was a catalyst for mindful attention, an orientation that Asma hopes to bring back to his life in America. He intends to slow down and enjoy what life has already given rather than chasing after ephemeral satisfactions and imagined successes. Buddhism can help a person train the mind to experience pleasure and joy without craving, because one understands their impermanence. Sounding like Aristotle, Asma holds

242 Encounters with Theravada Buddhism

that we find happiness not by pursuing it directly, but obliquely, as we are immersed in daily activities in the right way. Abandoning one's cravings should lead to altered relationships with friends and to one's work. Of his own work as a writer, he resolves not to pursue fame, ersatz immortality, or external markers of success; instead, he will write in order to learn something and to enjoy the process of writing.

Using the title of Bhuddhadasa Bhikku's book, Asma characterizes his transformation as "the movement from 'me and mine' to emptiness and no-self" (238). One expression of this change is greater compassion and service to others: "To serve is to lose your self" (216). His resolution to serve focuses especially on a commitment to be a good father for the son who is born just after he returns to Chicago. The birth of this child, to whom the book is dedicated, offers Asma his best opportunity to live out the paradigm shift that he believes he has gone through.[16]

The ending of *The Gods Drink Whiskey* affirms the value of travel for discovering the "transcendental everydayness" that a traveler can learn to find at home:

> Like many other searching Americans, I had turned the exotic spiritualism of a faraway land into a holy grail of sorts, and I had to journey there to discover the exotic, mysterious, and transcendental qualities of my own Chicago life. Whether in Bangkok, Angkor Wat, or Chicago, the mundane becomes transcendental because every moment and event of our lives can take us out of ourselves and connect us to the larger web of being simply by our attending to it with mindfulness. (239)

To see wherever one is as exotic and transcendent requires a perspective that Asma describes in terms of the Buddhist idea of no-self: the shift from "me and mine" to an appreciation of interdependence and the life one already has. Although he is modest about claiming too much and admits that, every day, he fails to realize his aspiration, Asma shows how his life was transformed by Buddhism and living in Cambodia. His memoir explores in a distinctive way our common focus in Western Buddhist travel narratives: the role of no-self as an intellectual framework that inspires, shapes, and precipitates certain experiences and provides a language and theory for interpreting the process of self-transformation. In Asma's version of unselfing, the everyday becomes transcendental when a person feels taken beyond the habits of egocentric consciousness and connected to the world with clear perception, diminished craving, and renewed compassion.

[16] Asma pursues the theme of no-self in relation to parenting in "A Natural Exercise in No-Self: Buddhism and Parenting," in his *Why I Am a Buddhist: No-Nonsense Buddhism with Red Meat and Whiskey*, ed. Stephen Asma (Charlottesville, VA: Hampton Roads Publishing Company, 2010).

CHAPTER 9

Searching for Chan Buddhism after Mao

After Mao Zedong and the Communist government established the People's Republic of China in 1949, all religions were subject to strict control and severe persecution, especially during the Cultural Revolution (1966–1976). For Western writers interested in the fate of Buddhism in China, travel made clear the massive scale of destruction and the pathos of individual stories of suffering. We have already seen how witnessing this historical experience plays a large role in stories about encounters with Tibetan Buddhism. In this chapter, I discuss four narratives about attempts to discover what remains of Chan (Chinese Zen) Buddhism after Mao: Gretel Ehrlich's *Questions of Heaven: The Chinese Journeys of an American Buddhist*, George Crane's *Bones of the Master: A Journey to Secret Mongolia*, and two works by Bill Porter: *Road to Heaven: Encounters with Chinese Hermits* and *Zen Baggage: A Pilgrimage to China*. In different ways, for each of these authors searching for Chan Buddhism in the People's Republic of China precipitates experiences of unselfing.[1] Partly because of Chan's suspicion of talk about oneself, and because these authors focus more on documentation than on self-disclosure, they are rather guarded or discreet about disclosing how their journeys affected them, at least compared to those who write about Tibetan Buddhism. Yet each one shows how a Chinese journey stirred the initial stages of self-transformation.

In 1991, Gretel Ehrlich viewed an exhibition of medieval Chinese scrolls depicting sacred mountains at the Metropolitan Museum of Art. Moved by this artwork, and knowing that mountain pilgrimages are an ancient practice in all Chinese religions, Ehrlich decided in 1995 to climb Emei Shan, one of the four peaks sacred for Buddhists. In "The Road to Emei Shan," the first chapter of her *Questions of Heaven: The Chinese Journeys of*

---

[1] "Chan" is used in contemporary pinyin and is standard, but I retain "Ch'an" in quotations that use this version.

243

244   Searching for Chan Buddhism after Mao

an American Buddhist (1997), Ehrlich describes a dispiriting climb up this traditional pilgrimage route. In visiting this and other sites in Sichuan and Yunan Provinces, Ehrlich hoped to find remnants of traditional Chinese culture, although she knew that much had been destroyed during Mao's regime: "I had come to China to pick up the threads of a once flourishing culture and thought I would find it in their sacred mountains" (4).[2] She finds only discouraging signs and the detritus of China's religious traditions. When she shows her taxi driver ancient poems and reproductions of landscape paintings, he shrugs, "as if to say, if that's what you came to China for, you're a thousand years too late" (3). The taxi driver, like many other people she meets, tells a grim story of how he survived the brutal years under Mao.

Pollution makes it difficult even to see Emei Shan. The Chinese government has turned the mountain into a tourist destination so that its religious character is all but overwhelmed by buying and selling. Tin cans for contributions might as well be labeled "the god of greed" (26). The monks on the mountain admit that they are there because they can't find a job and spend most of their time watching television. Even the monkeys on Emei Shan have become beggars or violent thieves who grab food and jewelry from visitors. When Ehrlich finally reaches the summit, she finds three Las Vegas-style hotels and a loudspeaker blaring Strauss waltzes. At the top of the mountain, exhausted and suffering from bronchitis, she breaks down in tears. She tells her guide, Vivian, "Nobody cares. Nobody is indignant about what has happened here" (34–35). Yet Vivian can't understand; earlier she had "said she was too young to know what had been lost and didn't see that there was a problem" (20).

As Ehrlich describes this depressing environment, she seems intermittently aware that her jaundiced perspective may need to be corrected. Her purpose in climbing Emei Shan is not only to document the state of contemporary China but to make a spiritual pilgrimage. She understands that "the mountain was a mirror and my itinerary up its paths was a diagram of spiritual progress. Nor was the mountain a single, simple place. It was a center of power whose weathers and textures kept changing, a trope for ongoing transformation" (6–7). The shifting moods of the mountain and her brooding consciousness reflect each other, and neither has a fixed identity. The book's epigraph, lines by the Japanese poet Nanao Sakaki, is one of the few references to no-self:

---

[2] Gretel Ehrlich, *Questions of Heaven: The Chinese Journeys of an American Buddhist* (Boston: Beacon Press, 1997).

Searching for Chan Buddhism after Mao

Why climb a mountain?
Look! A mountain there.
I don't climb mountain.
Mountain climbs me.
Mountain is myself.
I climb on myself.
There is not mountain
nor myself.
Something moves up and down in the air.[3]

Something is moving in Ehrlich, too, but what? Feeling as if she is walking through "a beautiful country that had been made into a living hell" (17), she wants to describe its contours as she climbs out. It takes great effort and discipline to complete the mountain pilgrimage route and the rest of her Chinese journey, and the spiritual transformation that she hopes for remains incomplete, a work in progress.

It is never clear to the reader what motivates Ehrlich's quest or what the circumstances of her life are before and after the Chinese journey. The suffering that she undergoes seems a form of penance or expiation – but for what? Several times she mentions having personal "questions of heaven," using the title of a Chinese poem that refers to quandaries about the human condition and the universe: "Are mountains really mountains? Are mountains a form of enlightenment? Are rivers mountains running? Can we walk through them? Why do mountains walk through us?" (9). Nearing the peak, she asks: "Was the 'I' the same as the 'one' of the mountain? Would ascent confer *samadhi*?" (28). While poetic and suggestive, these questions seem abstract, disconnected from the author's life, about which we learn very little. We get only a glimpse of her state of mind as she undergoes the first stage of her purgatory and wonder whether her travels will change Ehrlich so that she views China through different eyes. Will her journey bring about a "peak" experience that lifts her to a more positive view of China and hope for the future of Buddhism there? Or is hope a set-up for disappointment? The first chapter ends with a mountain metaphor that suggests the need for openness to whatever comes: "There are many false summits along the way and at the top, there is only emptiness. The beginning and the end are the same" (36).

---

[3] Nanao Sakaki, "Why" from *Break the Mirror* (New York: [North Point Press] Farrar, Straus, and Giroux, 1966). Reprinted by permission of North Point Press, a division of Farrar, Straus & Giroux.

246   Searching for Chan Buddhism after Mao

Things don't get much better when Ehrlich visits the Wolong Panda Preserve, northwest of Chengdu. As much of the natural habitat for pandas has disappeared, China has established reserves for this threatened species. Yet the pandas at Wolong are confined to dirty cement stalls and obviously miserable and ailing. These bears are sacrificial hostages kept for the donations given to protect them. Sick at heart, Ehrlich leaves this depressing place. She asserts that how humans treat animals is "a mirror of how we think of ourselves" (47). This claim is illustrated by the way she interweaves the narrative of her journey to visit the preserve with stories about Mao's tyranny, disastrous policies, and callous indifference to suffering. In response to this brutal treatment, China's people are now fixated on survival. Six years after the massacre at Tiananmen Square, it is evident that the Chinese government is suppressing democratic rights. Given these uncertain and dangerous conditions, people seek security in money. Ehrlich views the effects of globalization negatively, as undermining Chinese ingenuity, self-reliance, and what was once "the most sophisticated culture in the world" (59). Her lament and protest of the destruction of China's culture are the dominant theme through most of *Questions of Heaven*: "Almost everything spiritual, intellectual, and creative was purged and erased; the heart was ripped out of the culture and its people. Beauty had been considered a mockery by the Maoists; no corner in Han China seemed to offer any gracenotes, and I felt profoundly sad" (70).

When Ehrlich leaves Sichuan Province and enters Yunan, she endures a hair-raising taxi ride on perilous mountain roads with a driver who may be suicidal. In the city of Lijiang, she finally has an encounter that gives her a shred of hope. Yunan is the home of thirty minority nations, including the Naxi people. Because the Chinese government realizes that ethnic minorities are a tourist attraction, some aspects of traditional culture are allowed to continue, carefully monitored. Ehrlich seeks out an orchestra of Naxi musicians who perform music from eighth-century China. This tradition, suppressed and revived many times, is making a comeback: "For the first time during my stay in China, I knew I was seeing a fragment of culture, like a very sick patient, being brought back to life" (95). The leader of the group, Xuan Ke, was tortured while incarcerated from 1958 to 1978. His determination, courage, and political savvy were crucial in the survival of Naxi music. Telling his story to Ehrlich, he describes how humming sacred music kept him alive in prison. Singing and music arose originally from humanity's fear of death, he says, and early Naxi songs still have the power "to chase away demons, to chase away tigers" (107). Music is a powerful medicine that can bring life or death; it must be performed and listened to very carefully.

Before he performs, Xuan Ke instructs the audience to close their eyes and let the music enter them. He points out places on the body where music might enter, such as between the eyebrows, the palms, and the bottom of the feet. Ehrlich says just a bit about what it felt like to hear this music: "My eyes were closed and sounds entered me in elliptical sequences like Chinese narrative, recurring cycles and spheres oscillating within more spheres." Sixty years earlier, another Western visitor described Naxi music as "a recital of cosmic life as it was unfolding" (95). Xuan Ke speaks of music's healing power: "This kind of music brings all listeners and all players into harmony with nature, eliminating noise and war while promoting peace. It is music that comes from an expression inside the heart, which is what makes it truly religious" (96). Naxi music moves Ehrlich to a more peaceful and harmonious state of mind and heart, at least while she is listening to it.

The final chapter of *Questions of Heaven* describes a performance of Xuan Ke's troupe several months later in London. It was probably the first time Naxi music was played outside of China. Again, Xuan Ke describes the beneficent power of music to "restore the balance and harmony of the world, if our bodies learn how to be receptive to it" (117). The sound of the music fills Ehrlich with a sense of the presence of China:

> That night the Naxi music sounded like mountains and rivers and reefs of clouds diving and filling the Yangtze River Valley, streaming out of Tiger Leaping Gorge where Xuan Ke's mother once sang, casting a green spell on Jade Mountain Peak where clouds are made, causing them to rain down rain and snow and more music. (118)

At the end of her book, Ehrlich has moved to a very different place, not only geographically but emotionally and spiritually. She has some hope that China's traditional culture will survive and be appreciated, based on her embodied experience of being "entered" by the music and moved by its harmonies to a more serene condition, including a balanced awareness of possibilities for good or evil. The book closes by considering the uncertain future of Xuan Ke and implicitly that of China. Xuan Ke requests that Ehrlich "use soft words" in her travelogue, because "there is still danger for all of us" (120). Honesty is the only way that people can find out what really happened in recent Chinese history, but it is often punished. Xuan Ke tells Ehrlich to remember his darkened teeth, which he refuses to have fixed and compares to the Great Wall: "the history of my life and therefore the history of the Chinese people shows in them, so they will stay like this" (121).

248   Searching for Chan Buddhism after Mao

This ending expresses Gretel Ehrlich's primary emphasis in *Questions of Heaven* on documenting contemporary conditions in China and conveying her alarm. Although she alludes to her own spiritual pilgrimage, we know little about it or the significance of her passing remark that she "had studied with a Rinpoche and had spent a day with the sixteenth Karmapa (an important incarnate lama)" (101). Yet the autobiographical hints in this text are significant, and the impact of what she witnesses on Ehrlich is a continuing theme. The book's ending suggests that Ehrlich has moved a little further on her path through purgatory, and perhaps sees light at the end of the tunnel. The arc of the narrative shows a tentative transformation as she begins with outrage and despair about conditions in China, has an experience of Naxi music that suggests a moment of unselfing, and ends with a tentative and fragile sense of hope. The final image in the book, the blackened teeth of smiling Xuan Ke, suggests both a warning about continuing dangers and the possibility of resilience in response to trauma. If Ehrlich has not undergone a radical transformation, her experience when hearing Naxi music has moved her to a new stage of a continuing spiritual journey. Her own future condition cannot be separated from the fate of the Chinese people and the culture about which she cares so much. The outcome of her journey remains in doubt as long as the fate of Buddhism in China is precarious.

*

George Crane's *Bones of the Master: A Journey to Secret Mongolia* (2000) traces two arduous journeys in China in 1959 and 1996. The first story follows the flight of Tsung Tsai, a young Chan monk, from his monastery in Inner Mongolia to safety in Hong Kong. A second, much longer, travel narrative recounts how Tsung Tsai, accompanied by Crane, returns on a pilgrimage to find the bones of his spiritual master, construct a stupa to honor him, and rebuild a ruined temple and monastery. As Crane and Tsung Tsai go through harrowing dangers and learn about the past and present suffering of the Mongolian people, their relationship deepens. Tsung Tsai's selfless character is a large part of his charisma and appeal, and the reader is interested not only in the journey's outcome but also in how George Crane's bond with his mentor will change him.

Like the relationship in *Circling the Sacred Mountain* between Robert Thurman and Tad Wise (who Crane thanks in his acknowledgments), Tsung Tsai is an older, wiser, and spiritually committed Buddhist who inspires the devotion of a young man who freely acknowledges addictive behavior, lust, literary ambition, and resistance to the self-discipline of a

Searching for Chan Buddhism after Mao

Buddhist path. Crane met Tsung Tsai in 1987, when the two men, neighbors in the Catskill Mountains, were each clearing a road after a snowstorm. Crane, an agnostic of Jewish background, admires Tsung Tsai's combination of practical abilities and spiritual power:

> To a spiritual skeptic like myself, Tsung Tsai was too good to be true, a Renaissance man: monk, poet, philosopher, house builder, scientist, doctor, and when necessary, kung fu ass-kicker. It would spoil everything if he began proselytizing. I was constantly on the lookout for him to begin to try to convert me to devotion and practice. But he never did. (24)[4]

Crane had long been interested in Zen: "It was my kind of religion, spontaneous and improvisational; it felt like the spirit of poetry, the spirit of freedom itself" (24–25). He loves Zen's freedom, but not its discipline, and meditation makes him nauseous. His only commitment is to write a poem every day. Writing is his religion, he says, and it resembles Zen's intense concentration leading to "the fierce face-to-face moment when you spit out the truth or die" (25). Crane had not been particularly successful as a poet, and when he begins to translate Tsung Tsai's poems, he feels he is doing his best work. Subordinating his own literary voice to Tsung Tsai's is one way that his somewhat egotistical and narcissistic personality changes as a result of his bond with the Chan monk.

At the time of the journey, Crane was married for the third time, enjoying a period of relative calm after a turbulent life of "barely contained chaos" (27). Tsung Tsai seems to embody for him an ideal but unattainable combination of discipline and spontaneity. Both in his literary ambitions and in his personal life, Crane indulged in undisciplined freedom that he both clings to and wants to end. To make Tsung Tsai his spiritual master would mean giving up his autonomy:

> I had never been able to humble myself. I hadn't the courage to surrender the controls and put myself in someone else's hands. Was I doomed to mediocrity by not being able to accept what was needed: technique and transmission? In Tsung Tsai's world, *teacher* meant "master," that most sacred and—for me—suspect of titles. (45)

Learning technique means internalizing standards and rules, not just doing what you want. To value transmission requires understanding your place in a lineage and scrupulous fidelity in passing on the tradition. Mastering technique and transmission would require the breaking down of Crane's sense of self and the formation of a new one based on a spiritual

---

4 George Crane, *Bones of the Master: A Journey to Secret Mongolia* (New York: Bantam, 2000).

250   Searching for Chan Buddhism after Mao

tradition handed on from teacher to student. Tsung Tsai wants to return to China to build a stupa that will honor his teacher, Shiuh Deng, as a Buddha, and thereby ensure the transmission of the dharma in China's future. Will he also transmit his tradition to George Crane? If so, what will this mean for Crane's life and for the way he writes this travel narrative?

Crane first recreates the desperate journey Tsung Tsai made in 1959 during Mao's disastrous Great Leap Forward. Born in 1925, Tsung Tsai had been a monk for eighteen years at Puu Jih, a small Chan monastery in the high plateau and mountains of Inner Mongolia between the Gobi Desert and the Ordos Desert. Tibetan Buddhism was the dominant form in Inner Mongolia; Puu Jih was probably the only Chan monastery north of the Yellow River. Tsung Tsai was the only one of the thirteen resident monks who survived when starvation and Communist persecution destroyed this monastery. During this period, possibly the worst famine in history, millions of people died of hunger. Tsung Tsai witnessed horrific scenes of suffering on his flight to Hong Kong. He was close to death on many occasions and believed he had given up all attachments. It was not desire for his own survival that gave him the will to go on but commitment to preserve his monastery's vision and way of life: "That is why I must live, Georgie. All my brother monks have gone down dead" (53). Tsung Tsai saw countless corpses and dying people as he staggered across China over the course of a year. In Crane's recreation of the journey, the monk meditates on death around him until it seems to fill his own being and he is no longer afraid of it:

> Death surrounded him in his own sticklike body with its sunken chest and bloated belly, in his yellowed cracking nails, the white film on his tongue. It was all the same body. He was the cannibal and the cannibalized; the corpse and minnows; the pigs squealing in their freight car stalls; Ho Chu, with her ponytail, hanging from a tree; his family in their stony graves. (55)

This nightmare journey through inconceivable horrors was a form of unselfing that "stripped him of all that was false" (58) and made him the compelling presence whom Crane met three decades later.

After living in Hong Kong for more than a decade, most of the time in the hills with a reclusive dharma master, Tsung Tsai went to teach in New York City in 1973 and eventually moved to Woodstock, where in 1987 he encountered Crane after the snowstorm. Nine years later, he persuaded Crane to accompany him on his pilgrimage to find his teacher's burial site in the Ordos Desert, dig up and cremate Shiuh Deng's bones with proper ceremony, and build a stupa for the ashes in a cave he had used for retreats near the summit of Crow Pull Mountain. He hoped, as well, to rebuild the Puu Jih monastery and encourage signs of a Buddhist revival

Searching for Chan Buddhism after Mao

in China. Crane goes along not as an act of pilgrimage but because he is looking for adventure and, with a book contract secured, for an exciting and moving story to focus his vague literary ambitions.

The two companions visit Tsung Tsai's childhood village, the dynamited ruins of Puu Jih monastery, and several people who knew Tsung Tsai or his teacher many decades earlier. The story climaxes with an exhausting and nearly fatal climb and descent of Crow Pull Mountain. This journey altered George Crane's sense of self and understanding of Buddhism. As the bond with Tsung Tsai is tested and grows stronger through shared travail, Crane admires his mentor's unfailing energy, patience, and commitment to his spiritual mission. Although Crane says his teacher "was operating with a sense of purpose that was totally beyond me" (198) and sometimes finds him incomprehensible, he continues to follow him, obey his commands, and serve him faithfully. Tsung Tsai teaches him about patience, acting decisively, disciplining lusts, stilling the mind, and other desirable capacities and virtues. Although Crane usually does his best to comply, he often fails and feels like giving up. He persists, however: "I had decided on this trip to follow him. No matter what. What he did I would do. It was an experiment. I thought to learn something about discipline, about meditation" (101). In this intimate teacher–student relationship, Tsung Tsai and Crane put into practice one of the central teaching vehicles of Chan Buddhist tradition: submission to a master's demanding guidance in order to overcome self-centered ways. Crane also learns compassion for his teacher's frail and vulnerable body and for many sufferers they meet along the way.

A different kind of unselfing takes place when Crane looks at his past life with new eyes and feels shame and remorse. He and Tsung Tsai finally arrive at the site of Puu Jih and find – nothing. Even the stones remaining after the monastery was destroyed by the Red Guard were carried away to build houses for cadres. Tsung Tsai hears the voices of ghosts and is immensely saddened. Crane is moved to pity and to judge his own life:

> Standing there in judgment, I felt a wave of guilt. It was not his life but my life I saw, with its half-assed enthusiasms, its endless evasions, desires, and profound selfishness. If Puu Jih had not been destroyed, Tsung Tsai would have been surrounded by living disciples, good students, men of seriousness and purpose to carry on the Dharma. What was left to him? A plastic Buddha, an outhouse for a temple, and me—a spiritual ignoramus, a parody of a disciple. (145)

When Crane realizes that a true seeker would give anything to be in his place with a spiritual master, he is overcome by self-loathing and despair. A moment of shame, when he sees himself as if from the outside and wants to be a different person, could be the catalyst for a spiritual transformation. Like Augustine's moment of revulsion in the garden scene in Book 8 of his *Confessions*, this moment involves a splitting of the self as a man sees his worst qualities as if from another place. Unlike Augustine, Crane does not go on to assert that this experience was the pivotal moment in a completed transformation of identity. Yet it seems to be an important milestone on a journey still underway.

Tsung Tsai's version of Buddhism embraces and affirms emotion, in contrast with Crane's view of Japanese Zen: "Tsung Tsai's Ch'an was passionate, emotional, a far cry from Zen's philosophic cool no-mind, its insistence that emotion was fantasy, like nothing" (269). He sees meditation as a mixture of mind and emotion. He is filled with pity, sadness, and deep compassion for his people's suffering. His understanding of Buddhism highlights a particular emotional response: "Emotion is every human being's roots. Difficult to control. Very good monk have deepest heart. So very sad for world. Highest pity. Buddha nature, so kindness" (269–270). Tsung Tsai presents the Buddhist path as an exuberant embrace of all of life, not a purification or distillation of part of it: "Ch'an is completely world. Happy and sad, anger and peace, hate and love is meditation's branch and flower. Today cry, tomorrow laugh; it means nothing. Like fantasy. But Ch'an like mountain you cannot move. Doubt. No doubt. I give you both. That is Ch'an" (263). This affirmation of all of human nature and the world, which resembles the vitality and *joie de vivre* of Zorba the Greek, appeals greatly to Crane, who is not about to give up life's pleasures or ups and downs, however much they make him suffer.

Tsung Tsai is not only a devout Chan monk with a distinctive understanding of Buddhism but also a shaman who possesses uncanny powers. He depends on "monk power" when doing battle with ghosts and spirits. In one puzzling scene, Crane describes an exorcism when Tsung Tsai treats a boyhood friend haunted by dreams about being an axe murderer. As Crane watches, the friend goes into a trance and a walnut-sized tumor appears on his neck. Crane wonders whether Tsung Tsai is a monk, a shaman, or both: "He moved fluidly, seemingly untroubled by the contradictions between the universe of numbers, Zen's strict rationalism, and the older world of spirit possession and voodoo—of superstition, divination, and curses" (199). Although the monk asserts that Chan does not rely on magic, he acts as an exorcist, faith healer, and medium who communicates with spirits or ghosts. It is Tsung Tsai's "mind power" as much as anything that attracts Crane; his desire to acquire this power often seems to be his chief aspiration, with Buddhism being simply one possible means to this end. Tsung Tsai uses

Buddhism and other resources to make Crane aware of his own potential and power. He weaves together crucial Buddhist themes with Taoist and shamanistic motifs in cryptic remarks to his American student, for instance, this response to a question about the meaning of the idea that "everything is Ch'an": "What means is I never lose my mind. Always keep and you can see east, west, sky, earth. Everything pure. Everything coming you can see. Even can see in shadow. That is Ch'an. Nothing can move Ch'an mind. Understand?" (213–214). To this Crane responds: "Clear as mud." Tsung Tsai smiles and affirms that this is a good answer: "Ch'an mind talk. Now you've got it really. Please, you be learning" (214). That last sentence is both indicative and imperative. In a classic Chan manner, Tsung Tsai implies that Crane already understands the Buddha nature of all of life, yet he also says that his friend has more to learn and must practice with diligence.

As well as the "mind power" in Tsung Tsai and in Chan Buddhism, there is another kind of power that Crane already knows firsthand and wants more of: fox power. In Chinese mythology, the fox is a creature associated with the night, the feminine, erotic pleasure, and sensual desire. Tsung Tsai warns: "Fox is incarnation of too much desire. Too much sex. Be careful" (171). He does not say that everything related to the fox should be avoided or ignored but rather that Crane has a fox problem. Crane takes his teacher's warning seriously, admitting that his desires, especially for passing women, often dominate his better judgment. Yet he cannot overcome his own nature. In a chapter entitled "Fox knows Fox," he goes to a party, gets drunk, and flirts with an attractive woman who Tsung Tsai claims also has a fox problem. The generosity and lust for life that Crane witnesses during this wild party remind him of his own Jewish forbears, whose vitality similarly grew out of a long history of suffering:

> Like my family, like the Jews of Eastern Europe, these people had suffered a holocaust. From 1959 to 1969, they all had members of their families who were beaten, tortured, sent to the gulags. Monks, like rabbis, were murdered and exiled. The books, temples, the artifacts of their sacred culture, were destroyed. In all this suffering and bloody history, they had endured. They were still singing and dancing, embracing life. (176)

Crane does not want to give up the desire, excess, danger, and full humanity he sees around him:

> This was what I believed in, thought the drunk. Not the ascetic monk next to me with his celibacy, Buddha breath, and metaphysics. I toasted again, the wine sloshing over and dripping down my sleeve. "To what counts," I shouted. "To the seasons, to cooking, to wives and babies, to poetry, to everything impregnating, to-being-drunk-god-damnit-to-growing-old." (177)

Does this mean that he rejects Chan and his teacher's advice? Or would embracing the fox as a metaphor of self be a way of living out the teaching that "everything is Ch'an" (213), since Chan mind is present in everything, including his foxy nature?

The final chapter in *Bones of the Master*, entitled "The Black Master," gives an enigmatic answer to this question. Crane describes a strange confrontation between Tsung Tsai and Lei Shu Bao, his old friend and student who has become "badly black" (279) and involved in sex and magic. Having survived their ordeals in Inner Mongolia and on their way home, Crane and Tsung Tsai visit Lei at his temple in Hong Kong. Lei is apparently a Tantric master: "Did he strive for enlightenment by transgressing all taboos and embracing lust, the unholy trinity: power, money, and sex ... In Lei, I saw my fox, my basest desires, my overwhelming ego" (286). Lei recognizes him as a kindred spirit: "fox knows fox." Like several other male authors of Western Buddhist travel narratives, Crane is attracted to the Tantric way because it apparently blesses his lusts and addictions. When Crane suggests to Tsung Tsai, "Maybe I'm already Buddha," his teacher says maybe – or "maybe not. Who can know?" (288).

That night, Crane and Tsung Tsai are present when Lei leads a shamanic ritual involving hours of chanting and ringing bells. Crane describes how these sounds "drowned my mind," time disappeared, and his sense of self dissolved:

> The ringing went on and on. Tsung Tsai sat, his back no longer resting against the wall, but ramrod straight, his chin tucked, his eyes only on Lei. I was pushed to utter aloneness, that place where self disappears and merges with space, where everything is hallucinatory and where cause and effect mix. I'm losing it: my comfortable Western paradigm; all surety of reason, all sense of what is and isn't. There are no answers and no questions. (289)

He falls asleep, and on awakening Tsung Tsai tells him: "Mr. Lei is finished. He tries to chant me. Take my power" (290). Tsung Tsai is too strong for Lei to cast a spell on him; mind power vanquishes fox power. His freedom and power make him invulnerable to Lei's black magic: "I am monk, and emptiness" (290).

Crane does not explain what this confrontation means to him. I interpret the scene as dramatizing his recognition that Tsung Tsai's spiritual path is more powerful than Lei's Tantric way of excess. In an experience of unselfing, Crane has a moment of clarity when "self disappears" and he can observe the two men and what they represent as possible alternatives and choices for his future life. He does not say which metaphor of self he will adopt, the monk or the fox. He seems inclined to accept his own

Searching for Chan Buddhism after Mao 255

nature as a fox, an identity, nature, or destiny that he can't and doesn't want to escape. The brief epilogue, which shows Crane and his teacher back in New York, dreaming of someday returning Tsung Tsai's bones to Mongolia, does not make clear the nature of Crane's subsequent life. Tsung Tsai had predicted that Crane would "find his power" on the journey. That power and energy, as expressed both in daily living and his way of writing, may be rooted in accepting his fox nature instead of fighting it or trying to be a Tsung Tsai. To accept this about himself, to get over his self-doubt and internal conflict, would be to be a different person. It is ambiguous whether Crane exhibits wisdom in acknowledging that he does not have his mentor's spiritual maturity or whether he has succumbed to earlier temptations and adopted a Tantric worldview to rationalize satisfying his desires. Being a fox may be a good source of literary ambition and energy. Could a monk write a compelling travel narrative?

Crane's life does not change outwardly after the journey. The best evidence that he has been affected by his travels is his success in portraying Tsung Tsai. If he can't yet imitate the selfless energy of his charismatic mentor, it may be that his evident admiration and love for Tsung Tsai will eventually influence him to become more like the Chan master. Although Crane was not transformed by his travels, he hints that a long-term process is underway. If a fox can't be a monk, he can have an experience of unselfing and a moment of clarity when he recognizes what he should strive for.

*

Bill Porter has written many travel narratives set in China, including three stories about his quests to find hermits, sites associated with the first six patriarchs of Zen, and the graves of classical poets. He published book-length works describing his passages along the Yellow River and Yangtze Rivers, the Silk Road, and through Yunan Province. Sometimes using the nom de plume "Red Pine," he has translated Lao-tzu, the Heart Sutra, other classics of Chinese religious traditions, and the poems of Cold Mountain, Stonehouse, and other Buddhist and Taoist writers. In this voluminous literary corpus, Porter's own spiritual journey is subordinated to his effort to make Chinese literature and religious wisdom accessible to a Western audience. He provides only hints about how his far-reaching travels changed him and no extended description of pivotal events of transformation or experiences of unselfing. In spite of Porter's reticence or modesty about his own religious orientation and development, there are several ways in which ideas about self-transformation and its relation to no-self run through his work. I will explore this theme in two travel narratives: *Road to Heaven: Encounters with Chinese Hermits* (1993) and *Zen Baggage: A Pilgrimage to China* (2009).

In 1972, when he was twenty-nine, Bill Porter left a program of graduate studies in Chinese at Columbia University and went to a Buddhist monastery in Taiwan. For the next twenty years, he lived in Taiwan and Hong Kong, including several years alone on a mountain near Taipei. While translating the works of Chinese hermit-poets, he began to wonder whether there were still any hermits on the Chinese mainland, as well as about the condition of Buddhism in the People's Republic. Most people told him that probably no hermits had survived the Cultural Revolution's brutal campaign to rid China of its traditional culture. Yet Porter surmised that "if Buddhism were to survive in China, or anywhere else, it would depend not so much on monks and nuns living in temples as it would on them living in huts and caves" (9).[5] In 1989, he began to search for hermits and soon heard reports that some lived in the Chungnan Mountains, south of Sian. For several years, Porter explored the hidden recesses of this mountain range, which turned out to be "Hermit Heaven," a refuge for perhaps 200 solitary practitioners. *Road to Heaven* recounts his wandering journeys in search of these scattered hermits and his interviews with them.

The term "Chungnan Mountains" today refers to only the northern and eastern ridges of a larger range called the Chinling, which divides northern and southern China and extends west through the Kunlun range as far as Pakistan. These mountains have been a center of Chinese religious practice since Neolithic times, when the central figures were shamans. Archeological evidence suggests that the Chungnan Mountains were the earliest home of shamanism in China. Radiocarbon testing has dated to 5,000 years ago carbonized buds of hemp, which was used to induce spiritual states. Using Mircea Eliade's account of shamanism as a guide, Porter explains the continuity between this ancient tradition and the practices of China's hermits. Particularly important for our purposes is the common quest of shaman and hermit for ecstatic experience. A shaman leaves his body to pass through a series of heavens and receive messages and visions. He communicates with spirits and brings their enigmatic sayings back to his society. In ecstasy (whose etymology, from the Greek, means "standing outside" oneself), a shaman undergoes a form of unselfing, becoming other than his usual identity.

---

[5] Bill Porter, *Road to Heaven: Encounters with Chinese Hermits* (San Francisco: Mercury House, 1993).

Searching for Chan Buddhism after Mao

Being alone is conducive to this kind of experience. According to Eliade, a shaman "seeks solitude, becomes absent-minded, loves to roam in the woods or unfrequented places, has visions, and sings in his sleep."[6] Shamans became hermits in the third and second millennium BCE, when urbanization and social stratification during the first dynastic states created an institutionalized religion with rituals controlled by the rulers. The priestly bureaucracy viewed independent shamans with suspicion. Yet shamans continued to practice in the fastness of the remote Chungnan-Kunlun range; they were esteemed as sages and sought out by kings, emperors, and other leaders. Hermits were in touch with the forces of nature, could talk to Heaven, and were healers, herbalists, and diviners of signs. Their independence from society made them at once marginal figures and performers of established roles that connect city and court to nature, the mythic past, and spiritual powers.

The ability of shamans and hermits to stand outside society had a formative influence on Taoism. Lao-Tzu is said to have written the *Tao-te Ching* in the Chungnan Mountains and to have vanished beyond them. Before Taoism became organized as an institution in order to obtain patronage (what Porter calls "housebroken shamanism"),[7] following the Tao could mean either a life of seclusion or a life of public service, and these two alternatives were often in dialectical relationship. Some recluses were exiles from a corrupt court, and others were invited to return to the political world, bringing along the virtues and detached perspective that they had cultivated in the wilds:

> Seclusion and public service were seen as the dark and light of the moon, inseparable and complementary. Hermits and officials were often the same people at different times of their lives ... Whether or not they have come out of retirement to serve, hermits have influenced the entire culture as springs of pure thinking and pure living that sooner or later find their way to town. (33)

Porter interviews hermits who see themselves as Taoists, asking them about their daily activities, religious practices, and how they view China's political changes. Like the hermit-poets that he admires, Porter does not advocate any specific political stance or criticize particular policies or leaders. Instead, he points to the world beyond conflicting factions and struggles for power. Such a perspective transcends politics and yet

---

[6] Porter, *Road to Heaven*, 19, quoting Mircea Eliade's article on Shamanism in the first edition of *The Encyclopedia of Religion*, vol. 13, 202.

[7] Bill Porter, in a lecture on hermits at St. Olaf College, April 5, 2017.

258   Searching for Chan Buddhism after Mao

is finally essential to wise participation in it. When society rejects the harmony, balance, and effortless calm of the Tao, a sage withdraws and practices alone. As *Chuangtzu* puts it: "When the Tao prevails in the world, he lives in harmony with others. When the Tao doesn't prevail, he cultivates his virtue in seclusion" (61). Although Porter does not explicitly connect this view with contemporary China, the implication is clear: today's hermits can be a source of spiritual guidance in China's future and in the West.

Chinese Buddhism emerged and developed in the same region: "Of the eight major Buddhist schools that flowered in China, seven of them shed their first petals in or near the Chungnan Mountains" (89), including the Pure Land, Tantric, and Zen schools. Porter's interviews with Buddhist hermits often elicit brief mentions or allusions to no-self. Practitioners of Zen speak of the challenge of overcoming the self's habits and desires. In contrast, an advocate of the Pure Land approach views Zen as too demanding for most people and argues that one should not rely on one's own efforts but instead on the Buddha: "Nowadays, Pure Land practice is the only practice suitable for everyone. The difference is that Pure Land practice depends on the power of the Buddha. You don't need deep roots. Zen practice depends completely on yourself. It's much harder, especially now" (112). Each school sees its approach as the truly selfless one.

These hermits must integrate the ideal of no-self with the determined resolution, clarity of purpose, and sheer willpower required to pursue a spiritual path alone. Whatever school of Buddhism one adheres to, living in solitude in the mountains demands that one overcome attachments. Close to tears in her loneliness, a nun tells Porter:

> You can't live in the mountains if you're still attached, if you haven't seen through the red dust. Life in the mountains is hard. But once you've seen through the illusions of this world, hardships aren't important. The only thing that matters is practice. If you don't practice, you'll never get free of the dust of delusion. (114)

The metaphor of red dust recurs in interviews as a favorite term for all a hermit must leave behind, all the self's attachments.

Most of these mountain Buddhists are not well educated and have rather vague explanations of their practice, for instance, "I just pass the time" (142) and "I teach all sorts of odds and ends" (158). It is not surprising that the hermits are reticent and guarded about any topic related to religion and often tell Porter that they would prefer not to respond to his questions. He began his quest just after the massacre of protesters at Tiananmen Square, when memories of the trauma of the Cultural Revolution were still vivid. Evasion and indirect allusion are at once modes of religious communication and necessary for survival in China's uncertain future. Certain monks and nuns that Porter calls intellectual hermits have more sophisticated understandings of the dharma and may spend a good deal of time studying texts. Yet the suspicion of wordiness and merely intellectual understanding runs deep, and few hermits speak at length about no-self or any other idea. Although their references to no-self are brief, a number of related concepts recur, such as seeing into one's own nature, nothingness, and seeing all things as ephemeral. After he visits a stupa where visitors are spitting, smoking, and shouting, Porter recalls a passage in the *Diamond Sutra* in which the Buddha teaches: "Whatever has form is empty. When you see all forms as without form, you see the Buddha" (188). While Gretel Ehrlich would have lamented the sad state of contemporary practice, Porter simply records a key teaching and passes on. In the brevity of his discussions of Buddhism, Porter takes after the hermits. To make too much of any action or concept, including no-self, would be grasping red dust.

The effect on Bill Porter of his extensive search for hermits is somewhat uncertain and suggested rather than stated. He does not describe incidents of unselfing or summarizes how the journey changed him. The entire narrative, like the many months he spent prowling the mountains, is devoted to understanding people who have given their lives to the quest for self-transformation through the way of solitude. Yet the interviewed hermits do not refer to decisive moments of insight into the self or long-term changes of perspective. Self-transcendence is not an achievement to be proclaimed; its main sign is that the insistent self vanishes. This version of unselfing is evident in the penultimate chapter of the book, "Visiting Wang Wei, Finding Him Gone." In the eighth century, Wang Wei withdrew into the Chungnan Mountains to paint, write poetry, and meditate. "Long before he died, he seems to have already disappeared into one of his paintings or poems" (204). Having long appreciated and memorized Wang Wei's poems, Porter tries to visit the site of his hermitage. Wang Wei's retreat turns out to be on the grounds of a nuclear weapons factory, and Porter is arrested by the police. This incident resembles the search of an ancient poet, Tu Fu, who found the revered sage absent:

> Visiting Censor Wang's retreat
> why the silent pines bamboos
> Bramble gate closed and locked (207)

The venerable poet-painter who vanished into his artwork and the natural world continues to be an irresistible attraction to people caught in the world of social striving and struggle, policemen, and nuclear bombs. Yet he evades those who seek him.

In "When the Tao Comes to Town," the final chapter of *Road to Heaven*, Porter affirms the value for society of what hermits learn by leaving it.[8] A solitary sage will share what he learns with others: "Sooner or later, wisdom gives rise to compassion" (208). Whether Buddhist and Taoist sages come to town to teach or are sought out by city-dwellers who visit their retreats, other people need the hermit's perspective. What a hermit can offer to a seeker is elusive and not easily put in words, like a gesture suggesting a different direction in which to gaze. The political implications of hermit wisdom are vague yet significant. Chinese officials and police are uneasy about Westerners talking to these people over whom they have little control. They warn Porter to stop interviewing hermits or he will be deported. However, they release him and his friend after deciding that "we were too dumb to be spies" (213).

In the book's final scene, Porter visits Wolung Temple, which he thought was destroyed by the Red Guard. In this dilapidated place, he finds precious art treasures and a community of fifty happy monks who tell him that they are all hermits. The man who is obviously the abbot denies that he is so while explaining: "If we choose an abbot, he has to be approved by the government. We prefer to be left alone. That's why we don't fix up the temple. The government has offered us money to repair the buildings. But this is a Zen temple. We don't need fancy buildings. Fancy buildings just attract tourists" (220). After talking with the abbot, Porter remembers a Chinese saying: "The small hermit lives on a mountain. The great hermit lives in a town" (220). The book ends with a parable about the value of solitude for society. The community of hermits seems to be a harmoniously ordered anarchy with no official authority or structure, ruled by a common spirit of appreciation for inner freedom. It represents the ideal of the "great hermit": the paradox of living in society with the detachment and equanimity that are sought and sometimes learned in solitude.

Solitude is a form of unselfing, a detachment from social identity. A hermit discerns the limitations of the social roles with which he once identified. Yet, in the end, the hermit's perspective should be integrated into the life of society: the Tao must come to town. What that means for Porter's own life

---

[8] This is also the theme of John D. Barbour, *The Value of Solitude: The Ethics and Spirituality of Aloneness in Autobiography* (Charlottesville, VA: University of Virginia Press, 2004).

Searching for Chan Buddhism after Mao

remains undefined in this book, as does the relevance of the Tao for Chinese people in 1989 coming to terms with traumatic events at Tiananmen Square, strict police surveillance, and the beleaguered status of Buddhism and other religions. There is no overt political criticism or advocacy in the hermit community or in *Road to Heaven* but rather sly evasion of the people and institutions that try to control everything. Yet the hermit's disappearing self remains significant and relevant, even for the world of politics. For the Buddhist and Taoist sages that Porter encounters as he wanders through the Chungnan Mountains, the quest for self-transcendence focuses on insights and experiences that come in solitude and relativize the claims of the social self. The hermit sees beyond the self defined by society.

*

In the spring of 2006, Bill Porter undertook a ten-week journey from Beijing to Hong Kong, visiting sites connected to the first six patriarchs of Zen Buddhism (as he calls it, rather than Chan). In *Zen Baggage: A Pilgrimage to China* (2009), he weaves together the story of this journey, the history of Zen, interviews with contemporary monks, and autobiographical vignettes from his past life. The early patriarchs from Bodhidharma to Hui-neng lived between the late fifth and early eighth centuries CE and gave Zen its distinctive character, especially the emphasis on meditation, communal organization in monasteries, the ideal of finding enlightenment in everyday life, and, in paradoxical tension with all of these efforts, "the usefulness of doing nothing and getting nothing" (115).[9] Porter's emphasis on "nothing" continues throughout the text; every chapter title uses a "no" format, such as No Buddha, No Home, No Mind, No Day Off, and No Floating Belly-Up. Each "no" probes an important dimension of human experience while undermining any attempt to formalize or fix its meaning as a doctrine or belief.

For example, the first chapter of the book, "No Word," does two contradictory things. It tries to put in words the essential meaning of Zen, as when Porter holds that Zen isn't exclusively Chinese or Japanese any more, for it "belongs to anyone willing to see their nature and become a Buddha, anyone who lives the life of no-mind and laughs in these outrageous times" (3). Another in-a-nutshell formulation of what makes Zen stresses the interrelationship between meditation (the Sanskrit term for which, *dhyana*, was shortened in Chinese to *chan*) and wisdom (*prajna*). "It was the

---

[9] Bill Porter, *Zen Baggage: A Pilgrimage to China* (Berkeley: Counterpoint, 2009).

combination of dhyana (zen) with prajna that resulted in the tradition we know today as Zen … The practice of Zen involves the manifestation of both simultaneously and without distinction, whether walking, standing, sitting, or lying down" (8). Parallel to these pithy summaries of Zen are numerous reminders of the limitations of words, as revealed in anecdotes about masters who dismiss their value: "To talk about it is to go right by it" (2). The ideal of becoming free of concepts and language is a crucial characteristic of Zen. Yet a Zen master uses words (as well as gestures) to help the student realize their limitations.

Zen is prolific in generating stories and discourse about the right understanding and use of language. Zen has spawned more literature than any other school of Buddhism, including its own hermeneutics, a built-in theory of interpretation that is often conveyed in images such as a finger pointing to the moon. A Zen teacher uses words to suggest an orientation or perspective but undermines the attempt to take those words literally as defining the truth. Porter calls Zen's modes of discourse "the not-this, not-that, no-form type of forms" and asserts that "when buddhas use language, they do so to make us let go of language" (16). The teacher uses "skillful means" to adapt the teaching to a student's capacities; understanding this helps one assimilate their wisdom rightly rather than clinging to particular words and definitions.

Porter's first chapter can be taken as a theoretical commentary on *Zen Baggage*. He puts in fresh terms many central topics in Mahayana Buddhism's philosophical tradition: language, the relation between words and the wordless, ultimate truth and conditional truth, and direct apprehension in contrast to mediated interpretation. Porter weaves traditional Zen wisdom into his descriptions of conversations with a Buddhist abbot, a visit to Pailin Temple, ruminations on the words inscribed on a huge bell at Big Bell Temple, the mystery of what happened to the remains of Peking Man, and the sutras carved into a cave's stone walls. In all of these situations, Porter insists on the enigmatic significance and potent elusiveness of words. For instance, the sutras carved into Thunder Cave seem like a time capsule intended for future readers. They were carved in the eighth century, at the beginning of "the Dharma Ending Age," and their message is obscure: "How, I wondered, were we beings from the future expected to understand these words of the Buddha more than a thousand years later? There comes a time when language, even sacred language, becomes mumbo-jumbo" (31). In "No Words," then, Porter gives the reader a theory of language as an orientation to Zen Buddhism and to *Zen Baggage* itself.

Searching for Chan Buddhism after Mao

Although this book is far more revealing of the author than *Road to Heaven*, much of what the reader wants to know about Porter, especially his religious journey, remains suggestive and implicit rather than stated outright. We get lots of details about Porter's life on the road but not much introspection or interpretation of deeper meanings. In keeping with the theme of Zen as awareness of all of life, Porter describes meals, the prices of taxi rides and hotel rooms, daily naps, random sights, street life, and passing encounters with ordinary Chinese people and monks. He tells us what he had for breakfast and complains that the Chinese still haven't learned to make a decent cupcake! Porter is a rambling, even garrulous narrator, and some readers may tire of accumulating details that don't elicit an emotional or intellectual response. Yet this is an accurate representation of a typical day traveling, and it reveals more about China than more self-indulgent Western accounts. Porter's memoir involves a lot of quirky and ironic humor that makes him an enjoyable travel companion. He takes setbacks cheerfully and often turns them into comic adventures, as when he tries to dry his soaked clothes by wearing them one at a time in bed, distracting himself by writing in his journal: "A brief account of Third Patriarch Temple got me through the socks, and my meeting with the abbot got me through the T-shirt. Finally, for the pants, I opened the edition of *On Trusting the Mind* K'uan-jung had given me" (177). Before he knows it, his clothes are dry. He surmises that whoever cleans the room and puzzles over his wet sheets will blame ghosts.

Interspersed with these reports that resemble travel log entries are a few flashbacks to scenes in Porter's past, such as a time when he went AWOL from the Army, an intensive Chinese class at Columbia, and glimpses of his life as a hermit in Taiwan. Although these incidents don't have an obvious religious dimension or disclose dramatic experiences of unselfing, their rarity and brevity make them stand out, and they are apparently important moments in his life. The closest Porter comes to describing a transformative event or conversion is a brief and enigmatic account of how he became a Buddhist. This story is given in the context of Porter's visit to Wutaishan, a mountain that is a preeminent place for monks and nuns to practice in solitude. There, Porter visits the grave of Shou-yeh, the first Buddhist monk he met, whom he encountered when he was in graduate school. Among other endeavors, in 1936 Shou-yeh wrote out a 600,000-character sutra – in his own blood, three times! This almost killed him, and his devotion and indifference to dying impressed others enough that he was elevated to become the abbot of a temple and monastery on Wutaishan. After he fled China in the aftermath of the

Communist Revolution, Shou-yeh lived in Hong Kong, Vietnam, and eventually New York, where Porter met him at a weekend retreat in 1971. The only English word the monk knew was "watermelon," and Porter says his Chinese was only slightly better. When Shou-yeh showed Porter the sutra he had written out in his own blood, Porter was inspired to take refuge in the Buddha, the Dharma, and the Sangha. This is all that Porter reveals about this crucial, life-altering encounter. Visiting his teacher's stupa in 2006, he regrets "not being able to thank him for connecting me with the living Dharma, not just the Dharma in books" (72).

Their limited possibilities for verbal communication, together with the Chinese monk's combination of calm demeanor and utter commitment, had a huge impact on Porter just when he was starting to doubt that the academic world was where he wanted to be. Too many words, too much analysis of the pointing finger. Shou-yeh's example suggested an alternative way of being, including a different relationship to language: not forgoing words altogether but writing them with his blood. Porter's life work would come to focus especially on translation, a form of writing where his own personality disappeared as he attempted to render not only the words but also the spirit and worldview of Chinese poets, sages, and sutras. His own name disappeared when he adopted the pseudonym or pen name "Red Pine" as an author. The concise and cryptic account of his conversion to Buddhism is appropriate for a book that stresses the challenges of conveying deep truths in words. The story of how Porter became a Buddhist could have been a mini-chapter called "No Conversion."

While reminders of China's recent traumatic history surface repeatedly throughout Porter's journey, he also sees copious evidence of renewed interest in religion, including Buddhism. Although during the Cultural Revolution monastic life was almost eliminated, in 2006 Porter discovered many thriving monasteries and temples. On Wutaishan, the biggest pilgrimage center in northern China, there were once 300 temples and 10,000 monks and nuns. Very few survived into the 1980s, but Porter found a dozen or so large temples and busloads of visiting tourists: "The monks and nuns living in temples welcome them anyway, up to a point, figuring it is going to take another generation to reintroduce Buddhist practice to a traumatized, and now materialistic, public" (67). A more subtle danger to Buddhism than repression is the threat to dedicated monastic practice of hosting massive crowds of curious tourists. Tour guides with bullhorns, hawkers of souvenirs, and sincere questioning from Chinese and foreign visitors all distract monks from meditation, study, and rituals. There is also the seductive lure of yuan and the danger of being controlled by the

Searching for Chan Buddhism after Mao 265

government, which strictly regulates both tourism and religion. Several abbots explain their efforts to balance traditional practice with the task of educating the public about Buddhism. Compared to many other Western writers in China, such as Gretel Ehrlich, Porter spends little time lamenting or criticizing the state of contemporary Buddhism as he describes in a matter of fact way new challenges to the dharma. He suggests that Zen monasteries will deal with the temptations of tourism in the same way that they survived periods of governmental suppression: by oblique ways of evasion that partially accommodate others' demands. Like the hermits, monasteries will not confront others overtly but simply do their own thing. This reflects Porter's temperament, too. When one Chinese traveler remarks that he seems happy, Porter responds: "it was because I didn't have high standards and was adept at avoiding anything that looked like trouble. When I was in school, my favorite sport was dodge ball" (263).

Zen Baggage chronicles two "plots": Porter's travel itinerary through China and the historical evolution of Zen. Neither of these plots is correlated with Porter's spiritual development. Yet the ways in which Porter describes Zen history reveal much about his present orientation, if not how he got to it. He proposes a theory of Zen's emergence in three stages, beginning with Buddhism's arrival in China and its adoption by a series of dynasties between the third and sixth centuries. A second stage involved the new teaching of Bodhidharma, the first Zen patriarch, who said that we are all buddhas and enlightenment requires only an instant of insight, not a lifetime of ascetic practice and meditation. Visiting sites associated with Bodhidharma, Porter echoes the First Patriarch when he responds to a question about the essential teaching of Zen: "I told them that the only way out of this bitter sea—and where wasn't it on the salty side—was to see things as they are, made of your own mind. As far as I knew, that was the most essential teaching of Zen" (120). Although the idea that we are all buddhas is older than the early patriarchs, until their breakthrough it remained only a theory, not "a realization that affected one's life" (158).

A third and decisive development came when Zen became a communal practice. Porter argues that the success of Zen depended on finding a suitable location for a group to practice together. When Zen moved south and up into the flat, well-watered valleys and mountain basins in the Yangtze River watershed, it found an ecological niche in which it could thrive. There, starting with Tao-hsin, the Fourth Patriarch, Zen became a self-sustaining community whose motto was "No work, no food." Manual work became as important as meditation and monks supported each other materially and spiritually. The cooperative effort to practice mindfully in all activities is what "put the Z in Zen" (190). The perspective cultivated in Zen monasteries spread far beyond their walls and affected understandings of gardening, art, and many aspects of life.

This historical transformation of Zen finds a parallel in Porter's own spiritual outlook and one striking difference. Porter shares the Zennish emphasis on mindfulness in daily life, in contrast to separating a supposedly purified spiritual consciousness from the mundane. His travel narrative relishes the details of life on the road: whether his bath water is warm enough, how many blankets it took to stay warm, backaches and massages, and snacks of Snickers bars or pumpkin cookies. His total engagement in travel's satisfactions and irritations is contagious and surprisingly interesting in a long narrative full of such details. He acknowledges times of tedium or discomfort, then suddenly takes alert interest in an unexpected sight or conversation. Porter's travel writing does something analogous to what Yen-ying, the contemporary abbot at Shaolin, says that he does to orient recent arrivals:

> When new monks at Shaolin ask me about the Dharma, I tell them to have a cup of tea. If they still don't understand, I tell them to taste the tea. The Way is in everything we do. Drinking a cup of tea, eating, shitting, it doesn't matter, it's all the Way. You can read all the books you want, but unless you find the Way in your daily life, you're wasting your time. It's the same with martial arts. Every kick, every blow is the Way. You can't separate yourself from what you do. If you do, it's not the Way. At Shaolin we don't separate the inside from the outside. We must have a karmic connection for you to show up here in my room and be drinking tea with me. Have another cup. (136–137)

As he makes his way through China, Porter describes many cups of tea, coffee, or port.

He shares Zen's emphasis on the everyday here and now, but not its practice of living in a settled community. Although Porter appreciates how important a supportive community was for the flourishing of Zen, he wants no part of communal life. In particular, the ritual and ceremonial performances of Zen leave him cold. He hates ceremony in churches, the Army, or a Buddhist monastery: "As far as I was concerned, they were the denatured version of shamanistic rituals. Maybe if there was more dancing" (14). Even though he knows that rituals are supposed to foster a sense of community, he admits "as soon as I become part of a group, I'm looking for a way out" (14). For some people, an experience of being immersed in a group gives rise to unselfing, the overcoming of an individual's feeling of separateness. Yet for Porter, ceremonies reinforce his sense of being an outsider looking in:

Searching for Chan Buddhism after Mao

> It must be my karmic inheritance. I've always preferred to stand outside the shrine hall rather than inside … Give me the wind in the pines any day, and a pumpkin cookie from time to time. I've always wondered what kind of ceremonies the Buddha performed in his day. I don't recall ever reading about any. Did he even say grace before meals? (185)

Zen's evolution from the utterances of wandering solitary practitioners to the practices of a stable community is not duplicated in Porter's own life. He is not moved toward engagement with communal life.

Yet a significant shift took place in the seventeen years between *Road to Heaven* and *Zen Baggage*, in that the latter work interprets and celebrates a much more organized and extensive form of community than the looser affiliations of like-minded hermits. Furthermore, we can see Porter's decades-long labors to translate Chinese texts as a form of community building; his literary endeavors foster a transcultural group of people who share an appreciation for Chinese literature and religious wisdom. By giving the English-speaking world access to masterpieces of Chinese culture and by sharing his own entertaining explorations of contemporary China, Porter stretches the boundaries of what his readers can understand and value. In this sense, the written work of this translator and tale-telling traveler is, in its way, analogous to the labor of creating a Zen community. Porter's books are textual versions of the mind-to-mind transmission of awareness that is Zen's essential method.

In the index of *Zen Baggage*, there is an intriguing item: "self, 330." This lonely entry describes, first, Porter's account of his encounter with Yi-ch'ao, a monk who at fourteen had been the attendant of the great Zen master Empty Cloud (Hsu-yun). Porter then recalls what he was doing at that age. His "monastery" was a military boarding school in Hollywood and his "Zen master" was a man named George who taught Porter to fish and hunt in Idaho. "When you're fourteen you're glad someone wants to teach you something, and learning to use a fly rod and a shotgun was my world of Zen. It was not a religious experience. But then again, maybe it was. It got me into the wilderness and being alone a lot, both of which I liked" (330). Solitude and being in the natural world were Zen for him and – maybe or maybe not – a religious experience. Porter describes this discovery of a new and vital way of being in a low-key, understated, and matter-of-fact manner. This moment of unselfing gave him a new sense of self that continues to orient him.

Why is this the only passage in the book that Porter chose to index as referring to his self? It depicts a significant change in his sense of himself, but so do several other passages, especially the one recounting his encounter with the monk who inspired him to take the Three Refuges. This passage goes on to explicitly link self and no-self. The monk who had attended Empty Cloud says of a photograph of himself with the great master: "There is no self in anything. Whatever we see, we discriminate according to our delusions" (330). This vignette reveals something essential about the author even as it warns against trying to identity self with anything: photograph, story, or definition of particular characteristics or religious beliefs. Porter suggests that his journey ends at this point, when Yi-ch'ao hands him the photograph and says that there is no self, which prompts him to remember the incident when he was fourteen. As he concludes this autobiographical reflection, Porter invokes the title of the book: "There is so much baggage we burden ourselves with over the years that keeps us from seeing things the way they are. Some baggage we carry with us for a single thought, some for years, and some for lifetimes. But there isn't one piece that isn't our own creation" (330). The baggage is ours but we aren't the baggage.

Bags are a recurring motif in *Zen Baggage*. Porter accumulates books and tea along the way, and his back aches as his heavier pack weighs him down. His mood becomes lighter and happier when he mails the latest pile of souvenirs back to America. His relationship to his travel baggage is a metaphor for his interest in the burdens of selfhood and the moments of unselfing when this weight is set down. The baggage we burden ourselves with, including our understanding of our self, is real, and it weighs us down. It is also an illusion that prevents us from "seeing things the way they are." Although Porter would gladly discard his baggage and lose his sense of self, telling his story also involves (to extend the metaphor) opening his bags and displaying what's "inside." *Zen Baggage* describes the burdens of selfhood that Porter carries and moments when, unburdened, he forgets himself and simply attends to the world.

In the final chapter, "No Going Back," as Porter returns to his home in Port Townsend, Washington, he recalls another transpacific flight, when in 1972 he first went to China. He describes his estrangement from his father and a chance encounter with a hobo who shares an enigmatic story about being cared for by "the Monkey People" when his plane was shot down over the Philippines. The hobo regrets not going back to thank the Monkey People. He tells Porter not to leave China and walks off. Porter's reaction:

> I went back to my father's apartment, opened a beer, and joined him staring at the TV. The next day I got on the plane and never saw my father again. Four years later, the abbot brought me a letter he sent the day before he

Searching for Chan Buddhism after Mao   269

died. He asked if it wasn't about time I did something useful with my life. I moved out of the monastery not long after that and began translating poems and sutras. Thirty years later, I still haven't found anything better to do. (334)

This cryptic ending has many meanings. Porter's estrangement from his father seems related to his finding father figures in several abbots and in George, the hunting guide. There is "no going back" to his father ("no father"), no overcoming of estrangement, yet the history of that relationship influences later encounters and bonds. This passage locates the moment when Porter began his life's work as a translator, a vocation that to some people, including his father, seems useless, little different than being a hobo. The hobo whom Porter met was a wanderer with no interest in contributing to the gross national product or conforming to expectations; he says: "At least I won't die inside of some cracker-box house working some meaningless job" (334).

The ending of the book is full of Zennish paradoxes, such as Porter suggesting there is "no going back" just as he returns to his home in Port Townsend. He implies that there is no return to the autobiographical past, either: no point in searching for or clinging to the roots of one's present identity in earlier experiences. Yet this passage, like other autobiographical snippets scattered throughout *Zen Baggage*, is evidence that the past is still present. As a persisting sense of self takes new forms, it reveals ancient traces: the consequences of karma, heredity, and experiences that shape character. Porter concludes with this suggestive vignette that expresses the mystery of self and no-self, much like the Zen poems he translated. The book's title is a metaphor of self. Porter's baggage of selfhood includes Zen concepts and intuitions that help him understand that "there isn't one piece that isn't our own creation" (330).

Zen Baggage portrays Porter's understanding of no-self by portraying the mundane details of life on the road. He invites the reader to stop looking for something extraordinary, such as a dramatic episode of unselfing, and instead "have a cup of tea." To be able to do this may depend on a subtle kind of transformation wrought by "the wordless, buddhaless, mountainless, homeless, beginningless, formless, mindless teaching of Zen" (324).

Conclusion
Theories of No-Self, Stories of Unselfing, and Transformation

This book has explored various ways in which writers have understood the concept of no-self and used it to interpret experiences that were pivotal in a process of personal transformation. In the five sections of this Conclusion, I correlate my conclusions about Western Buddhist travel narratives with theories of no-self as this concept is used in the history of Buddhist thought. Copious and detailed information about *anatta* is readily available in encyclopedia articles, textbooks, and focused studies such as Steven Collins's *Selfless Persons*.[1] I first highlight several salient points about the concept of no-self that shed light on how contemporary Western writers portray experiences of unselfing and interpret their significance. In the following section, I reflect on the value of autobiographical narratives for understanding no-self and experiences of unselfing, in contrast to more abstract and systematic forms of discourse. Third, I discuss an eighteenth-century Tibetan autobiography that is analogous in certain ways to Western Buddhist travel narratives. I reflect in a fourth section on why travel narratives often portray experiences of unselfing. Finally, I propose a theory about the role of experiences of unselfing and the significance of autobiographical writing in the process of religious transformation. My approach invites and orients further work on narratives about transformation in Buddhism, other religious traditions, and diverse forms of autobiographical writing.

Theories of No-Self

On the face of it, the Buddhist concept of no-self is incompatible with the Western fascination with and commitment to the self. The Buddhist critique of the self would seem to undermine the autobiographical impulse

---

[1] Steven Collins, *Selfless Persons: Imagery and Thought in Theravada Buddhism* (Cambridge: Cambridge University Press, 1982).

that is prominent in many travel narratives. However, certain theoretical accounts of no-self illuminate the sense of contradiction, paradox, and irony in the idea of a literary genre devoted to the autobiographical investigation of the self's illusory nature. First, consider accounts of the historical context of Buddhist ideas about no-self. According to scholars of early Buddhism, the denial of self was directed toward a particular view of the self: the *atman* of the Upanishads. This mysterious ultimate metaphysical entity is indestructible, unchanging, immortal, and unaffected by suffering or worldly experience. *Atman* was identified with *Brahman*, the underlying ground of all reality. It is this specific conception of the self that is questioned and denied by the Buddha, early thinkers, and the complex systems of philosophical analysis known as Abhidharma. So, for example, Buddhist thinkers analyzed human experience in terms of impersonal constituents such as five "aggregates" (*skandhas*) or basic types of physical and mental events: bodily phenomena, sensations or feelings, perceptions, mental formations, and conscious awareness. Early Buddhist texts argue that the self depends on yet cannot be identified with any of the five aggregates. The idea of self, they argued, is a convenient label used to connect certain mental and physical phenomena that are causally linked.[2]

This historical contextualization of the early Buddhist critique of self highlights its dependence on a specific metaphysical conception: *atman*. This philosophical agenda did not, however, prevent or prohibit reliance on ideas about the self in most social situations, including monasteries and religious instruction. When the Buddha says "I" and refers to himself as he teaches, he obviously does not mean *atman*, the unchanging being beyond experience. According to Collins, "the linguistic items translated lexically as 'self' and 'person' … are used quite naturally and freely in a number of contexts, without any suggestion that their being so used might conflict with the doctrine of *anatta*."[3] Buddhists from early times until the present assume and refer to selves when they are involved in everyday practices and social interactions and when they discuss karma and ethical matters such as responsibility for deeds. Attention to the distinctive character of an individual was important in assigning a particular teacher or meditation practice to that person. While Buddhist tradition "insisted fiercely on *anatta* as a doctrinal position," in practice the doctrine did not play a role in daily religious life.[4]

---

[2] Ibid., 97–103 and Rupert Gethin, *The Foundations of Buddhism* (Oxford: Oxford University Press, 1998), 138–139.

[3] Collins, *Selfless Persons*, 71.

[4] Ibid., 94–96.

272   Conclusion

For the elite who used it, the doctrine of no-self had social, intellectual, and soteriological functions: "Among those Buddhists who are concerned with, and pay explicit allegiance to, the doctrine of *anatta*, it provides orientation to social attitudes and behavior (particularly *vis-à-vis* Brahmanical thought and the ritual priests who purveyed it), to conceptual activity in the intellectual life of Buddhist scholastics, and to soteriological activity in the life of virtuoso meditators."[5] *Anatta* was used by Buddhist thinkers to explain their difference from and opposition to Brahmanical thought. In technical philosophical discourse, *anatta* is a "linguistic taboo" for scholars that prohibits references to the self and replaces them with impersonal elements (*dhamma*). For monks, ideas about *anatta* are connected to soteriology in that they explain strategies for advanced meditators trying to become free from desire. In these limited contexts, no-self is a helpful tool. In other settings, references to the self are not only unproblematic but necessary for many purposes.

Bernard Faure goes further in contrasting everyday practices to doctrinal speculations, even criticizing those who insist on no-self as a fundamental component of Buddhist belief:

> The emphasis the majority of scholars have placed on the orthodox dogma of the *anatman* again reflects an elitist or even ideological vision of Buddhism: in fact, it is clear that the majority of followers of mainstream Buddhism believe in the existence of a self and that their observance of the religion is based on this very belief. The so-called "orthodox" or rather monastic conception of the nonexistence of the self fails to take account of the complexity of the Buddhist tradition and the diversity of its responses to the serious question of subjectivity.[6]

This view makes no-self an esoteric theory invoked only by scholars and monastic practitioners, not an essential part of the Buddhist worldview. Faure and Collins analyze tensions between doctrinal assertions about no-self and a Buddhist society's practical need for a conception of self.

I have at many points noted a similar tension at work in Western Buddhist travel narratives. Yet theories about no-self are not just speculative ideas but influential in many ways in these books, especially as they shape ideals of religious experience and moral character. Selflessness as a spiritual goal and ethical norm is fundamental in Buddhism, and these twin concerns are central in Western Buddhist travel narratives. In a few cases, such as van de Wetering's *Empty Mirror* and Schettini's *The Novice*,

---

[5] Ibid., 78.
[6] Bernard Faure, *Unmasking Buddhism* (Chichester: Wiley-Blackwell, 2008), 52.

selflessness does not have much to do with how a person treats others but simply means escape from misery or self-consciousness. Other works, such as Pistono's *In the Shadow of the Buddha*, emphasize the ethical meaning of selflessness as expressed in compassion and concern for justice. What being a selfless person means for each writer is shaped by differing understandings of no-self, personal experiences of unselfing, and the entire context of the author's life.

Ideas about no-self play a crucial role in orienting Western writers to seek experiences of unselfing and to interpret them in accordance with this Buddhist idea rather than in some other way. Collins uses the term "introjection" to describe the way in which monastic practitioners of meditation gain deepening insight into the truth of the doctrine of *anatta*. *Vipassana*, insight, is the application of the categories of Buddhist psychology to a monk's personal experience. A monk learns to analyze the arising and ceasing of phenomena that cannot be equated with the self and to classify experiences in terms of non-valued, impersonal constituent parts: "It is precisely the introjection of these categories and formulas—their 'point,' if not all their 'details'—and the 'realising' of them personally through meditation, which forms in practice the most important part of the Buddhist Path to *nirvana*."[7] This formulation views "experience" as the reproduction of traditional teaching when a monk interprets his meditative practice.

The relationships between experience and interpretation are more complicated and various than this in Western Buddhist travel narratives. Most writers already knew a lot about Buddhism before the journey, and some had studied or meditated for many years. In some cases, their experiences of unselfing were, indeed, a "realizing" of ideas that they "introjected" previously over many years. In other cases, the memory of a compelling experience of unselfing stayed with a writer for a long time without being shaped by Buddhist concepts. An example is Peter Matthiessen recollecting his experience as a young man alone on his watch on a naval vessel during a wild Pacific storm. Descriptions of unselfing in first-person narratives are not simply illustrations of Buddhist categories; they have multiple sources and dimensions, such as, in Matthiessen's case, the influence of Western texts by Rilke, Hesse, Jung, Kierkegaard, and others. The

---

[7] Collins, *Selfless Persons*, 263. See also Robert M. Gimello, "Mysticism and Meditation," in *Mysticism and Philosophical Analysis*, ed. Steven Katz (Oxford: Oxford University Press, 1978), 193: "Rather than speak of Buddhist doctrines as interpretations of Buddhist mystical experiences, one might better speak of Buddhist mystical experiences as deliberately contrived exemplifications of Buddhist doctrine."

274   Conclusion

relationship between theories of no-self and stories of unselfing – between
conceptual thought and accounts of experience – must be investigated in
each individual case.

For traditional and contemporary Buddhists, it is especially the practice
of meditation that confirms the theory of no-self. This is the arena where
the truths of the dharma are realized or recognized. In meditation, the
ordinary sense of self dissipates as attention is directed to a focus such as
the breath or a mantra, and interrupting thoughts are analyzed in terms
of impersonal Buddhist categories. In the experiences of unselfing "off the
cushion" that we examined in travel narratives, ordinary consciousness is
disrupted or suspended so that a different way of organizing experience
becomes possible. As in the practice of meditation, during these experiences the usual structures of thought, awareness of boundaries, and habits of consciousness are temporarily altered. For Western Buddhists, the
theory of no-self helps a person make sense of this experience, integrate it
into the sense of ongoing identity, and, in an extended first-person narrative, explore its significance in a long-term process of transformation.

Most ordinary Buddhists are not bothered by a need to reconcile no-self
and self, but Buddhist thinkers worked out ways to do this. One way to
ease the sense that these ideas are contradictory distinguishes between conventional, provisional, or superficial truth (*samvti-satya*) and ultimate truth
(*paramrtha-satya*). It is an ultimate truth that the self is not an independent
and enduring substance or entity, yet as a matter of convention and practical convenience, we refer to selves. Several Western Buddhist travel writers refer to this distinction as a way to reconcile ideas about no-self with
the needs of ordinary life. This allows them to have their cake (self) and
"eat" it, too – that is, to see the self consumed or absorbed into something
else. Yet most storytellers do not interrupt their narrative with this kind of
analysis. They assert that there is no essential self and then, without seeing
any need for explanation or justification, they describe how they journeyed
in Asia, had experiences that helped them understand Buddhism, and carried on with life, making decisions and feeling responsible for the things
an ordinary person cares about. Contemporary Western writers vacillate
between the rhetoric of no-self and assertions that they searched for or
found a true self, without trying to reconcile these claims. Are they hope-
lessly confused and inconsistent or trying to hold on to two crucial insights
even if they apparently contradict each other?

A traditional strategy by which certain thinkers dissolve the apparent contradiction of no-self and self is to find a "middle way." In the
Dharmacakrapravartana Sutra ("Sutra Turning the Wheel of Dharma"),

the first teaching the Buddha gave after awakening, he proposes a middle way, a strategy that later thinkers saw as applying not only to the right orientation toward sense pleasures but also to other questions. Taking this central Buddhist metaphor as an orientation to the nature of the self, they held that one must avoid belief in either the self's permanence or its annihilation. The third-century thinker Nagarjuna, in the "Examination of Self-Existence" chapter of his *Madhyamakakarika*, refutes the extremes of "is" and "is not" without explaining the correct middle course when understanding the self. Roger Jackson summarizes how Nagarjuna used the Buddhist concept of the middle to articulate how the self both is and is not, according to the two kinds of truth, superficial and ultimate:

> The "middle" decreed by Nagarjuna here is, taken negatively, a path between the "is" implied by interpreting the cosmos in terms of self-existence and the "is not" implied by applying emptiness in too thoroughgoing a manner; stated more positively, it is the mutual implication between dependent origination and emptiness, whereby understanding that entities and concepts arise conventionally in dependence upon causes and conditions entails automatically that they are ultimately empty, while the recognition that their ultimate nature is emptiness means that they must be conventionally established dependent arisings. In this sense, Nagarjuna's middle avoids the extremes of eternalism and nihilism taken as absolutes, but permits the assertion of "is" and "is not" as conventional designations as long as *both* of the truths are kept in mind.[8]

Jackson describes the "middle" not as a mean or halfway position but rather as a combination of views that, when either is taken alone, would be erroneous.

Nagarjuna's classic way of reconciling contradictions philosophically has a parallel in contemporary narratives about unselfing. In Western Buddhist travel memoirs, a middle way is presented in narrative form. This middle is a matter of both/and rather than in-between.[9] A story is a way to keep in mind *both* the truths of no-self and selfhood. In particular, a portrayal of personal transformation can show the author's self to be neither permanent nor annihilated but rather changing as she passes through an experience so unusual that it calls into question the nature or reality of the self. Particular incidents in such a narrative may focus on one or the other truth: either times when the ordinary self feels real and substantial or moments of

---

[8] Roger R. Jackson, "In Search of a Postmodern Middle," in *Buddhist Theology: Critical Reflections by Contemporary Buddhist Scholars*, eds. Roger R. Jackson and John J. Makransky (Richmond: Curzon: 2000), 231.

[9] Technically, however, Nagarjuna rejected "both" as one of the four extremes.

unselfing when a person's usual identity seems illusory or empty. The full story of a transformation needs to depict both kinds of truth.

Another point made in theoretical accounts of no-self also resonates with travel narratives by Western Buddhists. No-self means one thing for thinkers trying to clarify and coordinate Buddhist ideas and something else for monks engaged in meditation and trying to attain enlightenment. For people seeking nirvana, no-self is what Collins calls "a strategy in mental culture" intended to release them from clinging to particular views.[10] An important theme in the Buddhist critique of self is that there are often strong elements of attachment, possessiveness, and desire for control at work when a person strongly identifies with an idea. This is relevant to *anatta*, too: one shouldn't be attached to a concept or theory about no-self any more than any other idea. The Buddha once refused to reply to a question about the existence of the self, just as he did for other "unanswered questions" that foster unproductive speculation, conflict, and stress.[11] When a wandering ascetic, Vacchagotta, asked the Buddha if there is a self, the Buddha remained silent. Nor did he respond when asked if there is not a self. He explained why to his disciple Ananda:

> To say there is a s/Self would be to be associated with "eternalists"—namely those who believe in an eternal Self—and be in contradiction with the knowledge that "all *dharmas* are not-Self" (i. e. "no *dharma* is a Self"). To say that there is not a s/Self would be to be associated with "annihilationists"—namely those who believe only in a "this-life" self which is totally destroyed at death, such that there is no changing empirical *self-process* flowing on to a new rebirth—and would be confusing to Vacchagotta as he would think he had lost a s/Self that he formerly had.[12]

The Buddha refused to answer in order to cut off Vacchagotta's identification with and clinging to views, which can produce as much suffering as other forms of attachment. He did not want the perception of the self and all reality in terms of no-self – or, in Mahayana tradition, emptiness – to generate a dogmatic conviction that "there is no self." He was as cautious about views of no-self as about the self, and the tradition that he began influences Western Buddhist travel narratives. This perspective on the danger of clinging to fixed ideas makes it easier for them to reconcile

---

[10] Collins, *Selfless Persons*, 111.
[11] Collins, *Selfless Persons*, 131–38.
[12] Peter Harvey, "Not-Self (Anatman)," in *Encyclopedia of Buddhism*, ed. Damien Keon and Charles S. Prebish (London: Routledge, 2007), 570.

self and no-self. Using another common Buddhist metaphor, several of them compare the idea of no-self to a raft used to cross a stream, which can be discarded when it has served its proper function.

Collins helpfully distinguishes between two Buddhist approaches to non-self, one of which is concerned to formulate the "right view" of *anatta* as this doctrine describes ultimate reality. The second approach stresses not right view but "*no*-view," insisting on the danger of being attached to any view. This pragmatic and agnostic orientation sees *anatta* as a strategic instrument in mental culture: "The dichotomy between right and wrong views is replaced, one might say, by a continuum, along which all conceptual standpoints and cognitive acts are graded according to the degree to which they are held or performed with attachment."[13] Both of these orientations are at work in Western Buddhist travel narratives. Sometimes authors approach ideas about no-self as explanations of the character of ultimate reality and present it as a component of "right view." At other moments, Western authors more closely resemble the second traditional approach to no-self; they avoid or dismiss metaphysical speculations and say only that this idea helped them, and perhaps remind the reader that Buddhism is not a religion based on faith in doctrines and dogmas. For such a writer, no-self functions as a catalyst and useful support for the capacity to say farewell to the old self that must be abandoned or "die" in the process of transformation.

Western Buddhist travel writers do not spend much time or energy arguing about the existence or nonexistence of the self; the kinds of discussion that philosophers engage in do not preoccupy them. Yet the idea of no-self plays several important roles in the process of spiritual transformation that they describe. They emphasize no-self's soteriological meaning or, for those averse to seeing Buddhism as a religion of salvation, its therapeutic value. In contrast to the traditional Buddhist focus on meditation practice, these authors explore other areas of experience in which they found ideas about no-self to be illuminating. They show how Buddhist ideas about no-self helped them understand unusual experiences that were pivotal in a process of change that led to greater calm, wisdom, and compassion. These writers show how the idea that the self lacks permanent substance and is interrelated with all things enabled them to better understand their lives. They often use no-self in conjunction with psychological ideas about a true, larger, deeper, or more authentic self that emerged in the course of their travels. In this, they resemble Buddhists in traditional

[13] Collins, *Selfless Persons*, 117.

278   Conclusion

societies who speak of a true self that is not based on social role or location but identified with Buddha nature, "pure mind," or some other reality beyond ordinary consciousness.

In Western Buddhist travel narratives, a conception of no-self shapes authors' accounts of a compelling experience of unselfing, and their rhetoric varies greatly when they describe this event and what replaces the old self. The authors skirt difficult philosophical questions about how to reconcile understandings of no-self with narration of the self's ongoing life. Instead of addressing this issue in abstract terms, they tell a story whose tensions disclose a middle way, a both/and awareness of contrasting insights. Let us turn from theories about no-self to the ways in which travel writers construct stories about unselfing.

Stories of Unselfing

Unselfing is the general term I've proposed for experiences when a person's sense of self is dramatically altered. Unselfing may be explained in terms of a theory such as the Buddhist concept of no-self or described in the form of a story. In this section, I reflect broadly on the value of narrative for understanding experiences of unselfing; the next three sections discuss the specific contributions of autobiography and a particular kind of first-person writing, travel memoirs.

Narratives and theories each have a distinctive value as well as limitations. Narratives illuminate certain dimensions of religious experience that are obscured by abstract and systematic thought; they also present insights that seem ambiguous, inconsistent, or contradictory and so prompt systematic thinking. Yet to contrast theory and narrative so starkly simplifies the complex ways in which individuals seek to understand profound experiences such as religious conversion, transformation, and unselfing. Abstract thinking about religious experience is usually based on particular cases and an implicit narrative, an ideal model of the temporal order of events when a person encounters and understands the ultimate reality. Narratives depend on concepts and theories, for instance about the nature of God, the meaning of enlightenment or conversion, or the ethical virtues and duties expected of members of a religious community. The word "theory" derives from the Greek verb *theorein*, which means to look at, perceive, or behold. With the aid of a theory, one beholds and recognizes what one believes is reality: "Look! There it is!" In the case of a narrative about unselfing, the author does not usually explain what theory underlies this story of religious experience or what counts as being a state other than ordinary selfhood. Yet a conception of these things enables him to say: "Behold! My religious experience!"

Although I have attempted to approach Western Buddhist narratives with an open mind, so as to avoid imposing an overly restrictive definition of unselfing and transformation, I, too, have depended on an implicit theory about a certain kind of religious experience. At this point, I want to provide a sketch of that theory, drawing on several scholars of religion.

In her theory of religious experience, Ann Taves builds on the work of the French sociologist Emile Durkheim, who defined religion as "a unified system of beliefs and practices relative to sacred things, that is, things set apart and forbidden."[14] For Taves, religion is a process of meaning-making and valuation in which a group of people deem certain things to be special and set them apart from others. She explores the process of "singularization" involved when people claim that certain things are special, and she analyzes the ways that special things are incorporated into social institutions such as religious traditions and spiritual disciplines. Special things include experiences, objects, acts, and agents. They are set apart as special because they are either ideal or anomalous when compared to ordinary things of their kind. For Taves, as for Durkheim, the sacredness or religious quality of something is not an inherent quality but a value placed on it by a social group and tradition. She focuses on "deeming," the ways in which people ascribe value to and set apart special things. Although individuals within groups may argue about which things should be set apart and on what grounds, religious traditions develop norms that distinguish, for example, between authentic religious experiences and other events that may resemble them but are viewed as something else. What counts as a religious object or experience is not a stable and fixed matter and changes through a process of social negotiation as people attribute meaning to their lives. Taves urges scholars of religion to reframe the concept of religious experience in terms of "experiences deemed religious" and to explore the ways groups "make and unmake" religious experience.

From Taves's theory of religious experience, I want to adapt the concepts of deeming and specialness as useful for thinking about unselfing. This approach points us toward investigating *what counts* as an experience of unselfing and why. We should ask these questions about particular cases

---

[14] Ann Taves, *Religious Experience Reconsidered: A Building-Block Approach to the Study of Religion and Other Special Things* (Princeton: Princeton University Press, 2009), 16, quoting Durkheim's *The Elementary Forms of Religious Life* (1912). See also Ann Taves, "Special Things as Building Blocks of Religion," in *The Cambridge Companion to Religious Studies*, ed. Robert A. Orsi (Cambridge: Cambridge University Press, 2012), 58–83.

280 Conclusion

rather than define unselfing in advance. That is what I have been doing in examining Western Buddhist travel narratives. We witnessed an amazing variety of experiences that authors view as radically different than their ordinary sense of life. Think of Ian Baker gazing at a rock cliff that seems to dissolve, and of Maura O'Halloran feeling that she left her body and returned to it, suddenly empowered to resist her Zen master's attempt to coerce her into marriage. Recall Thomas Merton's encounters with the statues at Polonnaruwa, and the reaction of Ajahn Sucitto and Nick Scott to their nearly fatal encounter with bandits in India. Jamie Zeppa felt that her decision to marry and stay in Bhutan was like a dizzying leap off a cliff into another life. Stephen Asma describes several moments of "transcendental everydayness" when ordinary life was transfigured so that he became aware of his interconnectedness with all of reality. In some narratives, such as Peter Matthiessen's two travel memoirs or Janwillem van de Wetering's account of his Zen training, authors are frustrated when they are not able to have the experience of satori they long for. They, too, have an implicit concept of a special and ideal kind of religious experience, an expectation that shapes what happens to them, including their disappointment. In the preceding chapters, we examined a great variety of experiences deemed to be singular and special in comparison with the author's ordinary sense of self.

Unselfing is one of the "special things" of great concern for the world's religious traditions, and it is central to mysticism – perhaps even the common denominator of the many expressions of this elusive aspect of religion. Unselfing is also sought after and experienced by people unaffiliated with any religion. Consider the many ways in which a person's sense of self can change and how similar experiences can be interpreted in very different ways. One may feel that one no longer has agency, as if some other power has taken over and is acting. In a later book, Ann Taves studies people who speak or write with voices that they claim are not their own.[15] Possession by spirits is a widespread phenomenon and belief system in many of the world's religious traditions, which explain in these terms experiences when agency seems to be temporarily exercised by another being.[16] Another form of unselfing involves feeling dissociated from the physical body: observing it from outside, leaving it to travel elsewhere on a spiritual journey, or

---

[15] Ann Taves, *Revelatory Events: Three Case Studies of the Emergence of New Spiritual Paths* (Princeton: Princeton University Press, 2016).

[16] For a fascinating study of spirit possession, see Kristin C. Bloomer, *Possessed by the Virgin: Hinduism, Roman Catholicism, and Marian Possession in South India* (New York: Oxford University Press, 2018).

Stories of Unselfing 281

sensing that the body is inanimate or belongs to someone else. Unselfing has many of the common features of mystical experiences, such as the blurring of boundaries between self and the world, so that a person feels identity or kinship with what is usually thought to be not the self. Visions, trances, and intuitive insights may seem to come from a deeper self: a form of consciousness or wisdom beyond the ordinary mind. The sense of self can also change dramatically when a person experiences overwhelming emotions or first becomes aware of new desires and longings.

In all of these ways, an individual may undergo puzzling experiences that seem so inconsistent with all that he or she has previously known that his or her personal story no longer makes sense and he or she needs to create a new narrative – an account of transformation or conversion – to make sense of how the old and new identities are connected. Whether or not, or to what degree, the *self* actually changes, these startling experiences are evidence that a person's *sense of self* can be dramatically transformed. This kind of experience, the feeling that one's identity has changed, dissolved, or stretched to incorporate what was not the self, is one of the most mysterious and significant things that can happen to a person. Such an event needs to be interpreted and integrated into a person's life narrative and made part of "the story of who I am."

Religious traditions understand experiences of unselfing in specific and distinctive terms: for instance, as Buddhist awakening, Christian conversion, Muslim submission to Allah, Hindu *bhakti* (ecstatic devotion), or a Siberian shaman's otherworldly journey while in a trance. Religions provide an intellectual framework and normative perspective that establishes what these puzzling experiences mean and what they should lead to. The ways in which experiences of unselfing are believed to have meaning reflect a particular community's history, values, and language. Religious traditions often link experiences of unselfing to transformation and view them as a crucial step that brings a person into a new role in the community. Many religious rituals attempt to engender such experiences in an initiate and to define their meaning. At such a time of transition, religious ideas and values become real and significant in a new way to an individual: they are existentially grasped, felt in the bones, known as matters of conviction and commitment.

John Hick's approach to religion explains why unselfing is so often a crucial religious experience. Like Taves, Hick proposes a general theory of religion that integrates the details of many specific religious traditions. He uses the generic term "the Real" for that ultimate reality to which every religious tradition is committed. He argues that in "the great post-axial traditions" (a term that leaves out tribal and orally based cultures), salvation or liberation is seen as a transformation of human life from a focus on the self to ultimate reality:

> This may be by self-committing faith in Christ as one's lord and saviour; or by the total submission to God which is *islam*; or by faithful obedience to the Torah; or by transcendence of the ego, with its self-centered desires and ravings, to attain *moksa* or Nirvana. As I shall now try to show, these are variations within different conceptual schemes on a single fundamental theme: the sudden or gradual change of the individual from an absorbing self-concern to a new centring in the supposed unity-of-reality-and-value that is thought of as God, Brahman, the Dharma, Sunyata or the Tao. Thus the generic concept of salvation/liberation, which takes a different specific form in each of the great traditions, is that of the transformation of human existence from self-centeredness to Reality-centeredness.[17]

The pivotal moment in an individual's transformation to Reality-centeredness is what I call unselfing. Religious traditions use specific terms to describe this shift to a new understanding of life and new way of being. In the case of Buddhism, ideas about no-self play a crucial role in the awakening from self-centeredness to understanding the true nature of reality: "This turning from ego to reality is both illuminated and enabled by the *anatta* ('no self') doctrine, which D. T. Suzuki translates as 'non-ego,' 'selflessness,' and which he says 'is the principal conception of Buddhism, both Hinayana and Mahayana.'"[18] No-self *illuminates* the turning to Reality: this concept interprets and explains the meaning and significance of the experience. It also *enables* the turning away from suffering that is rooted in the powerful illusion of self: "The *anatta* or no-self doctrine is thus not offered merely as a theoretical truth but above all as a practical prescription for liberation."[19] The implications of *anatta* for how Buddhists should live are elaborated in such teachings as the Eightfold Path, monastic codes of conduct, ideal descriptions and narratives about bodhisattvas, and the techniques and goals of meditation. No-self is not only an interpretation of but also a vehicle for self-transformation.

As mentioned in the Introduction, Hick describes how religious traditions teach their adherents new ways of "seeing-as" and "experiencing-as." He summarizes the essential shift of perspective taught by Mahayana Buddhism:

---

[17] John Hick, *An Interpretation of Religion: Human Responses to the Transcendent* (New Haven: Yale University Press, 1989), 36.

[18] Ibid., 41, quoting D. T. Suzuki's *The Zen Doctrine of No Mind* (1972).

[19] Ibid., 42.

Stories of Unselfing

In the Mahayana development, particularly as represented by Zen, we have a very clear example of religious consciousness as a distinctive mode of experiencing-as. For the startling central insight of the Mahayana is that Nirvana and Samsara are identical. In the classic words of Nagarjuna, "There is not the slightest bit of difference between these two."[20]

The world-process is no longer seen as Samsara but as Nirvana. Relying heavily on D. T. Suzuki's works on Zen, Hick presents *satori* or enlightenment as the "hinge" that turns a person from one way of experiencing the world to another. *Satori* involves a "sudden conversion from one mode of experiencing to another, from the samsaric to the nirvanic mode; and this latter is, according to the Buddhist claim, Reality itself manifested within a purified human consciousness."[21] Although Suzuki has been criticized for ahistoricism and reliance upon a notion of religious experience derived from modern Western philosophy, I find helpful Hick's use of Suzuki's account of *satori* as one aspect of Hick's attempt to discern commonalities in diverse religious traditions. Hick's *An Interpretation of Religion* provides a theoretical context for understanding the significance of experiences of unselfing in many traditions. His remarks about *anatta* describe how this concept both explains and precipitates the fundamental Buddhist transformation, awakening, as well as the limited glimpses and tentative movements toward it that some Buddhists think they have made and may describe in stories such as Western Buddhist travel narratives.

Unselfing is one of the "special things" that recur in religious experience and are interpreted in distinctive ways by each tradition in narratives and more abstract forms of discourse such as sutras, sermons, theological treatises, and systematic analysis of doctrines such as Buddhist Abhidharma texts. Another level of analysis and abstraction takes place in theories of religious experience encompassing many religious traditions, such as those of William James, Ann Taves, John Hick, or the theory of unselfing that orients my study of narratives. Taves describes the special value of autobiographical accounts of religious experience:

> The closer we are to the experience in question the more we can see of the way it is embedded in and connected to other things. The more we abstract or disconnect "experience" from *the narrating of experience* in order that it may participate in more abstract discourses, the more it is fragmented or, as James says, "decomposed." First person narratives allow us to focus on the

---

[20] Ibid., 157.

[21] Ibid., 158. In *An Autobiography* (Oxford: Oneworld Publications, 2002), 223, Hick mentions an incident of unselfing while practicing Buddhist meditation when he "experienced what was to me a startling breakthrough into a new form or level of consciousness."

narrating of experience and provide historians with our primary means of access to the experience-in-practice of an individual or community. Such narratives provide a means of reconstituting the links between experience and the bodily knowledges, cultural traditions, and social relations that went into making or composing the experience. Third-person narratives are a step removed, although they often contain and rework first-person narratives. Theories of experience whether theological, spiritual, philosophical, sociological, or psychological, are the farthest removed and the most fragmented. Nonetheless, as we have seen, they inform the making and unmaking of experience at the level of narrative in varied and complicated ways.[22]

What do we learn from stories of unselfing that are often lost in the abstract, nonnarrative discourses of religious traditions and the theorizing of academic disciplines, including religious studies?

In contrast to an explanation in general terms, a narrative conveys the meaning and significance of a specific instance of unselfing in a detailed and illuminating way, weaving together many features of experience that are passed over by more abstract discourses. Taves mentions links between experience and three things: "bodily knowledges, cultural traditions, and social relations that went into making or composing the experience." Western Buddhist travel narratives provide a detailed record of the bodily condition and awareness of an author who undergoes unselfing, revealing how this affects the construal of the experience. Narratives also disclose how particular cultural traditions shape every version of unselfing: for instance, the influence of Zen encounter dialogues, stories about enlightened masters, and literary models and precedents from Buddhist history and the West, including accounts of conversion and mystical experience. Social relationships, such as connections with teachers, mentors, family members, friends, and other practitioners, play a large role in determining how an author makes sense of unusual incidents. Narratives reveal these dimensions of experience as a writer construes, debates, questions, and confirms or rejects what happened as an event that discloses the meaning of no-self.

There is another reason why stories, especially first-person ones, are indispensable in understanding unselfing. One of the problems with interpretations of *anatta* that view it simply as a metaphysical theory is that it becomes irrelevant to the lives of ordinary people. According to Buddhists through the ages, understanding *anatta* has a profoundly transformative effect. If it is only the philosophical theory that the self – like all

---

[22] Ann Taves, *Fits, Trances, and Visions: Experiencing Religion and Explaining Experience from Wesley to James* (Princeton: Princeton University Press, 1999), 360–361.

entities – keeps changing, it is hard to see why recognizing this should have a profound effect that radically reorients a person. When theories about no-self try to reconcile it with ordinary human life by seeing it as reserved for the separate discourse of specialist scholars and monks, its soteriological significance slips away. A narrative, in contrast, portrays the transformative effect of realizing the meaning of no-self on a deep existential level, not just as a matter of intellectual comprehension and assent, and not only for philosophers and monks. Stories of unselfing depict experiences that make clear for ordinary people the truth of the doctrine of *anatta*. Such narratives illuminate the life-changing effect of the concept of no-self when it is used to find significance in incidents that might be interpreted in other ways: as just a dream, the result of fatigue, or a weird feeling that passed. These stories disclose the complex relationships between religious experience and concepts and doctrines. Ideas shape what happens to people and are themselves shaped by specific events that people deem to be, in this case, examples and evidence of no-self. Narrative is invaluable for understanding the process of self-transformation that is important to every religious tradition because it integrates new intellectual comprehension with many other aspects of human existence: emotional, somatic, volitional, psychological, social, and cultural.

Narratives disclose how different understandings of no-self are rooted in particular conceptions of the self. What is the self that is lost in unselfing? What is the storyteller reacting against? Is it the sense that he is isolated, or feelings of guilt or shame, or terror of dying? Is what makes no-self appealing a way of life rejected as lacking meaning and purpose? Or a life consumed by overwhelming grief for a lost relationship? Is the sense of self that is overcome a detached observer who feels estranged from the vital life around him? Or is the writer simply tired of her current existence, bored, feeling stuck, or trapped in the same old, same old?

For Peter Matthiessen in *The Snow Leopard*, the old self is the devastated husband who mourns his wife's death. For Tad Wise, Stephen Schettini, and George Crane, the self they would gladly lose is a drug- or alcohol-abusing wastrel with little direction or purpose in life. For Matteo Pistono, the self that suffers is consumed with rage, unable to participate in political work effectively and with equanimity. For Jan Willis, the old sense of "me" lacks confidence and inner power, in contrast to the lioness that she intuits in dreams and portrays in *Dreaming Me*. In each story, it is not simply "the self" as an abstract metaphysical entity that is the problem but a very specific identity bound up with a form of suffering. No-self is a compelling idea because it suggests an alternative way to understand

286   Conclusion

and distance oneself from that particular kind of dissatisfaction or misery. Narratives reveal how the concept of no-self precipitates experiences of unselfing by orienting Western Buddhists to be alert to what goes beyond what they have known and felt. No-self suggests that things could be otherwise and that *I* can be different. Autobiographical narratives show how Buddhist ideas related to no-self help a writer to interpret disturbing and puzzling incidents by providing a perspective from which to construe these events and a rhetoric of transformation with which to incorporate them into a coherent life story.

A narrative about unselfing is not a description of a person somehow ceasing to be a person, nor a mere illustration of a theory of no-self. Rather, this kind of story dramatizes how a person learns to adopt a new perspective on a former identity and the changes that flow from this. When an individual undergoes an experience of unselfing and understands it in terms of no-self, he or she internalizes and knows in a personal way Buddhist ideas that were only theoretical or conceptual knowledge. One becomes able to view oneself as not a permanent, discrete, unchanging entity but rather as changing in response to many causes and conditions. The self is decentered, not destroyed. Unselfing is a momentary break in ordinary consciousness that, when interpreted in terms of the theory of no-self, becomes a lens for understanding all of life. It is not a permanent condition, and a person returns from this incident to ordinary consciousness; this "selfing" is part of the meaning and significance of the experience. Yet a person can act in ordinary life influenced by the perspective of no-self, according to Buddhist teachers. Although it isn't easy, takes a lot of practice, and inevitably involves many relapses, an experience of unselfing can be a catalyst for change in ordinary life. Many of our authors testify to the reality, significance, and joy of this transformation.

The relationship between theories of no-self and Western Buddhist travel narratives is not simply a matter of stories illustrating a doctrine or theory. Narratives explore the difficulties of putting religious ideas into practice, as well as conflicts between different religious ideals. For instance, Jamie Zeppa describes conflicts between the Buddhist ideal of selflessness and other values important to her, such as romantic love and the educational ideal of articulate individual expression. The two jointly written narratives, *Circling the Sacred Mountain* and *Rude Awakenings*, each contrast the perspective of an advanced teacher and practitioner of a Buddhist path (Robert Thurman and Ajahn Sucitto) with that of a less committed friend who is still caught up in the world of desires (Tad Wise and Nick Scott). Memoirs about residence in a Zen or Thai monastery explore covert ways in which the self insists on getting its way even in fervent and dedicated attempts at renunciation. Writers who travel to Tibet or encounter its forms of Buddhism in diaspora wrestle with how to reconcile teachings about equanimity and compassion with their sense of outrage and determination to protest the Chinese stranglehold on Tibet and its religion. These varied difficulties in putting selflessness into practice or reconciling it with other important values are not peripheral issues but essential to understanding what no-self means in particular situations. Autobiographical narratives explore questions and problems that arise when people try to live according to religious ideals, usually with mixed success and ambiguous results. Some Western Buddhist travel narratives demonstrate practical wisdom as the authors reveal how they lived with uncertainty, complexity, and conflict rather than explaining these difficulties away or conforming their life story to an ideal paradigm. In all these ways, then, stories depict truths about living that often elude systematic thinking and theory.

A Tibetan Precedent and Parallel

An interpretation of an eighteenth-century Tibetan autobiography suggests a helpful perspective on no-self in modern Western narratives. Although autobiographical texts by Buddhists were unusual before the twentieth century, they are not unknown, especially in Tibet. Janet Gyatso's *Apparitions of the Self* examines the genre of "secret autobiography" (*rangnam*), focusing on two works by Lama Jigme Lingpa (1730–1798), an outstanding writer in the Nyingma school.[23] The genre of secret autobiography, which dates to the eleventh century, depicts the life and teaching of a spiritual master who attained liberation through visions, yogic practices, and memories of past lives. Tibetan visionaries discovered so-called Treasures revealed in their previous lives that they retrieve and transmit to disciples. In these texts, a visionary demonstrates awesome powers, describes profound meditative experiences, and conveys insights into the elusive nature of subjectivity. Autobiographical writings legitimize a lama's authority, inspire confidence in disciples, and distinguish among alternative interpretations of Buddhist thought. In the intense

---

[23] Janet Gyatso, *Apparitions of the Self: The Secret Autobiographies of a Tibetan Visionary* (Princeton: Princeton University Press, 1998). On Tibetan autobiography, also see Sarah Jacoby, *Love and Liberation: Autobiographical Writings of the Tibetan Buddhist Visionary Sera Khandro* (New York: Columbia University Press, 2015).

competition between charismatic teachers vying for disciples and patronage, first-person writing expresses self-assertion and even boasting. At the same time, these texts show the unstable and elusive quality of the states of mind typically identified with selfhood and individual identity.

Several aspects of Gyatso's study are relevant to understanding no-self in Western Buddhist travel narratives. Far from making autobiography impossible or absurd, ideas about no-self play a role in generating "apparitions of the self," images of Jigme Lingpa that, in spite of their questionable ontological status, validate his authority and establish his credentials as a disciple of Padmasambhava who discovers treasures and revelations worthy of devotion. In a chapter entitled "No-Self Self and Other Dancing Moons," Gyatso analyses the literary strategies with which Jigme Lingpa represents the self as elusive or "undecidable," at once real and illusory. She describes two ways in which no-self self is adumbrated or suggested without being firmly defined. One strategy deploys two contradictory rhetorical figures in tandem, "as in the two seemingly incompatible sets of self-characterizations that I will group under the headings of the 'full' and the 'unfull' self."[24] The full self refers to the ways that Jigme Lingpa strongly asserts his identity and personal uniqueness by celebrating his achievements and visions, boasting of his superiority to rivals, displaying confident independence and originality, and describing marks on his body that prove him to be an authentic treasure discoverer and heir to spiritual forbears. This full self expresses jubilation, joy, and exuberant pleasure in literary creativity. He delights in his "lion's roar" (which reminds us of this motif in Jan Willis's *Dreaming Me*). His signs of pride, bold individuality, and spontaneous self-expression for its own sake contrast dramatically with the conventional ideal of an enlightened master who is humble and speaks and acts only for the sake of others.

Along with Jigme Lingpa's depiction of a full self marked by unique identity, spiritual power, and complex subjectivity, his autobiographical narratives suggest an "unfull" self: emptiness behind the masks he puts on for display. With self-mocking epithets (such as Beggar Sky Yogin the Fearless and Noble Goof-Off Beggar!), he discloses a split identity. In his role as narrator, he punctures the pretensions of Jigme Lingpa the professed spiritual hero. He portrays failures, mistakes, frustrations, and grasping attachments. He is uncertain that he is truly an authentic Treasure discoverer; far from being confident, he craves others' approval and authorization. This version of Jigme Lingpa complains and laments that visions vanish quickly, he cannot understand enigmatic words that come to mind,

---

[24] Gyatso, *Apparitions*, 212.

A Tibetan Precedent and Parallel

and his spiritual powers are waning. He lacks power and coherent identity. According to Gyatso, the tension between a full and an unfull self produces the distinctive qualities of Tibetan secret autobiography:

> These very undecidabilities have enabled Jigme Lingpa to present a most illustrious autobiographical self. It is a self that has been portrayed as empty of essence, but this emptiness has been exploited as a background to make all the more salient the heady mastery and realization that Jigme Lingpa celebrates precisely in the process of discovering it.[25]

The unformulated self lacking a stable essence produces a narrative that exuberantly celebrates the author's literary and visionary powers.

This pattern in Tibetan spiritual autobiographies has analogies in Western Buddhist travel narratives. In these books, too, we find parallel depictions of a full and unfull self, although contemporary Western authors use different terms. I noted at many points how writers alternate between the rhetoric of no-self and that of a true, authentic, or deep self. They assert or show that every identity is a construction or even an illusion, and on the next page state unequivocally that they discovered their authentic or true self. These statements apparently contradict each other. Yet, as depictions of moments in a spiritual process and as incidents in an engaging narrative, they convey the rhythm of selfing and unselfing in the author's spiritual journey. An experience of unselfing marks the transition from the full self of conscious individual identity to awareness of an ephemeral or empty self. When a stable identity dissolves, something else emerges: a new sense of self, enlarged or altered because it now recognizes its own nature as constantly changing, connected with other beings, and dependent on causes and conditions beyond its control. As in Jigme Lingpa's self-portrait, this combination of self-assertion and depiction of the self's "undecidability" produces "Subjectivity Without Essence," as Gyatso titles her epilogue. Uncertainties and absences undermine self-assertion; they also make its artful display all the more striking and vivid: "This is the trick that makes Buddhist autobiographical selfhood possible, without essentializing it."[26] In similar ways, Western Buddhist travel narratives do not deny subjectivity, agency, and individuality but show these aspects of the self's experience to be impermanent, fragile, and conditioned. This insight takes on deeper resonance in an experience of unselfing. A narrative conveys its impact and consequences far better than any abstract and generalizing formulation, including this one.

[25] Ibid., 242.
[26] Ibid., 268.

290 Conclusion

In addition to the parallel representation of a full and an empty self, Tibetan autobiographers use a second strategy that Gyatso calls a "single self-deconstructing figure."[27] Jigme Lingpa figures his self as an optical illusion, especially in the image of a "Dancing Moon in the Water," the title of one of his secret autobiographies. This classic Buddhist trope for the self suggests the viewer's uncertainty about whether an apparition is real or not – or, more precisely, the question of in what sense it is real. Another ambiguous metaphor for Jigme Lingpa's self is the *dakini*, a playful and elusive female divinity. His second secret autobiography, "Dakini's Grand Secret-Talk," is named after this female "other" whom he encounters in visions. If this entire text not only represents but actually is itself her "talk," then the dakini who utters it is the author of the autobiography and Jigme Lingpa's secret self. When even the gender of the visionary lama is ambiguous, how can any aspect of selfhood be determinate and substantial? The dancing moon and the dakini figure are ephemeral images of a slippery self that appears, transforms, and disappears. The two metaphors that furnish the titles of the two secret autobiographies, the dancing moon and the dakini, each express both the author's reality and his illusoriness by suggesting the created, fictive nature of every self-representation.

Gyatso's analysis reveals the crucial roles of imagination and metaphor in autobiographical representations of the Buddhist self. This focus is a basic feature of literary theories of Western autobiography and the crucial move that created this scholarly field, for instance, in seminal works such as James Olney's *Metaphors of Self* and Paul John Eakin's *Fictions in Autobiography*.[28] There is a distinctive paradoxical quality about Buddhist metaphors of self, rooted as they are in an understanding of no-self. In Western Buddhist travel narratives, we encountered many "metaphors of no-self," single images that convey a complex sense of the self as a fiction. For example, Peter Matthiessen's snow leopard, which is never glimpsed but makes its presence felt throughout his Nepalese trek, is a metaphor for no-self self. Jan van de Wetering's empty mirror is another one. Maura O'Halloran used water imagery (ice melting; waves on the ocean) to express her sense of flowing or merging with the world. At another point, she imagines herself as a statue with a cloth draped over it, and then the cloth stretches to cover more and more. When Thomas Merton encounters the statues at Polonnaruwa, he has an aesthetic and

[27] Ibid., 212.
[28] James Olney, *Metaphors of Self: The Meaning of Autobiography* (Princeton: Princeton University Press, 1972) and Paul John Eakin, *Fictions in Autobiography: Studies in the Art of Self-Invention* (Princeton: Princeton University Press, 1985).

religious epiphany: "everything is emptiness and everything is compassion."[29] The massive scale and solidity of the statues combined with their image of flowing motion suggest the paradoxical interdependence of form and emptiness in all things. Merton's account of this intense experience expresses his sense that his own life was being transformed by encounters with Asian Buddhism. The statues are one of his metaphors of a no-self self; another is the mountain Kanchenjunga, whose rockslides and eroded slopes show its apparent permanence to be an illusion.

In *The Heart of the World*, Ian Baker realizes the meaning of no-self as he contemplates the long-sought Tsangpo River waterfall, whose majestic form lacks fixed boundaries and is a liquid image of continual becoming. Another striking image in this book is the rock cliff covered with lichen on which he concentrates, trying to discern why this place is supposed to give him the key to the Tsangpo Gorge and a path into the heart of the *beyul*. As rain pours over him and the rock, Baker feels that the cliff face is a doorway or veil through which he might pass to enter another reality just behind it. In this image, too, the rocklike solidity and stability of things, including his sense of selfhood, exists in tension with awareness of the fluid, insubstantial, and dissolving nature of all things, even stone.

We could add many more examples of images and metaphors of self that, like Jigme Lingpa's dancing moon, convey concisely the paradoxes of no-self self. Often a crucial metaphor for no-self strikes a writer as significant during an experience of unselfing. Put another way, some of the transformative power of an experience of unselfing comes because it provides a pithy, poetic image that becomes a new metaphor for the author's self that is closely linked to no-self. There is something uncanny about the way such an image appears or strikes a person, as if imbued with mysterious power from an unknowable source – like a revelation or epiphany, to use Western theological analogies. In the midst of a journey's constantly changing scenes, a single image stands out starkly and fixes the traveler's attention. This event frequently provides an author with a poetic image or metaphor that represents what Gyatso calls "no-self self" and Collins refers to as a "selfless person." Sometimes this image is a Roshi, Ajahn, or Rinpoche with a strong and vibrant personality who represents the possibility of enlightenment, boundless compassion, and selflessness.

Buddhist tradition supplies certain recurring tropes for no-self self, such as an empty mirror, a waterfall, and the moon reflected in a lake. In contemporary autobiographical narratives, these traditional metaphors are

---

[29] Thomas Merton, *The Asian Journal of Thomas Merton* (New York: New Directions, 1973), 235.

292   Conclusion

more than simply literary devices; they actively shape the author's experience of unselfing and interpretation of what it means. We have seen, as well, how writers find creative ways to dramatize the experience of unselfing and convey in images the insights at stake in the concept of no-self. They devise new metaphors: a snow leopard, a cloth draped over a statue, or a dream about a lion. A journey in Asia provides images and incidents that, when catalyzed by Buddhist ideas about no-self, can bring about a breakthrough in understanding oneself and the world.

Travel Narratives and Other Genres

Why is travel a significant catalyst for transformation and a rich source of metaphors of self? What is distinctive about Western Buddhist travel narratives as a lens for understanding unselfing, no-self, and transformation? What other forms of literature explore these issues?

Every definition of a literary genre is a debatable construction that includes or excludes various borderline cases. I limited the scope of this study to autobiographical prose narratives in English by Western authors who traveled to Asia to further their knowledge and experience of Buddhism. We could obviously enlarge this study and shift its focus by considering other sources of insight into Buddhist experiences of transformation. For instance, we might consider poetry by Allen Ginsberg, Gary Snyder, and others. Ginsberg's journals and interviews discuss experiences of unselfing, especially an incident in Harlem in 1948 when he heard William Blake's voice and knew "a breakthrough from ordinary habitual quotidian consciousness into consciousness that was really seeing all of heaven in a flower."[30] I considered adding to this book a chapter on "Buddhism and the Beats," because Gary Snyder, Allen Ginsberg, and Joanne Kyger each recorded their experiences of journeys in 1962 that overlapped in India and Japan.[31] At this point in his life, however, Ginsberg was drawn more to Hinduism and the search for a guru than he was to Buddhism, and he does not reflect on no-self. Gary Snyder's deep commitment to Buddhism is reflected throughout his works. It

---

[30] Michael Schumacher (ed.), *The Essential Ginsberg* (New York: Harper, 2015), 282. The 1965 *Paris Review* interview from which this quote is taken is the most revealing autobiographical account of Ginsberg's religious development.

[31] Allen Ginsberg, *India Journals* (New York: Grove, 1996); Gary Snyder, *Passage through India: An expanded and Illustrated Edition* (Berkeley: Counterpoint Press, 2009) and *Earth Household* (New York: New Directions, 1969); and Joanne Kyger, *Strange Big Moon: The Japan and India Journals* (Berkeley: North Atlantic Books, 2000).

Travel Narratives and Other Genres 293

would require another book to do justice to these works in diverse literary genres, the influence of Jack Kerouac, and scholarship on the Beats.

Many other genres, such as biography, probe transformative experiences in Asia. Deborah Baker's *A Blue Hand: The Beats in India* examines the journeys of Ginsberg, Snyder, and several companions who searched for God, love, peace, and a way of life different from what they fled in the United States.[32] Fiction such as Jack Kerouac's *Dharma Bums*, Charles Johnson's *Oxherding Tale*, and stories by Alice Walker, Maxine Hong Kingston, and others explore Buddhist ideas. The genre of "autofiction," which blurs the distinction between fiction and autobiography, highlights the self's constructed, ambiguous, and elusive nature. Examples of Buddhist autofiction are Zen priest Ruth Ozeki's *A Tale for the Time Being* and C. W. Huntington, Jr.'s *Maya*.[33] Film, YouTube presentations, graphic novels, new digital formats, and many other media that present Buddhist ideas and practices depict experiences of unselfing or the process of transformation.[34]

Even within the genre of prose autobiographical narratives, I have examined only a tiny subset of works. A search on Amazon for "Buddhist spiritual autobiography" returns more than 1,000 titles as of June 2021, and the list grows longer. Travel is an important event and no-self a recurring topic in many of these books. We could move beyond our focus on Western writers to consider the insights of Asian Buddhists such as Sinhalese monk Bhante Gunaratana, as well as complex identities such as the German Buddhist nun Ayya Khema and Sangharakshita, an Englishman ordained as a *bhikkhu* in the Theravada tradition who founded the Friends of the Western Buddhist Order.[35] These authors moved fluidly through many cultures, complicating the simplistic binary of Western and non-Western writers. It

---

[32] Deborah Baker, *A Blue Hand: The Beats in India* (New York: Penguin, 2008).

[33] Ruth Ozeki, *A Tale for the Time Being* (New York: Penguin, 2013) and C. W. Huntington, Jr., *Maya: A Novel* (Boston: Wisdom Publications, 2015). See also Huntington, "The Autobiographical Self," in Rafal K. Stepien, ed., *Buddhist Literature as Philosophy, Buddhist Philosophy as Literature* (Albany: SUNY Press, 2020), 339–359.

[34] On representations of Buddhism in film, and on film as a skillful means that teaches how to view the world from a Buddhist perspective, see Francisca Cho, *Seeing Like the Buddha: Enlightenment through Film* (Albany: State University of New York Press, 2017) and Sharon A. Suh, *Silver Screen Buddha: Buddhism in Asian and Western Film* (London: Bloomsbury Academic, 2015).

[35] Bhante H. Gunaratana and Jeanne Halmgren, *Journey to Mindfulness: The Autobiography of Bhante G* (Boston: Shambhala, 1998) and Ayya Khema, *I Give You My Life* (Boston: Shambhala, 1998). The memoirs and travel writings of Sangharakshita are listed on his website: www.sangharakshita.org/writings. See also Brooke Schedneck, "Buddhist Life Stories," *Contemporary Buddhism* 8:1 (May 2007), 57–68.

would be instructive to examine how travel to the West affected Zen roshis, Theravada monks, and Tibetan lamas who settled in Europe or America. Did these Asian Buddhists experience unselfing and feel transformed in their new environment? If so, how did they speak and write about this transformation?

I mention these other genres in order to acknowledge the limits of this study and to propose that the approach taken here could be useful in examining how other works explore similar religious questions. How do they depict experiences of unselfing? How do various authors understand the meaning of no-self? In what ways do they link unselfing to spiritual development and its consequences? A still more ambitious study would compare Buddhist accounts of unselfing to the different ways that other religious traditions encourage and interpret experiences that call into question the nature and identity of the self.

Travel is one context for unselfing and self-transformation. Another is the practice of meditation, especially during intensive retreats. We examined several memoirs set in Zen or Theravada monasteries that detail insights into no-self and experiences of unselfing garnered during meditation retreats. Portraying such experiences and correlating them with traditional ideas is an established form of Buddhist writing, for instance in the popular books of Pema Chodron, Jack Kornfield, Sharon Salzberg, and Tara Branch. These volumes are usually collections of "dharma talks" that merge autobiographical vignettes with theoretical teaching about Buddhist concepts, and no-self is a recurring topic. Guy Armstrong's *Emptiness: A Practical Guide for Meditators* is a more systematic exposition of how the concept of emptiness or no-self is the key to understanding how meditation liberates the mind and transforms suffering.[36] As in most introductions to Buddhism in the West, Armstrong interweaves conceptual teachings with brief personal asides, using a structure that is not narrative but organized by topic.

A recent genre that approaches no-self in a new way is stories of a Buddhist practitioner who must adapt to the shock of learning, or experiencing firsthand, that an esteemed teacher and spiritual guide is also a sexual abuser. Examples of this kind of writing include Natalie Goldberg's *The Great Failure* and Shozan Jack Haubner's *Single White Monk*.[37] Both

---

[36] Guy Armstrong, *Emptiness: A Practical Guide for Meditators* (Somerville, MA: Wisdom Publications, 2017).

[37] Natalie Goldberg, *The Great Failure: A Bartender, A Monk, and My Unlikely Path to Truth* (San Francisco: Harper Collins, 2004) and Shozan Jack Haubner, *Single White Monk: Tales of Death, Failure, and Bad Sex* (Boulder: Shambhala, 2017).

Travel Narratives and Other Genres

of these works deal with the upheaval that rocked the American Zen community when Katagiri Roshi, the founder of the Minnesota Zen Center and a teacher at the Los Angeles Zen Center, was accused of carrying on affairs with female students. The disbelief, anger, and disillusionment brought by these revelations required a long period of healing, the loss of an older identity bound up with an idealized teacher, and new self-understanding. Ideas about no-self are central in Haubner's memoir. When his conviction that he must openly confront the scandal brings bitter conflict, he decides to leave his home temple and teach Zen in a way that remains undefined as he concludes the book. He confronts several symbolic "deaths" in addition to Katagiri's demise, forcing him to invent a new identity:

> Roshi's four deaths woke me up. First I had to let go of him as my teacher. Then I had to let go of him as the ideal human being. Then I had to let go of the tradition he gave me. At this point something happened. I sat on the cushion without a teacher or an ideal to practice toward or a firm lineage to back me up. All I had was my breath. So I followed it.[38]

The profound dislocation and shock he feels when his teacher is disgraced elicits a radical change. The doctrine of no-self provides guidance in letting go of his old identity and moving into an unknown future.

Another relevant species of Buddhist memoir is illness narratives: accounts of how Buddhism helped an author come to terms with a traumatic accident or serious disease. An example is Natalie Goldberg's *Let the Whole Thundering World Come Home: A Memoir*, which recounts her struggle with cancer.[39] Being forced to confront the imminent prospect of dying spurs radical questioning of the meaning of her whole life and identity. The author of an illness narrative strives to face anxiety, suffering, and fear with honesty and courage. He or she may feel a terrifying sense of diminishment and discover unsuspected resources within. Buddhist ideas about no-self can help make sense of the altered sense of being that comes with severe illness. Like travel narratives, these other forms of Buddhist writing depict the author's recognition of impermanence and the self's elusive, vulnerable, and groundless nature. Illness narratives and memoirs about recovery from abuse, like travelers' tales, also typically affirm that unexpected events forced the author to discover or create a more authentic, true, or deeper self.

Although Western Buddhist travel narratives are not the only kind of writing that explores unselfing and no-self, these topics are central in them.

---

[38] Haubner, *Single White Monk*, 195.
[39] Natalie Golderg, *Let the Whole Thundering World Come Home: A Memoir* (Boulder: Shambhala, 2018).

296   Conclusion

There are several basic ways in which travel may precipitate moments of unselfing and eventuate in a life transformation.

1) An outward change of scene can catalyze inner changes. The physical movement, new sights, and encounters with others involved in travel may dislocate familiar perceptions and habits and call forth a fresh response. Geographical journeys have long been linked to spiritual growth in many religious traditions, and Buddhism is no exception. Travel has the potential to shake things up, disrupt predictable routines, and nurture resilience and adaptability. A new setting and the necessary mental adjustments required for a journey may elicit insights, nurture creative capacities, and call forth persistence and courage. One can feel like a different person on a journey: more aware, energetic, and responsive to the world. Sometimes this new sense of self endures after the baggage is unpacked, and sometimes it dissipates. Perhaps the greatest boon, blessing, or benefit of travel is the wanderer's discovery of unknown dimensions of the self and resolution to keep them alive after the journey.

2) For Buddhists, as for pilgrims through history in most traditions, the difficulties of travel are thought to foster the development of certain desirable dispositions and moral virtues. Suffering and dissatisfaction (*dukkha*) can be met with patience, courage, and equanimity. In Western Buddhist travel narratives, especially those recounting an arduous Tibetan trek or a long foot pilgrimage on Shikoku or through India, walkers put themselves in vulnerable positions where they must confront physical and psychological challenges and may develop states of mind that allow them to persist. For some wayfarers, the ascetic dimensions of their chosen form of travel are a large part of its appeal and value. Being on the road means going without the possessions, comfort, and security of home. Several writers describe times when, in extreme conditions of duress, they broke through their usual sense of limitations. A dramatic example is Lama Govinda's reported experience of *lung-gom*, the Tibetan practice of rapid trance walking over dangerous terrain. Other writers focus on more subtle qualities that travel may nurture. Even in the mundane aspects of a journey, one can learn to recognize and let go of aversions and cravings. At the interminable border crossing or in a chaotic urban environment, one can practice patience, moment-by-moment mindful presence, and gratitude for small mercies. Travel provides dramatic and mundane moments that illustrate the central theme of the Buddha's teaching: the

Travel Narratives and Other Genres 297

inevitability of suffering and the possibility of release from suffering through the cultivation of certain qualities of mind and spirit.

3) Geographical wandering may lead to scenes of beauty that stir one's being in profound ways. The effect of the Himalayan mountains on Lama Govinda, Peter Matthiessen, and many others was, as in Western accounts of the sublime, to produce at once a sense of one's own smallness and fragility and the feeling that one participates in a vast and magnificent reality. An encounter with beauty may also take a smaller scale, reminiscent of Iris Murdoch's paradigm case of unselfing: a sudden observation of a hovering kestrel. Like natural beauty, works of art may move a viewer to a state of mind with religious dimensions. Think of Merton's encounter with the statues at Polonnaruwa, Gretel Ehrlich's rapt attention while listening to Naxi music, and Robert Sibley's vision of a bento box lunch as a tiny landscape. These incidents involve a heightened, appreciative, and unusually receptive consciousness and forgetfulness of ordinary concerns and worries. Accounts of unselfing in response to natural and aesthetic beauty portray self-transcendence and the emergence of a more appreciative way of perceiving the world, which the author may resolve to cultivate. At its best, travel brings opportunities to receive such moments of unselfing as a gift and to hone one's consciousness to be more alert for them.

4) Travel to another culture brings one into contact with very different ways of doing things and organizing social relations. In Zen monastic memoirs and books about sojourns in Thai Buddhist centers, the writers make few physical movements; for many months, they traverse the same path from dormitory to meditation room to dining hall. Yet the challenges of understanding and functioning in a foreign culture are sometimes so disorienting that a writer doubts his identity and asserts that eventually his sense of self was transformed. Outside the monastery, other Westerners in Asia similarly question their cultural conditioning and realize how much it has determined their sense of self; think of Wurlitzer and Asma in the dense metropolitan areas of Southeast Asia, Zeppa teaching in rural Bhutan, and Porter making his bemused way through post-Mao China. A foreign culture suggests alternative ways in which to comprehend the world; it makes one aware that one's usual way of seeing is only one of many possibilities. Encountering another culture can call in question one's conditioned responses and teach a traveler other ways to react to suffering, participate in a ritual, or practice compassion.

Of course, increased competency in another culture's ways, like every other desirable outcome of travel, is never guaranteed or automatic but only a possibility that depends on various conditions. Understanding Buddhist ideas about emptiness, no-self, and impermanence is sometimes a crucial factor that makes possible a writer's creative adaptability to Asian ways, as well as awareness of the self's malleability in different cultural settings.

5) Travel makes a person vulnerable and dependent on the generosity and hospitality of others. Being on the receiving end of compassion can make one more appreciative of its importance in life and more aware of the central Buddhist idea of interdependence. A difficult journey also provides many opportunities to practice compassion for unhappy fellow travelers. A good example of this aspect of a journey is the increasing sense of connectedness that Oliver Statler and Robert Sibley feel to their fellow *henro* on the Shikoku circuit, which in both cases culminates in deep compassion for a pilgrim who commits suicide.

6) Bardwell Smith and Robert Sibley mention Victor Turner's theory of *communitas* as they discuss the effects of travel. They use Turner's anthropological account of pilgrimage to interpret how a journey fostered experiences of openness and camaraderie with fellow travelers and people encountered on the road. Many other travelers' tales show similar bonds developing. The discovery of commonality with people very different from oneself can lead to new forms of awareness and connection, in relation both to others and to one's own latent capacities. Comparing his own experiences to Merton's in Sri Lanka and Thailand, Smith speaks of "a resonance in the reciprocity of being. It was the quality of respecting each other and being transformed by the meeting."[40] Even though such feelings are ephemeral and a traveler returns to ordinary routines, what was experienced en route may leave its mark. William James puts it this way in his discussion of conversion: "that it should for even a short time show a human being what the high-water mark of his spiritual capacity is, this is what constitutes its importance—an importance which backsliding cannot diminish, although persistence might increase it."[41]

---

[40] Bardwell Smith, "In Contrast to Sentimentality: Buddhist and Christian Sobriety," in *Christians Talk about Buddhist Meditation; Buddhists Talk about Christian Prayer*, eds. Rita M. Gross and Terry C. Muck (New York: Continuum, 2003), 49.

[41] William James, *The Varieties of Religious Experience* (New York: Macmillan, 1961), 209.

Travel Narratives and Other Genres

After the boundaries of individual selfhood are inevitably restored, a returned wayfarer may yearn for renewed occasions of felt kinship with others and think in new ways about the meaning and possibility of community. From a temporary moment of unselfing when a traveler's sense of discrete identity and separateness from others dissolves, long-term effects may follow.

I stress once more that all of these optimum results of travel are possibilities, not inevitable outcomes. It is just as likely that, faced with the challenges of travel, a person will retreat to the conviction that one has a fixed nature and impermeable boundaries. One may see others as utterly foreign, cling anxiously to familiar ideas and habits, and return no wiser than before the journey. Perhaps it would have been better to stay home. Yet even this returned wayfarer, pondering his disappointment and missed opportunities, may still learn something, perhaps by writing about the journey. In a wry account of his vacation on a fantasized Caribbean island, Alain de Botton portrays his final arrival at the ideal beach in perfect conditions, only to discover that "I had inadvertently brought myself with me to the island," spoiling everything:

> My body and mind were to prove temperamental accomplices in the mission of appreciating my destination. The body found it hard to sleep and complained of heat, flies and difficulties in digesting hotel meals. The mind meanwhile revealed a commitment to anxiety, boredom, free-floating sadness and financial alarm ... I was to discover an unexpected continuity between the melancholic self I had been at home and the person I was to be on the island, a continuity quite at odds with the radical discontinuity in the landscape and climate, where the very air seemed to be made of a different and sweeter substance.[42]

Without an explicitly Buddhist framework, de Botton presents an implicitly Buddhist insight into the way that anxiety and perpetual dissatisfaction can turn the varied circumstances of travel into repeated occasions for misery. He shows, too, how a good writer turns a "failed" journey into an engaging narrative and source of wisdom. Bad trips often make the best stories and teach the most about oneself.[43]

The grass always seems greener somewhere else. This perennial human insight may take specifically Buddhist forms of expression. Many

---

[42] Alain de Botton, *The Art of Travel* (New York: Random House, 2002), 19, 21.

[43] For an entertaining anthology of harrowing and exhilarating travel narratives, none of them Buddhist except for an excerpt from Peter Matthiessen's *The Snow Leopard* (New York: Penguin, 1978), see *Bad Trips,* ed. Keath Fraser (New York: Vintage, 1991).

writers of Western Buddhist travel narratives warn against the illusion that simply going elsewhere will end *dukkha*, one's continually arising dissatisfaction with life. A recurring motif is returning from far-flung adventures and realizing that what one had sought elsewhere is readily available at home. After his quest for the hidden lands of Pemako, Ian Baker affirms: "There is no paradise beyond that which is already present, even if still hidden from our view. The gates of Yangsang pervade all space, and the portals are everywhere, as numerous, say the texts, as pores on the skin or blades of grass on the earth."[44] The climax of *The Outer Path* is Jim Reynolds's realization that travel in Tibet is strengthening his expectations, anxieties, and cravings. The greatest benefit of this young man's geographical journey is the self-knowledge that he is at last ready to commit himself to an inner path; he decides to become a monk – now named Ajahn Chandako – and explore the further reaches of the mind.

Some books about Asian journeys end with the author planning to begin another journey, as does Oliver Statler when he finishes the Shikoku circuit; for him, ongoing journeying symbolizes an important truth about spiritual life as a matter of searching and striving. Other writers conclude with a sense of completion or turning elsewhere, as is the case when Robert Thurman asserts that there is no need to return to Mount Kailash; he advises his companions not to long to go back to the holy mountain but instead "bring its blessings along with us and share them freely around the loving world. We will work within the nonduality of the extraordinary and the ordinary."[45] Cautions about yearning for a holy place or endless traveling also warn about fixating on intense experiences, including moments of unselfing (an issue to be discussed in the next section). Yet longings for a particular place, for the kind of awareness involved in religiously motivated travel (what Robert Sibley calls "pilgrim mind"), and for further experiences of heightened consciousness express spiritual aspirations that need to be incorporated into one's nontraveling life. At their journey's end, many writers say that its most important consequences were desire for more of the right kind of travel and increased commitment to continuing self-transformation. What they don't say, but show, is that their religious aspirations are also expressed by autobiographical writing. How is transformation furthered by the practice of writing about the self?

---

[44] Ian Baker, *The Heart of the World: A Journey to Tibet's Lost Paradise* (New York: Penguin, 2004), 406.

[45] Robert Thurman and Tad Wise, *Circling the Sacred Mountain: A Spiritual Adventure through the Himalayas* (New York: Bantam Books, 1999), 339.

Self-Transformation and Autobiography

To assert that one has been transformed by travel is a bold claim. There are several reasons to be skeptical about such assertions in Western Buddhist travel narratives. Postcolonial critics have shown how Western depictions of "the other" often project a shadow self and disguise attempts to control another culture. Adopting this perspective, we might similarly interpret ideas about another kind of other – no-self – as nothing more than disguised reflections of a writer's self, which find expression even – perhaps especially – when a person thinks he or she has transcended the self. Religious searching and traveling in another culture can be a subtle form of self-enhancement when a person appropriates that culture's ideas and rituals or claims to define the meaning of Buddhism or authentic religious experience. We could revisit each Western Buddhist travel narrative and convict the author of exploiting Asians, Buddhists, and fellow travelers as useful tools and foils for their own spiritual questing.

In light of their knowledge of imperialism, neocolonialism, and exploitative tourism, some authors question their motivations for journeying, writing, and publishing. Recall Thomas Merton's doubts about his Asian journey and how some writers recognize their power and status as Westerners in Asia. After their encounters with Tibetan Buddhism further their religious growth and advance their literary ambitions, several authors wrestle with their responsibility to participate in the struggle for Tibetan survival. Others seem remarkably blithe about the fate of Tibet; I questioned Andrew Harvey's views for this reason. Although they are not steeped in postcolonialist theory, most of these writers are forthright about how their own interests spur their travels, writing, and religious searching. They are frequently troubled by their privilege as Western travelers and discuss their scruples about representing Buddhism. Most writers include the voices of Asians who challenge their understanding of Buddhism. Still, the politics and ethics of global travel are not the central focus of their writing. For critics and readers concerned primarily with that set of issues, a writer who moves through Asia on a personal pilgrimage is highly suspect, and the claim that such travel led to self-transcendence invites criticism of naïveté, hypocrisy, or self-deception.

A second form of critique challenges these authors' focus on experiences of unselfing. Several scholars criticize as narcissism or unchecked individualism the tendency of many versions of Western Buddhist Modernism to celebrate mindfulness, personal transformation, or mystical experience that is supposedly free of cultural baggage. Robert Sharf traces this tendency to D. T. Suzuki's influential version of Zen, and

302　　　　　　　　　　　　　　Conclusion

further back to William James and Protestant traditions that construe religion as a matter of inner experience:

> Suzuki was fascinated by James's notion of religious experience as a kind of pure, direct experience that is unmediated by one's cultural or religious formation. Suzuki and other modernists argued that *satori*—the sudden experience of an enlightened state—was the unmediated experience to which James referred, and that this experience was not only the essence of Buddhism but the essence of all religion. By insisting that some specific, repeatable, ineffable experience is at the very core of the Buddhist tradition, they end up essentialising Buddhism.[46]

In the emphasis on personal transformation, especially when it is supposed to take place in a sudden dramatic event such as those I interpret as unselfing, several crucial dimensions of Buddhism may get lost. Neglected or omitted are the role of religious community (the Buddhist sangha), the need for persistent discipline, and the value of ancient traditions that do not readily translate into the secular idiom of psychotherapy. When all that does not fit within the perspective of contemporary therapeutic discourse is excised, "Buddhism becomes something less than a religion, something less than what it is."[47] Rather than transforming a practitioner through renunciation and displacement of the self's agenda, Buddhism is itself transformed into a tool for self-enhancement and worldly success.

This warning against turning ideas about no-self into a vehicle for the self's agenda comes also from within Buddhism. A contemporary teacher in the Vipassana tradition, Guy Armstrong, asserts that what is important about no-self is not special experiences but rather the understanding of the self reflected in this perspective. In Theravada tradition, a person's first realization or glimpse of *nibbana*, the liberated state of mind of an enlightened being, has a transformative effect: "The ability to believe in a self, also called the 'personality view' (Pali: *sakkayaditthi*), is uprooted from mind, never to return in quite the same way again. One sees through the

---

[46] Robert H. Sharf, "Losing Our Religion," *Tricycle* (Summer 2007), 47. See also Robert H. Sharf's "Buddhist Modernism and the Rhetoric of Meditative Experience" and "Is Mindfulness Buddhist (and Why It Matters)," *Transcultural Psychiatry* 52 (2015) 470–484, as well as David McMahon, *The Making of Buddhist Modernism* (Oxford: Oxford University Press, 2008) and Jeff Wilson, *Mindful America: The Mutual Transformation of Buddhist Meditation and American Culture* (New York: Oxford University Press, 2014). For an argument that, *contra* Sharf, at least one Asian Buddhist tradition was highly interested in cultivating personal experience, see Janet Gyatso, "Healing Burns with Fire: The Facilitations of Experience in Tibetan Buddhism," *The Journal of the American Academy of Religion* 67 (1999), 113–147.

[47] C. W. Huntington, Jr., "The Triumph of Narcissism: Theravada Buddhist Meditation in the Marketplace," *Journal of the American Academy of Religion* 83 (2015), 624.

Self-Transformation and Autobiography 303

self so thoroughly that one never again believes it truly exists."[48] Yet after "stream entry" into the deep waters of wisdom, the sense of self will return and remain until a person's full enlightenment. A practicing Buddhist should not rely on having repeated experiences that disrupt this persisting sense of self but rather on understanding all experience in terms of no-self:

> Many avenues lead to the truth of not-self. We practice to keep learning in all these areas, allowing each insight to chip away the bonds of self. Some insights might be dramatic, but many will come in ordinary circumstances to our ordinary mind. We can trust that wisdom is continuing to grow and that the growth of wisdom leads to greater freedom and awakening. In time, the understanding of not-self becomes the way we see the world. It has to be like that. If that were not the case, we would have to rely on altered states of experience for our freedom, and that would not be freeing at all.[49]

Armstrong's "practical guide for meditators" emphasizes equally the significant event of stream-entry (the first step in enlightenment) and the need for continuing practice: what Zen tradition calls "sudden awakening, gradual cultivation." He is therefore cautious and ambivalent about seeking particular experiences and skeptical about claims of full transformation and enlightenment. This balanced perspective has deep roots in Buddhist tradition.

Scholars and teachers of Buddhism in the West criticize what we can call the cult of experience that drives so much spiritual searching and is central in autobiographies, memoirs, and travel narratives. Some of the books we examined come to a similarly skeptical perspective on this desire, while others end with the author devoted to further pursuit of peak experiences. Some authors express frustration that intense experiences elude them. For instance, John Blofeld laments his failure to have continued moments of unselfing, which he thinks are necessary for wisdom that goes beyond intellectual comprehension of ideas. Several authors who stayed for long periods at Zen monasteries depict their unhappiness and disappointment about not attaining a breakthrough moment of satori; the motif of frustration and failure is especially prominent in the works of van de Wetering and Chadwick and to a lesser degree in Maura O'Halloran's diary. In contrast, other writers shift attention away from intense experiences to something else: the sangha, the discipline of steady practice for its own sake, compassion for suffering, or opportunities to live in accord with Buddhist precepts in ordinary interactions with others. An author

[48] Armstrong, *Emptiness*, 97.
[49] Ibid., 97.

may assert that the walls between self and world do not come down only in dramatic moments or require a strenuous Himalayan trek. Ian Baker holds that the opportunity for transformation is always at hand: "There is no real separation or boundary between our selves and the world around us, and an ever-present wildness and radiance lies at the heart of our tamest vistas" (442). Every Western Buddhist travel narrative acknowledges that the author's transformation remains incomplete, and many of them stress that a relentless focus on engineering one's own spiritual progress by seeking particular experiences undermines the movement toward selflessness that is the proper goal and ideal result of Buddhist practice. This was an important aspect of Peter Matthiessen's turn from Rinzai to Soto Zen practice.

To translate this perspective into the language of conversion, the authors of Western Buddhist travel narratives show that conversion is ongoing or continuous rather than a single past event. Calling stories about transformation convert*ing* narratives would better express the idea that this process, for Buddhists as for Christians and others, is still underway and a crucial dimension of writing autobiographically. Converting or transforming involves self-breaking and self-making: deconversion from past beliefs and detachment from a false sense of self, as well as a new perspective, reorientation of values, and identity. Buddhist memoirs are different in many ways from Christian conversion narratives that depict examination of conscience, confession of sin, the necessity of faith in God, and patterning of the author's life in terms of biblical paradigms and earlier Christian exemplars. Yet there are analogies between Buddhist and Christian accounts of transformation, such as joining a community, adopting a new discourse and rhetoric, renewed ethical purpose and commitment, and resolution of intellectual doubts and confusion.

Among many possible points of comparison, here I highlight two aspects of Buddhist and Christian transformation narratives. First, the temporal span and depth of analysis of most book-length stories of transformation reveal this process to be inconclusive and ambiguous. There is always unfinished business from the past. Moreover, Buddhists and Christians who write extended memoirs tend to be modest about their spiritual accomplishments. One can hardly imagine a serious Buddhist writer claiming to be selfless, enlightened, or a bodhisattva. Yet a Buddhist may depict convincingly an important change and radical reorientation. Similarly, Christian conversion narratives try to portray a genuine change in the author's life as a consequence of coming to faith in God, encountering

Self-Transformation and Autobiography 305

the risen Lord, or joining a church. Yet, to be convincing, they must also give a realistic depiction of the author's continuing temptation and sin, as Augustine does in Book 10 of the *Confessions*. For Buddhist writers, too, transformation is still underway, in process but incomplete. The frequent motif of failure or forgetting what one has learned suggests that more challenges lie ahead. Think of the final scene in *Great Patient One*, when after his long ordeal tramping the pilgrimage trail in India, Nick Scott gorges himself with food as he flies home from India, as if all his efforts and ascetic discipline taught him nothing. After exploring various ways in which the author came to recognize the limitations of his sense of self, every Buddhist travel narrative ends with "selfing," a return to the performances and preoccupations of a past identity, yet with a new perspective. A transformation has been initiated or catalyzed, not completed.

Along with this emphasis on transformation as a drawn-out and inconclusive practice, there is a second commonality between Western Buddhist travel narratives and Christian conversion narratives. They almost always include a highly charged dramatic scene: an experience of unselfing. The writers condense a long-term process of change into a moment of transition that symbolizes the crucial turning point away from an older sense of self to something new. Whether or not the author grasped the significance of this moment at the time it happened, a climactic scene of recognition seems to be built into narratives of transformation. This may be partly because Christian conversion narratives influence the form and focus of most Western spiritual narratives, even when authors describe Buddhist experiences. It may be that any narrative representation of a radical change in life orientation, if it is to be convincing in the modern world, requires a plot with a climax, turning point, and a scene dramatizing the recognition of the change. A narrative about transformation usually depicts the pivotal moment when a new self that is coming into being is first glimpsed, often with a shock experienced as unselfing. Or it may dramatize the moment when an old identity is perceived as other, alien, not the self, even before a new sense of identity can be articulated. A writer representing transformation typically expresses multiple dimensions and meanings of this complex process in a compressed and highly symbolic scene of unselfing.

Some of the layers of meaning in a scene of unselfing reflect insights garnered during a long period of reflection and later concerns that are projected back on the event. An analogy: Augustine's portrayal of his sudden conversion in the garden scene in Book 8 of the *Confessions* dramatizes a process that took many years. His presentation of this incident uses the conversion scene to serve his later rhetorical purposes as the bishop of Hippo engaged in conflicts and controversies.[50] In a similar fashion, when the author of a Western Buddhist travel narrative portrays an incident of unselfing, the meaning and significance of this event are shaped by a later perspective and concerns. Buddhist and Christian narratives of transformation usually portray both a long and unresolved struggle toward a new way of life and a highly charged scene of unselfing that implies that transformation was abrupt, complete, and immediately clear in its meaning. For all their dissimilarities, Western Buddhist travel narratives share this pattern with stories about Christian conversion.

In this way, the plot of a transformation narrative integrates two perspectives on religious change. In his discussion of "The Self and Narrative Identity," Paul Ricoeur describes emplotment as a dialectic between a person's sameness and discontinuity over time: "Emplotment allows us to integrate with permanence in time what seems to be its contrary in the domain of sameness-identity, namely diversity, variability, discontinuity, and instability."[51] Ricoeur defines "discordant concordance, characteristic of all narrative composition, by the notion of the synthesis of the heterogeneous."[52] Any extended narrative about a person reconciles identity and diversity over time, according to Ricoeur. The qualities of the plot are transferred to a character: "characters, we will say, are themselves plots."[53] Although Ricoeur's primary example is a novel rather than autobiography and not specifically religious, his comment on Robert Musil's *The Man without Qualities* suggests a helpful perspective on stories of transformation. Describing Musil's fiction about the loss of identity, he refers to conversion narratives using phrases that illuminate Western Buddhist travel narratives:

> The self refigured here by the narrative is in reality confronted with the hypothesis of its own nothingness ... But who is *I* when the subject says that it is nothing? ... It may well be that the most dramatic transformations of personal identity pass through the crucible of this nothingness of identity ... So many conversion narratives attest to such nights of personal identity. In these moments of extreme destitution, the empty response to the question "Who am I" refers not to nullity but to the nakedness of the

[50] Paula Frederickson, "Paul and Augustine: Conversions, Narratives, Orthodox Traditions, and the Retrospective Self," *Journal of Theological Studies* 37 (1986), 3–34.

[51] Paul Ricoeur, *Oneself As Another*, trans. Kathleen Blamey (Chicago: University of Chicago Press, 1992), 140.

[52] Ibid., 141.

[53] Ibid., 143.

Self-Transformation and Autobiography 307

question itself ... The narratives that recount the dissolution of the self can be considered interpretive narratives with respect to what might be called an apophantic apprehension of the self.[54]

"Apophantic" refers to apophasis, the rhetorical strategy of describing something implicitly by denying it, as in "I shall not mention Caesar's avarice" or "God is not confined by space or time." A person's sense of self, too, can be revealed by apparent negation. Accounts of unselfing in Western Buddhist travel narratives recount a "night of personal identity," a period of "dissolution of the self," and they incorporate it within the larger context of the author's life story, thereby making a paradoxical synthesis of discordance and continuity. Such a narrative creates a character whose identity is based not on staying the same but rather on a dialectic between continuity over time and instability and variability, including those striking moments when selfhood seems to dissolve, fragment, or merge with something else.

Because of the importance of narrative in the construction and deconstruction of identity, writing an autobiography or memoir can play an important role in religious transformation. In previous scholarship on autobiography, I argued that writing one's life story is more than a matter of recording past events; in various ways, it can be a religious activity or practice in the author's present moment, that is, in the act of writing.[55] In addition to Ricoeur's and other theoretical perspectives from which I have drawn (especially the works of Collins, Gyatso, Hick, and Taves), a crucial idea underlies and orients my approach in this book: autobiographical writing is in certain cases an inherently religious action.

We can use the terms of these theories of religion or of Buddhism to interpret how the portrayal of transformation in Western Buddhist travel narratives is a form of religious action. With Ricoeur, we can see the work of emplotment as the creation in the narrative of a religious identity based on radical change reconciled with sameness or continuity. Western Buddhist

---

[54] Ibid., 166–167.

[55] John D. Barbour, *The Conscience of the Autobiographer: Ethical and Religious Dimensions of Autobiography* (New York: Macmillan, 1992) explores writers' struggles with conscience as they attempt to be truthful in assessing their lives. Barbour, *Versions of Deconversion* interprets how autobiographers explaining a loss of faith clarify and defend the present convictions that led them to reject former beliefs as false or immoral. Barbour, *The Value of Solitude* explores how writers reconcile the values they sought when alone with their moral responsibilities to other people and commitments to communities. See also John D. Barbour, "Religion and the Self: Life Writing as a Literary Form and Religious Practice," in *Teaching Religion and Literature*, ed. Daniel Boscaljon and Alan Levinovitz (New York: Routledge, 2019), 148–157. All of these studies interpret the writing of memoir as an event in an author's present situation and a form of religious action.

travel narratives are a form of "converting narrative" in which the process of transformation is still underway as the author reconfigures her life in the light of a new understanding of Buddhism. With John Hick, we can view the books we have examined as expressing their authors' continuing attempts to understand "the Real" (in specifically Buddhist expressions such as *sunyata* or *nirvana*) and to turn away from self-centeredness. Like Janet Gyatso, we can interpret the ways in which portraying empty self and full self in tandem or in a single metaphor dramatizes basic Buddhist insights and integrates them with the author's life story. Like Steven Collins's analysis of traditional Theravada societies, we can explore the ways in which contemporary Western Buddhists reconcile claims about the ultimate truth of no-self with their practical needs to refer to selves involved in the ordinary interactions of daily life. This kind of negotiation of discrepancies between a religion's normative ideals and the practices of everyday life is a crucial concern of narratives. Finally, Western Buddhist travel narratives exemplify what Ann Taves, in her theory of religious experience, calls the "deeming" of the "significant thing" that I call unselfing. Deeming is a process of interpretation and evaluation that continues in the act of writing.

In their stories about journeys, authors interpret unusual events as evidence for Buddhist ideas about no-self. Their first-person narratives provide access to the ways in which individuals connect theoretical knowledge of Buddhism with their own lives. When they sense boundaries between self and world dissolving, feel disconnected from their bodies, or discover unsuspected dimensions of their being in moments of exhaustion, compassion, or joy, they interpret these events within the framework of Buddhist concepts. Their construction of what happened in an episode of unselfing reports a past event, and it is also a crucial aspect of the author's ongoing Buddhist practice.

Individual experiences are transitory and evanescent unless they are made accessible to others. Taves's theory of religion analyzes how experience is "made and unmade" as communities argue about what counts as authentic or not, and why. Our understanding of religious experience is truncated if we focus only on individuals without attending to the complex social formations of religious traditions and communities. A collective process of evaluation determines which claims about religious experience are recognized as genuine and meaningful for others. In the contemporary world, autobiography is one of the institutions that engage in this social process of influence, contestation, and validation. Such writing makes private and puzzling experiences available to others for scrutiny and integrates them with the discourse and rhetoric of a religious community.

Self-Transformation and Autobiography

Western Buddhism is still at an early stage of formation, with many competing interpretations of the dharma and the best way to practice. Contemporary memoirs about Buddhist experiences function very differently than, for instance, the public confessions made by seventeenth-century Puritans when they entered full membership in the church, for there is no comparable orthodoxy and no final authority to render a decisive judgment about what is acceptable or not. Yet in Buddhist first-person narratives, too, an individual's intuitions and ideas are preserved and made accessible to other Buddhists for scrutiny. A chain of influence, transmission, and modeling continues in readers. For reading, too, can be a spiritual practice that triggers recognition, insight, desire to learn more, commitment, and sometimes transformation. A reader may learn to construe his or her own life story with new resources, such as a better understanding of no-self. A reader may realize that no-self is more than an abstruse hypothesis or puzzling ancient doctrine: it is a perspective helpful for understanding one's own life. I emphasize once more how radically different this contemporary Western version of Buddhism is when compared to classical Asian forms such as the Theravada culture described by Steven Collins. There, no-self was an idea reserved for "virtuoso specialists" in a monastic context and only invoked when monks engaged in intensive meditation or technical scholarly debate. In Buddhist modernism in the West, by contrast, no-self has become a concept that describes certain desirable experiences that laypersons believe will confirm the truth of Buddhist teachings. Such experiences can occur not only in meditation but also in a wide variety of settings, including the unfamiliar and dislocating places visited on a journey. Autobiography articulates one person's understanding of what no-self means, how it was experienced in an event of unselfing, and the long-term significance of the event as insight and interpretation led to personal transformation.

Autobiography has a peculiar kind of authority for individualistic and anti-authoritarian seekers such as many Westerners drawn to Buddhism. Writers of first-person narratives describe the attractiveness of a religion that, in contrast to their view of monotheistic traditions, offers the possibility of picking and choosing what works for them. (They may not realize that Buddhism, in both Asian and Western institutional forms, has its own authority structures and orthodoxies.) Rather than demanding faith or obedience, many Westerners see Buddhism as inviting them to "try it and see." An autobiography can depict how a writer explored various types and teachers of Buddhism and, by trial and error, discovered what was helpful. Readers are invited to take what resonates with their own life and

310 Conclusion

leave the rest. In the spiritual marketplace of the contemporary West, this aspect of autobiographical writing has a powerful appeal.

Western Buddhist travel narratives attract not only committed Buddhists but also those readers who often call themselves "spiritual but not religious." This label usually refers to the personal, "inner," experiential dimensions of religion, in contrast to an organized community's doctrines, institutions, and rituals. In fact, however, particular traditions and communities shape every conception of experience, including radically individualist and antinomian ones. Western Buddhist travel narratives are a form of spiritual autobiography, a larger and loosely defined genre that I have discussed elsewhere. Such works reveal the interplay between communal norms for life stories and the distinctive features of a particular life:

> Spiritual autobiography is best conceived of as a testing of the adequacy of a religious community's norms for a life narrative, when not only the communal norms but the testing itself—the autobiographical act—is believed to be called for by God or that which the writer believes to be worthy of ultimate loyalty and trust.[56]

Western Buddhist travel narratives do not simply illustrate but test and assess Buddhist ideas, revealing a process of searching, insight, and discernment in the writer's present moment: a profoundly religious activity. They may also assess and challenge basic assumptions of Western culture, such as its individualism, materialism, and justifications for violence.

Many contemporary memoirs demonstrate the characteristics most valued by spiritual seekers: experimentation, distrust of authority, reflexivity and self-scrutiny, and close attention to details of personal experience. They express the Romantic desire to re-enchant the world desacralized by technocratic science and rationalism, as well as the ideal of an authentic self that is free of social roles and conditioning. These are the same values that shape Buddhist Modernism as analyzed by David McMahon and others. Western Buddhist travel narratives are arguably the fullest and most articulate expression of Buddhist Modernism and postmodern revisions and experiments that explore new understandings of the dharma.[57]

---

[56] John D. Barbour, "Spiritual Autobiography," in *Encyclopedia of Life Writing: Autobiographical and Biographical Forms*, ed. Margaretta Jolly (London: Fitzroy Dearborn, 2001), vol. 2, 836. See also John D. Barbour, "Autobiography," in *The Encyclopedia of Religion*, second edition, ed. Lindsay Jones (Detroit: Macmillan Reference, 2005), vol. 2, 697–704.

[57] It would take us too far afield to discuss theories of postmodernism, its influence on Buddhism, and its expressions in autobiography. On postmodern Buddhism, see the last chapter of McMahon's *The Emergence of Buddhist Modernism* and Ann Gleig, *American Dharma: Buddhism Beyond Modernity* (New Haven: Yale University Press, 2018).

The writing and reading of this kind of literature express values and concerns that are at once fundamentally religious, Buddhist in a very specific way, and characteristic of a broad segment of contemporary Western spiritual seekers.

If transformation is to be long-lasting, it must become deeply rooted in a person's character (yet, paradoxically, also open to further change). What is important about no-self is not an isolated and ephemeral experience but how particular events interpreted in light of this idea continue to influence a person. To view one's life from the perspective of ideas about no-self is a capacity or skill that must be learned and practiced. The fields of neurobiology and cognitive science explore how learning and practice alter the mind. While a thorough discussion of this topic would take us far from the scope of this book, I would highlight three dimensions of recent thinking about the mind that are relevant to autobiographical writing about transformation. First, neurobiology emphasizes the plasticity of the brain: the way neurons are altered by new learning. Second, this perspective highlights the way in which intense emotional arousal makes synaptic associations more durable. Third, neuropsychology points to the importance of repetition and disciplined practice in establishing connections in the mind that make possible the development of skills such as a child's learning to read or an advanced cello player's or basketball star's apparently effortless performance. An autobiographer's interpretation of pivotal life events involves an analogous kind of practiced learning that builds a capacity. In the case of Western Buddhist travel narratives, we see a reframing of experience in terms of ideas about no-self. Experiences of unselfing have an intense and indelible emotional component that resonates long afterward, including during the act of writing about them. The attempt to understand moments of unselfing and one's entire life in terms of ideas about no-self exercises and strengthens a Buddhist's capacity to internalize the meaning of *anatta*, just as a Puritan autobiographer's examination of conscience and confession of sin seared into his consciousness and character crucial aspects of the Puritan worldview.

Knowledge of no-self is therefore a matter not only of knowing *that*, or conceptual knowledge, but also of knowing *how*: it is understanding how to interpret one's experience in terms of no-self. Steven Collins uses this distinction (made by philosopher Gilbert Ryle) to address the question: "What are Buddhists *Doing* When They Deny the Self?" What Collins calls "the practice of no-self" is monastic forms of asceticism and meditation that train a person to see the world, especially one's own experience,

Conclusion

in terms of the categories of Buddhist thought. This spiritual practice of reframing is intended to realize *nirvana*, selflessness:

> The practice of mindfulness is supposed to be neither simply a matter of knowledge nor of knowledge events which exist only for a certain length of time, as one might enter into a meditative trance for a specific period; rather, it is supposed to become a continuous form of awareness, present throughout any and every activity. We might, I think, profitably regard training in mindfulness as akin to learning a skill or skills, as an education in certain capabilities and dispositions. It is as much a fact or process of self-cultivation as of self-knowledge ... To practice for enlightenment is to train oneself in living selflessly, without suffering; the capacity to live and act thus, and the fact of doing so, are an essential part of what it means to *know* that there is no self.[58]

Although Collins refers only to the monastic practice of meditation, his emphasis on knowledge of no-self as a matter of knowing-how illuminates a crucial dimension of autobiographical writing. By this means, too, a Buddhist cultivates a specific way of looking at the world as a form of continuous awareness, thereby nurturing the capacity to interpret all experience in the light of no-self. An incident of unselfing can be a lens that changes one's perspective on the rest of one's life. Thus the insights of two very different fields, neurobiology and a study of ancient Theravada texts, converge in their emphasis on the development of "knowing how," in this case the capacity to view all of one's experience in terms of ideas about no-self. In Buddhist autobiographical writing, knowing how to interpret one's life in terms of no-self is practiced, cultivated, and nurtured. This learned skill and wisdom takes its impetus and orientation from an event of unselfing. Such writing provides readers with a model of a practice of self-interpretation that they, too, might adopt and follow in their own lives.

The Buddhist concept of no-self helps authors of Western Buddhist travel narratives to understand incidents when their usual sense of self seems broken, transcended, or rendered other than itself. These stories articulate a new sense of self that emerges after an experience of unselfing, one that incorporates such qualities of no-self as impermanence, vulnerability, fragmentariness, and interdependent relatedness to what was formerly thought to be outside, beyond, or not the self. The experience of

---

[58] Steven Collins, "What Are Buddhists *Doing* When They Deny the Self?," in *Religion and Practical Reason: New Essays in the Comparative Philosophy of Religion*, ed. Frank E. Reynolds and David Tracy (Albany: State University of New York Press, 1994), 78–79.

losing the illusion of a fixed self can bring liberation from bondage to self-concern and a sense of new possibilities that has analogies with Christian and other religious understandings of salvation.

Transformation is not total alteration but a shape-shifting that preserves something of the past. It is identity-in-difference: something that is hard to define but can be disclosed in a story provides continuity and coherence to the events in the author's life. Not unchanging substance or essence but rather a narrative of transformation is what weaves together a former sense of self, experiences of unselfing, and the new perspective that emerges and is exemplified in an author's Buddhist interpretation of how he or she changed and goes on changing. Transformation is the central theme of contemporary spiritual autobiography and the deepest religious concern at work in Buddhist thinking about no-self. Western Buddhist travel narratives offer crucial insights and wisdom about the meaning of no-self, the nature of self-transformation, and the religious significance of travel for Western individuals who try to learn from Buddhism in its Asian settings.

Bibliography

I Western Buddhist Travel Narratives and Other Autobiographical Texts

Aitkin, Molly Emma, ed. *Meeting the Buddha: On Pilgrimage in Buddhist India.* New York: Riverhead Books, 1995.

Asma, Stephen. *The Gods Drink Whiskey: Stumbling toward Enlightenment in the Land of the Tattered Buddha.* San Francisco: HarperCollins, 2005.

Baker, Ian. *The Heart of the World: A Journey to Tibet's Lost Paradise.* New York: Penguin, 2004.

Bernstein, Richard. *Ultimate Journey: Retracing the Path of an Ancient Buddhist Monk Who Crossed Asia.* New York: Knopf, 2002.

Blofeld, John. *My Journey in Mystic China: Old Pu's Travel Diary*, trans. Daniel Reid. Rochester, VT: Inner Traditions, 2008. [Originally published in Mandarin in 1990]

   The Wheel of Life: The Autobiography of a Western Buddhist, 3rd ed. Boston: Shambhala, 1988. [Originally published in 1959; 2nd ed., 1972]

Botton, Alain de. *The Art of Travel.* New York: Random House, 2002.

Byles, Marie Beuzeville. *Journey into Burmese Silence.* London: Allen & Unwin, 1962.

Byron, George Gordon. "Childe Harold's Pilgrimage." In Jerome McGann, ed., *Lord Byron: The Major Works*, 19–206. Oxford: Oxford University Press, 1986.

Caplow, Florence, and Susan Moon, eds. *The Hidden Lamp: Stories from Twenty-Five Centuries of Awakened Women.* Boston: Wisdom Publications, 2013.

Chadwick, David. *Thank You and Okay!: An American Zen Failure in Japan.* New York: Penguin, 1994.

Chandako, Ajahn. *Tales of Tudong.* 2008. Available at: vimutti.org.nz/teachings/writings.

Coleman, John E. *The Quiet Mind.* New York: Harper & Row, 1971.

Cousineau, Philip. *The Art of Pilgrimage.* New York: MJF Books, 1998.

Crane, George. *Bones of the Master: A Journey to Secret Mongolia.* New York: Bantam, 2000.

David-Neel, Alexandra. *My Journey to Lhasa.* New York: Harper & Brothers, 1927.

Bibliography

Ehrlich, Gretel. *Questions of Heaven: The Chinese Journeys of an American Buddhist.* Boston: Beacon Press, 1997.

Franz, Tracy. *My Year of Dirt and Water: Journal of a Zen Monk's Wife in Japan.* Berkeley: Stone Bridge Press, 2018.

Fraser, Keath, ed. *Bad Trips.* New York: Vintage Books, 1991.

Ginsberg, Allen. *India Journals.* New York: Grove, 1996.

Goldberg, Natalie. *The Great Failure: A Bartender, a Monk, and My Unlikely Path to Truth.* New York: Harper, 2004.

   Let the Whole Thundering World Come Home: A Memoir. Boulder, CO: Shambhala, 2018.

Goullart, Peter. *Forgotten Kingdom.* London: J. Murray, 1955.

Govinda, Lama Anagarika. *The Way of the White Clouds: A Buddhist Pilgrim in Tibet.* London: Rider & Company, 1966.

Greenwood, Gesshin Claire. *Bow First, Ask Questions Later: Ordination, Love, and Monastic Zen in Japan.* Somerville, MA: Wisdom Publications, 2018.

Grousset, Rene. *In the Footsteps of the Buddha.* London: Routledge, 1932.

Gunaratana, Bhante H., and Jeanne Halmgren. *Journey to Mindfulness: The Autobiography of Bhante G.* Boston: Wisdom Publications, 2003.

Harrer, Heinrich. *Seven Years in Tibet.* New York: Penguin, 1953.

Harvey, Andrew. *A Journey in Ladakh: Encounters with Buddhism.* New York: Houghton Mifflin, 1983.

Haubner, Shozan Jack. *Single White Monk: Tales of Death, Failure, and Bad Sex.* Boulder, CO: Shambhala, 2017.

Hick, John. *An Autobiography.* Oxford: Oneworld Publications, 2002.

Huntington, C. W., Jr. *Maya: A Novel.* Boston: Wisdom Publications, 2015.

Johnston, William. *Mystical Journey: An Autobiography.* Maryknoll: Orbis Books, 2006.

Kamenetz, Rodger. *The Jew in the Lotus: A Poet's Rediscovery of Jewish Identity in Buddhist India.* New York: HarperCollins, 1994.

Kapleau, Philip, ed. "Eight Contemporary Enlightenment Experiences of Japanese and Westerners." In *The Three Pillars of Zen: Teaching, Practice, Enlightenment,* 189–268. New York: Harper & Row, 1965.

Kherma, Ayya. *I Give You My Life.* Boston: Shambhala, 1998.

Kyger, Joanne. *Strange Big Moon: The Japan and India Journals.* Berkeley: North Atlantic Books, 2000.

MacDonald, Sarah. *Holy Cow!: An Indian Adventure.* New York: Broadway Books, 2002.

Matthiessen, Peter. *Nine Headed Dragon River.* Boston: Shambhala, 1985.

   The Snow Leopard. New York: Penguin, 1978.

Merton, Thomas. *The Asian Journal of Thomas Merton.* New York: New Directions, 1973.

O'Halloran, Maura. *Pure Heart, Enlightened Mind: The Life and Letters of an Irish Zen Saint.* Boston: Wisdom Publications, 2007.

Ozeki, Ruth. *A Tale for the Time Being.* New York: Penguin, 2013.

Pallis, Marco. *Peaks and Lamas.* New York: Knopf, 1949.

Pannapadipo, Phra Peter. *Phra Farang: An English Monk in Thailand.* Bangkok: Bangkok Writers, 1997.

Pistono, Matteo. *In the Shadow of the Buddha: One Man's Journey of Discovery in Tibet.* New York: Plume, 2011.

Porter, Bill. *Road to Heaven: Encounters with Chinese Hermits.* San Francisco: Mercury House, 1993.

    Zen Baggage: A Pilgrimage to China. Berkeley: Counterpoint, 2009.

Reynolds, Jim. *The Outer Path: Finding My Way in Tibet.* Sunnyvale, CA: Fair Oaks Publishing, 1992.

Sakaki, Nanao. "Why" from *Break the Mirror,* 46. New York: [North Point Press] Farrar, Straus, and Giroux, 1966. [Reprinted by permission of North Point Press, a division of Farrar, Straus & Giroux]

Sangharakshita. Many short pieces are available at www.sangharakshita.org

Saran, Mishi. *Chasing the Monk's Shadow: A Journey in the Footsteps of Xuanzang.* New York: Penguin, 2005.

Schettini, Stephen. *The Novice: Why I Became a Buddhist Monk, Why I Quit, and What I Learned.* Austin, TX: Greenleaf Book Group Press, 2009.

Schumacher, Michael, ed. *The Essential Ginsberg.* New York: Harper, 2015.

Shattock, Ernest Henry. *An Experiment in Mindfulness.* New York: Dutton, 1960.

Shrady, Nicholas. *Sacred Roads: Adventures from the Pilgrimage Trail.* San Francisco: Harper San Francisco, 1999.

Sibley, Robert. *The Way of the 88 Temples: Journeys on the Shikoku Pilgrimage.* Charlottesville, VA: University of Virginia Press, 2013.

    The Way of the Stars: Journeys on the Camino de Santiago. Charlottesville, VA: University of Virginia Press, 2012.

Smith, Bardwell. "In Contrast to Sentimentality: Buddhist and Christian Sobriety." In Rita M. Gross and Terry C. Muck, eds., *Christians Talk about Buddhist Meditation; Buddhists Talk about Christian Prayer,* 45–52. New York: Continuum, 2003.

Snyder, Gary. *Earth Household.* New York: New Directions, 1969.

    Passage through India: An Expanded and Illustrated Edition. Berkeley: Counterpoint Press, 2009.

Sucitto, Ajahn, and Nick Scott. *Rude Awakenings: Two Englishmen on Foot in Buddhism's Holy Land.* Boston: Wisdom Publications, 2006.

    Where Are You Going: A Pilgrimage on Foot to the Buddhist Holy Places. Part II: Great Patient One. Chithurst, Petersfield: Cittaviveka Monastery, 2010.

Statler, Oliver. *Japanese Pilgrimage.* New York: William Morrow and Company, 1983.

Thubron, Colin. *Shadow of the Silk Road.* London: Chatto & Windus, 2007.

    To a Mountain in Tibet. New York: HarperCollins, 2011.

Thurman, Robert, and Tad Wise. *Circling the Sacred Mountain: A Spiritual Adventure through the Himalayas.* New York: Bantam Books, 1999.

van de Wetering, Janwillem. *Afterzen: Experiences of a Zen Student Out on His Ear.* New York: St. Martin's Press, 1999.

    The Empty Mirror: Experiences in a Japanese Zen Monastery. New York: St. Martin's Press, 1973.

A Glimpse of Nothingness: Experiences in an American Zen Community. New York: Pocket Books, 1975.

Ward, Tim. *What the Buddha Never Taught*. Toronto: Somerville House Publishing, 1995.

Willis, Jan. *Dreaming Me: An African American Woman's Spiritual Journey*. New York: Riverhead Books, 2001.

Wurlitzer, Rudolph. *Hard Travel to Sacred Places*. Boston: Shambhala, 1993.

Zeppa, Jamie. *Beyond the Sky and the Earth: A Journey into Bhutan*. New York: Penguin, 1999.

II Scholarly and Other Works

Antonaccio, Maria. *A Philosophy to Live By: Engaging Iris Murdoch*. Oxford: Oxford University Press, 2012.

Aitken, Robert. *Taking the Path of Zen*. San Francisco: North Point Press, 1982.

Almond, Philip. *The British Discovery of Buddhism*. Cambridge: Cambridge University Press, 1988.

Armstrong, Guy. *Emptiness: A Practical Guide for Meditators*. Somerville, MA: Wisdom Publications, 2017.

Asma, Stephen, ed. "A Natural Exercise in No-Self: Buddhism and Parenting." In *Why I Am a Buddhist: No-Nonsense Buddhism with Red Meat and Whiskey*, 59–84. Charlottesville, VA: Hampton Roads Publishing Company, 2010.

Baker, Deborah. *A Blue Hand: The Beats in India*. New York: Penguin, 2008.

Baldoquin, Hilda Gutierez, ed. *Dharma Color and Culture: New Voices in Western Buddhism*. Berkeley: Parallex Press, 2004.

Barbour, John D. "Autobiography." In Lindsay Jones, ed. *The Encyclopedia of Religion*, 2nd ed., vol. 2, 697–704. Detroit: Macmillan Reference, 2005.

The Conscience of the Autobiographer: Ethical and Religious Dimensions of Autobiography. New York and London: Macmillan, 1992.

"Religion and the Self: Life Writing as a Literary Form and Religious Practice." In Daniel Boscaljon and Alan Levinovitz, eds., *Teaching Religion and Literature*, 148–157. New York: Routledge, 2019.

"Spiritual Autobiography." In Margaretta Jolly, ed., *Encyclopedia of Life Writing: Autobiographical and Biographical Forms*, vol. 2, 835–837. London: Fitzroy Dearborn, 2001.

"Thomas Merton's Pilgrimage and Orientalism." In Eric Ziolkowski, ed., *Literature, Religion, and East/West Comparison: Essays in Honor of Anthony C. Yu*, 243–259. Newark: University of Delaware Press, 2005.

The Value of Solitude: The Ethics and Spirituality of Aloneness in Autobiography. Charlottesville, VA: University of Virginia Press, 2004.

Versions of Deconversion: Autobiography and the Loss of Faith. Charlottesville, VA: University of Virginia Press, 1994.

Batchelor, Stephen. *After Buddhism: Rethinking the Dharma for a Secular Age*. New Haven, CT: Yale University Press, 2015.

Bibliography

The Awakening of the West: The Encounter of Buddhism and Western Culture. Berkeley: Parallax Press, 1994.

Buddhism Without Beliefs. New York: Riverhead Books, 1997.

Beck, Kimberly. "Telling Tales Out of School." In Scott A. Mitchell and Natalie E. F. Quli, eds., *Buddhism beyond Borders: New Perspectives on Buddhism in the United States*, 125–142. Albany, NY: State University of New York Press, 2015.

Bishop, Peter. *The Myth of Shangri-La: Tibet, Travel Writing, and the Creation of Sacred Landscape.* Berkeley: University of California Press, 1989.

Bloomer, Kristin C. *Possessed by the Virgin: Hinduism, Roman Catholicism, and Marian Possession in South India.* New York: Oxford University Press, 2018.

Braun, Eric. *The Birth of Insight: Meditation, Modern Buddhism, and the Burmese Monk Ledi Sayadaw.* Chicago: University of Chicago Press, 2013.

Buddhadasa, Bhikkhu. *Me and Mine: Selected Essays of Bhikkhu Buddhadasa*, ed. Donald K. Swearer. Albany, NY: State University of New York Press, 1989.

Chadwick, David, ed., *Crooked Cucumber: The Life and Zen Teaching of Shunryu Suzuki.* New York: Broadway Books, 1999.

Zen is Right Here: Teaching Stories and Anecdotes of Shunryu Suzuki, Author of "Zen Mind, Beginner's Mind." Boulder, CO: Shambhala, 2007.

Cho, Francisca. *Seeing Like the Buddha: Enlightenment through Film.* Albany: State University of New York Press, 2017.

Clooney, Francis X. S. J. "Thomas Merton's Deep Christian Learning across Religious Borders." *Buddhist-Christian Studies* 37 (2017), 49–64.

Collins, Steven. *Selfless Persons: Imagery and Thought in Theravada Buddhism.* Cambridge: Cambridge University Press, 1982.

"What Are Buddhists *Doing* When They Deny the Self?" In Frank E. Reynolds and David Tracy, eds., *Religion and Practical Reason: New Essays in the Comparative Philosophy of Religion*, 59–86. Albany: State University of New York Press, 1994.

Cowell, E. B. ed. *The Jataka or Stories of the Buddha's Former Births.* London: Pali Text Society, 1957.

David-Neel, Alexandra. *Magic and Mystery in Tibet.* New York: Dover, 1932. [Originally published in French in 1929]

De Silva, Lynn. *The Problem of the Self in Buddhism and Christianity.* New York: Barnes and Noble, 1979.

Dodin, Thierry and Heinz Räther, eds. *Imagining Tibet: Perceptions, Projections, and Fantasies.* Boston: Wisdom Publications, 2001.

Downey, Jack. "'We Drank Many Gin and Tonics': Desire and Enchantment in Merton's Buddhist Pilgrimage." *Buddhist-Christian Studies* 37 (2017), 73–92.

Dowrie, William. *Peter Matthiessen.* Boston: Twayne, 1991.

Duncan, James, and Derek Gregory. *Writes of Passage: Travel Writing, Place and Ambiguity.* London: Routledge, 1999.

Eakin, Paul John. *Fictions in Autobiography: Studies in the Art of Self-Invention.* Princeton: Princeton University Press, 1985.

Eliade, Mircea, ed. "Shamanism." *The Encyclopedia of Religion*, vol. 13, 201–208. New York: Macmillan, 1987.

Bibliography

Epstein, Mark. *Thoughts without a Thinker: Psychotherapy from a Buddhist Perspective*. New York: Basic Books, 1995.

Faure, Bernard. *Unmasking Buddhism*. Chichester: Wiley-Blackwell, 2008.

Flanagan, Owen. *The Bodhisattva's Brain: Buddhism Naturalized*. Cambridge: MIT Press, 2011.

Forsthoefel, Thomas. "Merton and the Axes of Dialogue." *Buddhist-Christian Studies* 37 (2017), 65–72.

Foster, Barbara and Michael Foster. *Forbidden Journey: The Life of Alexandra David-Neel*. San Francisco: Harper & Row, 1987.

Frederickson, Paula. "Paul and Augustine: Conversions, Narratives, Orthodox Traditions, and the Retrospective Self." *Journal of Theological Studies* 37 (1986), 3–34.

Gadamer, Hans-Georg. *Truth and Method*, 2nd rev. ed., trans. Joel Weinsheimer and Donald G. Marshall. New York: Seabury Press, 2004.

Gethin, Rupert. *Foundations of Buddhism*. Oxford: Oxford University Press, 1998.

Gimello, Robert M. "Mysticism and Meditation." In Steven Katz, ed., *Mysticism and Philosophical Analysis*, 170–199. Oxford: Oxford University Press, 1978.

Gleig, Ann. *American Dharma: Buddhism Beyond Modernity*. New Haven: Yale University Press, 2018.

Gordon, David J., *Iris Murdoch's Fables of Unselfing*. Columbia: University of Missouri Press, 1995.

Gotami, Li. *Tibet in Pictures: A Journey into the Past*, 2 volumes. Cazadero, CA: Dharma Publishing, 1979.

Gregory, Peter, ed. *Sudden and Gradual: Approaches to Enlightenment in Chinese Thought*. Honolulu: University of Hawaii Press, 1987.

Gross, Rita. *Buddhism After Patriarchy: A Feminist History, Analysis, and Reconstruction of Buddhism*. Albany: State University of New York Press, 1993.

Gyatso, Janet. *Apparitions of the Self: The Secret Autobiographies of a Tibetan Visionary – A Translation and Study of Jigme Lingpa's Dancing Moon in the Water and Dakki's Grand Secret-talk*. Princeton: Princeton University Press, 1998.

"Healing Burns with Fire: The Facilitations of Experience in Tibetan Buddhism." *The Journal of the American Academy of Religion* 67 (1999), 113–147.

Hanh, Thich Nhat. *How to Walk*. Berkeley: Parallax Press, 2015.

Hart, Patrick, and Jonathan Montaldo, eds. *The Intimate Merton: His Life from His Journals*. San Francisco: Harper, 1999.

Harvey, Peter. "Not-Self (Anatman)." In Damien Keon and Charles S. Prebish, eds., *Encyclopedia of Buddhism*, 568–575. London: Routledge, 2007.

Hassan, Ihab. "The Writer as Seeker: The Example of Peter Matthiessen." In Mary Gerhart and Anthony C. Yu, eds., *Morphologies of Faith: Essays in Religion and Culture in Honor of Nathan A. Scott, Jr*, 245–265. Atlanta: Scholars Press, 1990.

Hick, John. *An Interpretation of Religion: Human Responses to the Transcendent*. New Haven: Yale University Press, 1989.

Hoffmann, Yoel, ed. and trans. *The Sound of the One Hand: 281 Zen Koans With Answers*. New York: New York Review of Books, 2016.

Holland, Patrick, and Graham Huggan. *Tourists with Typewriters: Critical Reflections on Contemporary Travel Writing*. Ann Arbor: University of Michigan Press, 1998.

Hopkirk, Peter. *Trespassers on the Roof of the World*. Los Angeles: Tarcher, 1982.

Huggan, Graham. *The Post-Colonial Exotic: Marketing the Margins*. London: Routledge, 2001.

Huntington, C. W., Jr., "The Autobiographical No-Self." In Rafal K. Stepien, ed., *Buddhist Literature as Philosophy, Buddhist Philosophy as Literature*, 339–359. Albany, NY: State University of New York Press, 2020.

"The Triumph of Narcissism: Theravada Buddhist Meditation in the Marketplace." *Journal of the American Academy of Religion* 83 (2015), 624–648.

Jackson, Roger R. "In Search of a Postmodern Middle." In Roger R. Jackson and John J. Makransky, eds., *Buddhist Theology: Critical Reflections by Contemporary Buddhist Scholars*, 215–246. Richmond: Curzon, 2000.

Review of Janet Gyatso's *Apparitions of the Self* by Janet Gyatso. *Journal of Asian Studies* 57 (1998), 1145–1146.

Jacoby, Sarah. *Love and Liberation: Autobiographical Writings of the Tibetan Visionary Sera Khandro*. New York: Columbia University Press, 2014.

James, William. *The Varieties of Religious Experience*. New York: Macmillan, 1961.

Keenan, John P. "Thomas Merton's Unfinished Journey in Dialogue with Buddhism." *Buddhist-Christian Studies* 37 (2017), 103–128.

King, Richard. *Orientalism and Religion: Post-Colonial Theory, India, and the "Mystic East."* New York: Routledge, 1999.

King, Sallie. *Socially Engaged Buddhism*. Honolulu: University of Hawaii Press, 2008.

Kitagawa, Joseph M. *Religions of the East*. Philadelphia: Westminster Press, 1960.

Knitter, Paul. *Without Buddha I Could Not Be a Christian*. London: One World, 2009.

Levering, Miriam. "Was There Religious Autobiography in China before the Thirteenth Century?: The Ch'an Master Ta-hui Tsung-kao (1089–1163) As Autobiographer." *Journal of Chinese Religions* 30 (2002), 97–122.

Lopez, Donald S., Jr., *Curators of the Buddha: The Study of Buddhism Under Colonialism*. Chicago: University of Chicago Press, 1995.

Prisoners of Shangri-La: Tibetan Buddhism and the West. Chicago: University of Chicago Press, 1998.

Lopez, Donald S., Jr., ed. *Strange Tales of an Oriental Idol: An Anthology of Early European Portrayals of the Buddha*. Chicago: University of Chicago Press, 2016.

Lopez, Donald S., Jr., and Thupten Jinpa. *Dispelling the Darkness: A Jesuit's Quest for the Soul of Tibet*. Cambridge, MA: Harvard University Press, 2017.

McMahon, David. *The Making of Buddhist Modernism*. Oxford: Oxford University Press, 2008.

Bibliography

McMillin, Laurie Hovell. "Enlightenment Travels: The Making of Epiphany in Tibet." In James Duncan and Derek Gregory, eds., *Writes of Passage: Reading Travel Writing*, 49–69. London: Routledge, 1999.

Merton, Thomas. "From Pilgrimage to Crusade." In *Mystics and Zen Masters*, 91–112. New York: Farrar, Straus, and Giroux, 1967.

"Wisdom and Emptiness: A Dialogue by Daisetz T. Suzuki and Thomas Merton." In *Zen and the Birds of Appetite*, 99–138. New York: New Directions, 1968.

Murdoch, Iris. *The Sovereignty of Good*. New York: Schocken Books, 1971.

Murti, Tirupattur Ramaseshayyer Venkatachala. *The Central Philosophy of Buddhism*, 2nd ed. London: Allen & Unwin, 1960.

Normand, Lawrence, and Alison Winch, eds. *Encountering Buddhism in Twentieth Century British and American Literature*. London: Bloomsbury, 2013.

Olney, James. *Metaphors of Self: The Meaning of Autobiography*. Princeton: Princeton University Press, 1972.

Oppenheimer, Mark. *The Zen Predator of the Upper East Side*. Washington, DC: Atlantic Books, 2013.

Paine, Jeffrey. *Re-enchantment: Tibetan Buddhism Comes to the West*. New York: Norton, 2004.

Pannapadipo, Phra Peter. *One Step at a Time: Buddhist Meditation for Absolute Beginners*. Bangkok: Bangkok Writers, 1999.

Parfit, Derek. *Reasons and Persons*. Oxford: Clarendon Press, 1984.

Parker, David. *The Self in Moral Space: Life Narrative and the Good*. Ithaca, NY: Cornell University Press, 2007.

Pistono, Matteo. *Fearless in Tibet: The Life of Mystic Terton Sogyal*. Carlsbad, CA: Hay House, 2014.

Roar: Sulak Sivaraksa and the Path of Socially Engaged Buddhism. Berkeley: North Atlantic Books, 2019.

Porter, Dennis. *Haunted Journeys: Desire and Transgression in European Travel Writing*. Princeton: Princeton University Press, 1991.

Power, Richard, ed. "Within the White Cloud: Life and Work of Lama Govinda." In *The Lost Teachings of Lama Govinda*, xvii–lviii. Wheaton, IL: Quest Books, 2007.

Pratt, Mary Louise. *Imperial Eyes: Travel Writing and Transculturation*. London: Routledge, 1992.

Prebish, Charles, and Kenneth Tanaka. *The Faces of Buddhism in America*. Berkeley: University of California Press, 1998.

Prebish, Charles, and Martin Baumann. *Western Dharma: Buddhism Beyond Asia*. Berkeley: University of California Press, 2002.

Prothero, Stephen. *The White Buddhist: The Asian Odyssey of Henry Steel Olcott*. Bloomington: Indiana University Press, 1996.

Rambo, Lewis R. *Understanding Religious Conversion*. New Haven, CT: Yale University Press, 1995.

Rambo, Lewis R., and Charles E. Farhadian, eds. *The Oxford Handbook of Religious Conversion*. Oxford: Oxford University Press, 2014.

Reader, Ian. *Religion in Contemporary Japan*. Honolulu: University of Hawaii Press, 1991.

Reid, Daniel. "Translator's Introduction: The Wheel of Life." In John Blofeld, ed., *My Journey in China: Old Pu's Travel Diary*, xv–xxvi. Rochester, VT: Inner Traditions, 2008.

Ricoeur, Paul. *Oneself as Another*, trans. Kathleen Blamey. Chicago: University of Chicago Press, 1992.

Ross, Nancy Wilson, ed. *The World of Zen: An East-West Anthology*. New York: Vintage Books, 1960.

Rudd, Anthony. "No Self? Reflections on Buddhist Theories of Personal Identity." *Philosophy East and West* 65 (2015), 869–891.

Schedneck, Brooke. "Buddhist Life Stories." *Contemporary Buddhism* 8 (2007), 57–68.

Sharf, Robert H. "Buddhist Modernism and the Rhetoric of Meditative Experience." *Numen* 42 (1995), 228–283.

"Is Mindfulness Buddhist (and Why It Matters)." *Transcultural Psychiatry* 52 (2015), 470–484.

"Losing Our Religion." *Tricycle* 16 (2007), 44–49.

Siderits, Mark. *Personal Identity and Buddhist Philosophy: Empty Persons*. Burlington, VT: Ashgate, 2003.

Siderits, Mark, and Evan Thompson. *Self, No Self?: Perspectives from Analytic, Phenomenological, and Indian Traditions*. New York: Oxford University Press, 2013.

Simmer-Brown, Judith. "Ambivalence in Shangri-La: Merton's Orientalism and Dialogue." *Buddhist-Christian Studies* 37 (2017), 93–101.

Solnit, Rebecca. *Wanderlust: A History of Walking*. New York: Penguin, 2001.

Suh, Sharon A. *Silver Screen Buddha: Buddhism in Asian and Western Film*. London: Bloomsbury Academic, 2015.

Swearer, Donald. *Conflict, Culture, Change: Engaged Buddhism in a Globalizing World*. Somerville, MA: Wisdom Publications, 2015.

Syedullah, Jasmine. *Radical Dharma: Talking Race, Love, and Liberation*. Berkeley: North Atlantic Books, 2016.

Taves, Ann. *Fits, Trances, and Visions: Experiencing Religion and Explaining Experience from Wesley to James*. Princeton: Princeton University Press, 1999.

Religious Experience Reconsidered: A Building-Block Approach to the Study of Religion and Other Special Things. Princeton: Princeton University Press, 2009.

Revelatory Events: Three Case Studies of the Emergence of New Spiritual Paths. Princeton: Princeton University Press, 2016.

"Special Things as Building Blocks of Religion." In Robert A. Orsi, ed., *The Cambridge Companion to Religious Studies*, 58–83. Cambridge: Cambridge University Press, 2012.

Trungpa, Chogyam. *Cutting through Spiritual Materialism*. Boston: Shambhala Publications, 1973.

Turner, Victor, and Edith Turner. *Image and Pilgrimage in Christian Culture: Anthropological Perspectives*. New York: Columbia University Press, 1978.

Bibliography

Tweed, Thomas. *The American Encounter with Buddhism, 1844–1912: Victorian Culture and the Limits of Dissent*. Bloomington: Indiana University Press, 1992.

Van Overmeier, Ben. "Portraying Zen Buddhism in the Twentieth Century: Encounter Dialogues as Frame-Stories in Daisetz Suzuki's *Introduction to Zen Buddhism* and Janwillem Van de Wetering's The Empty Mirror." *Japan Studies Review* 21 (2017), 3–24.

Waddell, Norman, ed. "Translator's Introduction." trans. Norman Waddell. *Wild Ivy: The Spiritual Autobiography of Zen Master Hakuin*, vii–xliv. Boston: Shambhala, 1999.

Whalen-Bridge, John, and Gary Storhoff, eds. *The Emergence of Buddhist American Literature*. Albany: State University of New York Press, 2009.

Williams, Angel Kyodo. *Being Black: Zen and the Art of Living with Fearlessness and Grace*. New York: Penguin, 2002.

Williams, Angel Kyodo, Lama Rod Owens, and Jasmine Syedullah. *Radical Dharma: Talking Race, Love, and Liberation*. Berkeley: North Atlantic Books, 2016.

Willis, Jan. "Teaching Buddhism in the Western Academy." In Todd Lewis and Gary DeAngelis, eds., *Teaching Buddhism: New Insights on Understanding and Presenting the Traditions*, 151–165. New York: Oxford University Press, 2017.

Wilson, Jeff. *Mindful America: The Mutual Transformation of Buddhist Meditation and American Culture*. New York: Oxford University Press, 2014.

Wright, Dale. *What Is Buddhist Enlightenment?* Oxford: Oxford University Press, 2016.

Wu, Pei-yi. "An Ambivalent Pilgrim to Tai Shan in the Seventeenth Century." In Susan Naquin and Chun-gang Yu, eds., *Pilgrims and Sacred Sites in China*, 65–88. Berkeley: University of California Press, 1992.

Yu, Dan Smyor. "Buddhist Conversion in the Contemporary World." In Lewis R. Rambo and Charles E. Farhadian, eds., *The Oxford Handbook of Religious Conversion*, 465–487. Oxford: Oxford University Press, 2014.

Index

Abe, Masao, 113
Abhidhamma ("higher teaching"), 240, 271
addiction, 165, 227
  self-, 162
  sexual, 160, 162, 166
adventure, *Heart of the World*, 166, 167
African Americans, 200
  racism and, 199
  suffering and, 195–197
*Afterzen: Experiences of a Zen Student Out on
  His Ear*, 69
Alpert, Richard, 119
Amida, 128
anatman (no-self), 2, 12–14, 111, 272. See also
  anatta; no-self; unselfing
anatta (no-self), 168, 171, 172, 208, 228, 235,
  236, 271, 276, 277
anger, 176–178, 222, 223
  microaggression and, 198
Angkor Wat, 231
anicca (impermanence), 105, 111, 228. *See also*
  impermanence
Animism, 221, 234
anyita, 11
Armstrong, Guy, 302, 303
  A Practical Guide for Meditators, 294
art, 40, 106
  Polonnaruwa, 106–108
  Tibetan Buddhism and, 34
  Tsaparang and, 41–42
  unselfing and, 297
asceticism, 136, 148
  pilgrimage and, 129
The Asian Journal of Thomas Merton, 99–112
  pilgrimage, 108
  pilgrimage as homelessness, 103, 104
  Polonnaruwa, 106–108
  searching, 104–106
  "spiritual materialism," 110
  sunyata ("emptiness"), 108–110
Asma, Stephen, 10, 23, 233–242, 280. See also
  The Gods Drink Whiskey: Stumbling

*Toward Enlightenment in the Land of
  the Tattered Buddha*
atman, 236, 271
  self and, 271
attachment, 113, 156, 191, 227, 250
  suffering and, 197
  to the ego, 238
Augustine, 24, 104, 160, 166, 252, 305, 306
  Confessions, 252, 305, 306
autobiography, 7, 301–313. See also *Mystical
  Journey: An Autobiography; Dreaming Me:
  An African American Woman's Spiritual
  Journey; The Novice*
Buddhist, 7
  self-transformation and, 301–313
  spiritual, 24, 41, 42, 293, 309, 310, 313
  Tibetan, 287–292
  traditional Buddhist literature and, 7
  Western Buddhist travel narratives
    and, 6
  Zen monastic memoirs, 63
autofiction, 293
Avalokiteshvara, vow of, 183–185
awakening, 13, 20, 21, 100, 113, 145. *See also*
  enlightenment
awareness, 175
  beyuls and, 168
  meditation and, 176
  yoin, 135

baggage, as metaphor, 268, 269
Baker, Ian, 23, 166–172, 280, 291, 304. See also
  Heart of the World
Baker, Richard, 85
bangai, 136
Basho, 134, 135
Batchelor, Stephen, 4, 201, 210
beauty, unselfing and, 297
Bertolucci, Bernardo, 228
Beyond the Sky and the Earth, 10, 187–195
  Zeppa's experience of unselfing, 192, 193
beyul, 166–168, 291

324

Index

Pemako region, 168, 169
waterfalls and, 170
Bhutan, 187–194
biographies, 293
Black Panther movement, 196
The Blade Wheel of Mind Reform, 159, 162
Blofeld, John, 4, 21, 24–31, 42, 179. See also
The Wheel of Life
account of unselfing, 28
conversion to Buddhism, 27
initiation in Vajrayana Buddhism, 27–28
The Wheel of Life, 21, 63
Bodhidharma, 265
bodhisattva, 6, 7, 70, 80, 83, 96, 159, 163, 164,
172, 173, 174, 177, 178, 184
*Bones of the Master: A Journey to Secret
Mongolia*, 248–255
unselfing, Crane's experience of, 251, 252
Boorstein, Sylvia, 119
Bow First, Ask Questions Later, 92–97
Brahman, 271, 272
Buddhadasa, Bhikku, *Me and Mine*, 236
Buddhism, 2, 3, 28, 101, 118, 139. *See also*
Chan Buddhism; Mahayana Buddhism;
Tantric Buddhism; Theravada Buddhism;
Tibetan Buddhism; Vajrayana Buddhism;
Zen Buddhism
anatman or *anatta* (no-self), 2, 12, 17, 108,
111, 168, 171, 172, 208, 228, 235, 236, 271,
272, 276, 277
anicca or *anyita* ("impermanence"), 11, 105,
106, 111, 228
art, 106, 107
autobiographical writings and, 7
awakening, 13, 20, 21
Blofeld's conversion to, 27
China and, 31
Christianity and, 102, 103, 116
contemporary Asian, 3
culture and, 8
"engaged," 172, 177, 178, 224, 231
enlightenment and, 6, 15, 17, 44, 57–58,
63–98
ethics and, 238
inner path, 158
jataka tales, 6
JUBUs, 119, 120
karma, 137
no-self, Sucitto's view of, 143
pilgrimage and, 9, 123–149
Pure Land, 258
reincarnation, 26
rituals and, 30
"secular," 201, 203, 210
selfhood, 12

self-transformation and, 9
sex and, 238
Shingon, 128
sunyata ("emptiness"), Merton's view of, 108,
109, 110
Tantric, 153, 159, 166, 168, 181, 198
Theravada, 23, 32, 69, 140, 157, 207–244
Tibetan, 150–206
tourism and, 264
Buddhist Modernism, 19, 42, 302, 309, 310
Burma. *See* Myanmar
Byles, Marie, 208–209
Journey into the Burmese Silence, 208

Cambodia, 23, 230–235, 237–239, 241, 242.
See also Theravada Buddhism
Khmer Rouge, 235
Camino de Santiago de Compostela, 10, 116,
117, 132
Catholic Worker Movement, 177
ceremonies, 93, 95. *See also* rituals
Chadwick, David, 85–91, 98. See also *Thank You
and OK!: An American Zen Failure in Japan*
Chah, Ajahn, 210, 214, 215
Chan Buddhism, 243, 245, 246, 249, 252, 258,
261–269
fox power, 253, 254
learning and, 249
"mind power" and, 252, 253
Zen Buddhism and, 252, 261
Chandako, Ajahn. *See* Reynolds, Jim
"child mind," 102
China, 9, 10, 23, 25, 27, 31, 165, 171, 172, 185,
243–269. *See also* Chan Buddhism
Buddhist persecution and, 174
Cultural Revolution, 41–42, 243, 246
hermits and, 258
monasticism in, 264, 265
Naxi people, 246–248
Zen Buddhism, historical development in,
265, 266
Christianity, 111, 112, 199. *See also* conversion
Buddhism and, 102, 103, 116
contemplation, 113
conversion, 13, 58, 304–307
kenosis, 113
monasticism and, 109
mysticism and, 112
Chungnan Mountains, 256–258, 261
Circling the Sacred Mountain, 159–166, 248, 286
mind reform, 162–164
selflessness, 160, 161, 166
unselfing, 160, 161
The Cloud of Unknowing, 112
coincidence of opposites, 114

Index

Coleman, John Earl, 208–209
  The Quiet Mind, 208
Collins, Steven, 271, 272, 276, 277, 309, 311, 312
  Selfless Persons, 270
communitas, 116, 117, 137, 138, 298
compassion, 75, 106, 113, 125, 138, 161, 174–176,
    215, 224, 231, 237, 239, 240–241, 251, 260,
    273, 287, 291, 297, 298
  suffering and, 239, 240, 241
consciousness, 101, 114, 135
contemplation, 113
conversion, 13, 14, 57, 112, 148, 177, 193, 304–307
  continuous, 82
Cousineau, Philip, *The Art of Pilgrimage*, 10
Crane, George, 248–255, 285. See also *Bones of
    the Master: A Journey to Secret Mongolia*
cult of experience, 303, 304
Cultural Revolution, 41–42, 243, 246, 247,
    256, 264

Dai Bosatsu, 56
dakini, as metaphor, 290
Dalai Lama, 9, 102, 104, 108, 118, 119, 121, 154,
    163, 167, 168, 172–174, 177, 186, 198, 199
  on waterfalls, 169
Danzo, Ichikawa, 130, 131
David-Neel, Alexandra, 3, 37, 151–153. See also
    My Journey to Lhasa
Davis, Lynn, 227, 229, 230, 232
Day, Dorothy, 177
de Botton, Alain, 299
"deeming," 279, 308
deity yoga, 198
detachment, 68, 70, 80, 193, 217, 260. See also
    attachment
Dharamsala conference, 118–120
Dharma, 25, 30, 32–34, 61, 62, 64, 93, 94, 146,
    148, 185, 202, 233, 264, 266
Dharmacakrapravartana Sutra ("Sutra Turning
    the Wheel of Dharma"), 274
dharmakaya, 107
Diamond Sutra, 259
Dogen, 54, 58, 82, 83, 88, 91, 93, 96
dokusan, 85
"double belonging," 112
*Dreaming Me: An African American Woman's
    Spiritual Journey*, 195–200
  dreams, 199
  unselfing, Willis' experience of, 197–198
dualism, 60, 92, 225
duhkha ("suffering"), 11, 155, 156, 157, 205, 226,
    228, 231, 238, 296, 300
Durkheim, Emile, 279

Eakin, Paul John, *Fictions in Autobiography*, 290
ecstasy, 256, 257

ego, the, 35, 40, 86, 87, 113, 182, 216
  attachment and, 238
  self-emptying, 115
  "spiritual materialism" and, 110, 111
  suffering and, 196, 197
egotism, 16
Ehrlich, Gretel, 23, 243–248, 259, 265. See also
    *Questions of Heaven: The Chinese Journeys
    of an American Buddhist*
Eliade, Mircea, 256
Eliot, George, 16
Emai Shan, 243, 244, 245
emptiness, 12, 107–110, 113, 121, 168,
    183, 184
The Empty Mirror, 63–69
  equanimity in, 67–69
  koans, 64–66, 68, 69
  satori, 66
"engaged" Buddhism, 172, 177, 178,
    224, 231
enlightenment, 6, 7, 15, 17, 32, 43, 44, 51,
    54, 58, 63, 64, 69, 72, 73, 75, 82, 86, 112,
    113, 123, 128, 145, 174, 236. See also
    awakening
  achievement and, 73
  achieving, 83, 90
  dai kensho, 55
  kensho and, 48
  meditation and, 89
  O'Halloran's achievement of, 81, 82
  Rinzai Zen and, 88
  unselfing and, 55–70
  Zen Buddhism and, 67, 69
equanimity, 67, 69, 70, 81, 220, 232, 238
  in *Afterzen: Experiences of a Zen Student Out
    on His Ear*, 69, 70
  in *The Empty Mirror*, 67–69
ethics, 203, 226, 238
  Buddhism and, 238, 239
  selflessness and, 272

faith, 127, 128, 154, 203
  personal transformation and, 127, 128
  pilgrimage and, 128, 129
Faure, Bernard, 272
fox power, 253–255

Gadamer, Hans-George, 19
gender
  in Japan, 77
  monasticism and, 209
  norms, 80, 81
  roles and marriage and, 77–79
Ginsberg, Allen, 9, 119, 292
Glassman, Bernard, 58, 119. See also Tetsugen
Go Roshi, 72, 73, 75–77, 79, 81, 82

Index

God, 104, 112–114, 120, 121
  emptiness and, 121
  kenosis, 113
  unknowability of, 113
The Gods Drink Whiskey: Stumbling Toward
  Enlightenment in the Land of the Tattered
  Buddha, 10, 207–208, 233–242
  no-self, Asma's interpretation of, 236, 237
  self-transformation, 242
  unselfing, Asma's experiences of, 239, 240
Goldberg, Natalie
  Let the Whole Thundering World Come
    Home: A Memoir, 295
  The Great Failure, 294
Goldstein, Joseph, 119, 120
  The Experience of Insight, 229
goma ritual, 127
Govinda, Anagarika, 24, 31–42, 154. See also
  The Way of the White Clouds
  account of unselfing, 34–36
  on meditation, 36–37
  on pilgrimage, 40
  on reincarnation, 38–39
Great Leap Forward, 250
Great Patient One, 146–148
Greenwood, Gesshin Claire, *Bow First, Ask*
  Questions Later, 92–97
grief, 227, 231. *See also* suffering
guru devotion, 203
Gyatso, Janet, 307, 308
  Apparitions of the Self, 287–292

Hard Travel to Sacred Places, 226–232
Harrer, Heinrich, *Seven Years in Tibet*, 153, 154
Harvey, Andrew, 23, 179–187, 206, 301. See also
  A Journey in Ladakh
Haubner, Shozan Jack, *Single White Monk*, 294
healing
  faith and, 127
  music and, 247, 248
  rituals and, 126, 127
  walking and, 129, 130
Heart of the World, 166–172, 291
  beyuls, 166–169
  self-transcendence, 171
  self-transformation, 171
  Tsangpo Gorge expedition, 169, 170
henro ("pilgrims"), 125, 129–131, 138
hermeneutics, Zen, 262
hermits, 255–261
  intellectual, 259
  no-self and, 258
  self-transcendence and, 259
  solitude and, 260
  wisdom and, 260
Hick, John, 15, 281–283, 308

An Interpretation of Religion, 281–283
Hilton, James, *Lost Horizon*, 150
Himalayas, 26, 48, 50, 51, 147, 153, 156,
  160, 167
  beyul, 166–168
  homelessness, pilgrimage as, 103
Hong Kingston, Maxine, 293
Hong Kong, 250
Hume, David, 12

identity construction, 199
illness narratives, 295
impermanence, 188, 215, 217, 231, 241, 242.
  See also *anicca*
"In Contrast to Sentimentality," 115–118
  meditation, 118
  Smith's account of unselfing in, 118
In the Shadow of the Buddha, 172–178, 181
India, 9, 22, 23, 25, 32–33, 99, 118–120, 141–148,
  201–202
  Dharamsala conference, 118–120
Inner Mongolia, 250

Jackson, Roger, 12
  on the middle way, 275
James, William, 71, 240, 241, 283, 302
  The Varieties of Religious Experience, 2
Japan, 10, 54, 59, 60, 86, 112. *See also* Shikoku
  pilgrimage
  ceremonies, 93
  gender norms in, 77–79
Japanese Pilgrimage, 123–132
  henro, 125
  Kobo Daishi, 10, 123–129, 132, 133
  rituals, 126, 127
jataka tales, 6
The Jew in the Lotus: A Poet's Rediscovery of Jewish
  Identity in Buddhist India, 22, 118–122
  Dharamsala conference, 118–120
  emptiness, 120, 121
  unselfing, 122
Jigme Lingpa, 288–291
  "Dakini's Grand Secret Talk," 290
  "Dancing Moon in the Water," 290
Jikmé Dhuntsok, Kenpo, 173
Johnson, Charles, 9
Johnston, William, 22, 112–115, 118, 121, 122. See
  also *Mystical Journey: An Autobiography*
journal, 5, 6, 44, 54, 56, 61, 71, 80, 81, 83, 99,
  101–102, 263, 292. See also *The Asian*
  Journal of Thomas Merton; Nine-Headed
  Dragon River; Pure Heart, Enlightened
  Mind
A Journey in Ladakh, 179–187
  unselfing, Harvey's experience of, 183
  self-transformation, 184, 185

Index

journey(s), 5–6, 9–11, 20, 22, 25, 31, 33, 44, 49, 51, 54, 100–103, 132, 140, 158, 167, 195, 209, 243, 261, 292–300. *See also* travel
 as metaphor, 5, 6, 115
 Merton on, 103
 pilgrimage, 9, 10
 searching and, 6, 300
JUBUs, 119, 120
Judaism, 118–122
 kabbalah, 120, 121
 Tibetan Buddhism and, 118–122
Jung, Carl, 113, 114
 synchronicity, 135, 136

kabbalah, 120, 121
Kalzang, Lama Ngawang, 32
Kamenetz, Rodger, 22, 118–122. See also *The Jew in the Lotus: A Poet's Rediscovery of Jewish Identity in Buddhist India*
kami, 134
Kapleau, Philip, 98
 The Three Pillars of Zen, 63
karma, 27, 137, 138, 234–236
Katagiri, Dainin, 85, 89, 295
kenosis, 113
kensho, 59, 74–76, 82, 223
 Matthiessen on, 48
 unselfing and, 55
Kerouac, Jack, 9, 156, 293
Khmer Rouge, 230, 234, 235
khwan ("life spirit"), 228
Kitagawa, Joseph, 131
koan, 64
koans, 17, 65, 69, 74, 75, 77, 82, 98
 "mu," 72, 75, 76, 88, 90, 91
Kobo Daishi, 123–125, 127–129, 132
Kornfield, Jack, 119, 210
Krishnamurti, Jiddu, 208
Kyger, Joanne, 292

Ladakh, 179–183
language
 Mahayana Buddhism and, 262
 translation and, 264, 267
 Zen Buddhism and, 262
Lei, Shu Bao, 254, 255
Lerab Lingpa, Tertön Sogyal, 172, 173, 176
Lieberman, Marc, 119
liminal identity of the pilgrim, 134, 137
literary genre, 194, 292–295, 310
 autobiographies, 7, 8
 jataka tales, 6
 philosophical journalism, 233
 poetry, 9
 secret autobiography, 287–292

Western Buddhist travel narrative as, 4, 5, 24, 33, 43, 153, 207
Zen monastic memoirs, 63
Little Buddha, 227–229, 232
Lonergan, Bernard, 112
Lopez, Donald, Jr., *Prisoners of Shangri-La*, 150
Love, Deborah, 43, 46, 48, 55
lung-gom, 37–38, 152, 296

Maha Ghosananda, 239, 241
Mahayana Buddhism, 7, 26, 236, 262, 282, 283
 sunyata ("emptiness"), 12, 15, 108–110, 276
 language and, 262
 makyo, 136
Malraux, André, 229
Mao, Zedong, 243, 246, 250
Mara, 231
Marpa, 163
marriage, 77, 78, 190
Matthiessen, Peter, 1, 11, 22, 43–62, 93, 97, 102, 154, 166, 273, 279, 280, 290. See also *Nine-Headed Dragon River; The Snow Leopard*
 account of unselfing, 45, 47–49, 55, 58, 59
 on *kensho*, 48
 Tetsugen and, 58
Maurin, Peter, 177
McDonald, Sara, *Holy Cow*, 10, 11
McMahon, David, 19, 42, 310
meditation, 35, 39, 52, 67, 73, 105, 112, 113, 118, 136, 164, 165, 178, 184, 198, 201, 209, 224, 236. *See also* contemplation
 awareness and, 176
 beyuls and, 168
 enlightenment and, 82, 89
 Govinda on, 36–37
 "introjection," 273
 koan, 64
 makyo, 136
 mind reform, 162, 163
 mindfulness and, 210, 213
 no-self and, 274
 pilgrimage and, 52–53
 Vipassana, 155, 207, 208, 218, 219
 walking as, 20
 wisdom and, 261, 262
 Zen Buddhism and, 46
Merton, Thomas, 11, 22, 33, 99–112, 117, 118, 122, 170, 280, 290, 297, 298, 301. See also *The Asian Journal of Thomas Merton*
 Mystics and Zen Masters, 100
 The Seven Storey Mountain, 102
 "Transcendent Experience," 101
 "Wisdom in Emptiness," 100
 Zen and the Birds of Appetite, 100, 102

Index

metaphor(s), 5, 20, 21, 29, 66, 72, 97, 101, 102, 104, 115, 116–118, 149, 162, 199, 200, 245, 275, 277, 290–292, 308
  baggage as, 268, 269
  blade wheel, 159
  dakini as, 290
  dancing moon as, 290
  dreams and, 200
  fox as, 254, 255
  journey as, 112, 115
  lion's roar, 199–200, 288
  mountain as, 245
  of self, 290–292
  red dust, 258
  secret autobiography and, 290, 291
microaggressions, 198
middle way, 275, 278
Milarepa, 163
"mind power," 252–254
mind reform, 162–163
mindfulness, 209–213, 215, 232, 242, 265, 312
monastic training, 66–72, 76, 85, 87, 93
monasticism, 93, 102, 109, 157, 211, 214–216, 218, 222, 224
  food and, 220
  gender and, 209
  in China, 264–265
  pahkow, 210, 212–213
  "spiritual materialism" and, 110, 111
  Theravada and, 207
  Vinaya, 210–213
Morikawa, Nobuo, 124
mountains. *See also* Himalayas
  as metaphor, 245
  Chungnan, 256–258, 261
  Crow Pull, 251
  Emai Shan, 243
  Kailash, 159, 160, 162, 164, 165
  Kanchenjunga, 105, 106, 111
  Kundu Dorsempotrang, 168
  Wutaishan, 263–265
mu koan, 72, 76, 88, 90, 91
Murdoch, Iris, 14
music
  healing power of, 247, 248
  unselfing and, 248, 297
My Journey to Lhasa, 151–153
  no-self, 153
  unselfing, 152
Myanmar, 230, 231
Mystical Journey: An Autobiography, 112–115
mysticism, 112–115, 135, 181, 186, 280, 301
  coincidence of opposites, 114
  kabbalah, 121

of the ordinary, 135, 136
self-emptying, 113
unselfing and, 115

Nagarjuna, *Madhyamakakarika*, 275–276
narratives, 278, 283–287. *See also* travel narratives
  Christian conversion, 304–307
  illness, 295
  unselfing and, 283–287
National Geographic Society, 171
Naxi people, 246–248
Nepal, 9, 22, 23, 43, 103–105
New Age, 180–181
New Zealand, 158
Nhat Hanh, Thich, 9
nibbana, 302, 303
Niebuhr, H. Richard, 116
nihilism, Zen Buddhism and, 70
Nine-Headed Dragon River, 54–62
  no-self, 59, 61
  student–teacher relationship, 59
  unselfing, Matthiessen's account of, 55
Nirvana, 15
non-dualism, 114
no-self, 9, 10–13, 16, 18, 19, 21, 27, 59–64, 71, 80, 86, 89, 91, 94, 95, 142–144, 153, 154, 159, 160, 181, 183, 187–188, 190–191, 194, 195, 198, 204, 205, 208, 209, 215, 217–220, 228, 233, 235, 237, 270, 274, 277, 285, 309. *See also* middle way; selflessness
  Abhidharma and, 271
  anatta and, 272
  Asma's interpretation of, 236–237
  atman and, 271
  Buddhist accounts of, 271
  Christianity and, 111, 112, 195, 199
  dogma and, 276
  hermits and, 258–259
  knowledge of, 311–312
  learning and, 311–312
  meditation and, 273–274
  New Age rhetoric and, 181–183
  patience and, 142
  self-emptying and, 113
  truth and, 274
  unselfing and, 274
nothingness, 113
The Novice, 200–205

O'Halloran, Maura, 70–84, 280, 290, 303. See also *Pure Heart, Enlightened Mind: The Life and Letters of an Irish Saint*
  account of unselfing, 72–74, 77–79, 83, 84
  enlightenment, achievement of, 81–82

330   *Index*

O'Halloran, Maura (cont.)
  monastic training, 71
  on suffering, 71
  vow of *bodhisattva*, 80
Olney, James, *Metaphors of Self,* 290
Orientalism, 105, 230
The Outer Path: Finding My Way in Tibet,
  155–158
Ozeki, Ruth, 293

Padmasambhava, 173
pahkow, 210, 212
Pali, 207
Pannapadipo, Phra Peter. *See* Robinson, Peter
patience, no-self and, 142
Paul (apostle), 113
Phra Farang: An English Monk in Thailand,
  217–226
  Robinson's experience of unselfing,
   219–224
  Robinson's self-transformation, 220–222
phurba ritual, 174–176, 178
pilgrim mind, 133
pilgrimage, 9, 33, 40, 49–50, 99–100, 103,
  108, 111, 115, 116, 130, 132, 139, 140,
  148, 149, 167, 168. *See also* Shikoku
  pilgrimage
  as homelessness, 103
  beyuls and, 168–170
  Camino de Santiago de Compostela, 132
  communitas and, 116, 117, 137, 138
  Emai Shan, 243–245
  faith and, 128, 129
  henro, 125, 138
  liminal identity of the pilgrim, 134, 137
  meditation and, 52–53
  Merton on, 100
  Mount Kailash, 159, 160, 165
  self-transformation and, 40, 129–131
  Shikoku, 10, 22, 37, 116–117, 123–139,
   298, 300
  Wutaishan, 264, 265
Pistono, Matteo, 23, 172–178, 181, 196, 285. See
  also *In the Shadow of the Buddha*
poetry, 9, 134, 135, 138, 244, 249, 259
Polonnaruwa, 106–109
Porter, Bill, 23, 243, 255–269. See also *Road to
  Heaven: Encounters with Chinese Hermits*;
  Zen Baggage: A Pilgrimage to China*
prajna, 44
Pure Heart, Enlightened Mind, 71–84
  narrative structure, 84, 85
  O'Halloran's account of unselfing in, 72, 74,
   77–79, 83, 84
Pure Land Buddhism, 258

*Questions of Heaven: The Chinese Journeys of an
  American Buddhist,* 243–248

racism, 199, 206
Ram Dass, 119
Rambo, Lewis, 177
Reader, Ian, 136
reading as spiritual practice, 309, 310
reincarnation, 26, 38–39
religion, 42, 110, 113, 115, 120, 129, 142–143, 150,
  151, 240, 279, 281–283, 308, 309
  ego and, 47
  no-self and, 143
  "sacred technology" and, 187
  "seeing as," 15
  spirituality and, 310, 311
  "spiritual materialism" and, 110
  theories of, 278–283, 307, 308
religious experience, 2, 7, 42, 100
  salvation, 282
  theories and, 279–283, 308
  unselfing, 281
Reynolds, Jim, 23, 154–158. See also *The Outer
  Path: Finding My Way in Tibet*
Ricoeur, Paul, 306, 307
"right view," of no self, 277
Rinzai Zen, 54, 56–60, 64–65, 85, 88, 90, 92,
  93, 304
  enlightenment and, 88
  rituals, 88
  Soto Zen and, 88
rituals, 40, 81, 86, 139, 152, 281
  Buddhism and, 30
  ceremonies and, 93
  Dharma combat, 93, 94
  goma, 127
  phurba, 174–176, 178
  Rinzai Zen and, 88
  shamanism and, 254
  Theravada Buddhism and, 220, 221
  unselfing and, 126, 127
  Zen Buddhism and, 66, 67, 76, 266
*Road to Heaven: Encounters with Chinese
  Hermits,* 256–261
Robinson, Peter, 23, 217–226. See also *Phra
  Farang: An English Monk in Thailand*
  on Vipassana meditation, 218, 219
  One Step at a Time, 218
Rude Awakenings, 139–146, 286
  alms gathering, 141
  no-self, 142–144
  unselfing, 144–146

sabbai, 221, 222
Sacred Activism, 186, 187

Index

Suzuki, Shunryu, 85
synchronicity, 136

Tantric Buddhism, 123, 152, 153, 159, 166, 168, 181, 198, 236, 254
Tao-hsin, 265
Taoism, 257, 258, 260
Taves, Ann, 16, 279, 283, 284, 308
Taylor, Charles, 19
teacher-student relationship, 59, 62, 163
Tetsugen, 58, 60–62
"Thai Forest Tradition," 207
Thailand, 23, 27, 158, 207, 210, 213, 219, 227, 230, 234. *See also* Theravada Buddhism
Thank You and OK!, 85–91
  narrative structure, 85, 90, 91
Tharpa Chöeling, 202
theories
  of no-self, 270–278
  of religious experience, 279, 281–283, 307–308
Theravada Buddhism, 23, 32, 69, 140, 157, 207–242. *See also* monasticism
  "forest tradition," 210
  karma and, 236
  monasticism and, 207
  nibbana, 302, 303
  rituals and, 220–222
  Vipassana meditation, 218, 219
  Zen Buddhism and, 235
Thubron, Colin, *To a Mountain in Tibet*, 155
Thuksey Rinpoche, 182–187
Thurman, Robert, 11, 23, 159–166, 248, 300. See also *Circling the Sacred Mountain*
Tibet, 9, 22, 118, 150–178. *See also* mountains, Kailash
  beyul, 165–168
  Tsangpo River gorge, 167, 170, 171
Tibetan Buddhism, 28, 31–32, 150–206
  art and, 34
  "child mind," 102
  Judaism and, 119–122
  lung-gom, 37–38
  reincarnation, 38–39
  rituals and, 40
  "Treasures," 287, 288
  tum-mo, 38, 152
Tibetan secret autobiography, 287–292
  "Dakini's Grand Secret Talk," 290
  "Dancing Moon in the Water," 290
  metaphors and, 290, 291
  single self-deconstructing figure, 290
  unselfing and, 289

Tolstoy, Leo, *Confessions*, 218
tourism, 265, 301
trance walking, 37–38
transcendence. *See* self-transcendence
transformation. *See* self-transformation
translation, 264, 267
travel, 6, 10, 11, 19–21, 201, 202, 210, 233, 241, 242, 293. *See also* journey
  leaving home and, 193
  narratives, 1–11
  pilgrimage, 33
  suffering and, 11, 227–228
  unselfing and, 19, 20, 36, 296–300
trekking, 154, 164. *See also* walking
  Sherpas and, 49
  unselfing and, 36
Trungpa, Chogyam, 109, 110
truth, ultimate and relative, 274
Tsangpo River Gorge, 167, 169, 170, 171
Tsung, Tsai, 248–255
tum-mo, 38, 152
Turner, Edith, 111
Turner, Victor, 111, 134, 298

U Ba Khin, 208
unselfing, 2, 14, 15, 16–19, 21, 29, 30, 40, 51, 54, 57, 65–66, 81, 83, 88, 95, 103, 114, 115, 182, 250, 278, 280, 281, 283, 294
  Asma's experiences of, 239, 240
  Blofeld's account of, 27, 70
  Crane's experience of, 251, 252
  David-Neel's account of, 153
  enlightenment and, 55, 58, 59, 70–71
  ethical implications, 16
  Govinda's experience of, 34–36, 41
  Harvey's experience of, 183
  Ichikawa Danzo, 130, 131
  in traditional Buddhist literature, 16–17
  "introjection" and, 273
  Kamenetz's experience of, 122
  kensho and, 55
  koan study and, 65, 69
  letting go and, 222
  long-distance walking and, 36
  Matthiessen's account of, 45–49
  Merton's experience of, 101, 106, 107, 108
  mindfulness and, 213
  Murdoch on, 14
  music and, 248
  narratives and, 283–287
  no-self and, 274
  O'Halloran's account of, 72–74, 77–78, 83, 84
  rituals and, 126, 127
  Robinson's version of, 219, 221–223
  satori and, 66

Index

"sacred technology," 187
Sakaki, Nanao, 244
salvation, 282
Salzberg, Sharon, 119
samsara, 15, 28, 29, 236
satori, 65–66, 68–69, 113, 283
Sayadaw, Ledi, 208
Sayadaw, Mahasi, 208
Schaller, George, 1, 43, 45, 52
Schettini, Stephen, 23, 200–206, 285. See also
    The Novice
Scott, Nick, 22, 139, 149, 280. See also *Rude
    Awakenings: Two Englishmen on Foot in
    Buddhism's Holy Land*
"secular" Buddhism, 201–203, 210
"seeing as," 15
self/selfhood, 12, 13, 17, 18, 39, 40, 60, 85,
    116–118, 133, 172, 196, 197, 199, 200, 203,
    206, 217, 218, 226, 267, 268, 273. See also
    middle way; no-self
    atman and, 271
    baggage and, 269
    Buddhist accounts of, 271, 272
    coincidence of opposites, 114
    culture and, 189–191
    metaphors of. See metaphors
    truth of, 274
self-addiction, 162
self-consciousness, 72
self-emptying, 113, 114
selfing, 21, 84, 98, 286, 289, 305
selflessness, 95, 160–164, 166, 213, 216, 272
    Thurman on, 161
self-transcendence, 14, 16, 47, 49, 101, 110, 111,
    162, 171, 214, 241, 259, 261, 297, 301. See
    also unselfing
self-transformation, 2, 9, 13–15, 19, 42, 64,
    127–129, 171, 181, 197, 198, 205, 226, 241,
    242, 294, 313
    autobiography and, 301–313
    conversion and, 304–307
    enlightenment and, 44
    faith and, 127–129
    of Harvey, 183–186
    of Pistono, 177, 178
    of Robinson, 220–222
    of Ward, 216
    pilgrimage and, 40
    poetry and, 9
    satori and, 66
sex, ethics of, 237, 238
sexuality, fox power and, 253, 254
shamanism, 252–254, 256–257
Shangri–La, 150
Sharf, Robert, 301

Shattock, Ernest Henry, *An Experiment in
    Mindfulness*, 208, 209
Sherpas, 49, 53–54
Shikoku pilgrimage, 10, 22, 37, 116–117,
    123–139, 298, 300
    Ichikawa Danzo and, 130
    Shingon Buddhism, 128
Shinto, 124
Shrady, Nicholas, 10
shunyata, 121
Sibley, Robert, 22, 132–139, 149, 298. See also
    *The Way of the 88 Temples: Journeys on the
    Shikoku Pilgrimage*
Sikhism, 142
small self, 95, 97
Smith, Bardwell, 22, 115–118, 122, 298. *See also*
    "In Contrast to Sentimentality: Buddhist
    and Christian Sobriety"
The Snow Leopard, 1, 8, 19, 43–54, 57, 58, 102,
    154, 166, 285
    unselfing, Matthiessen's account of, 45–49
Snyder, Gary, 9, 292, 293
solitude
    hermits and, 260
    unselfing and, 260, 267
Soto Zen, 22, 54, 56–60, 72, 82, 85, 88, 90, 92,
    93, 97, 304
    Rinzai Zen and, 88, 89
spiritual autobiography, 24, 41, 42, 293, 309, 310,
    313. See also *Tibetan secret autobiography*
Sri Lanka, 106
Statler, Oliver, 22, 123–132, 138, 141, 148–150,
    298, 300. See also *Japanese Pilgrimage
    Japanese Inn*, 124
Students' Education Trust, 224–226
Sublime, the, 35, 36
Sucitto, Ajahn, 22, 139–149. See also *Rude
    Awakenings: Two Englishmen on Foot in
    Buddhism's Holy Land*
suffering, 11, 104, 125, 133, 140, 146, 156, 158, 159,
    177, 191, 195, 204, 215, 226, 228, 231, 232,
    238, 239, 243, 245, 282, 285, 296, 297
    African Americans and, 195, 196
    compassion and, 239–241
    denial and, 201
    grief and, 227, 231
    O'Halloran on, 71
    pride and, 196
    selflessness and, 160
Sumedho, Ajahn, 210
sunyata ("emptiness"), Merton on, 108–109
sutras, 7, 76, 261–264, 274, 275
Suzuki, D. T., 47, 63, 98, 100–102, 282, 283,
    301, 302
Suzuki, Seido, 92

Index

333

Scott and Sucitto's account of, 143–148
secret autobiography and, 289
"seeing as" and, 15
self-transcendence and, 101, 111
Sibley's experience of, 134, 135, 136
Smith's experience of, 118
solitude and, 260, 267
Thurman's version of, 160–162
travel and, 19, 20, 36, 296–300
Ward's experience of, 213
Willis' experience of, 198
Zen Buddhism and, 46
Zeppa's version of, 192, 193

Vajrakilaya, 175
Vajrayana Buddhism, 12, 23, 25, 27–29, 41, 175, 176
Blofeld's initiation in, 27
Van de Wetering, Janwillem, 22, 63–71, 90, 214, 280, 303. See also *The Empty Mirror Experiences of a Zen Student Out on His Ear*, 69–71
Van Overmeier, Ben, 63
Vietnam, 234
Vinaya, 210–213
Vipassana meditation, 155, 207, 208, 210, 218, 219, 273
Vong, Tep, 235

wa ("group harmony"), 138
Walker, Alice, 293
walking, 123, 125, 133, 135, 140, 149, 154. *See also* trekking
as meditation, 20
healing and, 129, 130
trance, 35–38, 296
unselfing and, 36
Wallace, Alan, 201
Wang, Wei, 259
Ward, Tim, 23, 207, 210–217, 221, 222, 234. See also *What the Buddha Never Taught*
waterfalls, 170
Dalai Lama on, 169
The Way of Chuang Tzu, 100
The Way of the 88 Temples: Journeys on the Shikoku Pilgrimage, 117, 132–139
pilgrim mind, 133
unselfing, 135–137
The Way of the White Clouds, 21, 24, 31–42, 154
Western Buddhist travel narratives, 1–6, 13, 98, 148, 184, 310
accounts of residence in Asia, 10, 13–14, 63–64
as literary genre, 1–11, 24–25, 208–210, 292
autobiographies and, 6
Blofeld's influence on, 31

Buddhist Modernism and, 19
encounter stories and, 17
jataka tales and, 6
journey as metaphor, 5–6
pilgrimage and, 9–10
quests, 10
self-transformation in, 66
unselfing and, 15–19
What the Buddha Never Taught, 207, 210–217
Ward's experience of unselfing, 212–214
Ward's transformation, 215–217
The Wheel of Life, 25–31, 179
reincarnation, 26
second edition, 30
third edition, 30
unselfing, Blofeld's account of, 26–28
Where Are You Going: A Pilgrimage on Foot to the Buddhist Holy Places. See Rude Awakenings: Two Englishmen on Foot in Buddhism's Holy Land; Great Patient One
Willis, Jan, 23, 195–200, 206, 285. See also *Dreaming Me: An African American Woman's Spiritual Journey*
wisdom
hermits and, 260
meditation and, 261
Wise, Tad, 23, 159–166, 248, 285. See also *Circling the Sacred Mountain*
Wright, Dale, 7, 73
Wurlitzer, Rudolph, 23, 207, 226–233. See also *Hard Travel to Sacred Places*
Wutaishan, 263–265

Xuan, Ke, 246, 247

Yama taka, 162
Yeshe, Thubten, 196–199
Yi-ch'ao, 267, 268
yoga, deity, 198
yoin, 135
Younghusband, Francis, *India and Tibet*, 151

zazen, 88
Zen Baggage: A Pilgrimage to China, 261–269
Zen Buddhism, 17, 22, 47, 54, 60, 62, 78, 79, 84, 100–102, 112, 225, 261, 262. *See also* Soto Zen, Rinzai Zen
bodhisattva, 70, 80, 83, 84
Chan Buddhism and, 252
communal life and, 265–267
enlightenment and, 65, 67, 69–71, 73, 83, 113
equanimity and, 69
hermeneutics, 262
historical development
in China, 265, 266

334   *Index*

Zen Buddhism (cont.)
    kensho, 55, 74–76, 82
    koans, 50, 64–65, 68–69, 72, 74–76, 81,
        90, 91
    meditation and, 46, 47, 73
    mindfulness and, 265, 266
    monastic training, 69
    nihilism and, 70
    precepts, 95

    rituals, 66, 67, 76, 266
    satori, 65, 66, 68–69
    Theravada Buddhism and, 235
    training, 64–66, 68, 71, 76
    unselfing and, 56, 88, 89
    writing and, 60, 61
Zen monastic memoirs, 63
Zeppa, Jamie, 23, 187–195, 206, 280. See also
    Beyond the Sky and the Earth